Unity Cookbook

Core Recipes for Game Developers

Christopher Coutinho

Unity Cookbook: Core Recipes for Game Developers

Christopher Coutinho
Mumbai, India

ISBN-13 (pbk): 979-8-8688-0852-4   ISBN-13 (electronic): 979-8-8688-0853-1
https://doi.org/10.1007/979-8-8688-0853-1

Copyright © 2024 by Christopher Coutinho

This work is subject to copyright. All rights are reserved by the Publisher, whether the whole or part of the material is concerned, specifically the rights of translation, reprinting, reuse of illustrations, recitation, broadcasting, reproduction on microfilms or in any other physical way, and transmission or information storage and retrieval, electronic adaptation, computer software, or by similar or dissimilar methodology now known or hereafter developed.

Trademarked names, logos, and images may appear in this book. Rather than use a trademark symbol with every occurrence of a trademarked name, logo, or image we use the names, logos, and images only in an editorial fashion and to the benefit of the trademark owner, with no intention of infringement of the trademark.

The use in this publication of trade names, trademarks, service marks, and similar terms, even if they are not identified as such, is not to be taken as an expression of opinion as to whether or not they are subject to proprietary rights.

While the advice and information in this book are believed to be true and accurate at the date of publication, neither the authors nor the editors nor the publisher can accept any legal responsibility for any errors or omissions that may be made. The publisher makes no warranty, express or implied, with respect to the material contained herein.

> Managing Director, Apress Media LLC: Welmoed Spahr
> Acquisitions Editor: Spandana Chatterjee
> Development Editor: James Markham
> Coordinating Editor: Kripa Joseph

Cover designed by eStudioCalamar

Cover image designed by Freepik (www.freepik.com)

Distributed to the book trade worldwide by Apress Media, LLC, 1 New York Plaza, New York, NY 10004, U.S.A. Phone 1-800-SPRINGER, fax (201) 348-4505, e-mail orders-ny@springer-sbm.com, or visit www.springeronline.com. Apress Media, LLC is a California LLC and the sole member (owner) is Springer Science + Business Media Finance Inc (SSBM Finance Inc). SSBM Finance Inc is a **Delaware** corporation.

For information on translations, please e-mail booktranslations@springernature.com; for reprint, paperback, or audio rights, please e-mail bookpermissions@springernature.com.

Apress titles may be purchased in bulk for academic, corporate, or promotional use. eBook versions and licenses are also available for most titles. For more information, reference our Print and eBook Bulk Sales web page at http://www.apress.com/bulk-sales.

Any source code or other supplementary material referenced by the author in this book is available to readers on GitHub (https://github.com/Apress). For more detailed information, please visit https://www.apress.com/gp/services/source-code.

If disposing of this product, please recycle the paper

To my unwavering pillars of support and inspiration, this book is dedicated to my beloved parents, wife, and daughter, whose unwavering encouragement and boundless love have been the guiding stars of my journey into the world of Unity development. Your belief in my dreams has been the foundation upon which I've built my passion for game development.

In the world of Unity coding, where lines of code become adventures, and virtual worlds come to life, your love and support have been the ultimate power-up.

With all my love and appreciation,

Christopher Coutinho.

Table of Contents

About the Author ....**xvii**

About the Technical Reviewer ....**xix**

Acknowledgments ....**xxi**

Prologue ....**xxiii**

Chapter 1: Unity's Character Controllers **1**

   Recipe 1-1: Importing Character Controllers 2

      Problem 2

      Solution 2

      How It Works 3

   Recipe 1-2: Render Pipeline Converter 5

      Problem 5

      Solution 5

      How It Works 6

   Recipe 1-3: First-Person Character Controller 7

      Problem 7

      Solution 7

      How It Works 7

   Recipe 1-4: Implementing Dynamic Object Interaction......................................32

      Problem 32

      Solution 32

      How It Works 32

v

TABLE OF CONTENTS

Recipe 1-5: Implement Mobile Touch Controls 36
- Problem 36
- Solution 36
- How It Works 36

Recipe 1-6: Third-Person Character Controller 38
- Problem 38
- Solution 39
- How It Works 39

Recipe 1-7: Integrating Gamepad Support 51
- Problem 51
- Solution 51
- How It Works 51

Recipe 1-8: Customizing the Character Model 54
- Problem 54
- Solution 54
- How It Works 55

Summary 58

Chapter 2: Unity's New Input System 61

Recipe 2-1: Harnessing Unity's New Input System for Enhanced Control Flexibility 62
- Problem 62
- Solution 62
- How It Works 62

Input Action Asset 65
- Action Maps 66
- Actions 67
- Bindings 73
- Control Schemes 88

TABLE OF CONTENTS

Handling Input in Scripts 92
Character Controller Scripts 95
    Grounded Check 98
    Camera Rotation 99
    Move Method 101
    Jump and Gravity 105
    Clamp Angle 108
    OnDrawGizmosSelected 110
Recipe 2-2: Implementing a Player Attack Action 112
    Problem 112
    Solution 112
    How It Works 113
Expanding Player Attack with Animation 119
Recipe 2-3: Player Input Component Behaviors 129
    Problem 129
    Solution 129
    How It Works 130
    Invoke C Sharp Events 142
Recipe 2-4: Input Handling – Hybrid Approach 147
    Problem 147
    Solution 147
    How It Works 147
Recipe 2-5: Implementing UI Controls 157
    Problem 157
    Solution 157
    How It Works 157

TABLE OF CONTENTS

Recipe 2-6: Implementing Rebindable Controls 175
    Problem 175
    Solution 175
    How It Works 175

Recipe 2-7: Persisting Rebound Controls 211
    Problem 211
    Solution 211
    How It Works 211

Recipe 2-8: Dynamic Icons for Gamepad Actions 215
    Problem 215
    Solution 216
    How It Works 216

Summary 222

Chapter 3: Architecting Enemy AI with Finite State Machines 223

Recipe 3-1: Setting Up a NavMesh 224
    Problem 224
    Solution 224
    How It Works 224

Recipe 3-2: Setting Up a NavMesh Agent 230
    Problem 230
    Solution 230
    How It Works 230

Recipe 3-3: Managing NPC Behavior and Weapon Arsenal 235
    Problem 235
    Solution 235
    How It Works 236

TABLE OF CONTENTS

Recipe 3-4: Integrating the Actions Class with the SniperRifleController Animator 244
    Problem 244
    Solution 244
    How It Works 245

Recipe 3-5: Configuring NPC Health Management 252
    Problem 252
    Solution 253
    How It Works 253

Recipe 3-6: Coding the NPC State Machine 259
    Problem 259
    Solution 260
    How It Works 260

Recipe 3-7: Implementing Enemy AI Idle State 278
    Problem 278
    Solution 278
    How It Works 279

Recipe 3-8: Implementing Enemy AI Patrol State 284
    Problem 284
    Solution 284
    How It Works 284

Recipe 3-9: Implementing Enemy AI Wander State 291
    Problem 291
    Solution 291
    How It Works 291

Recipe 3-10: Implementing Enemy AI Chase State 298
    Problem 298
    Solution 299
    How It Works 299

TABLE OF CONTENTS

Recipe 3-11: Implementing Enemy AI Attack State 304
    Problem 304
    Solution 305
    How It Works 305

Recipe 3-12: Implementing Enemy AI Hit State 310
    Problem 310
    Solution 310
    How It Works 311

Recipe 3-13: Implementing Enemy AI Cover State 316
    Problem 316
    Solution 316
    How It Works 316

Recipe 3-14: Implementing Enemy AI Death State 331
    Problem 331
    Solution 331
    How It Works 332

Summary 336

Chapter 4: Architecting Melee Combat: Building the Core Framework 337

Recipe 4-1: Exploring the Warrior Game Object 339
    Problem 339
    Solution 339
    How It Works 340

Recipe 4-2: Implementing the NPC Manager 349
    Problem 349
    Solution 349
    How It Works 349

TABLE OF CONTENTS

Recipe 4-3: Implementing the Warrior State Machine 357
    Problem 357
    Solution 358
    How It Works 358

Recipe 4-4: Implementing the Chase State 374
    Problem 374
    Solution 374
    How It Works 375

Recipe 4-5: Implementing the Circling State 382
    Problem 382
    Solution 382
    How It Works 382

Recipe 4-6: Implementing the Attack State 394
    Problem 394
    Solution 395
    How It Works 395

Recipe 4-7: Implementing the Retreat State 411
    Problem 411
    Solution 412
    How It Works 412

Recipe 4-8: Implementing the Warrior Animation Events Class 421
    Problem 421
    Solution 421
    How It Works 421

Recipe 4-9: Implementing the Melee Weapon Damage Behavior 428
    Problem 428
    Solution 428
    How It Works 429

xi

TABLE OF CONTENTS

Recipe 4-10: Implementing the Health Script 434
    Problem 434
    Solution 434
    How It Works 434

Recipe 4-11: Implementing the Hit State 440
    Problem 440
    Solution 440
    How It Works 440

Recipe 4-12: Implementing the Wander State 446
    Problem 446
    Solution 446
    How It Works 447

Recipe 4-13: Implementing the Cover State 452
    Problem 452
    Solution 452
    How It Works 453

Recipe 4-14: Implementing the Death State 469
    Problem 469
    Solution 469
    How It Works 469

Summary 475

Chapter 5: Architecting Player Parkour Movement 477

Recipe 5-1: Exploring the Parkour Environment and Player Armature Game Object 478
    Problem 478
    Solution 479
    How It Works 479

TABLE OF CONTENTS

Recipe 5-2: Implementing the Obstacle Sensor 482
    Problem 482
    Solution 482
    How It Works 482

Recipe 5-3: Implementing the ParkourManager 489
    Problem 489
    Solution 490
    How It Works 490

Recipe 5-4: Implementing Scriptable Objects for Parkour Actions 505
    Problem 505
    Solution 505
    How It Works 506

Recipe 5-5: Implementing a Vaulting Parkour Action 518
    Problem 518
    Solution 519
    How It Works 519

Summary 529

Chapter 6: Implementing Shooter Weapon Mechanics 533

Recipe 6-1: Exploring the Player Weapon Setup 534
    Problem 534
    Solution 535
    How It Works 535

Recipe 6-2: The Weapon Component 539
    Problem 539
    Solution 539
    How It Works 540

TABLE OF CONTENTS

Recipe 6-3: The Weapon Audio Component 549
    Problem 549
    Solution 550
    How It Works 550

Recipe 6-4: The Weapon Raycast Component 557
    Problem 557
    Solution 557
    How It Works 558

Recipe 6-5: The Weapon Casing Component 566
    Problem 566
    Solution 567
    How It Works 567

Recipe 6-6: The Weapon Magazine Component 577
    Problem 577
    Solution 578
    How It Works 578

Summary 583

Chapter 7: Implementing Efficient Object Pooling 585

The Performance Impact of Object Creation and Destruction 586

Common Applications in Game Development 587

Recipe 7-1: Implementing Object Pooling for Enhanced Performance 589
    Problem 589
    Solution 589
    How It Works 590
    Key Components of an Object Pool 591

Unity's ObjectPool<T> Class 592
    Key Features and API Methods 593

TABLE OF CONTENTS

Setting Up Your First Object Pool 594
Recipe 7-2: Implementing a Centralized Object Pooler 608
    Problem 608
    Solution 608
    How It Works 608
Using the CentralizedObjectPooler 617
Summary 623

Index 625

About the Author

Christopher Coutinho is a seasoned Unity tools and game developer with over seven years of expertise in Unity 3D and Virtual Reality (VR) development. As founder of GameWorks, a premier game development studio based in Mumbai, Christopher has mastered the art of creating immersive VR experiences. His influence extends beyond commercial endeavors; he has significantly impacted the next generation of game developers through his educational efforts.

Christopher has been a key educator in video game development, sharing his extensive knowledge on platforms such as iDTech, a division of Emeritus. His instructional focus encompasses popular game engines like Unity and Roblox. Additionally, he has taught a specialized Augmented/Virtual Reality (AR/VR) Design program, created by the NYU – Tandon School of Engineering, for iDTech. His blend of practical experience and educational excellence positions him as a leading figure in the contemporary gaming industry.

Moreover, Christopher is an accomplished author and content creator, with a portfolio that includes two books and numerous instructional videos published by Apress. In conjunction with the FIFA World Cup 2022, he developed and released a free mobile game on the Google Play Store, further showcasing his diverse talents and contributions to the gaming community.

About the Technical Reviewer

Simon Jackson is a long-time software engineer and architect with many years of Unity game development experience as well as an author of several Unity game development titles. He loves to both create Unity projects as well as lend a hand to help educate others, whether it's via a blog, vlog, user group, or major speaking event. He is also a board member of the MonoGame Foundation.

His primary focus at the moment is on the Reality Toolkit project, which is aimed at building a cross-platform Mixed Reality framework to enable both VR and AR developers to build efficient solutions in Unity and then build/distribute them to as many platforms as possible.

Acknowledgments

Writing a book is never a solitary endeavor. It takes the collective efforts, encouragement, and support of many individuals to bring a project like this to fruition. I would like to express my heartfelt gratitude to those who have played a pivotal role in making *Unity Cookbook: Core Recipes for Game Developers* a reality.

First and foremost, I want to extend my deepest appreciation to the Unity community. Your passion for game development and C# scripting has been a constant source of inspiration. Your questions, feedback, and enthusiasm have shaped the content of this book.

I am immensely thankful to the talented Unity developers whose work has enriched the platform and provided valuable insights for this book. Your contributions to the Unity ecosystem are truly remarkable.

To my dedicated editor and the publishing team, thank you for your guidance, patience, and expertise in helping me refine and polish this manuscript. Your commitment to excellence has made this book a better resource for readers.

I want to acknowledge the mentors and teachers who have shared their knowledge and expertise in Unity and C# game development. Your guidance has been instrumental in shaping my own understanding and skills, which I now pass on to others through this book.

To my family and friends, thank you for your unwavering support and understanding during the long hours of writing and research. Your encouragement has kept me motivated throughout this journey.

Prologue

In the boundless universe of digital creation, game development is one of the most vibrant and exciting frontiers. It is a realm where imagination meets reality, where pixels and code blend to create worlds as real as our dreams. And in this world, the Unity game engine shines like a beacon, inviting creators from all walks of life to embark on an extraordinary journey.

The joy of creating, the thrill of problem-solving, and the satisfaction of sharing one's creation with others are no longer confined to the experienced few. Unity opens the gates to everyone, regardless of age or experience, and within these pages lies the map to navigate this wondrous landscape.

Who Is This Book For?

Whether you are an aspiring indie developer, a seasoned instructor, or a dedicated student, this guide is designed for anyone looking to elevate their skills in Unity development. It is a comprehensive resource, a trusted mentor, and a valuable companion for those who are ready to deepen their understanding, push their creative boundaries, and build captivating experiences in the Unity engine. You do not need to be a master; all you need is the determination to grow and the passion to create.

PROLOGUE

What You'll Learn

This cookbook serves as your essential guide as you

- Master Unity's Core Features: Delve deep into the core functionalities of Unity, from essential scripting techniques to advanced optimization methods.

- Implement Efficient Solutions: Learn how to craft robust and scalable game systems using proven design patterns and best practices.

- Enhance Game Performance: Discover techniques like object pooling and memory management that are critical for maintaining smooth and responsive gameplay.

- Design with Precision: Understand the principles of creating engaging and polished game mechanics that resonate with players, from intuitive UI to immersive experiences.

Book Prerequisites

Embark on this adventure with

- A computer running Windows 10 or 11 and Unity version 2023.2.20f1. All downloadable project files utilize this version of Unity.

- An Xbox Controller (optional).

PROLOGUE

How to Use This Book

Travel at your pace, starting at the very beginning, or leap to recipes that intrigue you. This book adapts to your journey, providing a comprehensive guide to your success. In the realm of programming, hands-on practice is often the most effective path to mastery. Engaging directly with the code, experimenting with each listing, and applying what you've learned through practical exercises is central to this book's approach. *Unity Cookbook: Core Recipes for Game Developers* is designed as a hands-on resource to enrich your learning experience, allowing you to read about and actively practice and internalize the essential concepts of C# programming within Unity. Your journey through these pages will be an interactive exploration, providing a tangible and immersive understanding of the subject.

Downloadable Content

Enhance your ease of learning with the downloadable project files available at https://github.com/Apress/Unity-Cookbook-Core-Recipes-for-Game-Developers – a treasure trove to deepen your understanding and skill.

> **Note** Starting with Unity version 2023.2.16f1 and continuing into Unity 6, there is a known issue where the scene may become unresponsive when attempting to play it for the first time. If you encounter this issue, simply close the Unity editor and reopen the project again using the Unity Hub.

CHAPTER 1

Unity's Character Controllers

This chapter is your comprehensive guide to mastering Unity's Starter Assets for character controllers, to empower you with the knowledge and skills necessary to create dynamic and immersive character interactions in your Unity games. Whether you're aiming to develop a fast-paced first-person shooter, a strategic third-person adventure, or anything in between, the insights provided here will help you craft engaging and responsive character controllers that elevate your game development journey. With a keen focus on both first-person and third-person perspectives, you will build a solid foundation that will serve as the cornerstone for creating compelling and interactive game experiences.

You first download and install Unity's Starter Assets: Character Controllers package freely accessible directly through Unity's Asset Store. You then begin learning about the fundamental concepts and components that make up Unity's character controllers. This section is designed to provide you with a comprehensive understanding of how Unity's character controllers function at their core, setting the stage for more advanced customization and implementation. You then learn to set up both first-person and third-person character controllers, learning about the unique properties of each controller type. You then delve into the properties of character controllers and explore the wide array of capabilities at your disposal. This section is all about tailoring the controllers to fit the specific

CHAPTER 1   UNITY'S CHARACTER CONTROLLERS

requirements of your game. From adjusting movement dynamics to refining camera controls, you'll discover how to customize your controllers to create a unique and engaging gameplay experience.

You will learn to configure the first-person and third-person character controllers to respond to the nuanced inputs of an Xbox controller, as well as incorporate mobile touch functionality, offering a tactile and responsive gaming experience. Lastly, you learn how to set up your very own character as your third-person character controller.

Recipe 1-1: Importing Character Controllers

Problem

When developing a game in Unity, one of the initial challenges is setting up functional and responsive character controllers. This task can be technically complex and time-consuming, especially for developers who may not have deep experience with animation and character physics. The difficulty lies in ensuring that the controllers not only perform well across various game scenarios but also provide a smooth and immersive player experience. Moreover, optimizing these controllers for performance and ensuring compatibility with different devices can further complicate the development process. Without a robust solution, developers might spend excessive time on foundational elements, delaying more creative aspects of game development.

Solution

Unity's Starter Assets: Character Controllers packages provide an ideal solution by offering pre-configured, customizable character controllers that are ready to integrate into any game project. These assets reduce the complexity of developing reliable and efficient character movement systems by supplying pre-built controllers for both first-person and third-person perspectives. Developers can directly import these assets into their Unity projects, allowing them to focus more on game design and less on the technical intricacies of character mechanics. By using these Starter Assets, developers not only expedite their development process but also ensure that their games are built on a foundation of proven, optimized, and cross-device compatible character control systems.

How It Works

Unity has provided developers with its Starter Assets: Character Controllers | URP package for setting up first-person and third-person character controllers out of the box. This character controller package offers significant advantages to developers, streamlining the game creation process and enhancing overall game quality. This asset serves as a robust foundation, enabling developers to quickly integrate sophisticated character movement and control systems into their games without having to build them from scratch. This not only accelerates development timelines but also ensures that the character controllers are optimized for performance and compatibility across a wide range of devices. Additionally, this starter asset is highly customizable, allowing developers to tailor character behavior to fit the unique needs and aesthetics of their game, thereby fostering creativity and innovation.

The Unity Asset Store offers the Starter Assets: Character Controllers | URP version 1.0.1 package by Unity Technologies, which combines prefabs for setting up both first-person and third-person character controllers. You need to download and import this package into a new project to learn about these character controllers.

Start by creating a new Unity 3D URP project using Unity version 2023.2.20f1. Within Unity's Asset store, search for abovementioned character controllers starter assets and add them to your My Assets download section. Launch the Package Manager from within the Unity

CHAPTER 1   UNITY'S CHARACTER CONTROLLERS

Editor, and within the Package Manager dialog box that shows up, locate the Starter Assets as shown in Figure 1-1. Select My Assets on the left and then select Starter Assets: Character Controllers | URP ensuring the version is 1.0.1 or newer. Download and finally import the latest version. Unity will prompt you about some dependencies that are lacking, so ensure that these dependencies are installed. You will also be prompted to restart the Unity Editor, so ensure that Unity restarts the editor.

Once the Starter Assets: Character Controllers | URP package has been imported, select the Project tab and navigate to the Assets/StarterAssets folder where you will find the Runtime and Samples folder. Open the Runtime folder, and you will note that it contains several folders, some of the more important ones being FirstPersonController, InputSystem, Mobile, and ThirdPersonController that comprise prefabs and scripts ready for use out of the box. Navigate to the Assets/StarterAssets/Sample/FirstPersonController folder and launch the Playground scene.

Figure 1-1. *Package Manager*

Recipe 1-2: Render Pipeline Converter

Problem

One common issue faced by Unity developers when switching to the Universal Render Pipeline (URP) from the built-in render pipeline is the appearance of pink textures in the game scenes. This pink color indicates missing or incompatible shaders, which can disrupt the visual aspects of the game and make it difficult to proceed with development. This problem arises because the assets and materials created or configured for the built-in render pipeline do not automatically adapt to the new rendering settings of URP, necessitating a manual conversion to ensure compatibility and maintain the intended aesthetic quality of the game.

Solution

To resolve the shader compatibility issues when transitioning to URP, Unity offers the Render Pipeline Converter tool. This tool simplifies the conversion process by automatically adjusting rendering settings, upgrading materials, and converting animation clips to be compatible with URP. By accessing the tool via the Unity Editor, developers can efficiently convert their entire project. The tool provides checkboxes to select specific elements for conversion, such as Rendering Settings and Material Upgrade, ensuring a thorough and tailored adaptation. After initializing the conversion process, the once pink scenes transform into properly lit and colored environments, ready for further development and testing. This streamlined approach not only corrects visual discrepancies but also enhances workflow efficiency, allowing developers to focus on game design and functionality.

CHAPTER 1   UNITY'S CHARACTER CONTROLLERS

How It Works

From within the Unity editor main menu, select Window ➤ Rendering ➤ Render Pipeline Converter (Figure 1-2). Ensure that the dropdown states Built-in to URP. Check the checkboxes for Rendering Settings, Material Upgrade, Readonly Material Converter, and Animation Clip Converter. Finally, click the Initialize and Convert button, allowing Unity to work its magic. After a while, you will note that the scene has been transformed from its all-pink color to being nicely lit and environmental objects colored.

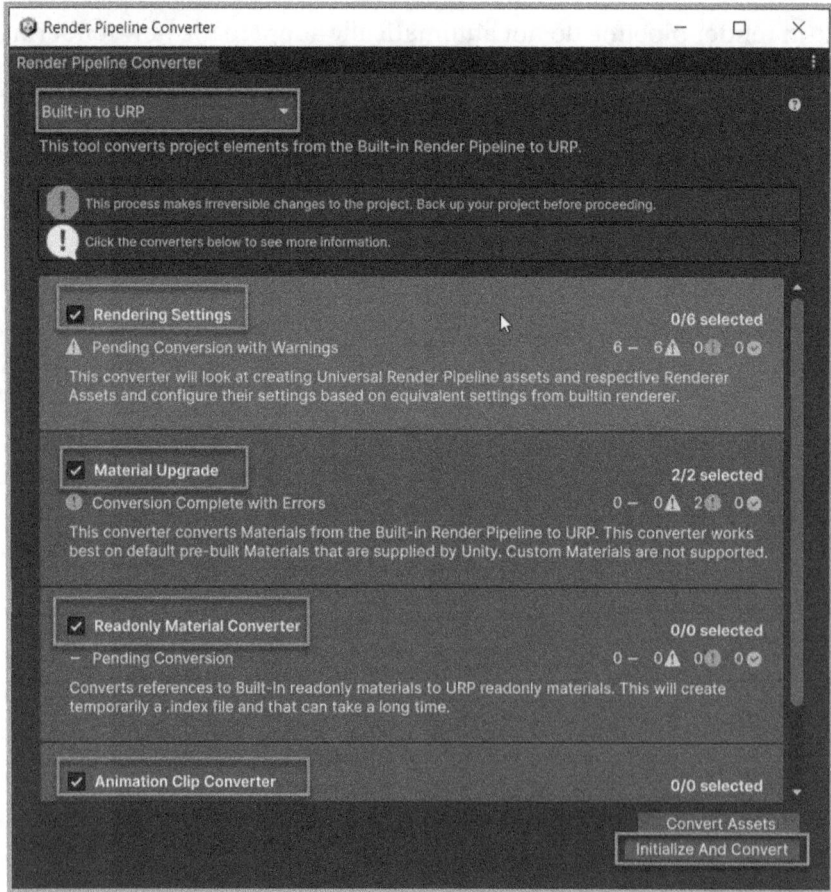

Figure 1-2. *Render Pipeline Converter*

Recipe 1-3: First-Person Character Controller

Problem

In game development, creating a responsive and immersive first-person player character controller is a fundamental challenge. Unity developers often struggle with configuring character controllers that handle complex interactions like movement dynamics, input management, and camera control effectively. This complexity can stall the development process, especially when aiming for high-quality, fluid gameplay across different platforms, including mobile devices.

Solution

Unity's Starter Assets for character controllers provide a comprehensive solution for these challenges. By leveraging these assets, developers can quickly implement sophisticated first-person controllers that are pre-configured with advanced input handling, mobile compatibility, and extensive customization options. These controllers include features like adjustable movement speeds, jump dynamics, and seamless camera integration using Cinemachine, allowing for rapid iteration and testing. This setup not only simplifies the initial stages of development but also ensures a high degree of polish and playability in the final game.

How It Works

At the heart of any immersive and dynamic game is how the player interacts with the game world, primarily through the character they control. Whether you're aiming to create a fast-paced action game, an expansive open-world adventure, or anything in between, mastering

CHAPTER 1   UNITY'S CHARACTER CONTROLLERS

these tools and features is your first step toward achieving dynamic and immersive character interactions. Unity's character controllers are complex systems that handle the physics and mechanics of character movement. At their core, these controllers manage input from the player and translate it into movement within the game world, taking into consideration factors like collision detection, physics interactions, and custom behaviors. The Starter Assets include both first-person and third-person controller setups, each with its unique components and configurations to cater to different gameplay styles.

Unity's Starter Assets: Character Controllers | URP package goes beyond basic movement, offering several special functionalities that set it apart:

- Advanced Input Handling: Unity's new Input System is fully supported, allowing for seamless integration with various input devices, including gamepads, keyboards, and touchscreens. This system makes it easier to create games that can be played across different platforms without extensive modifications for handling input.

- Mobile Compatibility: With the rise of mobile gaming, the Starter Assets have been optimized for touch input, ensuring that games developed with these assets can easily be adapted for mobile devices. This includes virtual joysticks and buttons that can be customized and scaled across different screen sizes.

- Customization and Extensibility: While the Starter Assets provide a solid foundation, they are designed to be highly customizable. Developers can easily modify parameters such as movement speed, jump height, and camera controls to fit the specific needs of their game. Furthermore, these assets are structured in a way that

CHAPTER 1   UNITY'S CHARACTER CONTROLLERS

allows for the addition of new behaviors and features, such as crouching, climbing, or swimming, with minimal effort.

- Camera Control: The package includes sophisticated camera systems for both first-person and third-person views, providing smooth and intuitive control over the game camera via the use of its suave Cinemachine Virtual Camera. These systems can be adjusted to change the feel of the game, from a tight, over-the-shoulder view for intense action games to a more laid-back, wide-angle view for exploration games.

With the Playground scene for the first-person controller open in the scene view, initiate a test run by pressing the Play button. This action activates the scene and allows for real-time interaction with the first-person character controller. Navigate through the scene using the "W," "A," "S," and "D" keys or the arrow keys for directional movement. The space bar key facilitates jumping, enabling the character to overcome obstacles. For rapid movement, hold down the "Shift" key while pressing the movement keys to sprint. To adjust the character's viewpoint, simply move the mouse to look around the scene. This comprehensive control scheme ensures a robust and immersive testing experience, out of the box, laying the groundwork for further customization and development of engaging first-person gameplay. Press the stop button to end the test run and return to the scene view.

Within the hierarchy of the Playground scene, essential game objects for the first-person character controller are distinctly organized. Beyond the Lighting and Environment objects, the core elements include the MainCamera, PlayerFollowCamera, PlayerCapsule, UI_Canvas_StarterAssetsInputs_Joysticks, and UI_EventSystem. These objects collectively form the fundamental structure of the first-person character controller setup, providing the necessary tools for visual rendering, player movement, and interaction within the game environment. This

CHAPTER 1   UNITY'S CHARACTER CONTROLLERS

arrangement facilitates a streamlined development process, allowing for easy customization and enhancement of the character controller's functionality (Figure 1-3).

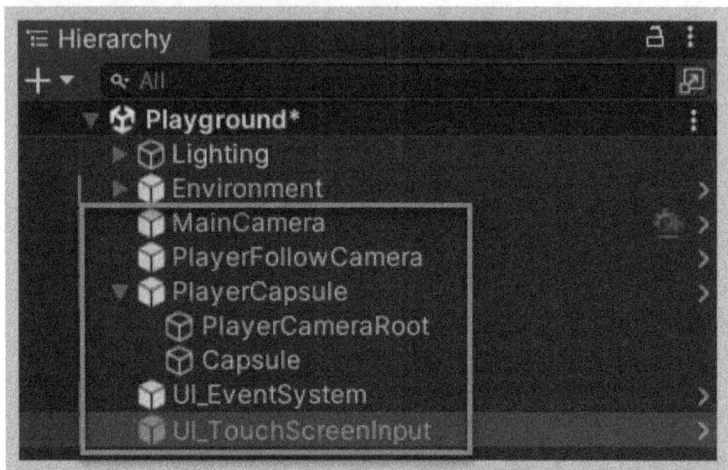

Figure 1-3. *First-Person Character Controller Setup*

Let's take a look at the Player Capsule game object, which plays a pivotal role in comprising the core components that make up the first-person character controller. Embedded within this object is a child game object named Capsule, which is equipped with a capsule collider to facilitate collision detection, ensuring realistic interactions within the game environment. Additionally, the PlayerCameraRoot game object, a crucial component for camera positioning, dictates the vertical placement of the camera through its Transform Position Y value. This setup is instrumental in controlling the first-person viewpoint. The Cinemachine Virtual Camera, integrated into the PlayerFollowCamera game object, dynamically follows the player's movements. It achieves this by referencing the Transform of the PlayerCameraRoot, ensuring the camera's position remains consistent with the player's perspective. This architecture provides a comprehensive framework for developing engaging and interactive first-person gameplay experiences.

CHAPTER 1   UNITY'S CHARACTER CONTROLLERS

Select the Player Capsule game object in the hierarchy, and let's explore the components it has been fitted with. Note that within the inspector it has been tagged as Player.

Unity's CharacterController component (Figure 1-4) is a powerful, non-physics-based controller that allows for sophisticated character movement and collision detection within a game environment. It's designed to simplify the process of creating complex character interactions without the direct application of physics, providing a more controlled and customizable approach to character movement. The CharacterController moves a character through the world using the Move method, which applies a displacement vector to the character's position. It takes into consideration the character's height, radius, and the slope it can climb. It automatically handles collisions with the terrain and other game objects marked as obstacles, sliding along surfaces without penetrating them. Collision detection is automatically handled, preventing the character from moving through other colliders in the scene. It automatically adjusts character movement on slopes, preventing the character from climbing slopes that are too steep and sliding down slopes when standing still, based on configurable parameters. The CharacterController can be set to automatically step over small obstacles or changes in elevation, enhancing realism in movement without additional coding for such interactions. The CharacterController component also includes methods for checking if the character is grounded (isGrounded property), enabling developers to implement jumping logic or adjust animations based on whether the character is in the air or on the ground. This combination of properties and methods provides a flexible framework for character movement. Some of the publicly available properties of Unity's CharacterController include

- Slope Limit: The maximum angle (in degrees) of slopes that the character can climb. Slopes steeper than this are treated as impassable barriers, and such steeper slopes will cause the character to slide down.

- Step Offset: The maximum height that the character can step up without needing to jump. It helps the character navigate environments and move up stairs or small ledges smoothly.

- Skin Width: A small, extra space around the character's capsule to prevent the collider from getting stuck in walls or objects directly beside it. This acts as a buffer zone, and it's used in collision detection to improve movement smoothness.

- Min Move Distance: The minimum distance the controller moves the character. Movements below this threshold will not be processed, helping to reduce jitter in character movement.

- Center: Specifies the center of the character's capsule relative to the local space of the GameObject. It is useful for adjusting the collider's position to match the character's visual representation. By changing this value, you can see the character's capsule collider position changing.

- Radius: Determines the radius of the character's capsule, affecting how close the character can get to other objects like obstacles or walls before a collision is detected.

- Height: The height of the character's collider capsule. This can be adjusted to fit the character model or to change the bounding area for collision detection. Ideally, this is set based on the character's size in the game to ensure accurate collision detection.

CHAPTER 1   UNITY'S CHARACTER CONTROLLERS

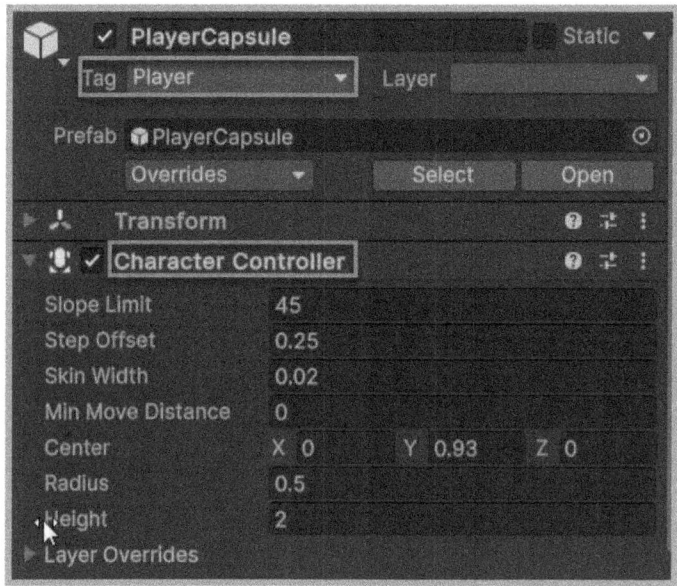

Figure 1-4. *Character Controller Component*

Unity's FirstPersonController component, showcased in Figure 1-5, is a pivotal element of the Starter Assets package, designed specifically for Unity's new Input System. This component excels in streamlining the development of first-person games by encapsulating complex functionalities such as movement, input handling, and camera control into a unified, easily modifiable script. Tailored to enhance the creation of immersive first-person experiences, it offers developers, both novice and experienced, an invaluable tool. The script's comprehensive implementation, as detailed below, covers critical aspects of first-person gameplay, ensuring a robust foundation for customizing character movement and interaction.

- CharacterController Component: At its core, the FirstPersonController script utilizes Unity's CharacterController component for movement and collision detection, ensuring that character interactions with the game environment are realistic and consistent.

13

CHAPTER 1   UNITY'S CHARACTER CONTROLLERS

- Movement and Sprinting: The script facilitates basic movement using the "W," "A," "S," and "D" keys or a gamepad's analog stick, along with sprinting functionality to increase movement speed. This is accomplished by interpolating between walking and sprinting speeds based on player input, providing a smooth transition that enhances the gameplay experience.

- Jumping and Gravity: It introduces a custom gravity and jumping system, allowing the player to jump to a specified height and ensuring that the character adheres to the game world's gravitational pull. This system works independently of Unity's built-in physics engine, offering developers more control over the character's movement dynamics.

- Grounded Check: An essential feature of the script is its ability to check whether the player is grounded, utilizing a physics sphere check. This grounded status is crucial for enabling or disabling the ability to jump and for applying gravity correctly, ensuring realistic character interactions with the game environment.

- Camera Control and Rotation: The script handles camera movements and rotation, linking it to mouse or gamepad input. This allows for a first-person perspective where the player can look around the environment fluidly. The camera's vertical movement is clamped to prevent unrealistic rotation, improving the player's experience and orientation in the game world.

- Cinemachine Integration: It integrates with Cinemachine, a powerful Unity tool for camera setups, to manage the camera's target and rotation. This ensures that the camera follows the player's character smoothly, contributing to a polished first-person perspective.

- Input System Integration: The script is designed to work seamlessly with Unity's new Input System, supporting a variety of input devices and control schemes, thereby enhancing the game's accessibility and player experience.

- PlayerInput and StarterAssetsInputs: For input handling, it leverages the PlayerInput component in conjunction with StarterAssetsInputs, a custom script part of the Starter Assets package, to process player commands for movement, jumping, and sprinting.

- Visual Feedback through Gizmos: For development and debugging, the script uses Unity's Gizmos to visually indicate whether the character is grounded, aiding developers in adjusting and fine-tuning the character's interaction with the terrain.

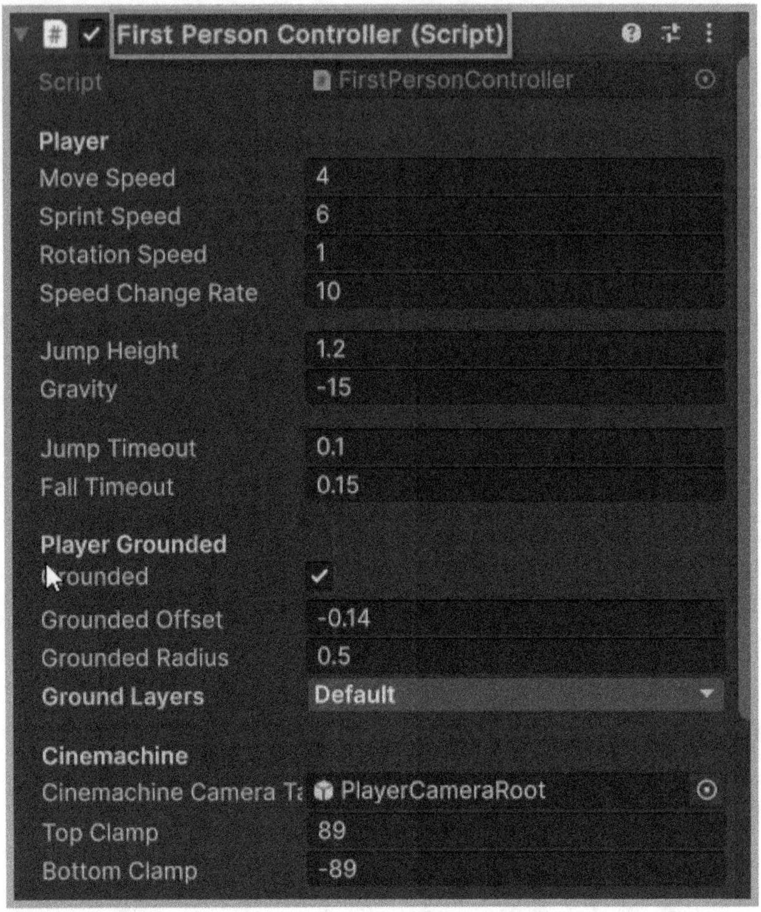

CHAPTER 1   UNITY'S CHARACTER CONTROLLERS

Figure 1-5. First-Person Controller Component

Let's look at each of the properties available under the heading Player (Figure 1-5) that provide developers with extensive control over the character's movement and behavior. Here's a detailed look at each of these properties and how manipulating them can affect the gameplay:

- Move Speed: This property defines the character's walking speed in meters per second (m/s). Increasing MoveSpeed from the default 4.0f to 6.0f will make the character move faster. This could be useful for a game

CHAPTER 1   UNITY'S CHARACTER CONTROLLERS

where the character needs to cover large distances quickly. A higher value results in faster movement across the game world, while a lower value will slow the character down, affecting how players navigate through the environment.

- Sprint Speed: This property determines the character's speed in meters per second (m/s) when the sprint button is held down. Setting SprintSpeed to 10.0f would significantly increase the character's speed when sprinting, which could be ideal for action-packed sequences or to escape from enemies quickly. Modifying this value alters the character's sprinting speed, allowing for quick bursts of movement, and enhancing the gameplay dynamics, especially in situations requiring fast reflexes or evasion.

- Rotation Speed: This property controls how quickly the character can rotate or turn around. Adjusting RotationSpeed to a higher value, such as 2.0f, makes the character turn faster, which can be useful in combat situations or when quick navigation is essential, but depending on your game play situation, you don't want the rotation to be too fast. Changing this value affects the responsiveness of character rotation to player input, with higher values leading to quicker turns and improved maneuverability.

- Speed Change Rate (Acceleration and Deceleration): This property governs the rate at which the character accelerates to maximum speed and decelerates to a stop. If SpeedChangeRate is increased to 20.0f, the character will reach its top speed or come to a stop more rapidly. This could be used to mimic the agile

17

movements of a nimble character. It influences how fluidly the character moves from a standstill to full speed and vice versa, with higher values making these transitions more immediate and lower values creating a smoother acceleration and deceleration curve.

- Jump Height: This property determines the maximum height (in meters) that the player can jump. Increasing JumpHeight from the default 1.2f to 2.0f allows the player to reach higher platforms or overcome taller obstacles, enhancing exploration or puzzle-solving aspects of a game. A higher value enables the player to jump higher, directly impacting gameplay by allowing access to previously unreachable areas or providing a tactical advantage in platforming or combat scenarios.

- Gravity: This property sets the gravity value applied to the player, distinct from Unity's global gravity settings. It's defined in meters per second squared (m/s^2) and is usually a negative value to simulate downward force. Setting Gravity to -20.0f makes the character fall faster after jumping or walking off a ledge, which could be used to create a game with more challenging platforming elements or a heavier, more impactful feel to the movement. Manipulating this value alters the speed at which the player falls, affecting the feel of jumps and how the player interacts with airborne mechanics. Larger negative values result in quicker descents, while smaller negative values offer a floatier, slower fall.

- Jump Timeout: This property sets a cooldown period in seconds that must pass before the player can initiate another jump. It's used to prevent players from jumping again immediately after landing or during a jump, which can be crucial for controlling the pace of gameplay and the mechanics of platforming challenges. Suppose JumpTimeout is adjusted from a default of 0.1f to 0.5f. In this scenario, after the player jumps, they must wait half a second before being able to jump again. This modification can be employed to enforce a more rhythmic or strategic approach to platforming sections, where timing and planning of jumps become critical to progression. Manipulating JumpTimeout directly impacts the gameplay feel and challenge. A longer timeout enforces deliberate pacing, making players think more carefully about when and where to jump. Conversely, a shorter timeout allows for a more fluid and rapid sequence of jumps, which might be preferable in fast-paced action or runner-style games.

- Fall Timeout: This property determines a grace period in seconds after the player has left a platform but can still initiate a jump, often referred to as "coyote time." This mechanic is particularly useful for improving the feel of platforming by forgiving slight misjudgments in jump timing at edges. By increasing the FallTimeout from its default of 0.15f to, say, 0.3f, players gain a longer window to react and execute a jump after inadvertently walking off a ledge. This adjustment can make platforming feel more forgiving, reducing frustration without significantly diminishing the game's challenge. Altering FallTimeout changes how forgiving the game is about platforming accuracy. A more extended FallTimeout allows for more lenient platforming, accommodating a wider range of player skill levels by mitigating the penalty for minor errors in jump timing. A shorter timeout demands more precision, increasing the difficulty and potentially catering to players seeking a more rigorous platforming challenge.

Let's now look at each of the properties available under the heading Player Grounded (Figure 1-5) that are pivotal for managing how the player character interacts with the ground. These properties collectively ensure that the character controller can accurately detect and respond to the ground, which is fundamental for a realistic and enjoyable player experience. Proper configuration of these properties can significantly enhance the character's interaction with the game world, affecting everything from movement mechanics to the feasibility of certain game designs.

- Grounded: This boolean property indicates whether the player is currently touching the ground. It's a dynamic value updated by the character's interactions with the game environment, not manually adjustable but crucial for scripts that conditionally execute actions based on whether the player is airborne or grounded. While not directly manipulable through the Inspector (since it's a runtime property), game logic can use its state to enable or disable actions, such as jumping only when Grounded is true, thereby preventing air jumps.

- Grounded Offset: This property adjusts the position of the ground check relative to the player character's position. It's a vertical offset that helps fine-tune where the ground detection sphere (or point) is placed. If a character is floating slightly above the ground due to the collider setup, setting a Grounded Offset to a small negative value (e.g., -0.14f) can lower the ground check position to accurately detect the ground. Adjusting this value helps in making the grounded detection more reliable, especially in cases where the character model or collider doesn't perfectly align with the visual ground level. It's critical to ensure that features like jumping behave correctly in response to the character's actual interaction with the terrain.

- Grounded Radius: This property specifies the radius of the sphere used to check if the player is grounded. This spherical check allows for more flexible and forgiving detection of the ground beneath the player character. Increasing the Grounded Radius (e.g., from 0.5f to 0.7f) can make the ground detection more generous and useful in scenarios where precise platform edges might otherwise lead to frustrating misses in jump initiations. Manipulating this radius affects how easily the character is considered to be grounded. A larger radius can smooth over small gaps and irregularities in the terrain, making the game feel more forgiving, while a smaller radius requires more precision in player movement.

- Ground Layers: This LayerMask determines which layers of objects in the scene are considered as ground. It allows developers to specify what the character can stand on, making it possible to exclude certain objects that shouldn't be considered ground (like water or certain types of obstacles). Setting the Ground Layers to only include the "Floor" and "Platform" layers means the character will only recognize objects in these layers as ground, ignoring others like "Enemy" or "Item" layers. By adjusting which layers are considered ground, developers can control the player's interaction with different elements of the game world. This can be used to create areas where the player is unable to stand or jump, adding a layer of challenge or strategy to the game design.

Lastly, let's look at the properties available under the heading Cinemachine (Figure 1-5), specifically designed to manage how the camera behaves in response to player input, ensuring a smooth and intuitive first-person camera experience. These properties integrate with Cinemachine, a powerful suite for camera management in Unity, to provide precise control over the player's view. Let's examine each of these properties:

- Cinemachine Camera Target: This GameObject serves as the focal point for the Cinemachine Virtual Camera. It determines where the camera is looking. By moving or rotating this target, you can adjust the camera's position and orientation about the player character. It references the PlayerCameraRoot game object discussed earlier. If the CinemachineCameraTarget is positioned above the player character, the camera will focus on that point, giving a view that might simulate

CHAPTER 1   UNITY'S CHARACTER CONTROLLERS

looking through the eyes of the character. Adjusting the target's position to be further ahead can create a view that's more akin to looking forward from the front of a helmet. Manipulating the position and orientation of the camera target changes the player's viewpoint and can significantly impact gameplay and immersion. For instance, a higher camera target can make the game feel taller, affecting how players perceive and navigate the environment.

- Top Clamp: This property defines the maximum upward angle (in degrees) that the player can tilt the camera. It effectively clamps the player's ability to look up, preventing disorienting or unrealistic views. Setting TopClamp to 70 degrees restricts the camera from tilting too far upwards, maintaining a realistic field of view that doesn't allow the player to look directly up, thereby keeping the horizon in view for orientation. Adjusting this value can tailor the player's experience by limiting how high they can look. This is particularly useful in environments where you want to keep the player's attention on certain levels of verticality or prevent them from spotting out-of-place elements above them.

- Bottom Clamp: Similar to TopClamp, this property sets the maximum downward angle (in degrees) the player can tilt the camera. It ensures that players cannot look too far down and lose orientation. A BottomClamp value of -60 degrees might be used to prevent the player from looking directly at their feet, which can be helpful in games where such a view would either reveal a lack of a character model or break immersion.

CHAPTER 1   UNITY'S CHARACTER CONTROLLERS

By controlling how low the player can look, this setting affects gameplay and exploration, guiding the player's interaction with the game world. It's essential for creating a balanced and immersive first-person perspective, ensuring that players remain engaged with the environment and action around them.

Now let's look at the StarterAssetsInputs script, which is integral to the Unity Starter Assets CharacterController, specifically designed to handle input for the Character Controller in a Unity project that utilizes the new Input System. It serves as an intermediary between player inputs (from devices like keyboards, mice, or gamepads) and the character movement and camera look functionality. It encapsulates complex input logic within a manageable and customizable script, ensuring that developers can easily adapt and extend their control schemes to fit the gameplay experience they aim to create. This script exemplifies the modularity and adaptability of Unity's input system, streamlining the development process for a wide range of gaming projects.

The script captures and processes player inputs related to movement (walking, sprinting), camera orientation (looking around), and actions (jumping). It translates these inputs into values that can be used by other components, such as the character controller or camera system, to affect the game world. By abstracting input handling into its own component, the script allows for easier modifications and additions to how inputs are processed, making the system more adaptable to different game types and control schemes. Designed with the new Unity Input System in mind, it ensures that inputs are managed in a way that's consistent with modern Unity development practices, supporting a wide range of input devices.

This script directly impacts the functionality of the Character Controller by providing the necessary input values for movement and actions. The move and sprint variables dictate the character's movement direction and speed, respectively, allowing for responsive and intuitive control over walking and running. The look variable influences the orientation of the camera or character's view, essential for first-person or third-person game perspectives. The jump variable triggers the character's ability to jump, making gameplay more dynamic and enabling interaction with the game environment in vertical dimensions.

The variables exposed within the Inspector for this component are designed to store and update the player's current input state regarding movement, camera orientation (look), jumping, and sprinting. These variables act as a bridge between raw input data (like pressing a key or moving a joystick) and the game mechanics that respond to these inputs. Here's how each of these input values works within the context of the script:

- Movement (move): The move variable is a Vector2 that captures two-dimensional input data, typically from a keyboard's arrow keys or a gamepad's joystick, representing forward/backward and left/right (strafing) movement. This variable is updated every frame based on player input. It's then accessed by movement-handling scripts, often those controlling a character controller or a custom movement script, to translate the input data into actual character movement within the game world.

- Look (look): Similar to move, the look variable is a Vector2 that stores input data for camera or character orientation, typically from mouse movement or a gamepad's right joystick. It represents horizontal and vertical camera rotation. Scripts responsible for camera control or character orientation use the look input to adjust the camera's or character's view direction accordingly, allowing the player to look around the environment.

CHAPTER 1   UNITY'S CHARACTER CONTROLLERS

- Jumping (jump): The jump variable is a boolean that indicates whether the player has pressed (and possibly is holding) the jump input, usually mapped to a key (like the spacebar) or a gamepad button. When the jump input is detected (i.e., jump is true), scripts that handle jumping mechanics can trigger a jump action, allowing the character to leap off the ground. This variable often interacts with physics components to apply an upward force to the character.

- Sprinting (sprint): Similar to jump, the sprint variable is a boolean that signifies whether the player is pressing the sprint input, typically to run faster than the default base movement speed. Movement scripts check the sprint variable to adjust the character's movement speed accordingly, enabling a faster traversal mode that consumes the input as long as the sprint key or button is held down.

These variables are dynamically updated in real-time based on the player's interactions with the input devices. The script's input handling methods (OnMove, OnLook, OnJump, and OnSprint) are designed to capture input events and update these variables accordingly. Other components in the game can access these variables to determine the current state of player input and to react accordingly, ensuring that the character's movements and actions on-screen reflect the player's intentions.

The analogMovement setting in the StarterAssetsInputs script plays a crucial role in how movement inputs are interpreted and applied to character movement, especially in distinguishing between analog and binary inputs. Understanding how this setting is used necessitates diving into the differences between these types of inputs and how they affect movement control.

CHAPTER 1 UNITY'S CHARACTER CONTROLLERS

- Analog Inputs: Analog inputs come from devices like gamepad joysticks, where the input is not just on or off but can vary in intensity or degree. For example, lightly pushing a joystick might move a character slowly, while pushing it all the way results in full-speed movement. Analog inputs can provide a wide range of values, typically normalized between -1.0 and 1.0, allowing for nuanced control over movement speed and direction.

- Binary Inputs: Binary inputs are digital and only have two states: on or off. Keyboard keys are a common source of binary inputs. Pressing a key for movement typically moves the character at a fixed speed, irrespective of how hard or lightly the key is pressed.

When analogMovement is enabled, the character's movement can smoothly transition between speeds, creating a more natural and responsive feel. This is in contrast to binary input handling, where movement is either on or off, causing more abrupt speed changes. The nuanced control schemes facilitated by analog input include

- Gradual Acceleration and Deceleration: Instead of instantly reaching full speed or stopping, characters can accelerate and decelerate smoothly.

- Directional Precision: Players have finer control over the direction of movement, as slight rotational adjustments to the joystick position can result in corresponding subtle changes in movement direction.

In game development, using the analogMovement setting allows developers to create games that feel more immersive and responsive, particularly on platforms where gamepads are commonly used. It enhances gameplay in genres requiring precise movement, such as stealth

CHAPTER 1   UNITY'S CHARACTER CONTROLLERS

games, where players might need to control their speed closely, or in racing games, where nuanced control over acceleration and turning is essential.

For games that need to support both keyboard and gamepad input, developers can use the analogMovement flag to switch between input modes, ensuring that the control scheme remains intuitive and enjoyable across different devices. This adaptability enhances the player experience by catering to the strengths of each input method, offering immediate and full-speed movement with keyboard inputs while providing variable speed and smoother control with analog inputs.

Finally, the Mouse Cursor Settings, manage the state of the mouse cursor, including locking it during gameplay for immersive first-person perspectives and determining whether mouse input should affect camera orientation. You would want to ensure that these checkboxes are checked as default.

Now let's look at the Player Input component, whose primary purpose is to abstract the process of input handling, making it easier to manage and more adaptable to different input devices without needing to hard-code device-specific controls. It works in tandem with Unity's new Input System's Input Actions asset (Figure 1-6), which defines various input actions and binds them to specific keys or buttons across different devices.

CHAPTER 1   UNITY'S CHARACTER CONTROLLERS

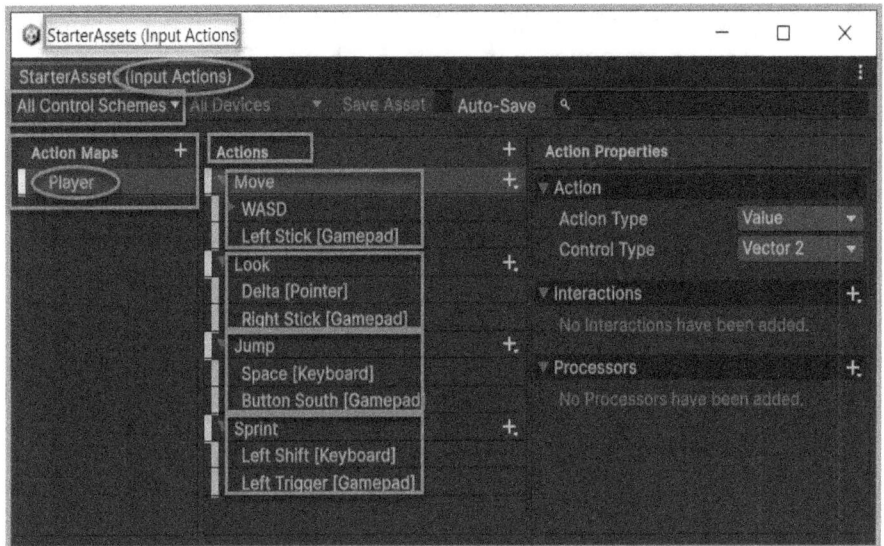

Figure 1-6. *StarterAssets (Input Actions) Window*

For the Player Input component, you'll see several key properties exposed in the Inspector:

- Actions: This property is where you assign the Input Actions asset (Figure 1-6) that contains the mappings of all the input actions (e.g., move, look, jump, sprint). This asset allows you to define complex input behavior, like combining keyboard and mouse inputs for a first-person shooter, or gamepad inputs for a console-style adventure game. The Actions you see provided here are the defaults provided with the Starter Assets: Character Controller. You can add your own specific action, for example, a crouch action, should you want to.

- Default Map: Allows you to select which set of actions (defined within the Input Actions asset) is currently active. This is useful for games with different control contexts (e.g., on-foot vs. vehicle controls) and can be switched dynamically in-game. Looking at Figure 1-6, you will note that there currently exists just one Action Map, i.e., Player and that has been assigned as the Default Map within the Inspector.

- Default Scheme: Specifies the preferred control scheme (e.g., Keyboard/Mouse, Gamepad, Xbox Controller, PS4 Controller) that the game should default to, particularly useful for games targeting multiple platforms. If a value is set from the dropdown list, that scheme will be tried first. However, if it fails, it will fall back to trying out the other control schemes in order.

- Behavior: Determines how the input actions are triggered. Options include "Send Messages," "Broadcast Messages," "Invoke Unity Events," and "Invoke C# Events." Each option controls how input events are communicated to the rest of your game, with "Invoke Unity Events" being a popular choice for directly connecting input actions to MonoBehaviour methods via the Inspector.

- Auto-Switch: The Auto-Switch property determines whether the Player Input component automatically switches the current control scheme based on the last device type that input was received from. For example, if a player is using a keyboard and then starts using a gamepad, the input system can automatically switch to the gamepad control scheme. This feature is particularly useful in games that aim to support multiple input devices, ensuring a seamless transition for players who might switch between controllers and

CHAPTER 1   UNITY'S CHARACTER CONTROLLERS

keyboard/mouse setups. It enhances user experience by adapting to the player's preferred input method without requiring manual configuration.

- UI Input Module: The UI Input Module property is expected to be populated with a reference to an Input System UI Input Module component, which is typically attached to an Event System object in the scene. This component bridges the Unity Input System with the game's UI elements, allowing the input system to interact with and control UI interactions (like button clicks, menu navigation, etc.). By populating this property, you ensure that the game's UI can properly respond to player inputs, integrating the control scheme with the game's menus, inventory screens, or any other interactive UI elements. It's essential for creating a cohesive input experience that covers both gameplay and UI navigation.

- Camera: You don't need to populate this property with a camera object, and it's safe to leave it empty. Typically, this Camera property is used to assign the main camera of the game to the Player Input component. By specifying which camera is controlled by player inputs, you could have the game directly tie camera movements to input devices, allowing for dynamic and responsive camera control based on the player's look or aim actions. This setup could allow the creation of immersive and interactive gameplay experiences where the player's viewpoint is a critical part of the game mechanics.

CHAPTER 1   UNITY'S CHARACTER CONTROLLERS

Recipe 1-4: Implementing Dynamic Object Interaction

Problem

In game development, creating a dynamic and interactive environment can significantly enhance the player's experience. However, developers often face challenges in implementing realistic interactions between the player and objects within the game world, such as pushing obstacles. These interactions require a system that can manage physics-based movements without compromising game performance or realism.

Solution

Unity's BasicRigidBodyPush script addresses this by enabling characters to apply physical forces to objects in the environment, simulating realistic pushing interactions. To set this up, developers need to assign the script to the character controller, configure pushable objects with Rigidbody components, and define specific layers for interaction. By adjusting parameters like push ability and strength, the script facilitates nuanced control over how objects react to being pushed, enhancing the game's interactivity and realism. This allows players to engage more deeply with the game environment, pushing obstacles and navigating through dynamic scenarios effectively.

How It Works

The BasicRigidBodyPush script is a versatile tool in the Unity game developer's arsenal, offering a straightforward method to make game environments more dynamic and interactive. It fits seamlessly into the broader functionality of the Unity Starter Assets CharacterController, providing a template for further customization and refinement based on the specific needs and vision of a game project. The script utilizes Unity's physics system to apply a force to rigid bodies the character collides with, simulating a pushing effect. This functionality hinges on a few key components:

- Layer Mask (pushLayers): Determines which layers contain objects that the character can push. This allows developers to specify which objects in the game world are interactive in this way, avoiding unintended interactions with non-pushable objects.

- Push Ability (canPush): A boolean flag that enables or disables the ability for the character to push objects. This can be toggled in-game to provide or restrict the player's ability to interact with the environment dynamically.

- Strength (strength): A modifiable value that dictates the force magnitude applied to pushed objects. This allows for the customization of how impactful the push interaction is, affecting how far or fast pushed objects are moved.

This script extends the functionality of Unity's CharacterController component by reacting to collision events through the OnControllerColliderHit method. When the character collides with an object, the script checks if the object is pushable based on its Rigidbody state (non-kinematic), its layer (as defined in pushLayers), and the direction of the collision (to avoid pushing objects downward, which could simulate unrealistic strength or create gameplay imbalances).

By integrating this script with the CharacterController, developers can enhance the physical presence of the player in the game world. Objects react to the player's movements, adding a layer of realism and interactivity.

CHAPTER 1   UNITY'S CHARACTER CONTROLLERS

For example, navigating through a cluttered environment becomes more engaging as the player can push obstacles aside rather than simply navigating around them. This can be particularly effective in puzzle games, exploration games, or any genre where environmental interaction enriches the gameplay experience.

Let's set up the first-person character controller in the Playground scene to be able to push boxes around using the BasicRigidBodyPush component. You need to follow a series of steps to properly configure both the character controller and the boxes that will be pushed.

- Create a New Layer: Using the Layer dropdown in the inspector, create a new layer "Pushable." Within the hierarchy, expand the Environment game object and further expand the game object Greybox and locate the boxes Box_100x100x100_Prefab (16) and Box_100x100x100_Prefab (17), which will be the boxes you can push around. Set their layer to "Pushable" in the Inspector.

- Rigidbody Component: Each box that you want to be pushable must have a Rigidbody component attached. This component is what allows the object to be moved via physics forces. In the hierarchy, select boxes Box_100x100x100_Prefab (16) and Box_100x100x100_Prefab (17) and add a Rigidbody component to each of them. Make sure the Rigidbody is not marked as kinematic, as kinematic objects cannot be affected by forces. You would also note that each of these boxes has already been fitted with box colliders that are necessary for the Unity physics engine to detect collisions between the player character and the box.

CHAPTER 1   UNITY'S CHARACTER CONTROLLERS

- Attach the Script: Ensure your character controller GameObject (in this case referred to as "PlayerCapsule" in the hierarchy) has the BasicRigidBodyPush script component attached to it.

- Push Layers: Set the pushLayers to match the layer(s) your pushable boxes are assigned. This ensures the script only tries to push objects on the correct layer. Your boxes are on a layer named "Pushable"; you need to add this layer to the pushLayers mask in the script's properties.

- Can Push: Ensure the canPush boolean is checked to enable pushing functionality.

- Strength: Adjust the strength value to control how forcefully the player can push the boxes. A higher value means more force is applied, making the boxes move faster or further when pushed. The default value is fine for testing purposes.

Once everything is set up, enter Play mode in Unity. Move your first-person character to collide with the boxes. Given the correct setup, the first-person character should now be able to push the boxes around the Playground scene, with the force of the push governed by the strength parameter of the BasicRigidBodyPush component.

Recipe 1-5: Implement Mobile Touch Controls

Problem

Integrating touch controls for mobile gameplay in Unity can be challenging, especially when ensuring the game functions seamlessly across different devices. Developers need an efficient way to implement and test touch inputs within the Unity Editor without the immediate need for actual mobile devices.

Solution

Unity facilitates the integration of mobile touch controls through its comprehensive UI elements and input simulation features. This process includes enabling and disabling certain mouse cursor settings and using the Input Debugger to simulate touch input from the mouse or pen. This setup allows for a straightforward testing environment within the Unity Editor, making the development and debugging of mobile games more accessible and efficient.

How It Works

Implementing touch screen controls for Unity's Starter Assets: Character Controllers involves a few steps to get everything up and running within the Unity Editor. This ensures that your first-person or third-person character can be controlled via touch inputs, like on a mobile device, without needing an actual device for testing purposes. Here's how you can set it up and test it within the Unity Editor:

CHAPTER 1   UNITY'S CHARACTER CONTROLLERS

1. In the hierarchy, find the UI_TouchScreenInput game object. This canvas contains the buttons configured for touch input. By default, this game object is not already active, so enable the game object to make the touch controls visible in your game view when the experience is played.

2. Select the PlayerCapsule game object in the hierarchy and locate its Starter Assets Inputs component. Under the heading Mouse Cursor Settings, you will note that the checkboxes – Cursor Locked and Cursor Input For Look are checked by default. To enable testing touch controls within the Unity Editor, you need to uncheck both these checkboxes.

3. To test touch controls within the Unity Editor, go to Window ➤ Analysis > ➤ Input Debugger. You could also use the Open Input Debugger button available at the bottom of the Inspector. In the Input Debugger window that opens (Figure 1-7), go to Options and enable "Simulate Touch Input From Mouse or Pen." This allows you to use your mouse as a stand-in for touch inputs.

4. Enter Play Mode in the Unity Editor. You should now be able to interact with the virtual joysticks and buttons using your mouse, simulating how a player would use touch controls on a mobile device.

Lastly, when you're done testing and decide to return to the standard keyboard/mouse scheme, ensure that you check the checkboxes – Cursor Locked and Cursor Input For Look available within the Starter Assets Inputs component, beneath the Mouse Cursor Settings heading. Also ensure that you deactivate the game object UI_TouchScreenInput.

Finally, using the Open Input Debugger button available at the bottom of the Inspector, launch open the Input Debug window. Click on the Options dropdown and ensure that "Simulate Touch Input From Mouse or Pen" is unchecked. Only then will you be able to go back to using mouse and joystick rotational inputs to rotate your character.

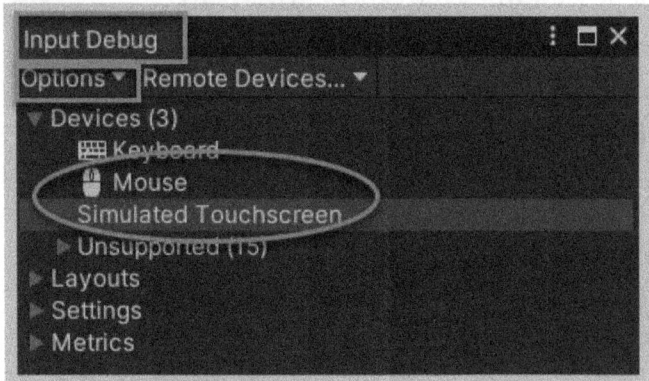

Figure 1-7. Input Debugger Window

Recipe 1-6: Third-Person Character Controller

Problem

Developing a third-person character controller in Unity that offers smooth and responsive character movements, versatile camera control, and effective animation integration can be challenging. Ensuring that these components work seamlessly together to create a fluid gameplay experience while accommodating a range of input devices adds to the complexity.

CHAPTER 1   UNITY'S CHARACTER CONTROLLERS

Solution

Unity's Third-Person Character Controller provides a comprehensive solution that integrates advanced movement dynamics, camera control through Cinemachine, and responsive animation behaviors. By setting up the Player Armature game object with essential components like the Character Controller, Basic Rigid Body Push, Starter Assets Inputs, and Player Input, developers can efficiently manage character interactions and movements. Additional customization is facilitated through properties such as Rotation Smooth Time for natural turning and audio integration for enhanced sensory feedback. This setup ensures that developers can focus on creating immersive and dynamic gameplay experiences in a third-person perspective, leveraging Unity's robust framework for character control and animation management.

How It Works

Unity's Third-Person Character Controller provides developers with a robust and customizable foundation for creating third-person perspective games. This controller is designed to offer smooth and intuitive character movement, including walking, running, jumping, and crouching, all while ensuring seamless camera control with Cinemachine integration for dynamic camera movements. With support for both keyboard and gamepad inputs out of the box, it also includes mobile touch inputs for broader platform compatibility. The Third-Person Character Controller is built to work with Unity's new Input System, ensuring a modern and efficient approach to handling player inputs. Additionally, it features an animator component that allows for easy integration of character animations, making it an excellent starting point for developers looking to create immersive third-person games in Unity.

CHAPTER 1   UNITY'S CHARACTER CONTROLLERS

Select the Project tab, navigate to the Assets/StarterAssets/Sample/ThirdPersonController folder, and launch the Playground scene. With the Playground scene for the third-person controller open in the scene view, initiate a test run by pressing the Play button. This action activates the scene and allows for real-time interaction with the third-person character controller. Navigate through the scene using the "W," "A," "S," and "D" keys or the arrow keys for directional movement. The space bar key facilitates jumping, enabling the character to overcome obstacles. For rapid movement, hold down the "Shift" key while pressing the movement keys to sprint. To adjust the character's viewpoint, simply move the mouse to look around the scene. You will note that this control scheme is similar to that of the first-person controller.

Within the hierarchy of the Playground scene, for the third-person controller, you will note that the game objects are the same as were available for the first-person character controller, with the exception that the first-person character controller had a PlayerCapsule game object (Figure 1-3), while the third-person character controller has a PlayerArmature game object that comprises the Armature_Mesh and Skeleton that make up the third-person character as depicted in Figure 1-8.

CHAPTER 1   UNITY'S CHARACTER CONTROLLERS

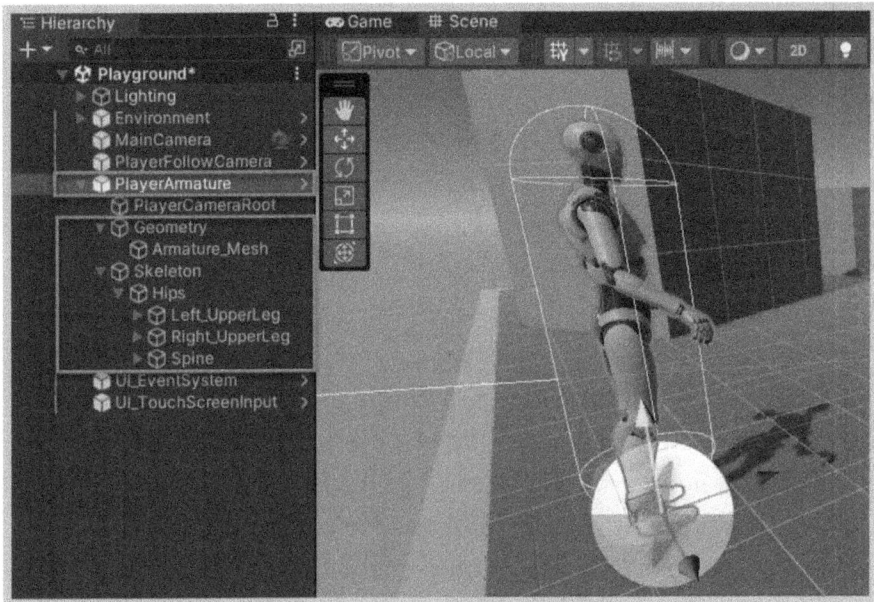

Figure 1-8. *Third-Person Character Controller Setup*

Let's take a look at the Player Armature game object, which plays a pivotal role in comprising the core components that make up the third-person character controller. Embedded within this object are several child game objects, namely, PlayerCameraRoot, Geometry, which has the child game object Armature_Mesh, and the Skeleton game object. The PlayerCameraRoot game object, a crucial component for camera positioning, dictates the vertical placement of the camera through its Transform Position Y value and is instrumental in controlling the third-person viewpoint. Its Transform Position Y value is 1.375, which is the same value used within the first-person character controller. The PlayerFollowCamera and MainCamera game objects setup is similar to that of the first-person character controller.

In the project hierarchy, upon selecting the Player Armature game object, one will observe it has been appropriately tagged as "Player." This tagging is crucial for identification and interaction purposes within

CHAPTER 1   UNITY'S CHARACTER CONTROLLERS

the game's scripts and logic. Notably, the Player Armature game object is equipped with a suite of components identical to those found on the Player Capsule game object of the first-person character controller. These components include the Character Controller, Basic Rigid Body Push, Starter Assets Inputs, and Player Input. Each of these components functions in a manner consistent with their implementation and description provided in the earlier sections of this chapter, where the intricacies of the first-person character controller were dissected. The consistent use of these components across both first- and third-person controllers underscores a unified approach to character movement, interaction, and input handling within Unity's Starter Assets, facilitating a seamless development experience while working with either character controller setup. The Third-Person Controller component on the Player Armature game object has a lot of properties similar to those that were available on the First-Person Controller component. You will go on to examine those properties of the Third-Person Controller component that did not exist within the First-Person Controller component in the next section. The Player Armature game object also comprises an Animator component that brings the third-person character to life by managing animations based on player inputs and game events.

The Third-Person Controller is specifically designed to manage the behavior and interaction of a third-person character within a game environment. This script facilitates a wide range of character movements and actions, such as walking, sprinting, jumping, and turning, in response to player inputs. It ensures smooth and responsive control over the character, enhancing the gameplay experience by providing a natural and intuitive feel to character movement and camera control. It ensures that third-person character control is both intuitive and versatile, supporting a wide range of gameplay styles. By managing complex interactions between player inputs, character movements, camera controls, and animations, it stands as a comprehensive solution for third-person game development in Unity. It differs from the First-Person Controller in a few ways, namely:

- Perspective and Camera Control: Unlike the First-Person Controller, which is designed for first-person perspective games, the Third-Person Controller is tailored for third-person perspective gameplay, necessitating different approaches to camera control and character rotation to accommodate the visibility of the character's body. It works closely with Cinemachine for camera movement, providing settings for camera follow targets, clamping angles, and camera locking, to create dynamic and cinematic views that follow the character's action.

- Animation Integration: The Third-Person Controller script includes extensive support for animations, using an Animator component to visually represent the character's actions and states based on inputs and movements. It manages an array of animation states such as walking, jumping, and falling, providing a more immersive experience.

- Rotation Smoothness: It introduces a rotation smooth time setting to gradually adjust the character's facing direction, offering a more natural transition as the character turns. This is particularly important in a third-person view to maintain a cohesive visual experience.

- Audio Integration: Additionally, the Third-Person Controller supports audio feedback for actions like footsteps and landing, enhancing the sensory experience by linking audio clips to specific movements and animations through Animation Events.

CHAPTER 1   UNITY'S CHARACTER CONTROLLERS

Let's look at the properties available under the heading Player (Figure 1-9) that are unique to the Third-Person Controller.

- Rotation Smooth Time: This property determines the smoothness of the character's rotation toward the direction of movement. It is a time interval over which the rotation from the current orientation to the target orientation is smoothed out. A lower value (close to 0.0f) results in quicker, almost instantaneous turning of the character, which might be suitable for fast-paced action games. A higher value, closer to the maximum of 0.3f, makes the character turn slower and more gradual, which can enhance realism or be preferable in exploration-based games. For example, setting RotationSmoothTime to 0.05f would make the character more responsive to direction changes, while 0.25f would ensure a smoother, more deliberate rotation.

- Landing Audio Clip: This property allows you to assign an audio clip that is played when the character lands after jumping or falling. It adds auditory feedback to the act of landing, enhancing the sensory experience of the game. By assigning different Landing Audio Clips, developers can adapt the sound to match the surface type the character lands on or the intensity of the fall. For instance, a soft landing on grass could have a muted, low-volume clip, while landing on metal could use a sharper, echoing sound. Changing this clip based on the context can significantly improve immersion and realism.

CHAPTER 1   UNITY'S CHARACTER CONTROLLERS

- Footstep Audio Clips: This array of audio clips is used to provide auditory feedback for the character's footsteps. By assigning multiple clips, the game can randomly play different sounds for each step, avoiding repetitive audio that can break immersion. Developers can fill this array with various sounds corresponding to different surface types or footwear to reflect the character's environment and actions more accurately. For example, adding clips with muffled steps for sneaking or heavy, distinct steps for running in armor allows the audio to contribute to the storytelling and gameplay experience. Randomly selecting from these clips as the character moves ensures the footsteps sound natural and varied.

- Footstep Audio Volume: This property controls the overall volume of the footstep sounds. It is a global multiplier that affects how loudly the footstep audio clips are played. Adjusting the Footstep Audio Volume enables developers to balance the footstep sounds against the game's overall audio mix. For stealth segments, the volume could be reduced to emphasize quiet movement, while louder steps could enhance the weightiness of a heavily armored character. For instance, setting the volume to 0.2 might be used to indicate cautious movement, whereas a value of 0.8 could reflect a confident, unconcerned approach. This control allows the footstep audio to be dynamically adapted to different gameplay scenarios.

CHAPTER 1   UNITY'S CHARACTER CONTROLLERS

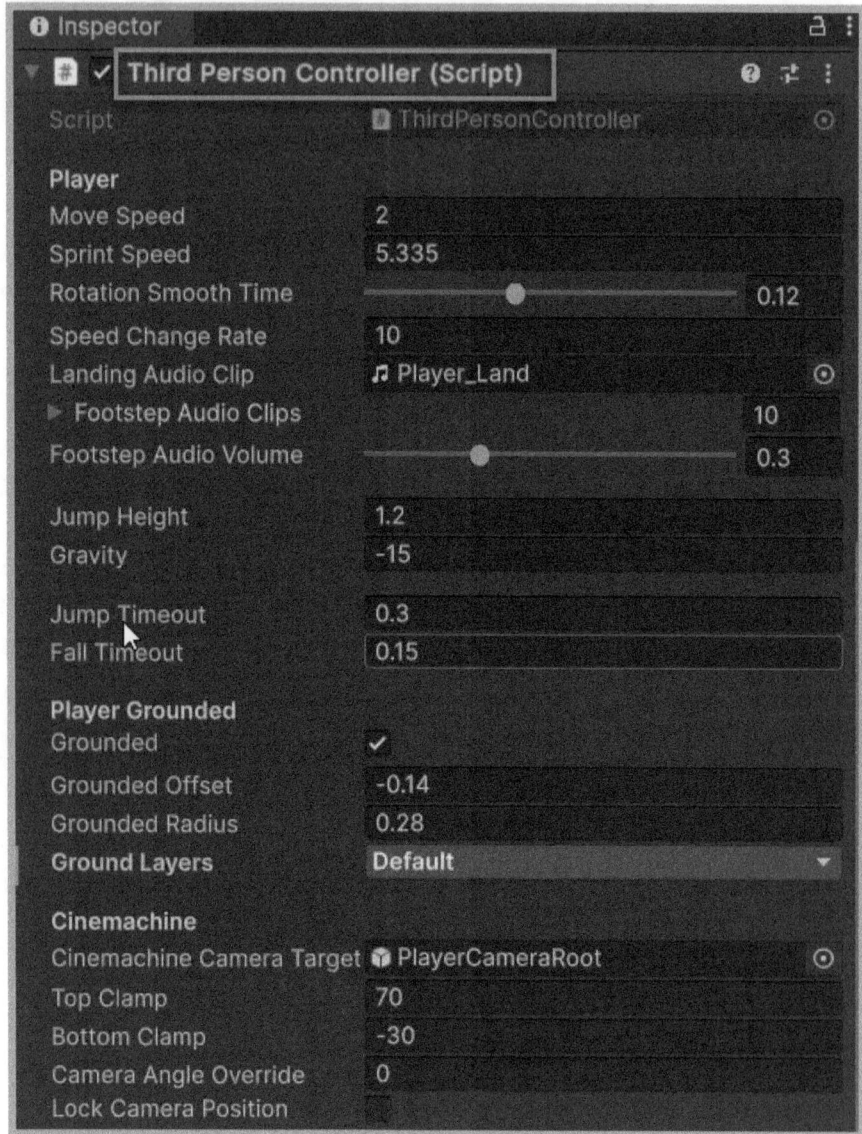

Figure 1-9. *Third-Person Controller Component*

CHAPTER 1   UNITY'S CHARACTER CONTROLLERS

Now, let's look at the properties available under the heading Cinemachine (Figure 1-9) that are unique to the Third-Person Controller.

- Camera Angle Override: This property allows developers to manually adjust the camera's angle, overriding the automatic angle calculated by Cinemachine based on the player's input and movement. It's expressed in degrees and can affect the pitch (up and down) orientation of the camera. By modifying the Camera Angle Override, developers can fine-tune the camera's default viewing angle to better suit specific gameplay requirements or aesthetic choices. For instance, setting a positive value might tilt the camera downwards, offering players a better view of the ground or objects below them, useful in platforming sections where precise jumps are necessary. Conversely, a negative value tilts the camera upwards, which could be used to emphasize the vastness of an environment or to focus on aerial elements of gameplay. Adjusting this property allows for creative control over the player's perspective, enhancing the visual storytelling or gameplay experience without altering the character's orientation or movement mechanics directly.

- Lock Camera Position: The Lock Camera Position property enables developers to fix the camera in a specific position, preventing it from moving or rotating in response to player inputs. This can be useful in scripted events or specific gameplay scenarios where maintaining a consistent view is crucial. Enabling Lock Camera Position effectively freezes the camera's orientation and position, offering a steady viewpoint. This could be

47

particularly effective during narrative-driven sequences, where the focus is on dialogue or environmental storytelling, and player control over the camera might distract from the intended focal points. For gameplay, it can be used to create challenge segments where the player must navigate obstacles with a fixed camera angle, introducing a layer of difficulty or variety to the gameplay. However, it's important to use this feature strategically or as a gameplay mechanic, as it removes a layer of player agency over camera control, which can be frustrating if overused or poorly implemented.

The Third-Person Controller makes use of the Animator component to control and transition between different animations based on the player character's actions and movements. This setup allows for a fluid and dynamic portrayal of the character's interactions within the game world. Here's an overview of how the Animator component is set up and utilized within this context (Figure 1-10):

- Animator Controller: The Animator component is linked to an Animator Controller (Figure 1-11), which contains a state machine defining various animation states (e.g., idle, walking, running, jumping, in air, etc.) and the transitions between them. These states are typically associated with animation clips that visually represent each state.

- Parameters: The state transitions within the Animator Controller are governed by parameters (e.g., speed, grounded, jump, freefall, etc.) that are dynamically set via script based on the player's input and the character's interaction with the environment. These parameters are used to trigger the appropriate animations at the right time.

CHAPTER 1   UNITY'S CHARACTER CONTROLLERS

- Animation Blend Trees: For movements like idle, walking, and running, blend trees are often used within the Animator Controller. Blend trees allow for seamless blending between animations (e.g., from walking to running) based on a parameter, typically the movement speed, ensuring smooth transitions that reflect the character's change in pace. In Figure 1-11, the state "Idle Walk Run Blend" is a blend tree that blends these individual animations based on the speed parameter. Likewise, the state "JumpLand" represents another blend tree.

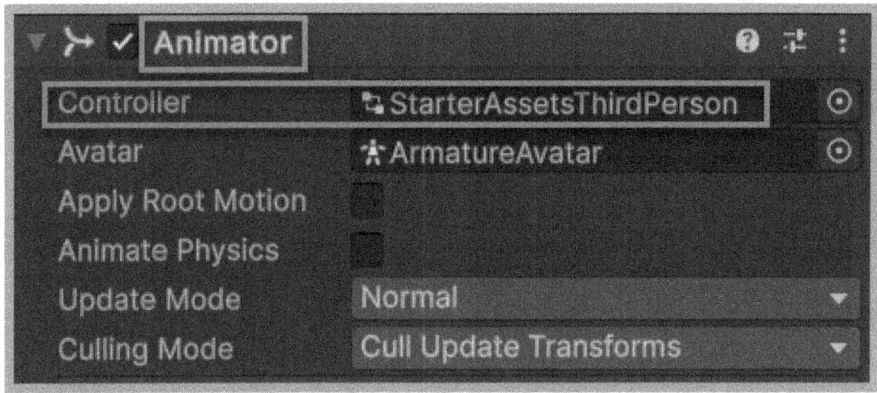

Figure 1-10. *Animator Component*

The ThirdPersonController script continuously updates the speed parameter based on the player's movement input, causing the Animator to transition between idle, walking, and running states. This is typically done by measuring the magnitude of the movement vector and applying it as a speed value to the Animator.

CHAPTER 1   UNITY'S CHARACTER CONTROLLERS

The jump action updates a boolean parameter in the Animator controller when invoked, triggering the jump animation. Upon landing (detected through the grounded check), the Animator transitions to the landing animation before returning to the base locomotion state.

For directional movement and rotation, the Animator controller parameters are adjusted to align the character's animation direction with the input direction, ensuring that the character visually moves and turns in a manner consistent with player inputs.

By carefully managing these parameters and understanding the Animator Controller's setup, in conjunction with the Third-Person Controller script, developers can create a responsive and visually appealing character movement system for third-person games.

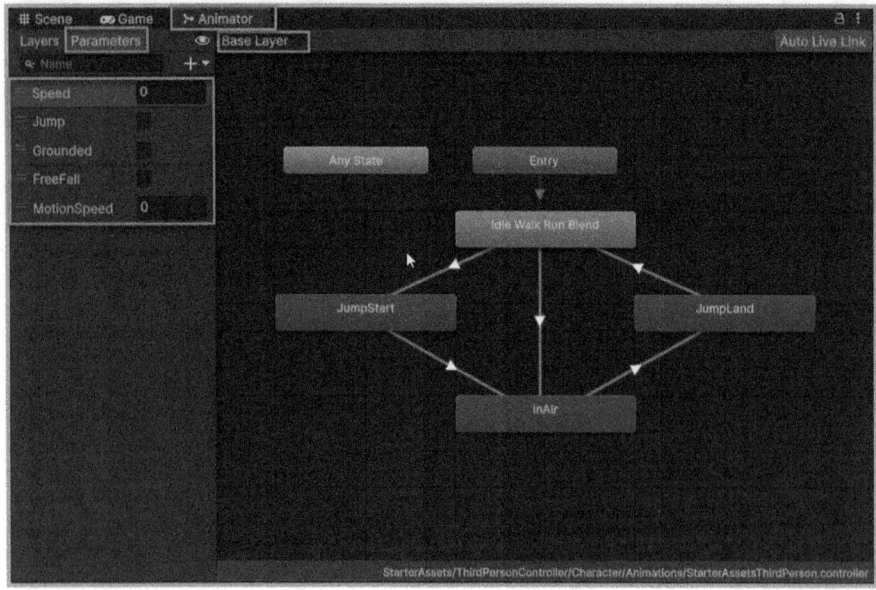

Figure 1-11. *Animator Controller*

Recipe 1-7: Integrating Gamepad Support

Problem

In modern game development, catering to players who prefer various input methods is crucial for accessibility and user satisfaction. However, integrating gamepad support can be challenging, especially ensuring that the game responds well across different gamepad brands and configurations while maintaining a seamless and intuitive control experience.

Solution

Unity's new Input System, combined with the pre-configured Starter Assets, simplifies the integration of gamepad support by allowing developers to map gamepad controls to in-game actions effectively. By utilizing the "Player Actions Map" within the Starter Assets (Input Action Asset), developers can easily assign actions like moving, looking, jumping, and sprinting to gamepad buttons and axes. This system supports a broad range of gamepads, ensuring that players can use their preferred controllers. Further customization and testing with various gamepads are encouraged to fine-tune control sensitivity and responsiveness, ensuring a high-quality gameplay experience across all devices.

How It Works

The new Unity Input System that you have been using throughout this chapter is a flexible and customizable system that allows for easy setup of various input devices. It supports a wide range of devices, including gamepads, enabling you to define actions and bindings that can be easily mapped to different controls.

CHAPTER 1   UNITY'S CHARACTER CONTROLLERS

Unity's Starter Assets are engineered with inclusivity in mind, offering out-of-the-box support for various input methods, including gamepads. Central to this support is the Input Actions system, which simplifies the process of mapping gamepad buttons and axes to in-game actions. This chapter section delves into the "Player Actions Map" provided within the Starter Assets, highlighting the pre-configured gamepad actions and their direct correlation to gamepad inputs, ensuring a robust and intuitive control scheme for gamepad users.

With the Player Armature game object selected in the hierarchy, locate the Player Input component within the Inspector. You will note that its Actions property has been populated with the default "Starter Assets (Input Action Asset)," which could serve as the building block upon which you configure further actions. Double-click on the "Starter Assets (Input Action Asset)" within the Inspector to launch the Starter Assets (Input Actions) window (Figure 1-6). This Input Actions asset can contain several action maps. Here the "Player Actions Map" is pivotal for gameplay. This map outlines all the primary actions a player can perform, such as moving, looking around, jumping, and sprinting. Each action is then linked to specific gamepad controls, demonstrating a thoughtful integration that caters to a seamless gamepad gameplay experience. Some preconfigured Gamepad Actions have been listed below:

- Move: The Move action is typically bound to the left analog stick of a gamepad, allowing players to navigate the character through the game world. The input from the analog stick is translated into a Vector2 value, representing the character's intended movement direction and speed based on the stick's displacement.

- Look: The Look action leverages the right analog stick, enabling players to control the camera or character's viewpoint. Similar to Move, it produces a Vector2 value

CHAPTER 1 UNITY'S CHARACTER CONTROLLERS

that dictates the camera's or character's orientation, facilitating a smooth and responsive aiming or looking mechanism.

- Jump: Bound to a face button (e.g., "A" on an Xbox controller or the South button on other gamepads), the Jump action allows players to perform jumps or leaps. This discrete input is detected as a button press, triggering the character to jump in response to the player's command.

- Sprint: The Sprint action is often associated with another face button or a trigger. Here it is associated with the left trigger on gamepads, enabling players to increase the character's movement speed. Holding down the associated button or trigger activates sprinting, allowing for faster navigation at the expense of stealth or precision.

Each action defined within the Player Actions Map is meticulously crafted to correspond with natural gamepad usage, ensuring that the transition between different input methods is seamless. The Unity Input System's architecture allows these mappings to be universally applied across various gamepad models and brands, offering broad compatibility.

Testing these pre-configured gamepad actions is crucial to fine-tuning the gameplay experience. Developers should engage in iterative testing processes, using different types of gamepads to ensure that the mappings are intuitive and responsive. Adjustments may be required to account for factors like dead zones and sensitivity, particularly for analog inputs like the Move and Look actions, which can be achieved by fine-tuning the Binding Properties values.

CHAPTER 1   UNITY'S CHARACTER CONTROLLERS

Within the Player Input component, the Default Scheme option allows for specifying the input device, including the Gamepad, Xbox Controller, or PS4 Controller, tailoring the setup to the specific hardware in use. Opting for "Gamepad" provides a generic configuration suitable for a wide range of controllers. Alternatively, selecting "<Any>" from the dropdown ensures universal compatibility, accommodating any connected controller. To verify functionality and ensure an optimal gameplay experience, it is recommended to conduct playtesting with your controller connected to observe the interaction and responsiveness of the input scheme in action.

Recipe 1-8: Customizing the Character Model

Problem

Integrating a new character model into Unity's third-person controller can be challenging due to the need for compatibility with pre-existing animations and control schemes. Ensuring that the new model adheres to specific rigging standards and scales correctly within the existing game environment is crucial for seamless functionality and animation fidelity.

Solution

To effectively swap the default character model with a new humanoid model, begin by ensuring the new model is rigged as a humanoid and positioned in a T-pose. Import the model, adjust its rig settings in Unity to match the humanoid configuration, and assign the correct Avatar. Replace the existing character model in the third-person controller's hierarchy with the new model, ensuring it is properly nested under the appropriate parent objects. Update the Animator component on the controller to use the new model's Avatar. Through careful testing and adjustments, such as

CHAPTER 1 UNITY'S CHARACTER CONTROLLERS

fine-tuning the animations and scaling, you can ensure the new character model integrates flawlessly with the existing control and animation systems, enhancing the visual appeal and uniqueness of your game.

How It Works

Swapping out the default character in Unity's Starter Assets for a third-person controller with a new character model involves several steps. This process ensures that the new character integrates seamlessly with the existing animations and controls. Below are the necessary steps, including prerequisites for the new character model:

- Humanoid Rig: The new character model must be rigged as a humanoid. This setup allows Unity to map the character's bone structure to its animation system effectively.

- T-Pose: The model should be in a T-pose when rigged. This pose is crucial for correctly mapping the animations from the Unity Animator to the character's skeleton.

- Compatible Scale: Ensure the character's scale matches the scale used in your Unity project to avoid any discrepancies in movement or interaction within the game world.

If you choose to use a humanoid character model from Unity's Asset Store, you could use either Banana Man, which is a free asset provided by Banana Yellow Games, or you could use Unity's famous humanoid robot, Robot Kyle, which is available for URP as of version 2.1.0. If you choose to use Banana Man in your Unity project, you may need to utilize the Render Pipeline Converter to switch it to the Universal Render Pipeline (URP). Initially, download and import Banana Man using Unity's Package

CHAPTER 1   UNITY'S CHARACTER CONTROLLERS

Manager. Upon being downloaded, you will find it within your Assets/Plugins folder. Alternatively, if you prefer not to use Banana Man, you can download a humanoid model from Mixamo to use in your project. Configure the Rig: In the Project tab, navigate to the folder Assets/Plugins/Banana Yellow Games/Characters/Banana Man. Select the Banana Man imported character in the Project tab, go to the Rig tab in the Inspector, and ensure the Animation Type is set to Humanoid. Click Apply to save these settings if you have to make this change. Expand the Banana Man model, and you will note that there exists a Banana Man Avatar already. Verify that this Avatar is correctly set up by clicking the "Configure" button in the Rig tab and ensuring all bones are correctly mapped.

1. Swap the Character Model in the Third-Person Controller:

    - Return to the Playground scene. In the hierarchy, select, expand, and unpack the Player Armature prefab completely.

    - Now expand the game object Geometry so that the Armature_Mesh game object is visible. You may disable or remove this Armature_Mesh model (recommended to disable for initial testing).

    - Now from within the Project tab, drag and drop the Banana Man model into the hierarchy onto the Geometry game object, making it a child of it (Figure 1-12).

2. Update the Animator Component:

    - In the hierarchy, select the Banana Man prefab and unpack it completely. Within the Inspector, you will note that it has an Animator component. Remove this Animator component available on the Banana

CHAPTER 1   UNITY'S CHARACTER CONTROLLERS

Man game object. It's not needed as the Player Armature game object has an Animator component already.

- Select the Player Armature game object in the hierarchy, and within the Inspector, locate its Animator component. In the Animator component, replace the Avatar property with the Avatar available for Banana Man, namely, Banana Man Avatar.

3. Test and Fine-tune: Enter Play Mode to test the basic movements (walking, running, jumping) with the new Banana Man character to ensure animations are correctly applied. You may need to return to the model's import settings or the Animator configurations to adjust the mappings, scales, or other settings based on the testing outcome. Pay special attention to any clipping, animation stretching, or unnatural movements, and adjust the Avatar's configuration as needed.

Chapter 1 Unity's Character Controllers

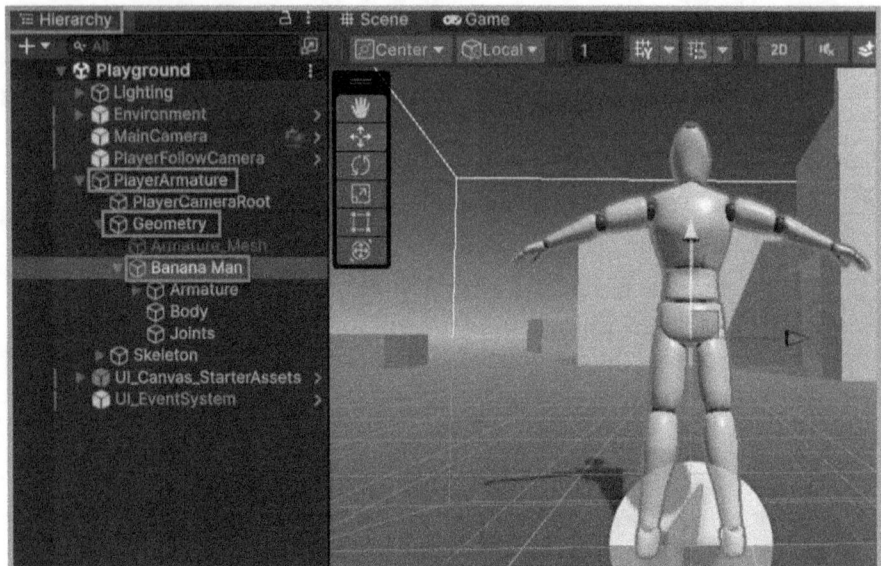

Figure 1-12. *Swapping Character Model to Banana Man*

Replacing the default character with a new model in Unity's Starter Assets for a third-person controller can significantly customize your game's look and feel. By following these detailed steps and meeting the prerequisites for the new character model, you can ensure a smooth transition and maintain the functionality of the character's controls and animations. Remember, patience and attention to detail during the setup and testing phases are key to a successful character swap.

Summary

This chapter provides an exhaustive guide on leveraging Unity's Starter Assets for character controllers, specifically focusing on first-person and third-person perspectives. It begins with instructions on accessing and integrating Unity's Starter Assets: Character Controllers package from the Unity Asset Store, emphasizing its usefulness in expediting game development through pre-built character controllers. This foundational asset enables developers to incorporate sophisticated character movement and control systems into their games efficiently, underlining its importance in creating dynamic and responsive gameplay experiences.

This chapter methodically guides the reader through downloading and importing the Starter Assets: Character Controllers | URP package into a Unity project, providing a hands-on approach to understanding the setup and customization of first-person and third-person character controllers. This section is particularly valuable for developers aiming to fine-tune character dynamics and camera controls to suit their game's unique gameplay mechanics.

The technical aspects of character controllers are then delved into, offering insights into Unity's character controller system's complexity and functionality. This segment educates on advanced input handling, mobile compatibility, and the extensibility of starter assets, thereby equipping developers with the knowledge to modify and enhance character controllers for a personalized gaming experience. The inclusion of practical exercises, such as configuring controllers for Xbox input and touch functionality, exemplifies the chapter's practical approach to teaching character controller customization.

In conclusion, this chapter serves as a comprehensive manual for game developers seeking to master Unity's character controllers. It seamlessly blends theoretical knowledge with practical application, ensuring readers are well-equipped to implement dynamic and immersive character interactions in their Unity games. From setting up starter assets to customizing character dynamics and integrating mobile controls, the chapter provides a step-by-step guide that is both instructive and insightful, catering to both novice and intermediate developers aiming to elevate their game development skills within the Unity ecosystem.

CHAPTER 2

Unity's New Input System

In this chapter, you explore Unity's New Input System, a cutting-edge framework that significantly improves game development through superior control and flexibility of player inputs. This system transforms input management with its scalable and intuitive approach to player interactions. Moving beyond the basic setup, you delve into the New Input System's complexities, focusing on the Player Input component and leveraging Starter Assets (Input Actions) introduced in the first chapter. This section also guides readers in setting up a prototype in-game menu, which is smoothly integrated with the input system, culminating in the creation of a re-bindable control system. Through detailed exploration, developers will gain essential insights and tools for advanced input handling, enhancing the overall gaming experience.

CHAPTER 2   UNITY'S NEW INPUT SYSTEM

Recipe 2-1: Harnessing Unity's New Input System for Enhanced Control Flexibility

Problem

Unity's legacy Input Manager is limited in its ability to handle dynamic control schemes and lacks support for modern controller features, hindering the development of games that require flexible and contextual input configurations.

Solution

Migrating to Unity's New Input System enables developers to utilize a more robust and flexible framework that supports a wide range of devices and input types, including touchpads and gyroscopes. This system allows for the easy implementation of re-bindable controls and contextual input adjustments, enhancing gameplay interactions and ensuring future-proof projects. Through its event-driven architecture, the system simplifies input management across different platforms and makes it easier to integrate complex input configurations, providing a better foundation for developing advanced game mechanics and improving player experience.

How It Works

Unity's legacy Input Manager falls short in several areas where the New Input System excels. Primarily, the older system's static nature makes it challenging to implement dynamic control schemes or adjust inputs based on contextual game states. It lacks direct support for modern controller features, such as touch pads and gyroscopes, limiting the scope of gameplay interactions that can be designed. Furthermore, the process of input rebinding in the legacy system is notably cumbersome for both developers and players, often requiring additional scripts and interfaces

CHAPTER 2   UNITY'S NEW INPUT SYSTEM

to achieve what the New Input System offers natively. By adopting the New Input System, developers not only gain access to a more robust and intuitive framework but also ensure their projects are future-proof, ready to embrace the evolving landscape of game development and player expectations.

The migration to Unity's New Input System offers a myriad of benefits, marking a significant advancement in how developers handle player inputs within their games. The new Input System introduces a modular, event-driven architecture that enhances control and flexibility. This new framework supports a wide range of input devices out-of-the-box, facilitates complex input configurations, and enables seamless integration of custom input devices. Moreover, its ability to handle multiple input actions simultaneously allows for more sophisticated and responsive game mechanics, ultimately leading to a richer player experience. The system's design not only streamlines the development process but also significantly reduces the complexity involved in creating adaptable and cross-platform compatible controls.

In Chapter 1, upon integrating Unity's Starter Assets: Character Controllers package into a project, the new Unity Input System is automatically set up and ready to use, showcasing a practical implementation of this advanced input framework. The New Input System can be found within Unity's Package Manager, which serves as the hub for managing the software dependencies and libraries your project requires. To locate the New Input System within the Package Manager, one can simply navigate to the "Unity Registry" section, where the Input System package, alongside its documentation and version details, is listed. The package also includes a variety of samples that demonstrate its capabilities and usage, such as On-Screen controls, Rebinding UI, and UI vs Game Input. These samples are invaluable resources, offering practical examples and templates that can be directly applied or modified to suit the specific needs of your game development project (Figure 2-1).

CHAPTER 2   UNITY'S NEW INPUT SYSTEM

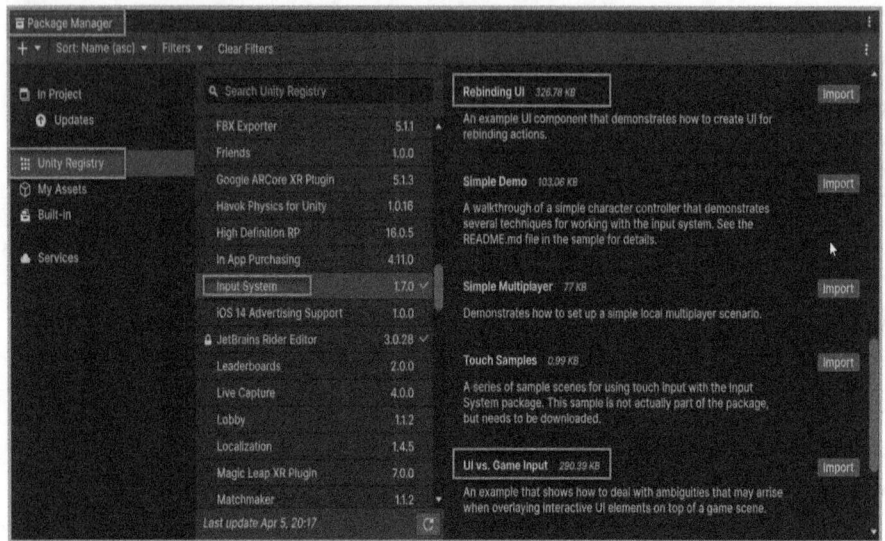

Figure 2-1. *Package Manager – Unity's New Input System*

Understanding the workings of the Input System Package within the context of the Starter Assets: Character Controllers package, developers gain a hands-on understanding of how to leverage the New Input System's features, unveiling the system's efficiency and adaptability in managing inputs for character movement and interaction. This integration exemplifies how the New Input System abstracts input handling away from hardware devices, allowing developers to focus on defining the actions and contexts relevant to their game mechanics. The Character Controller assets you used in Chapter 1, utilize Input Actions, a core feature of the New Input System, to map player commands to character actions such as moving, jumping, looking, and sprinting. This approach not only simplifies the input management process but also enhances the game's portability across different platforms and input devices. In this chapter, you will explore the provided "Starter Assets" Input Action Asset and learn to configure Action Maps, actions, and bindings to implement responsive and intuitive control schemes, thereby elevating the gameplay experience.

Input Action Asset

An Input Action Asset is a comprehensive container that encapsulates various input actions, action maps, and bindings in a single, manageable asset. This system represents a shift from the traditional polling-based input management to a more event-driven model, where inputs from different sources (like keyboards, mice, gamepads, etc.) are abstracted into actions (like jump, move, look, sprint, shoot, etc.) that are meaningful within the game. Instead of checking each frame whether a specific key is pressed, the system allows developers to define actions and associate those with any number of physical inputs, making it significantly easier to manage complex input schemes, remap controls, and support multiple input devices.

With the third-person controller playground scene open, in the hierarchy, select the PlayerArmature game object. Within the Inspector scroll down to the Player Input component and you will see the default "Starter Assets" Input Action Asset provided by Unity that comes pre-configured with a set of common actions and bindings designed to accelerate the development process, especially for character movement and camera control. Double-click on this "Starter Assets" Input Action Asset in the Inspector to have the Starter Assets (Input Actions) window open (Figure 2-2).

You will note that this default "Starter Assets" Input Action Asset is organized into a single Action Map, i.e., "Player," reflecting on the gameplay context within your game. This action map contains actions like "Move," "Look," "Jump," and "Sprint" with bindings that define how these actions are triggered by player inputs across various devices. This setup showcases the new Input System's flexibility, enabling a character to move using either keyboard or gamepad inputs without the need for separate code paths.

CHAPTER 2 UNITY'S NEW INPUT SYSTEM

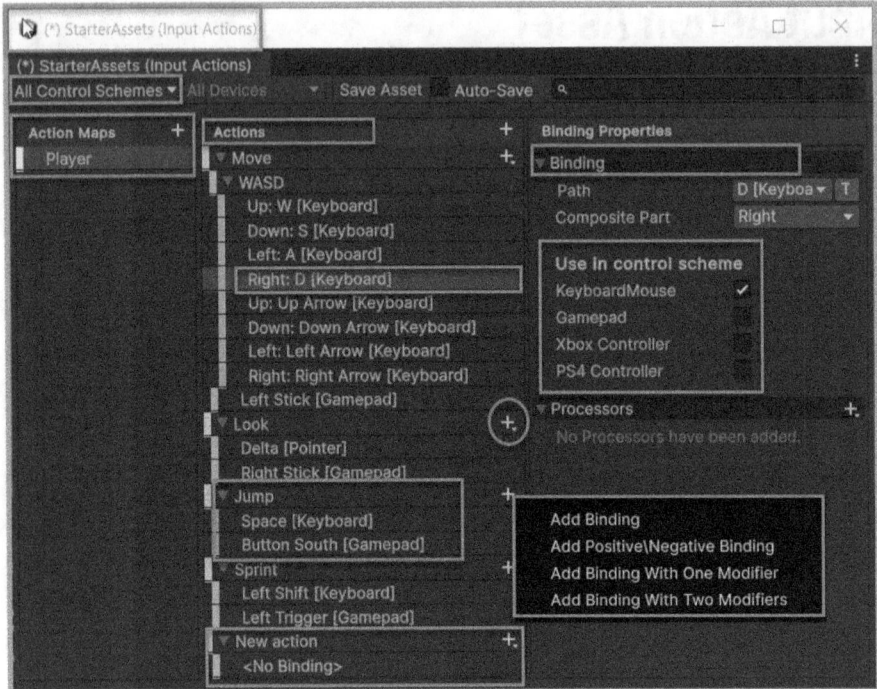

Figure 2-2. *Input Actions Asset – StarterAssets*

Action Maps

An Action Map is a conceptual grouping of related input actions that are intended to be used together under certain gameplay conditions. Each Action Map serves as a container for individual actions, such as "Move," "Jump," "Sprint," "Look," "Shoot," or "Interact," which represent meaningful inputs from the player. These actions are then mapped to specific physical inputs, like keyboard keys, mouse movements, gamepad buttons, or touch gestures, depending on the device being used.

The "Starter Assets" Input Action Asset, depicted in Figure 2-2, consists of a solitary action map named "Player." This serves as a foundational example; however, in practice, an Input Action Asset can encompass multiple Action Maps tailored to various gameplay aspects. These can range from UI Navigation and Vehicle Control to Inventory Management, Combat, and Dialogue, each facilitating specific interactive experiences within a game. This versatility allows developers to craft nuanced and responsive control schemes across different game states and functionalities.

The primary purpose of Action Maps is to organize and manage inputs logically and efficiently, allowing developers to easily switch between different sets of controls based on the current state of the game or application. For example, a game might have separate Action Maps for general gameplay, menu navigation, and vehicle control. This organization simplifies the process of enabling and disabling different control schemes as the player moves between gameplay modes, such as transitioning from on-foot exploration to driving a vehicle. A developer can easily switch between the different action maps via code.

In essence, Action Maps facilitate a modular approach to input management. They allow for the clean separation of different input contexts, making it easier for developers to design, maintain, and extend the input-handling logic within their projects. This system not only enhances the developer's ability to create more complex and dynamic input schemes but also improves the end user's experience by providing more intuitive and context-sensitive controls.

Actions

An "Action" represents a specific input or a group of inputs that trigger a defined behavior or event within a game or application. Actions abstract the concept of player inputs away from specific devices or buttons, focusing instead on the intention behind the input. This allows developers to design controls based on the actions players need to perform, rather than the specific hardware they might be using.

Within the "Player" action Map, the actions that have been provided by default are Move, Look, Jump, and Sprint. Each action represents a specific type of player input that triggers certain behaviors in the game, such as moving the character, looking around, jumping, or sprinting.

An Action comprises several key components:

- Name: A unique identifier for the action, such as "Jump" or "Look," which helps in referencing it within the game's code.

- Action Type: Specifies the nature of the input, which can be a button press, a value change (like an analog stick movement), or a passive state. The action type determines how the input system interprets the incoming data. Common types include "Button" for simple on/off inputs, "Value" for inputs that have a range (like a joystick axis), and "Pass through" for raw input data.

- Interactions: Interactions modify how an action processes input, allowing for more complex input behaviors like tap, double-tap, or hold. They provide developers with the flexibility to create nuanced input responses beyond simple press-and-release mechanisms.

- Processors: Input processors apply modifications to the input data before it's used by an action, such as scaling, normalization, or dead zone processing. This is useful for adjusting the raw input data to fit the game's needs better.

CHAPTER 2   UNITY'S NEW INPUT SYSTEM

- Callbacks: Actions trigger callbacks (events) when they are performed. Developers can write code that responds to these events, linking the abstract input action (like "Jump") to a concrete response in the game (like making the character leap into the air).

- Bindings: These are the actual hardware inputs (e.g., keyboard keys, mouse buttons, and gamepad buttons) that are linked to the action. An action can have multiple bindings, allowing it to be triggered by different inputs across various devices.

1. **Move**: The "Move" action's type is set to "Value" and its control type to "Vector 2," as these types effectively translate the varied inputs from devices like keyboards (with discrete WASD keys) and gamepads (with analog sticks providing continuous input) into smooth, directional movement within the game.

   The "Value" action type is chosen for the "Move" action because movement typically involves continuous input rather than a binary press/release mechanism. This type is ideal for capturing inputs that vary over a range, such as the degree to which a joystick is tilted or the combination of keys pressed to move in a particular direction. The "Value" type ensures that the action can process and respond to the nuanced variations in input that are characteristic of movement controls, providing smooth and precise control over character movement within the game.

For the Control Type, a "Vector 2" is used because movement in a two-dimensional plane (or even simulating 3D movement on a 2D input device like a gamepad or keyboard) requires two values to represent both horizontal and vertical directions simultaneously. For example, moving diagonally requires both an X (horizontal) and a Y (vertical) input value. The "Vector 2" type allows the input system to capture and process these two-dimensional inputs as a single entity, making it easier to implement responsive and intuitive movement controls that can handle the full range of possible player movements.

2. **Look**: The "Look" action's type is set to "Value" and its control type to "Vector 2," to adeptly handle the complexities of camera or player viewpoint movement, which typically involves continuous, multi-directional input. This configuration effectively utilizes the input system's capability to handle complex, continuous inputs, ensuring that the "Look" action can provide players with a responsive and immersive camera control experience, essential for navigating and interacting with the game environment.

    The "Value" action type selected for the "Look" action captures the continuous and nuanced input necessary for controlling the camera or player's view direction. Unlike discrete actions that are either on or off (such as jumping or shooting), looking around in a game environment usually requires precise, variable input to smoothly transition the view across different axes. This continuous input allows for the gradual and precise adjustments needed for a player to look around with a high degree of control. The choice of "Vector 2" as the control type reflects the need to simultaneously process two-dimensional input data for looking around, which involves both horizontal (left/right) and vertical (up/down) movements. This is particularly relevant when using input devices like a mouse, where horizontal movement controls the rotation of the view along the yaw axis and vertical movement controls the pitch of the view. Similarly, for gamepads, the analog stick's X and Y positions provide this two-dimensional input. The "Vector 2" control type allows these inputs to be captured as a cohesive unit, facilitating a smooth and intuitive-looking mechanism within the game.

3. **Jump:** As jumping is typically a discrete, binary action within games, the "Jump" action's "Action Type" is set to "Button." Unlike continuous inputs that vary over time or have multiple degrees of input (like moving or looking around), jumping is usually an instantaneous action that occurs when a player presses a specific button. The "Button" action type is ideal for this kind of input because it is designed to handle on/off state changes, perfectly suiting actions that don't require gradual changes or sustained input. This configuration underscores the flexibility of Unity's new Input System in accommodating a wide range of action types, from the nuanced, continuous inputs required

for movement and looking to the simple, binary inputs needed for actions like jumping, ensuring developers can create intuitive and engaging gameplay mechanics.

Setting the "Action Type" to "Button" for the "Jump" action ensures that the input system listens for a clear, distinct press event to trigger the jump. This approach simplifies the detection and handling of jump inputs across various devices, whether it's a spacebar press on a keyboard, a button press on a gamepad, or any other designated jump control. It allows for immediate response to player inputs, providing a tactile and responsive gaming experience where actions like jumping feel direct and intentional.

4. **Sprint:** The "Sprint" action uses The "Pass Through" action type to ensure that the input is captured directly without any internal processing or state management by the Input System. This is particularly useful for actions that might be based on a combination of inputs or where the raw input data is important. For the "Sprint" action, using "Pass Through" allows the game to directly read the input state (e.g., whether the sprint button is being held down) at any given frame, enabling a more fluid and responsive control for actions that can be initiated or stopped rapidly, such as starting or stopping a sprint.

Setting the "Control Type" to "Any" signifies that the action can be triggered by any kind of input device or control, whether it's a keypress, button press, or another form of input. This level of inclusivity ensures that the "Sprint" action is accessible regardless of the player's input method, providing a universal approach that accommodates a wide range of player preferences and hardware setups. This setting is particularly advantageous for a function like sprinting, which is a common gameplay mechanic and may need to be accessible through various input devices to ensure all players can use it comfortably.

Bindings

A "Binding" is a link between a player's physical input on a device (e.g., pressing a key, moving a joystick) and an "Action" defined within the system. Bindings specify which actual hardware inputs should trigger the abstract actions (like "Jump," "Move," "Look," "Sprint," etc.) that developers have set up in their game. This allows for a clear separation between the input logic and the physical devices used, facilitating easier input management and greater flexibility in control schemes. Bindings are a crucial component of Unity's New Input System, providing the granularity and flexibility needed to create intuitive and accessible control schemes.

A Binding comprises several key aspects:

- Path: This is a device-specific identifier that points to the source of the input, such as a keyboard key (<keyboard>/a), mouse movement (<Pointer>/delta), or a gamepad stick (<Gamepad>/rightStick). The path uses a standardized syntax to refer to different input controls across various types of devices.

- Interactions: Bindings can include interactions that modify how the input is processed. Interactions determine the conditions under which an action is triggered by the input, like "Press" (input is considered when the button is pressed down) or "Hold" (action is triggered after the button has been held down for a specified duration).

- Processors: Bindings may also use processors, which modify the input data before it's passed on to the action. Processors can perform operations like normalization, dead zone adjustments, or scaling to ensure that the input data fits the game's needs more precisely.

- Composite Bindings: For more complex input scenarios, bindings can be composite, meaning they combine multiple physical inputs into a single action. For example, within the "Player" action map, the "Move" action comprises a composite binding named "WASD" that combines the "W," "A," "S," and "D" keys as well as the arrow keys into a single vector2 input. Hence, the "WASD" composite binding is of the composite type "2D Vector" as for these keyboard movements you need their X and Y axes values.

- Groups (Control Schemes): Bindings can be categorized into groups to facilitate switching between different control schemes or to enable/disable certain inputs under specific conditions. Groups can represent different, control schemes for different input methods (e.g., keyboard/mouse vs. gamepad).

CHAPTER 2   UNITY'S NEW INPUT SYSTEM

1. **WASD:** The "WASD" composite binding comprises several child bindings, namely, the keyboard keys "W," "A," "S," "D," "Up Arrow," "Down Arrow," "Left Arrow," and "Right Arrow." This composite binding combines these multiple individual inputs into a single action, in this case, mapping the familiar "WASD" and arrow keys to directional movement.

    - W/Up Arrow Key (Forward): The W or Up arrow key is bound to the forward movement, typically mapped to increase the value along the vertical axis in a Vector2, resulting in the character moving forward in the game. Its Composite Part has been set to the value "Up." This binding is configured to contribute a positive value along the Y-axis of the Vector2 when this key is pressed.

    - A/Left Arrow Key (Left): The A or Left arrow key is set up for leftward movement, mapped to decrease the value along the horizontal axis in a Vector2. Its Composite Part has been set to the value "Left." This causes the character to move left when this key is pressed, contributing a negative value along the X-axis of the Vector2.

    - S/Down Arrow Key (Backward): The S or Down arrow key corresponds to backward movement, inversely mapped to decrease the value along the vertical axis compared to the W key. Its Composite Part has been set to the value "Down." Pressing this key moves the character backward, adding a negative value to the Y-axis of the Vector2.

75

- D/Right Arrow Key (Right): The D or Right arrow key is configured for rightward movement, similarly inversely mapped to increase the value along the horizontal axis compared to the A key. Its Composite Part has been set to the value "Right." This results in the character moving right when this key is pressed, adding a positive value to the X-axis of the Vector2.

2. **Left Stick [Gamepad]:** The "Left Stick [Gamepad]" binding for the "Move" action demonstrates how Unity's new Input System can intuitively map analog inputs to character movement. This binding utilizes the analog nature of a gamepad's left stick to provide smooth, 360-degree movement control. Here's an explanation of its binding properties and setup:

    - Path: This property specifies the input source, in this case, the gamepad's left stick. It's defined with a syntax that the Input System recognizes, such as "<Gamepad>/leftStick." This path directly points to the physical control on the device, ensuring that the Input System listens for movements specifically from the left stick of any connected gamepad.

    - Interactions: While interactions can define how the input is processed (e.g., press and hold), for analog inputs like the left stick, interactions need not be explicitly set unless a specific behavior is needed, such as detecting a hard push. In many cases for movement, the raw analog input is preferred to allow for precise control over the character's speed and direction. Hence, you would note that here no interactions have been set up.

CHAPTER 2   UNITY'S NEW INPUT SYSTEM

- Processors: This property can apply modifications to the input data, such as dead zone adjustments or normalization. For a "Left Stick [Gamepad]" binding, a "Stick Deadzone" processor is used to ensure that slight, unintentional movements of the stick don't affect the character's movement. This processor filters out inputs that fall within a specified dead zone range, ensuring that only deliberate stick movements translate into in-game action.

- Groups (control scheme): This optional property allows developers to organize bindings into groups for specific control schemes or platforms. For instance, here the Left Stick [Gamepad] binding is assigned to the "Gamepad" group (control scheme) to distinguish these controls from those intended for keyboard and mouse or touch.

- Action: While not a direct property of the binding itself, the action to which this binding is attached ("Move" in this case) determines how the input data is used. For the left stick, the action's type is typically set to "Value" with a control type of "Vector2," allowing the stick's two-dimensional input (X and Y axes movement) to directly control character movement in the game space.

3. **Delta [Pointer]:** The "Delta [Pointer]" binding for the "Look" action is an excellent illustration of how Unity's new Input System can handle precise, two-dimensional input from devices like a mouse, gamepad, or touchpad, particularly for camera control or aiming mechanisms in games.

77

"Pointer Delta" refers to the change in position (delta) of a pointer device (like a mouse or finger on a touchscreen) between the current frame and the previous frame. This delta is represented as a two-dimensional vector (Vector2), where the X component corresponds to the horizontal movement, and the Y component corresponds to the vertical movement. This data is crucial for implementing responsive and intuitive look controls in games, allowing players to control the camera or their viewpoint with precision. By measuring the delta, or change in position, rather than the absolute position, the system can accurately track and respond to the speed and direction of the player's input, translating it into smooth and continuous camera movements. The "Pointer Delta" effectively captures the essence of how the player interacts with the game through the pointer device, providing a direct link between physical movement and in-game action. Here's a breakdown of its binding properties and setup:

- Path: This specifies the source of the input, in this case, "Pointer/delta." The path directs the Input System to listen for the delta movement of the pointer device, which includes mice, touchpads, or even touchscreens when used with a dragging motion.

- Interactions: For the "Delta [Pointer]" binding, interactions are typically not specified because the interest lies in the raw, continuous movement data. The focus is on capturing every minute change in position, crucial for aiming or looking around in a 3D environment.

- Processors: Processors might be applied to modify the raw input data for a more consistent or customized experience. Here the processors for pointer delta input include "Invert Vector 2" (to invert the input axis, useful for inverting the Y-axis in camera controls) and "ScaleVector2" (to scale the input values, adjusting sensitivity). These allow developers to fine-tune how pointer movements translate into in-game actions.

- Groups (control scheme): While optional, groups can be used to categorize this binding under specific control schemes. Here it has been categorized under the "Mouse & Keyboard" control scheme, ensuring that the game responds appropriately to different input methods.

- Action: Attached to the "Look" action, which has been configured with an action type of "Value" and a control type of "Vector2." This setup is chosen because the pointer delta provides two-dimensional data (movement along the X and Y axes), which would directly influence the direction and speed of the camera or crosshair movement in the game.

4. **Right Stick [Gamepad]:** The "Right Stick [Gamepad]" binding for the "Look" action is configured to facilitate camera control via a gamepad's right stick. This setup is crucial for providing a smooth and intuitive look mechanism in games. To ensure the input from the right stick translates effectively into game actions, several

processors have been applied to the binding. While the exact processors used may vary based on specific game design requirements, the processors used here include:

- Invert Vector 2: The "Invert Vector 2" processor may be used to invert the input from the stick along one or both axes. Inverting the Y-axis is a common preference among players for look controls, where moving the stick up results in looking down and vice versa. This processor adjusts the input data to match player expectations and comfort.

- Stick Deadzone: This processor is applied to manage the dead zone of the analog stick. A dead zone is a threshold below which input is ignored, helping to prevent unintended camera movement when the stick is near its neutral position. The Stick Deadzone processor ensures that slight, unintentional movements of the stick don't register as input, providing a cleaner and more intentional control experience.

- Scale Vector 2: This processor scales the input from the stick, effectively adjusting the sensitivity of the look controls. By scaling the vector, developers can fine-tune how much the camera moves in response to stick movement, allowing for precise control over camera behavior and player aim.

The other binding properties are similar to the "Left Stick [Gamepad] discussed earlier.

5. **Space [Keyboard]:** The "Space [Keyboard]" binding for the "Jump" action is a straightforward example of mapping a key press to a specific game action using Unity's new Input System. This setup allows for the detection and handling of the jump action initiated by pressing the spacebar on a keyboard. Here's a detailed look at the binding properties for this configuration:

    - Path: This property specifies the input source, which in this case is the spacebar on the keyboard. It is defined using a specific syntax recognized by the Input System, such as "<Keyboard>/space." This path directs the Input System to listen for press events specifically from the spacebar, linking this physical action with the in-game jump behavior.

    - Interactions: The interactions property can be used to further define how the input is processed in relation to the action. For a jump action triggered by the spacebar, a common interaction is "Press," which ensures the action is triggered the moment the key is pressed down. This provides immediate feedback to the player, making the jump feel responsive. However, this is not a mandatory requirement to have the jump action triggered so has not been used here.

    - Processors: For a digital button press like the spacebar, processors are generally not necessary because the input is binary (pressed or not pressed) without any variable magnitude that needs adjustment. Therefore, this property is not used in the "Space [Keyboard]" binding for the "Jump" action.

- Groups (control scheme): This optional property allows developers to categorize bindings into control schemes or groups for organizational purposes or for supporting multiple input methods. The "Jump" action bound to the "Space [Keyboard]" is a part of the "Keyboard & Mouse" control scheme, distinguishing it from gamepad controls.

- Action: This isn't a direct property of the binding itself but is crucial in understanding the context. The "Jump" action, to which the "Space [Keyboard]" binding is attached, has been configured with an action type of "Button," indicating it's a discrete action triggered by a binary input. This setup aligns with the nature of jumping in games, which typically requires a single, decisive input to initiate.

6. **Button South [Gamepad]:** The "Button South [Gamepad]" binding for the "Jump" action is designed to map the action of jumping to the most accessible button typically found on the face of a gamepad, often labeled as "A" on Xbox controllers, "X" on PlayStation controllers, and "B" on Nintendo systems. This setup exemplifies the Input System's ability to abstract input commands across different hardware, ensuring a consistent gameplay experience regardless of the controller brand or model. Here's an overview of the binding properties for this configuration:

- Path: The input source is specified here, targeting the "Button South" on any connected gamepad, which is universally recognized by the Input System through a standardized identifier like "<Gamepad>/buttonSouth." This path ensures that the Input System listens for press events from this specific button across all supported gamepad types.

- Interactions: For jump actions, the "Press" interaction is commonly used, configured to trigger the action as soon as the button is pressed down. This provides a responsive feel to the jump command, crucial for timing jump-sensitive gameplay. The interaction ensures that the jump occurs immediately, offering players precise control over their character's jumping movements. However, this is not a mandatory requirement and has not been used here.

- Processors: Typically, processors are not used for binary (pressed/not pressed) inputs like a gamepad button. The input from a "Button South" press is straightforward and does not require additional processing to interpret its intention or adjust its value.

- Groups (control scheme): This property is being used here to categorize this binding under a specific control scheme group, such as "Gamepad." For the jump action, being part of a "Gamepad" group helps differentiate it from other input methods like keyboard and mouse or touch controls.

- Action: While not a property of the individual binding, it's important to note that the "Jump" action to which this binding is attached has been set up with an "Action Type" of "Button." This reflects the binary nature of the input, suitable for actions that are either in an active or inactive state, without gradations in between.

7. **Left Shift [Keyboard]:** The "Left Shift [Keyboard]" binding for the "Sprint" action demonstrates how Unity's new Input System allows developers to map specific gameplay functions to keyboard inputs, in this case, enabling a sprint action through the left shift key. This setup enhances player control by assigning an easily accessible key to a commonly used game mechanic. Here's a breakdown of the binding properties for this configuration:

    - Path: This property specifies the exact input source, here being the left shift key on a keyboard, defined with a precise identifier such as "<Keyboard>/leftShift." This path directs the Input System to listen for input events specifically from the left shift key, ensuring that the sprint action is triggered accurately when the key is pressed.

    - Interactions: The "Press" interaction is commonly applied to actions like sprinting, where the desired outcome is to initiate the sprint as soon as the key is pressed down. Alternatively, the "Hold" interaction might be used if the intention is for the sprint to only be active while the key is continuously held down. This ensures a responsive and intuitive control mechanism for the sprint action, allowing for immediate player feedback.

- Processors: For a binary input like a key press, processors are typically not necessary, as there's no need to modify the raw input data. The input from pressing the left shift key is straightforward, capturing the press without requiring adjustments or interpretations.

- Groups (control scheme): This optional property allows the binding to be categorized within a specific control scheme or group, such as "Keyboard & Mouse," distinguishing it from other input methods like gamepad controls. Grouping bindings in this manner facilitates the management of multiple control schemes within the game.

- Action: The "Sprint" action would be configured with an "Action Type" of "Button" or possibly "Pass Through" depending on how the sprint mechanic is designed to function within the game. The "Button" type is suitable for discrete actions that are either on or off, while "Pass Through" could be used for actions where continuous input state information is necessary. Here, the "Sprint" action has been configured with the "Action Type" of "Pass Through."

8. **Left Trigger [Gamepad]:** The "Left Trigger [Gamepad]" binding for the "Sprint" action is a strategic choice that utilizes the analog nature of the gamepad's left trigger to control sprinting in games. This setup could allow for nuanced control over the sprint action, such as enabling variable sprint speeds based on how far the trigger is pressed. However, this kind of setup has not been programmed for use within the provided "Starter Assets – Input Action Assets." Here's an explanation of the binding properties for this configuration:

- Path: The property identifies the specific input source, in this case, the gamepad's left trigger. It's defined with a precise path, like "<Gamepad>/leftTrigger," which tells the Input System to listen for input specifically from the left trigger of any connected gamepad. This direct path ensures that the sprint action can be tied to the analog input provided by the trigger's position.

- Interactions: No Interactions have been set up here. However, for an action like sprinting, which might be designed to activate based on the degree of pressure applied to the trigger, the "Press" interaction would typically be used to determine the point at which the action triggers. However, developers might also consider custom interactions or thresholds to better match the desired gameplay dynamics, such as triggering sprint at a certain pressure level on the trigger.

- Processors: Even though no processors have been used with this binding, given the analog nature of the left trigger, processors could play a crucial role in this binding. A "Normalize" processor might be used to convert the analog input range of the trigger into a usable format, while a "Deadzone" processor could ensure that slight presses do not unintentionally activate sprinting. These processors could help in fine-
tuning how the input from the left trigger is interpreted and used within the game.

- Groups (control scheme): While optional, the "Groups" property categorizes this binding under a specific control scheme, namely "Gamepad." This helps in organizing the game's control configurations and ensures that sprinting behaves as expected when the player is using a gamepad.

- Action: While not a property of the individual binding, it's important to note that the "Sprint" action to which this binding is attached has been set up with an "Action Type" of "Pass Through." However, this binding could be configured as part of a different ("SprintGamePad" action), with an "Action Type" of "Value" given its analog input, allowing the game to detect varying levels of pressure on the trigger. This setup could then provide a range of responses, from a gradual increase in sprint speed to a binary sprint/no-sprint outcome, depending on how the game's mechanics are designed.

Control Schemes

Control Schemes in Unity's new Input System represent organized groups of input settings tailored for different types of input devices, such as gamepads, keyboards, mice, and touchscreens. Each Control Scheme defines a specific set of input bindings that correlate with the inputs available on the designated device or devices, enabling developers to easily manage and switch between different input methods based on player preferences or device availability.

Within the Starter Assets (Input Actions) window, depicted in Figure 2-2, the "All Control Schemes" dropdown menu allows developers to view and select from existing Control Schemes. This feature simplifies the process of designing, testing, and modifying input configurations across various devices. Control Schemes comprise

- Named Sets of Bindings: Each scheme is essentially a collection of input bindings that are named and saved under a specific scheme name, making them easily identifiable and selectable.

- Device Specifications: Control Schemes specify the input devices they support, organizing inputs in a way that matches the layout and capabilities of those devices.

From within the Starter Assets (Input Actions) window, depicted in Figure 2-2, select the "GamePad" control scheme available within the "All Control Schemes" dropdown menu. You will immediately note that within the "Actions" section of the window, you are now able to view just the "Gamepad" binding for each action, which makes it a lot easier to work with.

By default, Unity's Input Action-Starter Assets provide several common Control Schemes such as "Gamepad," "KeyboardMouse," "PS4 Controller," and "Xbox Controller," each set up with the basic actions and require

CHAPTER 2 UNITY'S NEW INPUT SYSTEM

you to set up only their input bindings. To manage Control Schemes the dropdown provides you with several menu items discussed below (Figure 2-3):

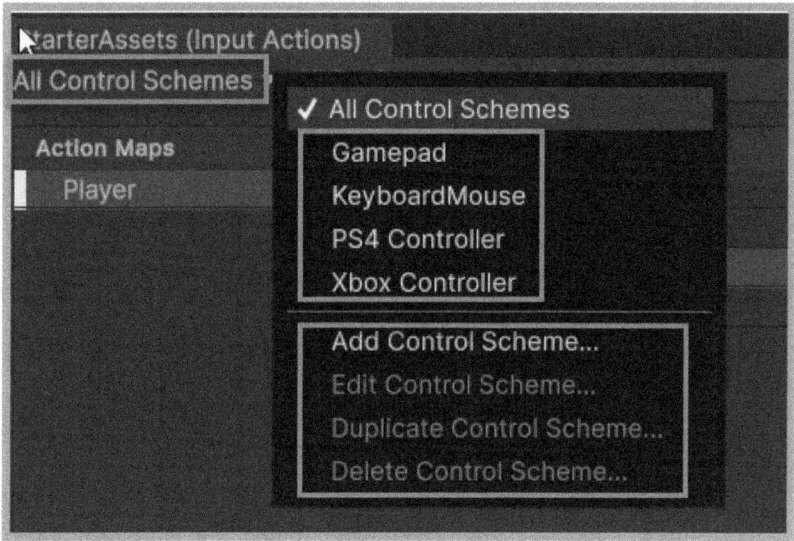

Figure 2-3. *All Control Schemes – Dropdown*

- Adding a New Scheme: Through the Input Actions window, developers can add a new Control Scheme by clicking on the plus icon or right-clicking in the Control Schemes area and selecting "Add Control Scheme."

- Editing a Scheme: Selecting a scheme allows for the modification of its name and associated devices. This is done through the same Input Actions window, where details can be directly edited. Here you need to first select the control scheme you want to edit and then select the "Edit Control Scheme" menu item.

- Duplicating a Scheme: This can be useful for creating variations of existing schemes. Duplication is typically done by first selecting the control scheme you want to duplicate and then selecting the menu item "Duplicate Control Scheme."

- Deleting a Scheme: Unneeded schemes can be removed by selecting them and choosing the "Delete Control scheme" menu item.

Adding a New Control Scheme

Let's create a new control scheme for XR controllers.

1. Add a New Control Scheme: With the Starter Assets (Input Actions) window open, select the "All Control Schemes" dropdown and from within it select the menu item "Add Control Scheme" to see the "Add Control Scheme" dialog pop-up (Figure 2-4).

2. Name and Configure the Control Scheme: Name your new Control Scheme appropriately, such as "XR Controller."

3. Choose Device: Where it states "List is Empty" click the plus icon and select "XR Controller" from the list that shows up and click Save. You might see options like "XR Controller," "XR HMD" or specific device names depending on the Unity version and the XR plugin you're using (Figure 2-4). Ideally, you would want to set up separate control schemes for the "XR Controller" and the "XR HMD."

4. Define Input Actions for the XR Controller: With the "XR Controller" control scheme setup, you will note that you have also been provided with the default actions from the "Player" Actions Map. Ideally, you would want to create a new Action Map for this new "XR Controller" control scheme and define new Input Actions specific to XR interaction. These might include actions like "Grab," "Point," or "Teleport," etc.

5. Define Bindings for Actions: For each action, specify the binding path that corresponds to buttons, triggers, or other controls on the XR Controller. Unity's Input System provides paths for common XR controller inputs.

6. Configure Additional Properties: Configure additional properties for each action as needed, such as interactions, processors, and groups, to fine-tune how inputs are handled.

7. Save and Test: After setting up your Control Scheme and defining the necessary Input Actions and bindings, save your changes in the Input Actions Editor window. Test the new Control Scheme in your project. Make sure the XR device is connected and properly configured in Unity. You may need to write or adjust scripts that use the Input System to respond to your newly configured actions.

CHAPTER 2   UNITY'S NEW INPUT SYSTEM

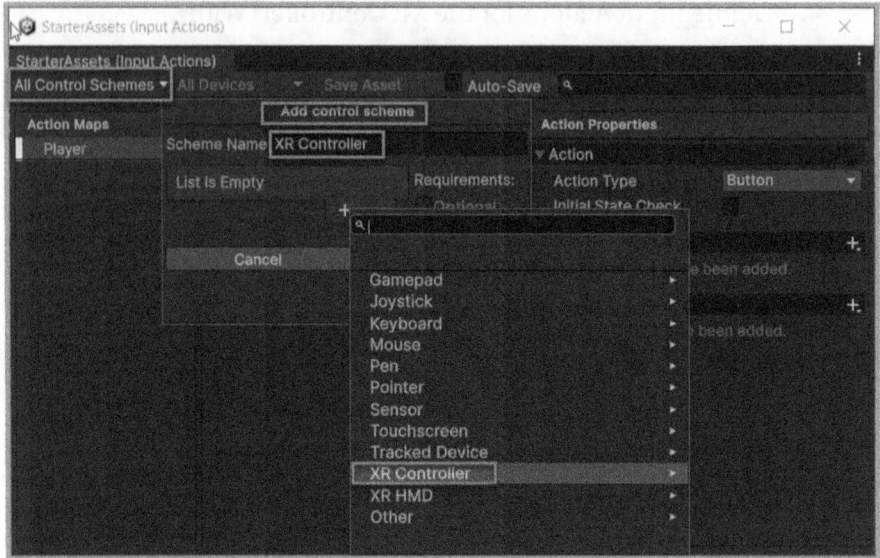

Figure 2-4. *Adding a new Control Scheme*

Handling Input in Scripts

Having explored the Input Action Asset (Starter Assets) and its various elements, namely, Action Maps, Actions, Control Schemes, Bindings, and their properties, you now need a way to use these input actions within your game scripts. This involves writing C# scripts that reference the Input Actions Asset and listen for input events. The Unity Input System offers several ways to handle input actions in scripts:

- Callbacks: You can register callback functions that the Input System will call when specific input actions occur.

- Polling: Alternatively, you can poll the current state of an input action (e.g., checking if a "Jump" action is being performed in the current frame).

CHAPTER 2 UNITY'S NEW INPUT SYSTEM

With the Player Armature game object selected in the hierarchy, within the Inspector you will note that there exists a Starter Assets Inputs script. This script is a comprehensive input handler for Unity projects that abstracts away the direct handling of keyboard, mouse, and gamepad inputs, providing a clean and accessible interface for controlling player characters. By responding to input actions defined in an Input Action Asset (Starter Assets) and updating public variables accordingly, it facilitates the creation of responsive and intuitive player controls within the Unity engine. This setup exemplifies a modular and scalable approach to input management, allowing for easy expansion or modification as the needs of your project evolve. Launch this script in the editor of your choice. This script serves as a bridge between the new Unity Input System's input actions and the game's character control logic available as part of either the ThirdPersonController script or the FirstPersonController script.

The use of the #if ENABLE_INPUT_SYSTEM directive ensures that this script only compiles and runs its input handling code if the project is set up to use the new Unity Input System. This allows for easier toggling between the legacy input system and the new Input System during development.

This script uses several public variables to hold the current state of various inputs such as movement direction (move), camera look direction (look), jump action (jump), and sprint action (sprint). These are public variables that can be accessed by other scripts in the game, typically the Character Controller script that moves and animates the player character based on these inputs.

This script defines methods that are called by the Input System (Player Input component) when specific input actions occur (e.g., moving, looking around, jumping, sprinting). These methods update the input states stored in the class. Within the Inspector locate the Player Input component and you will note that its "Behavior" property has been set to "Send Message," which determines how notifications should be sent when a player-related input event happens. You will note that beneath this dropdown the messages that will be sent, several method names have been listed (Figure 2-5).

CHAPTER 2   UNITY'S NEW INPUT SYSTEM

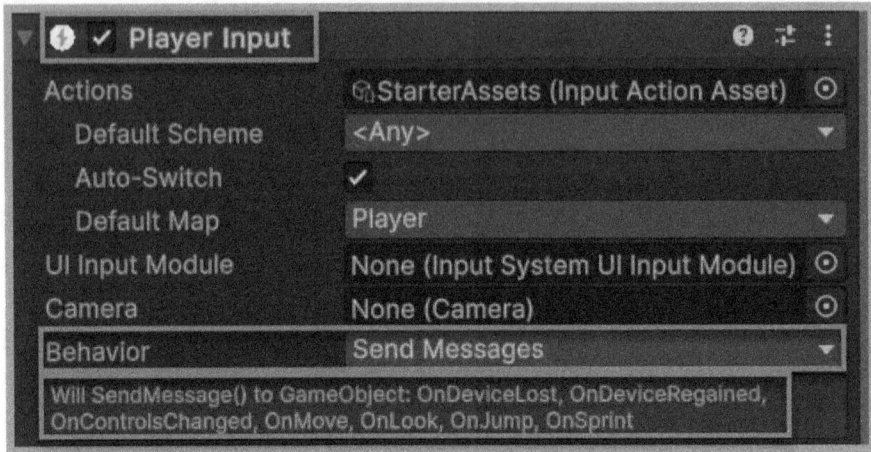

Figure 2-5. Player Input – Behavior property

These methods, namely, OnMove, OnLook, OnJump, and OnSprint, show up here on account of the Actions that have been set up within the Input Action Asset (Starter Assets). Launch the Starter Assets within the Unity Editor and create a new Action by clicking the plus icon beside "Actions." Name this new action "Attack." You don't need to create any binding for it for now. Close the Starter Assets (Input Actions) window and when prompted whether to save changes made, select "Save." You will immediately note that within the Player Input component beneath the Behavior property a new method "OnAttack" has been listed.

Now within the "StarterAssetsInputs" script, you can declare a new public method OnAttack. Of course, you will need to set up the bindings within the Input Action Asset for the keyboard and Gamepad.

You would have also noted that each method uses the "InputValue" parameter to extract the relevant data for its action. "InputValue" is part of the "UnityEngine.InputSystem" namespace. For movement (OnMove) and look (OnLook), this data is a Vector2 representing directions, where the direction data is being obtained using "value.Get<Vector2>()." For jump and sprint actions, the data is a boolean representing whether the action is being performed (isPressed). This data is obtained using "value.isPressed."

The script also manages the state of the mouse cursor through the OnApplicationFocus and SetCursorState methods. This is crucial for games that capture the mouse cursor during gameplay for aiming or looking around. When the game window gains or loses focus, it appropriately locks or unlocks the cursor.

Character Controller Scripts

The Character Controller scripts being referred to here are either the ThirdPersonController script or the FirstPersonController script. The properties of each of these components were discussed in Chapter 1. Let's explore the FirstPersonController script. You will note that it requires that the CharacterController and PlayerInput components be available. Several public field declarations are exposed in the Inspector, all of which were explained in Chapter 1. Among the private variables, it's important to note that you have variables to reference the Player Input, Starter Assets Inputs, Character Controller, and the main camera.

As the controllers don't use Rigidbodies the Update method is used instead of FixedUpdate. The methods JumpAndGravity, GroundedCheck, and Move within the Update method and CameraRotation within the LateUpdate method utilize the input values that were captured via the "StarterAssetsInputs" script.

Within the CameraRotation method, you will note that the "_input" variable references the Vector 2 "look" property obtained within the "StarterAssetsInputs" script and then utilizes this value to handle the rotation of the camera (Figure 2-6). It adjusts the pitch of the camera and rotates the player character left and right. The pitch is clamped between specified top and bottom angles to prevent unnatural camera movement.

CHAPTER 2   UNITY'S NEW INPUT SYSTEM

```
private void CameraRotation()
{
    // if there is an input
    if (_input.look sqrMagnitude >= _threshold)
```

Figure 2-6. *_input.look property referenced*

Within the Move method, you will note that the "_input" variable references the boolean "sprint" property within the "StarterAssetsInputs" script and then utilizes this value to determine targetSpeed. The "_input" variable is also used to reference the Vector 2 "move" property within the "StarterAssetsInputs" script whose value is then used to set targetSpeed. The "_input" variable then references the boolean property "analogMovement" to check if it's true in which case the variable inputMagnitude is set to the magnitude of the Vector 2 "move" property within the "StarterAssetsInputs" script. You will note that throughout this Move method, the "_input" variable is being used to reference properties within the "StarterAssetsInputs" script (Figure 2-7).

```
private void Move()
{
    // set target speed based on move speed, sprint speed and if sprint is pressed
    float targetSpeed = _input.sprint ? SprintSpeed : MoveSpeed;

    // a simplistic acceleration and deceleration designed to be easy to remove, replace, or iterate upon

    // note: Vector2's == operator uses approximation so is not floating point error prone, and is cheaper than
    // if there is no input, set the target speed to 0
    if (_input.move == Vector2.zero) targetSpeed = 0.0f;

    // a reference to the players current horizontal velocity
    float currentHorizontalSpeed = new Vector3(_controller.velocity.x, 0.0f, _controller.velocity.z).magnitude;

    float speedOffset = 0.1f;
    float inputMagnitude = _input.analogMovement ? _input.move.magnitude : 1f;
```

Figure 2-7. *_input.sprint, _input.move, _input.analogMovement properties referenced*

CHAPTER 2   UNITY'S NEW INPUT SYSTEM

An important point to note within the Move method is that the inputDirection is being normalized via code, instead of attempting to achieve this normalization via the Input Action Asset (Figure 2-8).

```
// normalise input direction
Vector3 inputDirection = new Vector3(_input.move.x, 0.0f, _input.move.y).normalized;
```

Figure 2-8. *Normalize input direction done via code*

Within the Input Action Asset, within its "WASD" composite binding you will note that the mode selected is "Digital" and not "Digital Normalized." (Figure 2-9) Also, you will note that the "Left Stick [Gamepad]" doesn't have any normalization applied (Figure 2-10).

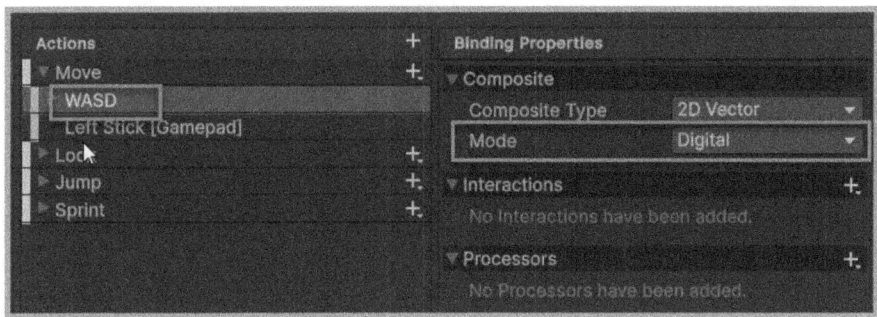

Figure 2-9. *Mode set to digital*

CHAPTER 2   UNITY'S NEW INPUT SYSTEM

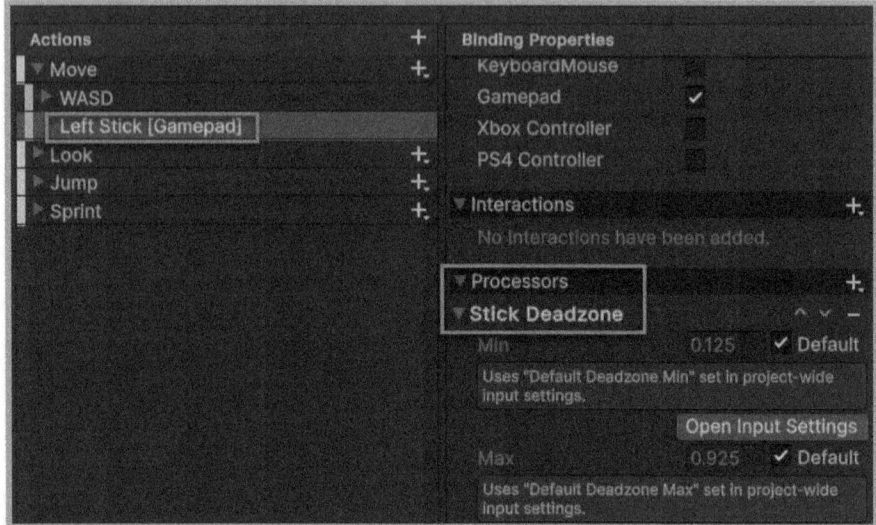

Figure 2-10. *No normalization processor setup*

Normalizing the input direction vector ensures that movement speed is consistent regardless of the input direction. Without normalization, moving diagonally (when input on both the *X* and *Y* axes is nonzero) would result in a faster speed than moving in a cardinal direction due to the way vector magnitude is calculated. By normalizing, the magnitude of the direction vector is set to 1 (or 0 if the vector is zero), ensuring consistent movement speeds.

This differs from using the Normalize Vector 2 Processors action in the Input System in that the normalization in code directly affects how the character moves in the game world, providing a more immediate and controlled way to manage input data.

Grounded Check

The GroundedCheck method uses Physics.CheckSphere to determine if the player is grounded by checking if a virtual sphere placed just below

CHAPTER 2   UNITY'S NEW INPUT SYSTEM

the player's feet intersects with any ground layer objects. This method is reliable because it can be adjusted for different ground surfaces and player dynamics (Figure 2-11).

```
private void GroundedCheck()
{
    // set sphere position, with offset
    Vector3 spherePosition = new Vector3(transform.position.x, transform.position.y - GroundedOffset, transform.position.z);
    Grounded = Physics.CheckSphere(spherePosition, GroundedRadius, GroundLayers, QueryTriggerInteraction.Ignore);
}
```

Figure 2-11. *GroundedCheck method*

Camera Rotation

The CameraRotation method is a critical component of the FirstPersonController script, handling the rotation of the player's view based on mouse or joystick input. This method ensures that the player can look around in a first-person perspective by adjusting the pitch (up and down movement) and yaw (left and right movement) based on input. Here's an overview of how this method functions (Figure 2-12):

- Check for Input: This method first checks if there is any look input from the player (_input.look.sqrMagnitude >= _threshold). The .sqrMagnitude property returns the squared length of the vector representing the look input. This is more efficient than using .magnitude because it avoids a square root calculation. The _threshold variable ensures that minor, unintentional movements are ignored, providing a cleaner input response.

- Delta Time Multiplier: A deltaTimeMultiplier is determined based on whether the current input device is a mouse (IsCurrentDeviceMouse). If the input device is a mouse, deltaTimeMultiplier is set to 1.0f; otherwise, it's set to Time.deltaTime. This differentiation is crucial because mouse movement is generally absolute (representing the distance moved since the last frame), while joystick input is relative (representing a direction and magnitude). Multiplying joystick input by Time.deltaTime ensures smooth and frame-rate independent rotation. In contrast, mouse input should not be frame-rate dependent, thus not multiplied by Time.deltaTime.

- Update Pitch Rotation: The pitch rotation (_cinemachineTargetPitch) is updated by adding the vertical component of the look input (_input.look.y) multiplied by the rotation speed and the deltaTimeMultiplier. This calculation adjusts the pitch based on player input, allowing looking up and down.

- Clamp the Pitch Rotation: The pitch rotation is then clamped to a specified range (BottomClamp to TopClamp) using the ClampAngle method. This prevents the camera from rotating too far up or down, which could disorient the player or result in unrealistic camera behavior.

- Update Cinemachine Camera Target Pitch: The pitch rotation is applied to the Cinemachine camera target (CinemachineCameraTarget) by setting its local rotation to a new Quaternion created with Quaternion.Euler. This effectively updates the camera's pitch while keeping its yaw and roll the same.

CHAPTER 2 UNITY'S NEW INPUT SYSTEM

- Rotate the Player Left and Right: Finally, the player's yaw rotation is updated by rotating the player object around the Y-axis (Vector3.up) by an amount determined by the horizontal component of the look input (_input.look.x) multiplied by the rotation speed and the deltaTimeMultiplier. This allows the player to look left and right.

Through this method, the script processes player input to rotate the camera and the player character smoothly and intuitively, accounting for different input devices and ensuring that the camera's pitch is constrained to realistic angles. The separation of pitch and yaw adjustments allows for precise control over how the player looks around in the game world, making for an immersive first-person experience.

```
private void CameraRotation()
{
    // if there is an input
    if (_input.look.sqrMagnitude >= _threshold)
    {
        //Don't multiply mouse input by Time.deltaTime
        float deltaTimeMultiplier = IsCurrentDeviceMouse ? 1.0f : Time.deltaTime;

        _cinemachineTargetPitch += _input.look.y * RotationSpeed * deltaTimeMultiplier;
        _rotationVelocity = _input.look.x * RotationSpeed * deltaTimeMultiplier;

        // clamp our pitch rotation
        _cinemachineTargetPitch = ClampAngle(_cinemachineTargetPitch, BottomClamp, TopClamp);

        // Update Cinemachine camera target pitch
        CinemachineCameraTarget.transform.localRotation = Quaternion.Euler(_cinemachineTargetPitch, 0.0f, 0.0f);

        // rotate the player left and right
        transform.Rotate(Vector3.up * _rotationVelocity);
    }
}
```

Figure 2-12. *CameraRotation method*

Move Method

The Move method in the FirstPersonController class is responsible for handling player movement based on input from the new Unity Input System. This method manages both the speed of movement and the direction, accommodating both walking and sprinting speeds and applies a simple model of acceleration and deceleration. Here's an overview of its functionality (Figure 2-13):

- Determining Target Speed: This method first determines the target speed (targetSpeed) based on whether the sprint input is active. If _input.sprint is true, the target speed is set to SprintSpeed; otherwise, it's set to MoveSpeed. This allows for dynamic speed changes based on player input. If there is no movement input (i.e., _input.move is Vector2.zero), the target speed is set to 0. This ensures the player stops moving when there's no input.

- Handling Acceleration and Deceleration: This method then calculates the player's current horizontal speed by creating a new vector from the player's velocity on the x and z axes (ignoring vertical velocity) and then finding its magnitude. This speed is used to determine how much the player needs to accelerate or decelerate to reach the target speed. If the current horizontal speed is not within a small offset (speedOffset) of the target speed, the player's speed (_speed) is adjusted towards the target speed using linear interpolation (Mathf.Lerp). This interpolation creates a smooth transition between speeds, providing a more organic feel to movement acceleration and deceleration. The SpeedChangeRate variable affects how quickly this speed change occurs. The calculated speed is rounded to three decimal places to ensure precision without floating-point errors.

CHAPTER 2 UNITY'S NEW INPUT SYSTEM

- Calculating Input Direction: The input direction is initially normalized to ensure it has a magnitude of 1. This prevents faster movement when moving diagonally. The method then proceeds to check If there is movement input (i.e., _input.move is not Vector2. zero), and the input direction is recalculated based on the player's orientation. It uses the player's right and forward directions multiplied by the input's x and y components, respectively. This calculation ensures the movement direction is always relative to where the player is facing.

- Moving the Player: The final step is to move the player using the CharacterController's Move method. The movement vector is the normalized input direction scaled by the calculated speed (_speed) and the frame's deltaTime, ensuring frame-rate independent movement. This vector is added to the player's current vertical velocity vector (to account for gravity and jumping) and then scaled by deltaTime again. The result is a smooth and responsive movement that respects both player input and game physics, such as gravity.

CHAPTER 2   UNITY'S NEW INPUT SYSTEM

```
private void Move()
{
    // set target speed based on move speed, sprint speed and if sprint is pressed
    float targetSpeed = _input.sprint ? SprintSpeed : MoveSpeed;

    // a simplistic acceleration and deceleration designed to be easy to remove, replace, or iterate upon

    // note: Vector2's == operator uses approximation so is not floating point error prone, and is cheaper than magnitude
    // if there is no input, set the target speed to 0
    if (_input.move == Vector2.zero) targetSpeed = 0.0f;

    // a reference to the players current horizontal velocity
    float currentHorizontalSpeed = new Vector3(_controller.velocity.x, 0.0f, _controller.velocity.z).magnitude;

    float speedOffset = 0.1f;
    float inputMagnitude = _input.analogMovement ? _input.move.magnitude : 1f;

    // accelerate or decelerate to target speed
    if (currentHorizontalSpeed < targetSpeed - speedOffset || currentHorizontalSpeed > targetSpeed + speedOffset)
    {
        // creates curved result rather than a linear one giving a more organic speed change
        // note T in Lerp is clamped, so we don't need to clamp our speed
        _speed = Mathf.Lerp(currentHorizontalSpeed, targetSpeed * inputMagnitude, Time.deltaTime * SpeedChangeRate);

        // round speed to 3 decimal places
        _speed = Mathf.Round(_speed * 1000f) / 1000f;
    }
    else
    {
        _speed = targetSpeed;
    }

    // normalise input direction
    Vector3 inputDirection = new Vector3(_input.move.x, 0.0f, _input.move.y).normalized;

    // note: Vector2's != operator uses approximation so is not floating point error prone, and is cheaper than magnitude
    // if there is a move input rotate player when the player is moving
    if (_input.move != Vector2.zero)
    {
        // move
        inputDirection = transform.right * _input.move.x + transform.forward * _input.move.y;
    }

    // move the player
    _controller.Move(inputDirection.normalized * (_speed * Time.deltaTime) + new Vector3(0.0f, _verticalVelocity, 0.0f) * Time.deltaTime);
}
```

Figure 2-13. *Move method*

In summary, the Move method dynamically adjusts the player's speed based on sprint input and smoothly transitions between speeds to provide organic acceleration and deceleration. It calculates the direction of movement based on player input and orientation, ensuring that movement is always relative to the player's current facing direction. This method exemplifies a responsive and intuitive movement system suitable for character controllers in Unity.

Jump and Gravity

The JumpAndGravity method is designed to manage jumping mechanics and apply gravity to the player's character, ensuring a realistic and responsive movement experience. This method is called every frame within the Update method to continuously assess and apply the necessary vertical velocity adjustments based on the player's grounded status, jump inputs, and the natural effect of gravity. Here's an overview of this method (Figure 2-14):

- Grounded Check: At the beginning, the method checks if the player is grounded using the Grounded boolean. Being grounded means the player is standing on a surface and is capable of jumping.

- Reset Fall Timeout: If the player is grounded, the method resets the fall timeout timer (_fallTimeoutDelta) to a predefined FallTimeout value. This timer is used to delay the transition to a falling state, allowing for more nuanced control when walking off ledges or down slopes or stairs.

- Resetting Vertical Velocity: To prevent the player's vertical velocity from decreasing indefinitely while grounded, it's reset to a small negative value (-2f). This ensures a slight downward force, keeping the player firmly on the ground, and helps with standing on sloped surfaces without sliding.

- Processing Jump Input: If the jump input (_input.jump) is active and the jump timeout (_jumpTimeoutDelta) has elapsed (i.e., the player is ready to jump again), the player's vertical velocity (_verticalVelocity) is set to a value calculated using the square root of the jump height multiplied by -2 and gravity (Mathf. Sqrt(JumpHeight * -2f * Gravity)). This formula derives from the kinematic equation for projectile motion, ensuring the player reaches the desired jump height based on the gravity value.

- Jump Timeout Countdown: The jump timeout delta (_jumpTimeoutDelta) is reduced by Time.deltaTime each frame while it's greater than or equal to zero. This delay ensures a brief period after jumping before the player can jump again, preventing rapid, unrealistic consecutive jumps.

- Handling Airborne Logic: If the player is not grounded, the method resets the jump timeout timer (_jumpTimeoutDelta) to the JumpTimeout value, preparing it for when the player lands again. Similar to the jump timeout, the fall timeout delta (_fallTimeoutDelta) decreases by Time.deltaTime each frame while it's greater than or equal to zero. This mechanism can be used to delay certain actions or animations when the player starts falling. Lastly, the jump input is set to false (_input.jump = false) when not grounded, ensuring the player cannot initiate a jump while airborne.

- Applying Gravity: Gravity is continuously applied to the player's vertical velocity (_verticalVelocity), increasing it by the gravity value multiplied by Time.deltaTime, simulating acceleration due to gravity over time. This effect is capped at a terminal velocity (_terminalVelocity), preventing the player from accelerating indefinitely and reaching unrealistically high speeds when falling for extended periods.

```
private void JumpAndGravity()
{
    if (Grounded)
    {
        // reset the fall timeout timer
        _fallTimeoutDelta = FallTimeout;

        // stop our velocity dropping infinitely when grounded
        if (_verticalVelocity < 0.0f)
        {
            _verticalVelocity = -2f;
        }

        // Jump
        if (_input.jump && _jumpTimeoutDelta <= 0.0f)
        {
            // the square root of H * -2 * G = how much velocity needed to reach desired height
            _verticalVelocity = Mathf.Sqrt(JumpHeight * -2f * Gravity);
        }

        // jump timeout
        if (_jumpTimeoutDelta >= 0.0f)
        {
            _jumpTimeoutDelta -= Time.deltaTime;
        }
    }
    else
    {
        // reset the jump timeout timer
        _jumpTimeoutDelta = JumpTimeout;

        // fall timeout
        if (_fallTimeoutDelta >= 0.0f)
        {
            _fallTimeoutDelta -= Time.deltaTime;
        }

        // if we are not grounded, do not jump
        _input.jump = false;
    }

    // apply gravity over time if under terminal (multiply by delta time twice to linearly speed up over time)
    if (_verticalVelocity < _terminalVelocity)
    {
        _verticalVelocity += Gravity * Time.deltaTime;
    }
}
```

Figure 2-14. *JumpAndGravity method*

This method intricately simulates realistic jumping and falling dynamics by applying principles of physics, such as gravity and projectile motion. It uses timeouts to create natural delays between jumps and falls, enhancing gameplay realism. This method ensures that the player's interaction with the game world feels intuitive and grounded in real-world physics, contributing to a more immersive gaming experience.

CHAPTER 2   UNITY'S NEW INPUT SYSTEM

Clamp Angle

The ClampAngle method is designed to normalize and constrain an angle within a specified range, ensuring it does not exceed certain limits. This is particularly useful in 3D games and applications where camera or object rotation needs to be controlled to avoid unnatural movement or disorienting the player. Let's break down how this method works (Figure 2-15):

- lfAngle: This parameter represents the current angle that needs to be clamped. This angle could be in any range and not necessarily normalized between 0 and 360 degrees.

- lfMin: This parameter defines the minimum allowed value for the angle. If lfAngle falls below this value, it will be clamped up to this minimum.

- lfMax: This parameter defines the maximum allowed value for the angle. If lfAngle exceeds this value, it will be clamped down to this maximum.

- Normalization: This method first checks if the angle is less than -360 degrees or greater than 360 degrees. If so, it adjusts the angle to bring it within a 0- to 360-degree range by adding or subtracting 360 degrees, respectively. This step ensures that the angle is within a standard range, making the clamping step (which follows) straightforward and predictable. It's important because rotation angles can theoretically become very large or very small numbers as a game runs, especially if an object or camera can rotate freely without restrictions.

CHAPTER 2   UNITY'S NEW INPUT SYSTEM

- Clamping: After normalization, the method uses Mathf. Clamp to ensure the angle is within the specified minimum and maximum limits (lfMin and lfMax). Mathf.Clamp takes a value and two bounds; if the value is between the bounds, it's returned unchanged. If it's below the lower bound, the lower bound is returned, and if it's above the upper bound, the upper bound is returned. This step is crucial for maintaining the angle within a desired range, such as limiting the vertical look angle of a camera to prevent it from flipping over.

In a first-person camera setup, this method could be used to clamp the pitch of the camera so the player can't look too far up or down, which would potentially invert the camera or look backward through the player model. For example, you might want to keep the vertical angle between -90 and 90 degrees to prevent the camera from going upside down.

The ClampAngle method is a utility function that normalizes and clamps an angle within a specified range. By ensuring angles do not exceed defined limits, it provides a robust way to control rotations in 3D environments, contributing to a smoother and more controlled user experience.

```
private static float ClampAngle(float lfAngle, float lfMin, float lfMax)
{
    if (lfAngle < -360f) lfAngle += 360f;
    if (lfAngle > 360f) lfAngle -= 360f;
    return Mathf.Clamp(lfAngle, lfMin, lfMax);
}
```

Figure 2-15. *ClampAngle method*

OnDrawGizmosSelected

The OnDrawGizmosSelected method in Unity is a special editor function that allows developers to draw visual cues or "gizmos" in the Scene View. These gizmos are visible when the GameObject with the script is selected, providing helpful visual feedback that aids in debugging and level design. The primary purpose of the OnDrawGizmosSelected method here is to visually indicate whether the player character is grounded by drawing a sphere at the player's feet. The color of the sphere changes based on the player's grounded status: green if grounded, red if not. Here's an overview of this method (Figure 2-16):

- Transparent Green: A color representing the grounded state. This color is set to green with a transparency of 35% (alpha = 0.35f). Transparency is used here so the sphere does not completely obstruct the view of any objects it may be overlapping in the Scene View.

- Transparent Red: A color representing the nongrounded (or airborne) state. This is set to red with the same level of transparency as the green. The use of red and green provides a clear, intuitive indicator of status at a glance.

- Conditional Coloring: The method checks the Grounded boolean variable to determine the player's grounded status. Depending on this status, it sets the Gizmos.color to either transparent green or transparent red, in preparation for drawing the gizmo.

- Drawing the Gizmo: The method Gizmos.DrawSphere() draws a sphere gizmo at a specified position and radius. The position is set to be directly beneath the player character (transform.position.y - GroundedOffset), ensuring the sphere represents the

CHAPTER 2 UNITY'S NEW INPUT SYSTEM

area checked for grounding. The GroundedRadius is used for the sphere's radius, visually indicating the size of the area being checked to determine if the player is grounded. This is especially useful for visualizing how large the grounding check is and can help in adjusting the GroundedOffset and GroundedRadius for different character sizes or when working with varied terrain.

By using this method, developers can visually debug the player's grounding mechanism without running the game. For example, if the player is unexpectedly not grounded on what appears to be flat terrain, the developer can select the player object and immediately see where the grounding check is happening and how large it is, allowing for quick adjustments to GroundedOffset or GroundedRadius values. Similarly, it helps to ensure the grounding logic is working as intended during development.

```
private void OnDrawGizmosSelected()
{
    Color transparentGreen = new Color(0.0f, 1.0f, 0.0f, 0.35f);
    Color transparentRed = new Color(1.0f, 0.0f, 0.0f, 0.35f);

    if (Grounded) Gizmos.color = transparentGreen;
    else Gizmos.color = transparentRed;

    // when selected, draw a gizmo in the position of, and matching radius of, the grounded collider
    Gizmos.DrawSphere(new Vector3(transform.position.x, transform.position.y - GroundedOffset, transform.position.z), GroundedRadius);
}
```

Figure 2-16. *OnDrawGizmosSelected method*

The OnDrawGizmosSelected method provides a powerful visual aid during game development in Unity. By visually indicating game state information such as grounded status, it enables developers to rapidly iterate on gameplay mechanics and ensures that their game behaves as expected, without the need for extensive logging or breakpoint debugging.

CHAPTER 2   UNITY'S NEW INPUT SYSTEM

The ThirdPersonController script encompasses additional methods beyond those outlined for the FirstPersonController, offering straightforward comprehension upon review of its code. This facilitates an intuitive progression for readers to familiarize themselves with its functionality within the context of this book chapter.

Recipe 2-2: Implementing a Player Attack Action

Problem

The default setup of Unity's Third Person Controller does not include an attack action, limiting gameplay dynamics. Players need the ability to perform attack actions using specific controls across different input devices such as keyboards and gamepads.

Solution

To introduce an attack action in Unity's Third Person Controller, modify the Starter Assets (Input Actions Asset) by adding a new "Attack" action linked to the "K" key and the Button East on gamepads. Update the StarterAssetsInputs script to include a boolean for attack status and a method to handle the attack action. Extend the ThirdPersonController script to incorporate the attack method that triggers an attack animation and logs the action. Test the implementation by running the Playground scene, ensuring the attack action is functional when triggered by the specified keys on both the keyboard and gamepad.

How It Works

In this recipe, you will implement a player attack action for your third-person controller, by building on the existing Starter Assets (Input Action Asset). This setup will allow for triggering an attack action with the "K" key for the KeyboardMouse control scheme and the Button East for the Gamepad control scheme. Upon activation, "Attack in Progress" will be displayed in the console.

1. **Modifying Starter Assets (Input Actions Asset):**
   Open up the Starter Assets (Input Action Asset) within Unity's Editor. You will need to create a new Attack action as part of the "Player" action map.

   For the KeyboardMouse Control Scheme:

   - Ensure the "Player" Action Map has been selected. Now click the plus button adjacent to 'Actions' to add a new action and rename this newly added action to Attack.

   - Beneath the Attack action select the item "<No Binding>." You can now set up a new binding using the "Binding Properties" section.

   - Click the "Path" field drop-down for the new binding, press the "K" key to set it as the binding key, or manually select it from the list. You will note that the item that was labeled "<No Binding>" now reads "K[Keyboard]." Also, note that the "Path" now states "K[Keyboard]" (Figure 2-17).

   - For the section "Use in control scheme" select the check box KeyboardMouse.

CHAPTER 2   UNITY'S NEW INPUT SYSTEM

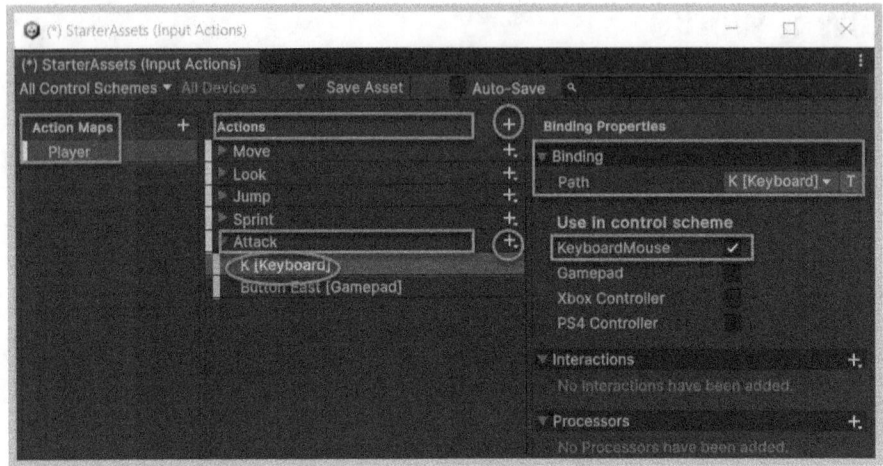

Figure 2-17. *Attack – Actions and Bindings for KeyboardMouse control scheme*

For the Gamepad Control Scheme:

- Ensure that the Attack action is selected under Actions. Now add another binding by clicking the plus with chevron button beside Attack and select the item "Add Binding" from the list.

- Beneath the Attack action select the newly added item "<No Binding>." You can now set up a new binding using the "Binding Properties" section.

- Click the "Path" field drop-down for this new binding, and set its path to Button East by pressing the respective button on your connected gamepad or selecting it manually from the list. You will note that the item that was labeled "<No Binding>" now reads "Button East [Gamepad]." Also, note that the "Path" now states "Button East [Gamepad]" (Figure 2-18).

CHAPTER 2   UNITY'S NEW INPUT SYSTEM

- For the section "Use in control scheme" select the check box Gamepad.

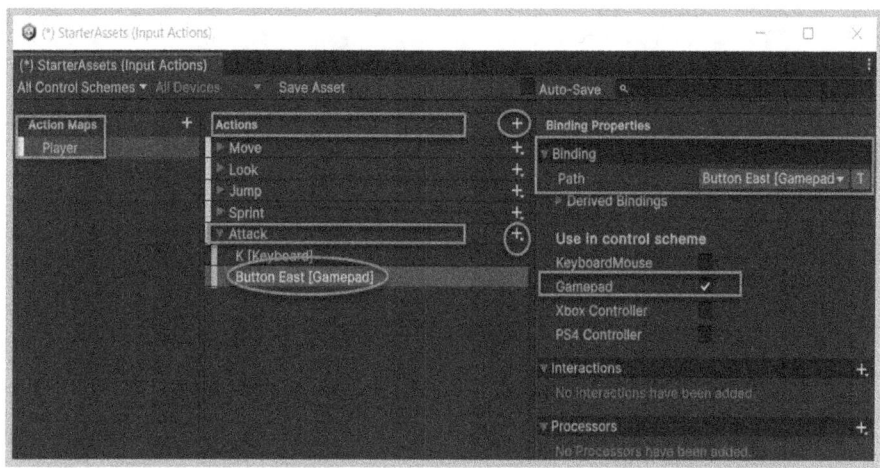

Figure 2-18. *Attack – Actions and Bindings for Gamepad control scheme*

2. **Modifying the Starter Assets Inputs Script:** In the StarterAssetsInputs script, under the "Character Input Values" header, add a public boolean variable named "attack" to correspond with the "Attack" action. This modification aligns with the example shown in Figure 2-19.

115

CHAPTER 2   UNITY'S NEW INPUT SYSTEM

```
namespace StarterAssets
{
    Unity Script (4 asset references) | 5 references
    public class StarterAssetsInputs : MonoBehaviour
    {
        [Header("Character Input Values")]
        public Vector2 move;
        public Vector2 look;
        public bool jump;
        public bool sprint;
        public bool attack;
```

Figure 2-19.   Added a public bool attack variable to the script

Implement an OnAttack method to be called through the Player Input component's "Behavior" property "end Messages" notification when pressing either the "K" key or the gamepad's Button East. This method is illustrated in Figure 2-20.

CHAPTER 2   UNITY'S NEW INPUT SYSTEM

```
#if ENABLE_INPUT_SYSTEM
        0 references
        public void OnMove(InputValue value)
        {
            MoveInput(value.Get<Vector2>());
        }
        0 references
        public void OnLook(InputValue value)
        {
            if(cursorInputForLook)
                LookInput(value.Get<Vector2>());
        }
        0 references
        public void OnAttack(InputValue value)
        {
            attack = value.isPressed;
        }
        0 references
        public void OnJump(InputValue value)
        {
            JumpInput(value.isPressed);
        }
        0 references
        public void OnSprint(InputValue value)
        {
            SprintInput(value.isPressed);
        }
#endif
```

Figure 2-20. *Implementation of the OnAttack method*

You will note that here you are not using an intermediary method to set the value of the "attack" variable as is done for the other methods listed in Figure 2-20.

CHAPTER 2   UNITY'S NEW INPUT SYSTEM

3. **Extending the ThirdPersonController Script:** Add an Attack method in the ThirdPersonController script to manage attack logic. To integrate this without modifications to the existing script, invoke Attack within the Update method, despite it not being the optimal approach. This aligns with Unity's conventional "Send Messages" behavior, allowing for straightforward implementation without overhauling the current script structure. The modified Update method is illustrated in Figure 2-21.

```
private void Update()
{
    _hasAnimator = TryGetComponent(out _animator);

    JumpAndGravity();
    GroundedCheck();
    Move();
    Attack();
}
```

Figure 2-21. Modified Update() within theThirdPersonController script to invoke Attack()

The Attack method is illustrated in Figure 2-22, where it checks to see if the variable "attack" within the StarterAssetsInputs script is true in which case it logs a message to the console. Before exiting the Attack method the "attack" variable is set to false ensuring that the Attack action is not spammed.

```
private void Attack()
{
    if(_input.attack)
        Debug.Log("Attack in Progress");

    _input.attack = false;
}
```

Figure 2-22. *Added Attack() within the ThirdPersonController script*

4. **Testing:** Run the Playground scene for the Third Person Controller and test both the "K" key and the Button East on a gamepad. Each press should result in "Attack in Progress" being printed to the console, indicating that your Attack action is correctly set up and triggered.

Expanding Player Attack with Animation

This section expands on the previously implemented player attack action by adding a melee attack animation for the third-person character controller. Begin by opening the "Playground" scene designed for the third-person controller. Access the Unity Asset Store, search for and download the "Melee Warrior Animations FREE" by Kevin Iglesias into your active Unity project. Within the project's Assets folder, you will note that a new "Kevin Iglesias" directory, has been created that holds various animations.

Within the hierarchy select the Player Armature game object and within the inspector locate the Animator component. For its controller property, double-click on the StarterAssetsThirdPerson Animator controller to have it open up within the Animator window. Within the

CHAPTER 2   UNITY'S NEW INPUT SYSTEM

project's Assets folder, locate the "Kevin Iglesias" directory, leading to Assets/Kevin Iglesias/Melee Warrior Animations / Animations / OneHanded / RightHand. Here, you'll find the "RightHand@Attack01" animation file, as shown in Figure 2-23. Use the Inspector to preview this animation.

Figure 2-23. *RightHand@Attack01 melee animation*

Drag the "RightHand@Attack01" animation into the Animator window, positioning it above the Entry state, and renaming this new animation state to "Attack" as shown in Figure 2-24. In the Animator window's Parameters tab, create a new boolean parameter named "Attack" (refer to Figure 2-24). Establish two transitions: one leading from the "Attack" state to the "Idle Walk Run Blend" state, and another from the "Idle Walk Run Blend" state back to the "Attack" state.

CHAPTER 2   UNITY'S NEW INPUT SYSTEM

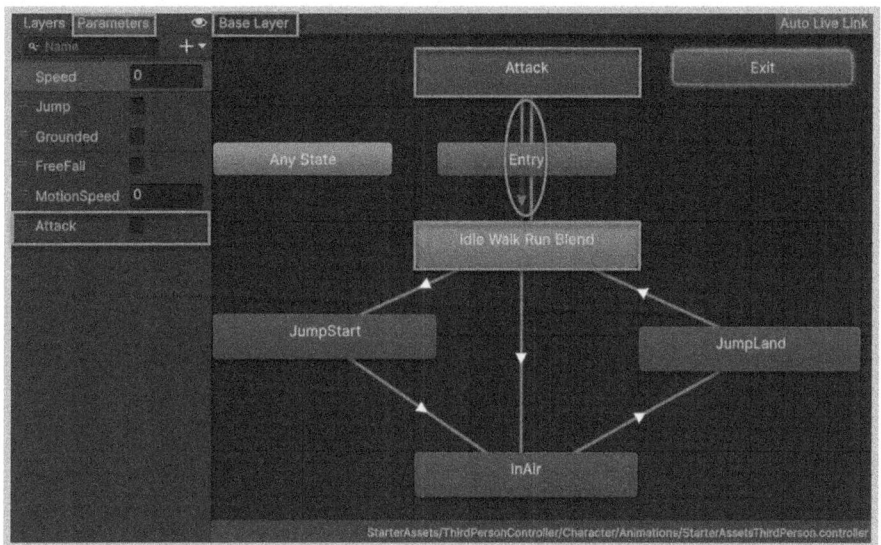

Figure 2-24. *Animator Window with newly added Attack State and its transitions*

Create a transition from the "Attack" state to the "Idle Walk Run Blend" state, and in the Inspector, uncheck "Has Exit Time." Set both the Transition Duration and Transition Offset properties to zero. Scroll to the Conditions section in the Inspector, choose the "Attack" parameter from the left dropdown, and set its value to false using the right dropdown. This setup mandates that the transition from the "Attack" state to the "Idle Walk Run Blend" state only occurs when the "Attack" parameter is programmatically set to false, enabling the transition (Figure 2-25).

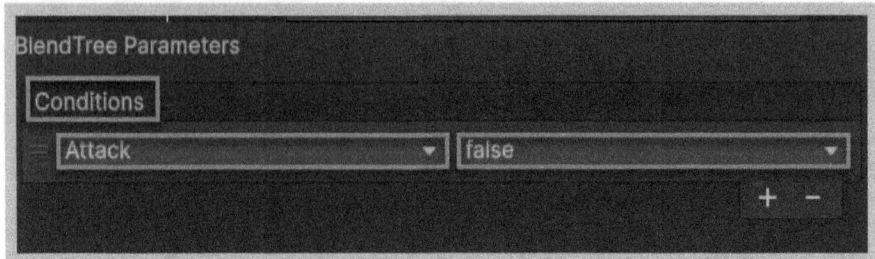

Figure 2-25. *Condition to move from the Attack state to the Idle Walk Run Blend state*

Create a transition from the "Idle Walk Run Blend" state to the "Attack" state, and in the Inspector, uncheck "Has Exit Time." Set both the Transition Duration and Transition Offset properties to zero. Scroll to the Conditions section in the Inspector, choose the "Attack" parameter from the left dropdown, and set its value to true using the right dropdown. This setup mandates that the transition from the "Idle Walk Run Blend" state to the "Attack" state only occurs when the "Attack" parameter is programmatically set to true, enabling the transition (Figure 2-26).

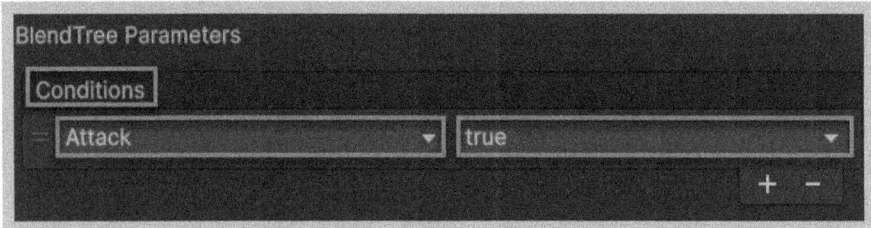

Figure 2-26. *Condition to move from the Idle Walk Run Blend state to the Attack state*

Following the setup of the Attack animation in the Animator, it's time to enhance the ThirdPersonController script. Open this script in your preferred editor and locate the section labeled "animation IDs," which contains declarations for private integer animation ID variables. Append to this section by declaring a new private integer variable, _animIDAttack, as illustrated in Figure 2-27. This variable is designated for storing the optimized integer hash

CHAPTER 2 UNITY'S NEW INPUT SYSTEM

of the "Attack" animation parameter, facilitating efficient referencing within the script. This optimization enhances game performance by negating the need for string comparisons in the Animator component.

```
// animation IDs
private int _animIDSpeed;
private int _animIDGrounded;
private int _animIDJump;
private int _animIDFreeFall;
private int _animIDMotionSpeed;
private int _animIDAttack; //ACC
```

Figure 2-27. *Declaring the variable _animIDAttack to store an optimized integer hash*

Locate the AssignAnimationIDs method within the script. At the very bottom of this method add the line of code depicted in Figure 2-28. This line of code converts the name of an animation parameter ("Attack") into an optimized integer hash and stores it in the variable, _animIDAttack. This stored hash can then be used throughout the script to reference the "Attack" animation parameter efficiently.

```
private void AssignAnimationIDs()
{
    _animIDSpeed = Animator.StringToHash("Speed");
    _animIDGrounded = Animator.StringToHash("Grounded");
    _animIDJump = Animator.StringToHash("Jump");
    _animIDFreeFall = Animator.StringToHash("FreeFall");
    _animIDMotionSpeed = Animator.StringToHash("MotionSpeed");
    _animIDAttack = Animator.StringToHash("Attack"); //ACC
}
```

Figure 2-28. *Initializing the _animIDAttack variable to an optimized integer hash*

The static method Animator.StringToHash() is provided by the Unity Engine's Animator class. Its purpose is to convert a string value into an integer hash. The method is efficient for performance because working with integers is faster than working with strings. This optimization becomes significant when you need to reference animation parameters frequently, such as in update loops or animation callbacks.

In the preceding section, a basic Attack method was introduced. This section will elaborate on that method, enabling the Attack animation within the Animator to be triggered by pressing either the "K" key or the Button East on a gamepad. The refined code for the Attack method is depicted in Figure 2-29(a).

```
private void Attack() //ACC
{
    if(_input.attack && _hasAnimator)
    {
        Debug.Log("Attack in Progress");
        _animator.SetBool(_animIDAttack, _input.attack);
    }

    AnimatorStateInfo stateInfo = _animator.GetCurrentAnimatorStateInfo(0);
    _input.attack = false;

    if (stateInfo.IsName("Attack") && stateInfo.normalizedTime >= 1.0f)
    {
        //Attack animtion has been completed
        Debug.Log("'Attack' Animation has completed.");
        _animator.SetBool(_animIDAttack, _input.attack);
    }
}
```

Figure 2-29(a). *Modified Attack() method*

The Attack method depicted in Figure 2-29(a) is designed to manage an attack action within a game. This method integrates input handling, animation control, and state management to execute and monitor an attack animation sequence. Here's a detailed breakdown of its functionality:

CHAPTER 2 UNITY'S NEW INPUT SYSTEM

1. Initial Conditions Check:

    - if(_input.attack && _hasAnimator): This conditional statement checks two conditions before proceeding with the attack logic:
    - _input.attack: A boolean value indicating whether the attack input has been triggered by the player. This would typically be set to true when the player presses the "K" key or Button East on a gamepad, designated for attacking.
    - _hasAnimator: A boolean flag indicating whether an Animator component is attached and available on the game object. This ensures that the script only attempts to control animations if the Animator is present.

2. Initiating Attack Animation:

    - Debug.Log("Attack in Progress");: Logs a message to the Console, useful for debugging to confirm the attack sequence is being initiated.
    - _animator.SetBool(_animIDAttack, _input.attack);: Uses the _animator reference to access the Animator component and sets a boolean parameter (identified by _animIDAttack representing the Attack parameter in the Animator) to the current state of _input.attack (which will be true). The _animIDAttack is a hashed integer representing the parameter name (Attack) for efficiency, as discussed previously. This line effectively starts the attack animation by setting the respective Animator parameter to true.

3. Managing Attack Animation State:
   - AnimatorStateInfo stateInfo = _animator. GetCurrentAnimatorStateInfo(0);: Retrieves the current state of the animation in the base layer (0) of the Animator and stores it in stateInfo. This is used to check the progress of the Attack animation.
   - _input.attack = false;: Resets the _input.attack flag to false. This is crucial for preventing the attack logic from triggering repeatedly without new input from the player as the Attack method is being called from within Update every frame.

4. Completing the Attack Animation:
   - if (stateInfo.IsName("Attack") && stateInfo.normalizedTime >= 1.0f): The if statement checks if the current animation state is the "Attack" animation and if it has completed (i.e., normalizedTime >= 1.0f). The normalizedTime represents the current time of the animation normalized to a range of 0 to 1, where 1 indicates the animation has finished playing.
   - Debug.Log("'Attack' Animation has completed.");: If the conditions above are met, it logs a message indicating the completion of the attack animation. This is useful for debugging and may also be used to trigger other events or actions in the game following an attack (e.g., allowing another attack to be initiated).

- _animator.SetBool(_animIDAttack, _input.attack);: Finally, the method sets the Animator parameter for the Attack back to false, using the _input.attack value which was reset earlier. This ensures that the animation will not replay until the attack input is triggered again by the player.

The Attack method orchestrates the execution and management of an attack action in a game. It initiates an attack animation based on player input, monitors the animation's progress, and ensures that the game's state is appropriately updated once the animation completes. This method elegantly combines input handling, animation control, and state management to facilitate a key gameplay mechanic.

Run the Playground scene for the Third Person Controller and test both the 'K' key and the Button East on a gamepad. Each press should result in the Attack animation being played.

You would have noted that upon the Attack animation having played, the transition from the Attack state back to the "Idle Walk Run Blend" state is not smooth, and ideally the Animator on your development team would need to address this issue to ensure a seamless animation flow. For this recipe to ensure a smooth transition without getting into the nitty-gritty of animations and blend trees, you can replace the Unity provided "Idle" animation within the "Idle Walk Run Blend" tree with the "1H@CombatIdle01" animation which can be located within the folder, Assets\Kevin Iglesias\Melee Warrior Animations\Animations\OneHanded. Select the blend tree in the Animator and within the Inspector where the three Motion fields are listed, drag and drop the "1H@CombatIdle01" animation into the Motion field that is currently populated with Unity's "Idle" animation.

CHAPTER 2 UNITY'S NEW INPUT SYSTEM

Now within the ThirdPersonController script locate the section labeled "animation IDs," which contains declarations for private integer animation ID variables as illustrated in Figure 2-27. Declare a new private integer variable, _IdleWalkRunBlend. This variable is designated for storing the optimized integer hash of the "Idle Walk Run Blend" animation state. Now locate the method AssignAnimationIDs() as illustrated in Figure 2-28. At the very bottom of this method add the line of code: _IdleWalkRunBlend = Animator.StringToHash("Idle Walk Run Blend");This line of code converts the "Idle Walk Run Blend" animation state into an optimized integer hash and stores it in the variable, _ IdleWalkRunBlend.

Now within the script locate the WaitForAnimation (string stateName) IEnumerator and incorporate the line of code commented as //ACC, as illustrated in Figure 2-29(b). The method CrossFadeInFixedTime() is part of Unity's Animator component and is used to smoothly transition between animations. This method is used to blend from the current animation state to a new animation state over a fixed duration, creating a smooth transition between animations, avoiding abrupt changes that can look unrealistic.

```
private IEnumerator WaitForAnimation(string stateName) //ACC
{
    // Wait until the animation state entered is nearly completed
    yield return new WaitUntil(() => IsAnimationNearlyComplete(stateName, 0.99f));

    // Set the boolean for the attack animation to false
    _animator.SetBool(_animIDAttack, false);
    _animator.CrossFadeInFixedTime(_IdleWalkRunBlend, 0.1f); //ACC
}
```

Figure 2-29(b). *Modified WaitForAnimation() method*

In the provided code, _animator.CrossFadeInFixedTime (_IdleWalkRunBlend, 0.1f); transitions the animation from the Attack state to the state identified by _IdleWalkRunBlend over a period of 0.1 seconds.

Recipe 2-3: Player Input Component Behaviors

Problem

In Unity, managing how input actions are communicated across various components and scripts in a game can be challenging. The Player Input Component's Behavior property offers several communication methods, each with unique implications for game architecture and performance. Understanding the nuances of these options – Send Messages, Broadcast Messages, Invoke Unity Events, and Invoke C# Events – is crucial for developers to optimize and tailor game input handling according to their specific needs and project requirements.

Solution

To effectively utilize the Player Input Component's Behavior options in Unity, developers should start by assessing the needs of their project to choose the appropriate behavior. For simpler projects or those requiring high modularity without strict performance constraints, using "Send Messages" or "Broadcast Messages" provides an easy setup with less coding overhead. For more complex scenarios where performance and precise control over input actions are crucial, "Invoke Unity Events" offers a flexible and efficient solution, allowing developers to link input actions directly to methods across multiple scripts and components. Setting up these behaviors involves configuring input actions in the Player Input component and linking these actions to appropriate methods or events, enhancing gameplay fluidity and responsiveness while maintaining clean and manageable code architecture.

CHAPTER 2   UNITY'S NEW INPUT SYSTEM

How It Works

In this recipe, you will delve into the Behavior property of the Player Input component exploring the functionality of each option available in the dropdown menu – Send Messages, Broadcast Messages, Invoke Unity Events, and Invoke C# Events. These options dictate the method through which the Player Input Component communicates player actions to the game, impacting how developers can design interaction systems to be more modular, efficient, and easy to maintain. By understanding the nuances and practical implications of each dropdown item, developers can tailor the input handling to fit the specific needs of their projects, enhancing gameplay fluidity and responsiveness.

Send Messages

So far you have been using the default Send Messages option to communicate binding key/button press actions to the game. This behavior is particularly useful in scenarios where you want to keep your scripts decoupled and are willing to trade off some performance for flexibility and simplicity in setup. It allows Unity developers to efficiently link player actions defined in the Input System to behavior scripts (StarterAssetsInputs) on their game objects, leveraging Unity's dynamic message-passing system for easy and flexible event handling.

- **Action Mappings**: In the Input Actions asset (Starter Assets), developers set up various input actions, such as "Jump," "Move," "Look," "Sprint," "Attack," etc. When these input actions are created and the Input Actions asset is saved, the Player Input component constructs a method name based on the action that was created. This name typically follows a convention, such as

CHAPTER 2   UNITY'S NEW INPUT SYSTEM

On[ActionName], where [ActionName] is the name of the created action. Thus, for the Sprint action, an OnSprint method is available as displayed beneath the Behavior property (Figure 2-5). These actions are linked to specific types of player inputs, like keyboard presses, gamepad buttons, or mouse movements.

- **Send Message Mechanism:** When the Player Input components Behavior property is set to "Send Messages," and an input action is triggered, it calls SendMessage to invoke a method with the constructed name on all scripts attached to the same GameObject (Player Armature). For example, if the action is named "Jump," SendMessage("OnJump") will be called. You would have noted that the OnJump method is available within the StarterAssetsInputs script that resides on the same game object (Player Armature) that the Player Input component resides on as well.

- **Method Invocation:** The SendMessages behavior will attempt to invoke the concerned method on any script attached to the GameObject that has a matching method name. For instance, if there is a method called OnJump in any of the attached scripts, it will be executed. You do have this OnJump method available within the StarterAssetsInputs script on the Player Armature game object. If no matching method is found, Unity can optionally log a warning or an error, depending on the project's settings for message handling.

131

Some of the advantages of using the Send Messages behavior option include the following:

- **Loose Coupling:** Scripts do not need to know about each other, which reduces dependencies among components and can simplify script interactions.
- **Flexibility:** New scripts can easily respond to input actions by implementing methods with the correct names, without needing to register explicitly with the input system.

Some considerations you would want to keep in mind:

- **Performance:** Using SendMessage is generally less efficient than calling methods directly (such as through delegates or events) because it involves reflection (inspecting the script's functions at runtime). This can lead to slightly increased processing times, especially if messages are sent frequently.
- **Error Handling:** There is less compile-time checking for errors. For example, if you misspell the method name or do not implement a corresponding method on any script, the error will only show up at runtime.

Broadcast Messages

The "Broadcast Messages" option within the Behavior property functions as a method for disseminating input-related events across the GameObject hierarchy. The "Broadcast Messages" behavior allows the Player Input component to send notifications about input events to not only the scripts on its own GameObject but also to all child GameObjects in the hierarchy. This approach is suitable for situations where multiple components or systems nested within a single GameObject hierarchy need to respond to the

CHAPTER 2   UNITY'S NEW INPUT SYSTEM

same input action. This behavior extends the communication reach of input actions beyond the GameObject to which the Player Input component is attached, promoting a broader, yet controlled, event broadcasting.

- **Action Mappings:** Developers begin by configuring input actions within the Input Actions asset, associating player actions (like "Move" or "Jump") with specific hardware inputs (keyboard keys, gamepad buttons, mouse movements, etc.).

- **Broadcasting Mechanism:** When an input action is triggered, the Player Input component automatically uses a method name based on the action's name, following the format On[ActionName] (e.g., OnMove for a "Move" action). It then uses BroadcastMessage, a Unity function, to invoke this method on the GameObject to which the Player Input component is attached and all of its child GameObjects in the hierarchy.

- **Recursive Method Invocation:** The BroadcastMessage function recursively searches through the GameObject and all its descendants for scripts that have a method matching the constructed name and invokes it. If a script with a matching method name is found on any GameObject in the hierarchy, that method is executed.

Some of the advantages of using the Broadcast Messages behavior option include the following:

- **Hierarchical Communication:** Enables a single input action to trigger responses across a range of components within a GameObject's hierarchy, ensuring that all relevant systems can react to input without requiring individual connections.

133

- **Ease of Setup:** Similar to "Send Messages," this approach requires minimal setup in terms of script connectivity and event handling, making it easy to use especially in complex hierarchies.

Some considerations you would want to keep in mind:

- **Performance Impact:** Like "Send Messages," the use of BroadcastMessage can lead to performance overhead due to the use of reflection to invoke methods dynamically. The impact is potentially greater with "Broadcast Messages" due to the recursive nature of the method calls across potentially large hierarchies.

- **Potential for Overbroadcasting:** If not carefully managed, broadcasting messages can lead to unintended side effects if multiple objects react undesirably to the same input, complicating debugging and game behavior.

- **Lack of Compile-Time Safety:** Errors in method naming or the absence of corresponding methods will only surface at runtime, which may lead to harder-to-track bugs.

The "Broadcast Messages" option is particularly useful in scenarios where a structured hierarchy of GameObjects needs to respond uniformly to player inputs, such as in complex interactive UIs or when multiple subsystems within a character model (e.g., animations, sound, and game mechanics) must react simultaneously to the same input.

In summary, the "Broadcast Messages" option within the Player Input component offers a powerful way to handle input events across a GameObject hierarchy, providing a broad yet simple mechanism for linking player actions to game responses in a unified manner.

Invoke Unity Events

The "Invoke Unity Events" option in the Behavior property of the Player Input component allows developers to directly link input actions to Unity Events, which can then trigger methods on any component within the scene, providing a highly flexible approach to input management. The "Invoke Unity Events" behavior leverages the Unity Event system, a powerful feature that allows events to be serialized in the editor and listeners to be added dynamically through the Unity Inspector. This system facilitates the decoupling of event producers and event consumers, enhancing modularity and flexibility in handling complex input scenarios.

- **Event Configuration:** Within the Unity Editor, developers map input actions to Unity Events in the Player Input component's configuration. Each action defined in the Input Actions asset has a corresponding Unity Event available as depicted in Figure 2-30. You need to select "Invoke Unity Events" as the Behavior option.

- **Unity Event Linkage:** For each input action (like "Jump" or "Attack"), a corresponding Unity Event is exposed in the Player Input component's Inspector (Figure 2-30). Developers can then add event listeners to these Unity Events directly in the Inspector. These listeners can reference any public method from any component in the scene, allowing the method to be invoked when the input action occurs.

- **Event Invocation:** When an input action is triggered (e.g., a key/gamepad button press or mouse click), the Player Input component fires the corresponding Unity Event. All methods attached as listeners to the Unity Event are automatically called. This can include methods across various components and GameObjects, as long as they are accessible and have been linked via the Inspector.

CHAPTER 2   UNITY'S NEW INPUT SYSTEM

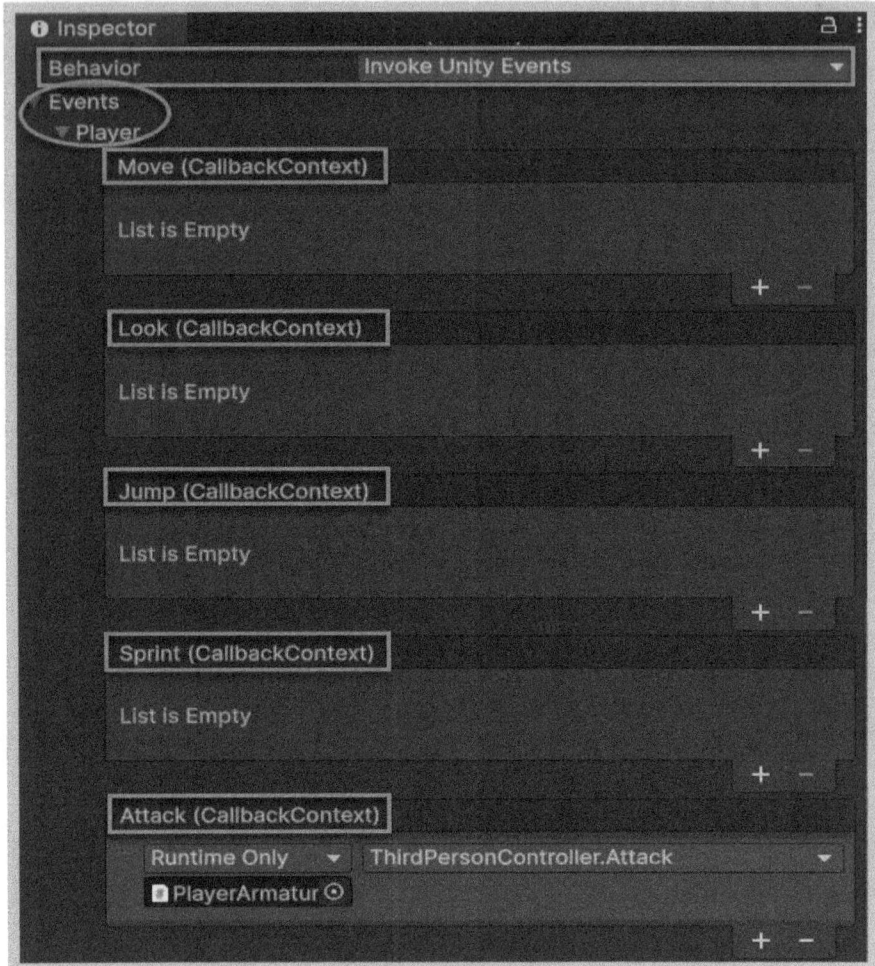

Figure 2-30. *Unity Events that are available as part of the Invoke Unity Events Behavior option*

CHAPTER 2   UNITY'S NEW INPUT SYSTEM

Some of the advantages of using the Invoke Unity Events behavior option include the following:

- **High Customizability:** Developers can customize exactly what happens when an input action is triggered, linking different actions to different methods across multiple scripts and GameObjects without writing additional code to manage these relationships.

- **Ease of Use:** The Unity Inspector provides a user-friendly interface for linking events to methods, making it accessible even to those less familiar with coding.

- **Strong Decoupling:** By using Unity Events, the components that generate input signals are decoupled from the components that react to these inputs, following good design principles and making the system easier to manage and extend.

Some considerations you would want to keep in mind:

- **Performance Considerations:** While Unity Events are versatile, they can be slower than direct method calls, particularly if the number of listeners is large or if the events are triggered very frequently.

- **Complexity in Large Projects:** Managing a large number of Unity Events through the Inspector can become cumbersome in complex projects. It may also make it harder to track and debug the flow of events through the system, as the connections are not as visible in the code itself.

- **Overhead of Unused Listeners:** Care must be taken to ensure that listeners that are no longer needed are properly removed, as lingering references can lead to memory leaks or unintended behavior.

The "Invoke Unity Events" option is particularly useful in scenarios where different subsystems of the game might need to respond differently to the same input action. For instance, pressing a button might need to trigger an animation, play a sound, and update the game state, each handled by different components or scripts. Unity Events makes it straightforward to manage these diverse responses in a centralized and easily adjustable manner.

In a previous section titled implementing a player attack action, I mentioned that invoking the Attack method within the Update method, was not an optimal approach, as the Attack method would be called every frame to check if it had been triggered. A more optimal approach would be to invoke this Attack method using the Invoke Unity Events behavior option and then hooking up the Unity Event "Attack(CallbackContext)" appropriately (Figure 2-30).

Let's set this up now. Within the Inspector for its Player Input Component, set its Behavior property to "Invoke Unity Events." Doing so makes an Events section available within which you have a section for where all your "Player" map actions have been provided with a corresponding Unity Event. For this example, you are concerned with setting up the Attack Unity Event (Figure 2-30).

Before configuring the Attack Unity Event, you will need to modify its code within the ThirdPersonController script. Another important point to note is that the Unity Event Attack as depicted in Figure 2-30 has a "CallbackContext" parameter which you will need to incorporate into your Attack method in the ThirdPersonController script.

Within the ThirdPersonController script locate the Attack method. Figure 2-31 depicts the changes that have been made to this Attack method to enable it to be invoked via the Attack Unity Event.

CHAPTER 2 UNITY'S NEW INPUT SYSTEM

```
public void Attack(InputAction.CallbackContext value) //ACC
{
    //if(_input.attack && _hasAnimator)
    {
        Debug.Log("Attack in Progress");
        //  _animator.SetBool(_animIDAttack, _input.attack);
        _animator.SetBool(_animIDAttack, true);
    }

    AnimatorStateInfo stateInfo = _animator.GetCurrentAnimatorStateInfo(0);
    //_input.attack = false;

    if (stateInfo.IsName("Attack") && stateInfo.normalizedTime >= 1.0f)
    {
        //Attack animtion has been completed
        Debug.Log("'Attack' Animation has completed.");
        //_animator.SetBool(_animIDAttack, _input.attack);
        _animator.SetBool(_animIDAttack, false);
    }
}
```

***Figure 2-31.** Modified Attack method within the ThirdPersonController script*

1. The Attack method is now declared "public" as it needs to be invoked via the Unity Event.

2. The Attack method now requires a parameter value "InputAction.CallbackContext" even though it is never used, as the Attack Unity Event listed within the Inspector has made this mandatory.

3. As you won't be using the StarteAssetsInputs script now to check for an Attack key press, the if conditional statement has been commented. For this example code, it is also assumed that an Animator component exists.

CHAPTER 2   UNITY'S NEW INPUT SYSTEM

4. As there is no purpose in referencing the StarterAssetsInputs script "attack" variable the code that uses it to set the boolean property for _animIDAttack has been commented out and a similar code statement replaces it where the boolean property for _animIDAttack is directly set to true, which will result in the attack animation playing.

5. The code that sets _input.attack to false is no longer required for the reasons explained above, hence it has been commented out.

6. Once the Attack animation has completed running, you directly set _ animIDAttack to false.

7. Now within the ThirdPersonController script, locate its Update method and within it comment out the Attack method as it will no longer be invoked every frame from within Update.

8. Within the StarterAssetsInputs script, you can comment out the code for its public OnAttack method as it will never be invoked as you are no longer using the "Send Messages" option. See Figure 2-32.

CHAPTER 2   UNITY'S NEW INPUT SYSTEM

```
#if ENABLE_INPUT_SYSTEM
    0 references
    public void OnMove(InputValue value)
    {
        MoveInput(value.Get<Vector2>());
    }
    0 references
    public void OnLook(InputValue value)
    {
        if(cursorInputForLook)
            LookInput(value.Get<Vector2>());
    }
    /***
    public void OnAttack(InputValue value)
    {
        attack = value.isPressed;
    }
    ***/
```

Figure 2-32. *Commented OnAttack method within StarterAssetsInputs script*

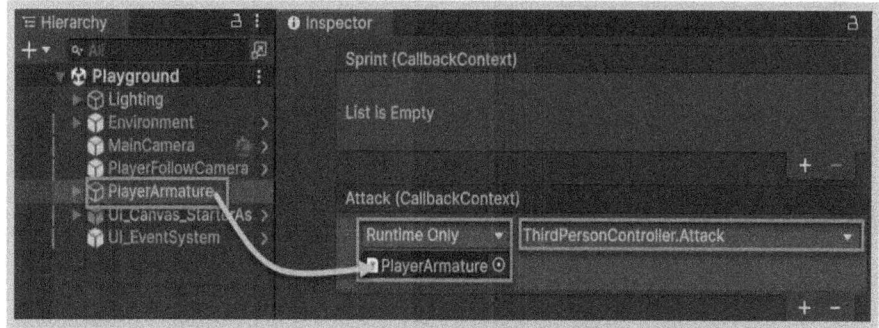

Figure 2-33. *Setup Attack Unity Event*

141

CHAPTER 2 UNITY'S NEW INPUT SYSTEM

Now you need to configure the Unity Event "Attack" in the Inspector. You will note that the ThirdPersonController script that hosts the Attack method resides on the Player Armature game object. To configure the "Attack" Unity event in the Inspector, drag and drop the Player Armature game object from the hierarchy onto the box below the "Runtime Only" drop-down. From the drop-down on the right select the menu item "ThirdPersonController" and then from the popup menu that shows up select "Attack" available at the very top beneath the header "Dynamic Callback Context." Your Attack Unity Event setup should then look like what is depicted in Figure 2-33.

Run the Playground scene for the Third Person Controller and test both the 'K' key and the Button East on a gamepad. Each press should result in the Attack animation being played. This has optimized your code, however, none of the above Move, Look, Jump, and Sprint actions will work as the code architecture they use was set up to work with "Send Messages." You would ideally need to re-write to some extent each of the methods associated with Movement, looking, Jumping, etc., to enable it to directly function with Unity Events and the Invoke Unity Events behavior.

In summary, the "Invoke Unity Events" behavior in the Player Input component offers a highly flexible and powerful tool for managing complex input scenarios in Unity, providing an intuitive interface for linking input actions with any number of diverse responses, thereby enhancing both development efficiency and gameplay sophistication.

Invoke C Sharp Events

The final Behavior property is the "Invoke C Sharp Events" option. This option leverages the power of C# events to handle input actions, offering a more code-centric approach to responding to player interactions. This method is particularly suitable for developers who prefer to keep all input handling encapsulated within their scripts, providing a clean, efficient, and type-safe way to manage input events.

CHAPTER 2   UNITY'S NEW INPUT SYSTEM

"Invoke C Sharp Events" provides a way to directly connect "Input Actions" to C# event handlers. When a player input action occurs, the Player Input component raises an event that can be handled by any subscribed method within the application. This approach aligns well with common programming patterns in C#, promoting good practices such as encapsulation and separation of concerns.

1. **Define Input Actions:** First, developers create and configure input actions in the Input Actions asset. Each action corresponds to a specific player input binding, such as pressing a button or moving a joystick. You are using the Starter Assets (Input Actions) asset that contains all actions.

2. **Subscribe to Events:** In C# scripts, developers subscribe methods to the events generated by these input actions. This is done by attaching event handlers to the events exposed by the Player Input component. Each action has an associated C# event that can be subscribed to.

3. **Event Handling:**

    - When an input action is triggered (e.g., the player presses the Attack button), the Player Input component triggers the corresponding phase/event.

    - The method that is subscribed to that phase/event is called, allowing the game to respond to the input without tight coupling between components.

To see the "Invoke C Sharp Events" in action let's wire it up to the Attack action. First, ensure that the Behaviors property within the Player Input component has been set to "Invoke C Sharp Events." Now within the ThirdPersonController script modify the OnEnable and OnDisable methods by adding two lines of code to each as depicted in Figure 2-36. Also, you will note that the lines of code used in the hybrid approach have been commented out, to ensure that it is the "Invoke C Sharp Events" that is driving the Attack action.

The caching of the _playerInput variable which was originally being done in the Start() method has now been moved to the Awake() method and commented out within the Start() method as shown in Figures 2-34 and 2-35.

```
private void Awake()
{
    attackAction = GetComponent<PlayerInput>().actions.FindAction("Attack"); //ACC
    #if ENABLE_INPUT_SYSTEM
    _playerInput = GetComponent<PlayerInput>();
    #else
    Debug.LogError( "Starter Assets package is missing dependencies. Please use Tools/Starter
    #endif

    // get a reference to our main camera
    if (_mainCamera == null)
    {
        _mainCamera = GameObject.FindGameObjectWithTag("MainCamera");
    }
}
```

Figure 2-34. *Modified Awake method responsible for caching _playerInput*

CHAPTER 2　UNITY'S NEW INPUT SYSTEM

```
private void OnEnable() //ACC
{
    //attackAction.Enable();
    //attackAction.started += OnAttackStart;
    //attackAction.canceled += OnAttackComplete;

    _playerInput.actions["Attack"].performed += OnAttackStart;
    _playerInput.actions["Attack"].canceled += OnAttackComplete;

}

private void OnDisable() //ACC
{
    //attackAction.Disable();
    //attackAction.started -= OnAttackStart;
    //attackAction.canceled -= OnAttackComplete;

    _playerInput.actions["Attack"].performed -= OnAttackStart;
    _playerInput.actions["Attack"].canceled -= OnAttackComplete;
}
```

Figure 2-35. Modified Start method where commented-out code has been moved to Awake ()

```
private void Start()
{
    _cinemachineTargetYaw = CinemachineCameraTarget.transform.rotation.eulerAngles.y;
    _hasAnimator = TryGetComponent(out _animator);
    _controller = GetComponent<CharacterController>();
    _input = GetComponent<StarterAssetsInputs>();
    /*** This commented out Code has been moved to the Awake() method.
    #if ENABLE_INPUT_SYSTEM
    _playerInput = GetComponent<PlayerInput>();
    #else
    Debug.LogError( "Starter Assets package is missing dependencies. Please use Tools/Starter
    #endif
    ***/
    AssignAnimationIDs();
    // reset our timeouts on start
    _jumpTimeoutDelta = JumpTimeout;
    _fallTimeoutDelta = FallTimeout;
}
```

Figure 2-36. OnEnable and OnDisable methods

The _playerInput is an instance of the PlayerInput component while actions are a property of the PlayerInput component that provides access to all the input actions defined in the associated Input Actions asset (Starter Assets). ["Attack"] accesses a specific action named "Attack" from the collection of actions. This name corresponds to an action that should have been set up in the Input Actions asset (Starter Assets) and is meant to handle the input related to attacking.

"performed" is an event/phase on the input action that is triggered when the action is fully performed according to its set criteria (for instance, when a button is pressed down completely). OnAttackStart and OnAttackComplete are event handler methods that the performed and canceled event/phase subscribe to. By using the += operator you subscribe an event to a method (listener), in this case, OnAttackStart and OnAttackComplete.

The OnAttackStart and OnAttackComplete event handler methods depicted in Figure 2-40 must match the expected signature for the event handler. For the performed event, the handler needs to accept a parameter of type InputAction.CallbackContext, which provides context information about the input action, such as its value or duration.

Run the Playground scene for the Third Person Controller and test both the 'K' key and the Button East on a gamepad. Each press should result in the Attack animation being played, using the code written exclusively for the "Invoke C Sharp Events" behavior. However, note that it's only the Attack binding that works here. Other key/button binding presses won't work.

Recipe 2-4: Input Handling – Hybrid Approach

Problem

Managing input actions efficiently in Unity can be challenging, especially when different actions require distinct handling methods for optimal performance and gameplay integration. Traditional input handling methods like 'Send Messages' might not be suitable for actions that should not run every frame, such as an Attack action, leading to potential performance issues and less efficient gameplay mechanics.

Solution

A hybrid input handling strategy can be implemented by combining Unity's built-in "Send Messages" feature for standard actions with a custom input handling approach for specific actions like Attack, which require more controlled and performance-optimized handling. This involves setting up the Input System to manage input actions with different lifecycle phases – Started, Performed, and Canceled – to precisely control when and how actions are triggered and terminated. This approach not only optimizes performance by reducing unnecessary function calls but also enhances the responsiveness and fluidity of gameplay by tailoring input handling to the specific needs of each action.

How It Works

Implementing a hybrid input handling strategy merges default functionalities with tailored solutions. Utilize Unity's "Send Messages" feature for predefined actions provided by Unity and implement a more

CHAPTER 2   UNITY'S NEW INPUT SYSTEM

intricate coding approach for custom actions such as Attack, which should not run every frame within the Update method. This approach enhances performance by minimizing redundant function calls.

All necessary code for the Attack action will be integrated within the ThirdPersonController script. Before adding this new code, ensure that the OnAttack method in the StarterAssetsInputs script is commented out (see Figure 2-32). This change is necessary because the "K" keypress and the Button East gamepad button bindings will no longer trigger the OnAttack method within the StarterAssetsInputs script. Also, ensure that the Behaviors property within the Player Input component has been set to "Send Messages."

Using this approach you will utilize the new Unity Input Systems concept where each action can be triggered in different phases of its lifecycle, primarily divided into three main phases: Started, Performed, and Canceled. Understanding these phases is crucial for effectively using the Input System to manage complex input scenarios in your games.

1. **Started Phase:** The Started phase signals the beginning of an action. For a button, this phase triggers the moment the button begins to be pressed down. This phase is particularly useful for actions where the initial activation moment is important – like starting to charge a weapon or beginning a jump. In code, handling the Started phase typically looks like subscribing to an event that fires when an action starts as depicted in Figure 2-37. This phase can be used to set up or initialize states that are needed while the action is being performed. The "started" phase is called when you press the binding.

CHAPTER 2 UNITY'S NEW INPUT SYSTEM

```
attackAction.started += OnAttackStart;
```

Figure 2-37. *Started phase for an Attack action*

The above code subscribes to the attackAction's "started" phase to the OnAttackStart method (event handler).

2. **Performed Phase:** The Performed phase occurs when the action is considered to be fully triggered or executed. For different types of actions, this means different things:

   - Button Presses: The Performed phase triggers when the button is fully pressed down.

   - Value Changes (like an axis on a joystick): This phase can trigger repeatedly as the value changes beyond a certain threshold.

   - Continuous Actions (like holding down a button): Can trigger repeatedly according to the repeat rate if set.

   This phase is most commonly used for executing the main response to an input action and is called when all interactions have been completed, if any. If no interactions have been set up, the Performed phase is called immediately after the Started phase (Figure 2-38).

```
attackAction.performed += OnAttackPerform;
```

Figure 2-38. Performed phase for an Attack action

> For gameplay mechanics, this might involve firing a weapon, jumping, or other immediate game behaviors that are triggered by player inputs.

3. **Canceled Phase:** The Canceled phase indicates that an ongoing action has been interrupted or ceased. For button inputs, this typically occurs when the button is released. This phase is crucial for actions that need to be cleaned up or for which there are specific behaviors when inputs are stopped prematurely. For instance, releasing a button to stop charging a weapon, ending a sprint when the shift key is released, or stopping a continuous movement or command. Figure 2-39 shows the attackAction canceled phase invoking the OnAttackComplete method (event handler).

```
attackAction.canceled += OnAttackComplete;
```

Figure 2-39. Canceled phase for an Attack action

> When setting up your input handling using Unity's Input System, these phases allow you to differentiate between the start of an action, the action's execution, and when an action ends. This can help in creating more nuanced input responses, such as:

CHAPTER 2 UNITY'S NEW INPUT SYSTEM

- Drag and Drop: Begin dragging on Started, update drag on Performed, and complete or cancel the drag on Canceled.

- Charging and Releasing Mechanisms: Start charging on Started, perform some action on Performed, and release or fire on Canceled.

You will be using the Started and Canceled phases to implement the Attack action. Within the ThirdPersonController script, locate the section beneath the animation IDs declaration. Note that a new variable of type InputAction, namely, attackAction has been created here (Figure 2-40). This variable references the Attack action available as part of the Starter Assets (Input Action Asset), available as part of the Actions property within the Player Input component.

```
#if ENABLE_INPUT_SYSTEM
private PlayerInput _playerInput;
#endif
private Animator _animator;
private CharacterController _controller;
private StarterAssetsInputs _input;
private GameObject _mainCamera;
private InputAction attackAction; //ACC
```

Figure 2-40. Declaring variable attackAction of type InputAction

In the Awake method, you initialize the attackAction variable by retrieving the "Attack" action from the PlayerInput component, by referencing its actions property. FindAction is the method used to retrieve the "Attack" action (Figure 2-41).

```
private void Awake()
{
    attackAction = GetComponent<PlayerInput>().actions.FindAction("Attack"); //ACC
    // get a reference to our main camera
    if (_mainCamera == null)
    {
        _mainCamera = GameObject.FindGameObjectWithTag("MainCamera");
    }
}
```

Figure 2-41. *Initialize the attackAction variable within the Awake method*

Next set up the OnEnable and OnDisable methods as depicted in Figure 2-42. These methods allow you to subscribe and unsubscribe to event handlers (methods) required for the Attack action's "started" and "canceled" phases. These methods manage the lifecycle of the attackAction input action when the GameObject is enabled or disabled in the scene.

```
private void OnEnable() //ACC
{
    attackAction.Enable();
    attackAction.started += OnAttackStart;
    attackAction.canceled += OnAttackComplete;

}

private void OnDisable() //ACC
{
    attackAction.Disable();
    attackAction.started -= OnAttackStart;
    attackAction.canceled -= OnAttackComplete;
}
```

Figure 2-42. *OnEnable and OnDisable methods for setting up the Attack Action*

CHAPTER 2 UNITY'S NEW INPUT SYSTEM

Within the OnEnable method, the attackAction is explicitly enabled, allowing it to start processing input. It subscribes to the started and canceled phases of attackAction. The OnAttackStart method is set to trigger when the action starts (typically when the binding is pressed down), and OnAttackComplete is set to trigger when the action is canceled (typically when the binding is released).

Within the OnDisable method, the attackAction is disabled, which stops it from processing inputs. It unsubscribes from the started and canceled phases to clean up and prevent potential memory leaks or unintended behavior when the GameObject is not active or has been destroyed.

Next setup the OnAttackStart and OnAttackComplete methods as depicted in Figure 2-43. These methods are event handlers linked to the input action. The Attack method you had modified earlier as depicted in Figure 2-31 has now been renamed to OnAttackStart.

```
private void OnAttackStart(InputAction.CallbackContext context) //ACC
{
    Debug.Log("Attack key was pressed");
    _animator.SetBool(_animIDAttack, true);
}

2 references
private void OnAttackComplete(InputAction.CallbackContext context) //ACC
{
    Debug.Log("Attack key was released");
    StartCoroutine(WaitForAnimation("Attack"));
}
```

Figure 2-43. *OnAttackStart and OnAttackComplete Event handlers*

The OnAttackStart event is triggered when the attack action starts (e.g., pressing the attack action binding). It logs this event and sets the _animIDAttack animator boolean parameter (which controls the attack animation) to true, starting the attack animation.

CHAPTER 2   UNITY'S NEW INPUT SYSTEM

The OnAttackComplete event is triggered when the attack action is canceled (e.g., releasing the attack action binding). It logs the event and starts a coroutine that handles the end of the attack animation sequence.

Next, you need to create the "WaitForAnimation" coroutine shown in Figure 2-44. This coroutine is designed to efficiently handle the timing of animation states, particularly ensuring that a specific animation reaches near completion before changing the state of an Animator parameter. By waiting until an animation is almost complete before changing states, you maintain a high level of polish in your game's visual feedback, which is crucial for actions like attacks where player perception of timing and the response is critical. However, it's important to note that this is not the only way to achieve this and you could use animation events instead.

```
private IEnumerator WaitForAnimation(string stateName) //ACC
{
    // Wait until the animation state entered is nearly completed
    yield return new WaitUntil(() => IsAnimationNearlyComplete(stateName, 0.99f));

    // Set the boolean for the attack animation to false
    _animator.SetBool(_animIDAttack, false);
}
```

Figure 2-44. *WaitForAnimation coroutine*

Ensure that at the very top of the ThirdPersonController script you add in the namespace "System.Collections" required by the IEnumerator type of the coroutine (Figure 2-45).

```
using System.Collections;
using UnityEngine;
#if ENABLE_INPUT_SYSTEM
using UnityEngine.InputSystem;
#endif
```

Figure 2-45. *Adding namespace System.Collections*

CHAPTER 2 UNITY'S NEW INPUT SYSTEM

When the attack key is released, OnAttackComplete is triggered due to the input action's canceled phase. This method logs a message and starts the WaitForAnimation coroutine, passing "Attack" as the stateName, which specifies the animation state to monitor.

Inside the coroutine, the statement "yield return new WaitUntil(...)" is used to create a pause in the coroutine's execution. The coroutine will resume execution only when the condition specified by WaitUntil returns true. In this case, it waits for the IsAnimationNearlyComplete method to return true, indicating that the specified animation state (stateName, i.e., Attack) is 99% (or 0.99f as normalized time) complete. In Unity, the normalized time of an animation state represents the current time of the animation divided by its total duration, thus a value from 0 to 1. A normalized time of 0.99f effectively means that the animation is 99% complete.

After the animation is nearly complete, the next line of code after the WaitUntil is executed, which sets the Animator Boolean parameter (_animIDAttack) to false. This typically is used to transition the animator from its Attack state back to another state (Idle Walk Run Blend) as the animation nears completion.

Lastly, you need to create the IsAnimationNearlyComplete method depicted in Figure 2-46. This method serves as a critical function within the coroutine WaitForAnimation, providing a conditional check to determine if a specified animation state is nearing completion based on a given threshold. By using IsAnimationNearlyComplete within a coroutine that utilizes "WaitUntil," you achieve a non-blocking delay that is both efficient and tightly controlled, ensuring that transitions and state changes in your game's animations occur precisely when needed.

CHAPTER 2   UNITY'S NEW INPUT SYSTEM

```
private bool IsAnimationNearlyComplete(string stateName, float threshold) //ACC
{
    AnimatorStateInfo stateInfo = _animator.GetCurrentAnimatorStateInfo(0); // Using layer 0
    return stateInfo.IsName(stateName) && stateInfo.normalizedTime >= threshold;
}
```

Figure 2-46. *IsAnimationNearlyComplete method*

The IsAnimationNearlyComplete method takes two parameters, a string stateName which is the name of the animation state to check. This parameter allows the function to be versatile and reusable for different animations. The other parameter, a float threshold is a decimal representing the normalized time threshold at which the animation is considered nearly complete. Normalized time is a value from 0 (beginning of the animation) to 1 (end of the animation), so a threshold of 0.99 indicates the animation is 99% complete.

The method then goes on to retrieve the current state information of the animation from the Animator's first layer (layer 0). This is typical in many game setups where layer 0 handles primary character animations and the Attack animation is currently on the base layer zero.

It then checks if the current animation state matches the provided stateName and if the normalized time of this state has reached or surpassed the specified threshold. This dual condition ensures that the function returns true only when the specific animation is both active and nearly finished. This effectively synchronizes the timing within the game, holding off any subsequent actions until the current animation is appropriately complete.

In summary, together, these methods provide a robust hybrid framework for managing input actions and efficiently managing resources by subscribing and unsubscribing to events as needed.

CHAPTER 2   UNITY'S NEW INPUT SYSTEM

Recipe 2-5: Implementing UI Controls
Problem

In Unity, effectively managing input for both gameplay and UI interactions can be challenging, especially when transitioning between different input contexts. Common issues include overlapping inputs, where game controls interfere with UI navigation, and maintaining a responsive UI system that adapts to various input devices like keyboards and gamepads.

Solution

To address these challenges, consolidate UI and player action maps into a single Input Action Asset for streamlined management. Utilize Unity's Player Input component to switch dynamically between these action maps based on game context. By setting up a universal action map for shared actions and configuring input bindings specifically for UI controls, you can prevent input conflicts and ensure smooth transitions. Implementing a toggle action, such as using the "Escape" key to switch between gameplay and UI modes, further refines control flow, allowing players to seamlessly interact with both game elements and UI without disruptions.

How It Works

This recipe guides you through the implementation of UI controls and their mapping to input devices such as keyboards and gamepads using Unity's new Input System. You will learn how to navigate between UI elements, set up a new UI map within the default Starter Assets (Input Action Asset), and programmatically switch between input maps depending on the game context.

Setup a Canvas with Two Buttons

To quickly set up two Text Mesh Pro (TMP) buttons within a Canvas, centered in the scene in Unity, follow these steps:

1. Install Text Mesh Pro: If not already installed, go to Window ➤ TextMeshPro ➤ Import TMP Essential Resources to add Text Mesh Pro to your project.

2. Create a Canvas:

   - In the Hierarchy panel, right-click and select UI ➤ Canvas. This creates a new Canvas in your scene.

   - Set the Canvas' UI Scale Mode property to Scale With Screen Size to ensure UI elements scale properly on different displays.

3. Add a Panel:

   - Right-click on the Canvas in the Hierarchy and select UI ➤ Panel. This Panel will act as a container for your buttons, helping to manage their layout.

   - Set the RectTransform tool of the panel to stretch in both directions (top, bottom, left, and right) to 0, making the panel cover the entire Canvas.

   - Optionally, modify the Image component of the Panel to change its background color or make it transparent by setting the Alpha channel to 35.

4. Create Text Mesh Pro Buttons:

   - Right-click on the Panel, and select UI ➤ Button - TextMeshPro. This creates a TMP button with default settings.

CHAPTER 2 UNITY'S NEW INPUT SYSTEM

- Duplicate the button by selecting it, then pressing Ctrl + D (or Cmd + D on Mac) to create the second button.

5. Center and Arrange the Buttons:

    - For each button, use the RectTransform tool, setting the Anchor Presets to the middle center with offsets. Adjust the width and height as desired.

    - Position the first button by setting Pos Y to a positive value (50) to move it upwards.

    - Set the Pos Y of the second button to a negative value (-50) to move it downward, ensuring symmetric positioning relative to the first button.

6. Customize Button Properties:

    - For each button, access the child object named Text (TMP) to modify the text properties including font, size, color, and alignment. You could call one button "Save" and the other "Load" should you want to.

    - Customize the button's appearance under the Button component by adjusting its selected color property and setting it to something like Red. This will enable you to easily visualize a button being selected.

7. Adjust Canvas and Panel Settings for Optimal Display:

    - Ensure that the Canvas is set to match the screen size or aspect ratio you anticipate your game will be viewed on.

    - Adjust the Panel if necessary to better align with the layout or design needs.

159

CHAPTER 2   UNITY'S NEW INPUT SYSTEM

UI Event System

In the hierarchy, you will note that there already exists an Event System for Unity's new Input System. Select this "UI_EventSystem" in the hierarchy and within the inspector expand its Input System UI Input Module component (Figure 2-47).

This Input System UI Input Module component uses the DefaultInputActions (Input Action Asset) as depicted in Figure 2-47. Double-click on it to open it. You will note that it comprises two action maps. However, it's the UI action map that will be used for the UI button elements you created. Ensure that you select this UI action map so that the actions it has been set up with are visible in the middle pane (Figure 2-48).

With the "UI_EventSystem" still selected in the hierarchy, in the Inspector within the Input System UI Input Module component (Figure 2-47), you will note several actions listed such as Point, Left Click, Right Click, etc. For example, Left Click is set to UI/Click from the dropdown, which in turn maps to the "Click" action within the UI action map. If you expand the "Click" action (Figure 2-49) within the UI action map you will note that this "Click" action has several bindings for the Left Mouse Button, Pen Tip, Touch/Press on a touch screen as well as a trigger binding for an XR controller. Similarly, if you look at "Move" within the Input System UI Input Module component, which is used for making a selection between UI elements (buttons), you will note that it maps to the "Navigate" action within the UI action map. This "Navigate" action has bindings for the Gamepad, Joystick, and Keyboard as depicted in Figure 2-49.

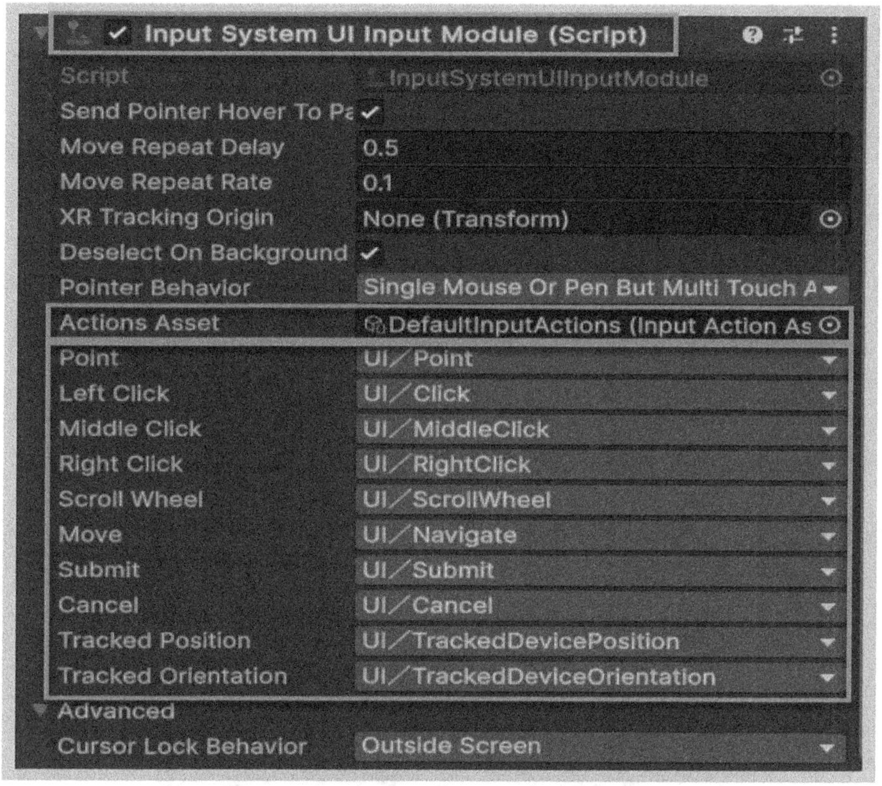

CHAPTER 2 UNITY'S NEW INPUT SYSTEM

Figure 2-47. Input System UI Input Module component

CHAPTER 2　UNITY'S NEW INPUT SYSTEM

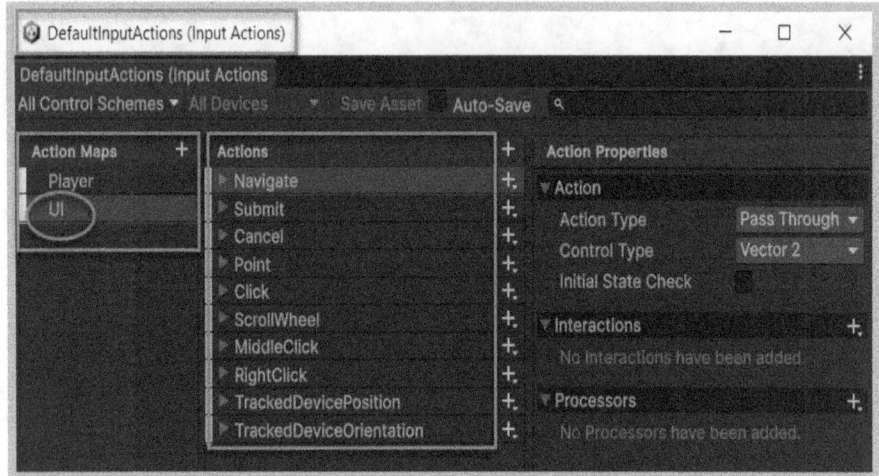

Figure 2-48. *DefaultInputActions with the UI action map selected*

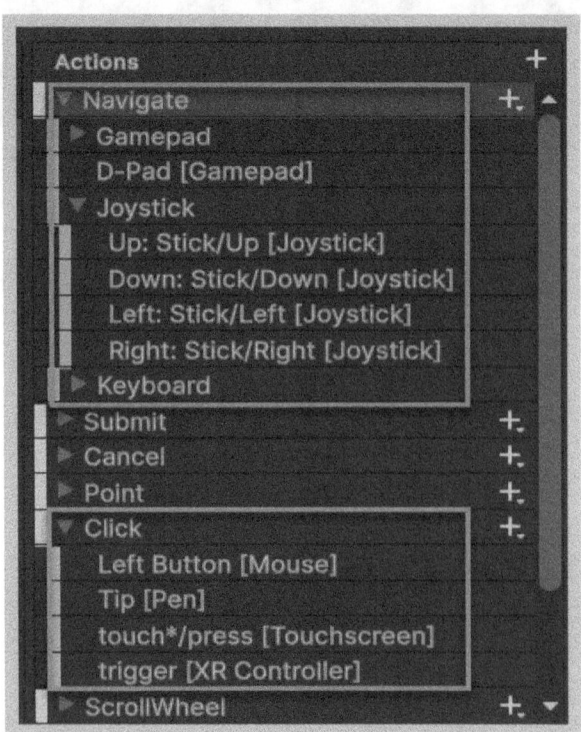

Figure 2-49. *Navigate and Click actions*

CHAPTER 2   UNITY'S NEW INPUT SYSTEM

Before testing out your buttons, drag and drop the "Button" game object from the hierarchy onto the "First Slected" property within the Event System component of the "UI_EventSystem game object as depicted in Figure 2-50. This ensures that your first button (Save) is selected by default.

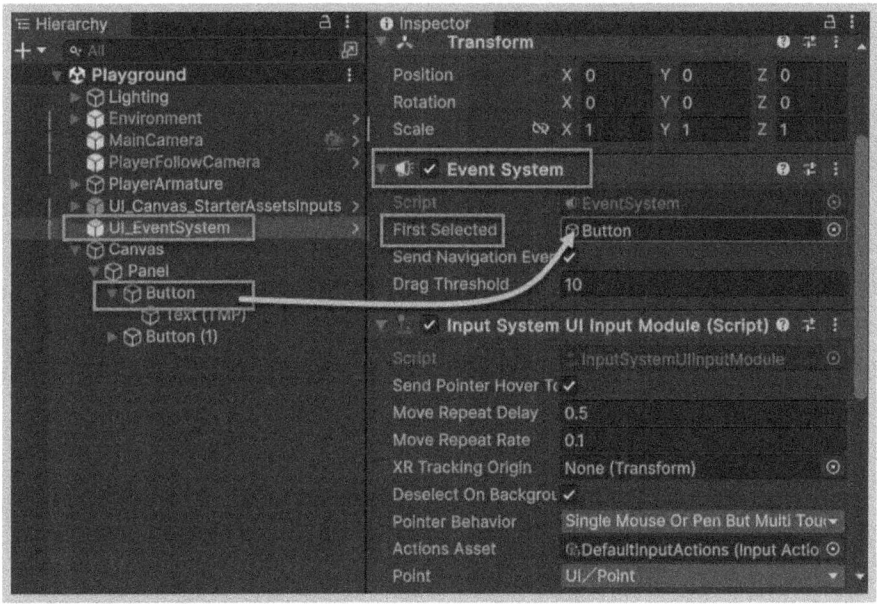

Figure 2-50. *Setting up the default selected button*

Run the Playground scene for the Third Person Controller and test the keyboard keys "W," "S," "Up Arrow," and "Down Arrow." You will note that you can now alternate between the two buttons "Save" and "Load." However, you would have also noted that the player character also moves and this is not the behavior you would ideally want. Moreover, if you click anywhere on the screen, you would lose the ability to select any of the buttons.

To fix the issue of losing the ability to select the buttons on account of clicking anywhere within the screen, you need to simply uncheck the check box that states "Deselect On Background Click," available within the Input System UI Input Module component (Figure 2-51).

163

Consolidate Action Maps

To streamline input management, you need to consolidate the UI action map from the "DefaultInputActions" and the Player action map from the "StarterAssets" into a single input actions asset. This consolidation allows for more efficient switching between action maps based on the game context. To achieve this, you need to copy the UI action map into the "StarterAssets" input action asset, ensuring that both sets of input controls are managed from one centralized location.

Open the "DefaultInputActions" input action asset and select "UI" within Action Maps. Right-click on it and select copy, then close this "DefaultInputActions" input action asset. Next, open the "StarterAssets" input action asset, and within its Action Maps section right-click and select paste. You have now consolidated both action maps into the "StarterAssets" input action asset. Ensure that you save your modified "StarterAssets" input action asset.

Select the UI action map and expand the Keyboard action. Review each child binding to confirm that a Control Scheme has not been set up. For each binding, ensure that the checkbox labeled "KeyboardMouse" is selected to designate it as the appropriate control scheme. This step is crucial for ensuring that all keyboard bindings are correctly configured within the specified control scheme. Do the same for the Click Action's Left Button [Mouse] binding, the Scroll Wheel – Scroll [Mouse] binding, Middle Click – Middle Button [Mouse], and Right Click – Right Button [Mouse]. Finally, ensure that you save "StarterAssets."

Now select the "UI_EventSystem" game object in the hierarchy and within the Inspector for its Input System UI Input Module, replace the Action Asset which is currently "DefaultInputActions" with "StarterAssets," which you can find within your project tab by navigating to Assets/StarterAssets/InputSystem (Figure 2-51).

CHAPTER 2   UNITY'S NEW INPUT SYSTEM

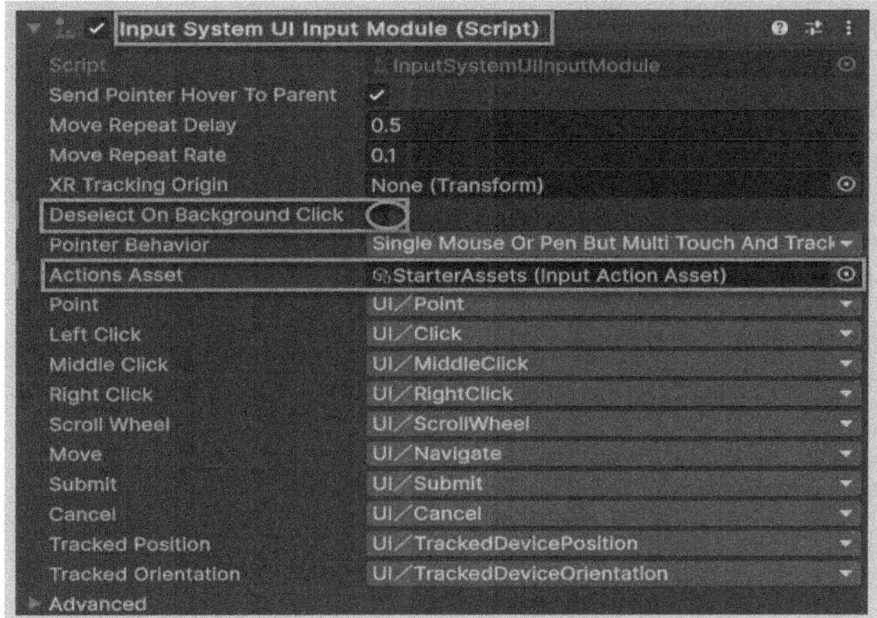

Figure 2-51. *Actions Asset set to StarterAssets*

Next, select the "PlayerArmature" game object in the hierarchy. Within the Inspector locate its Player Input component. Here you need to populate the property UI Input Module with the Input System UI Input Module component that is available on the "UI_EventSystem" game object. You can click on the target icon button available for the UI Input Module property and select the "UI_EventSystem" from the window that pops up. The setup Player Input component is depicted in Figure 2-52.

CHAPTER 2   UNITY'S NEW INPUT SYSTEM

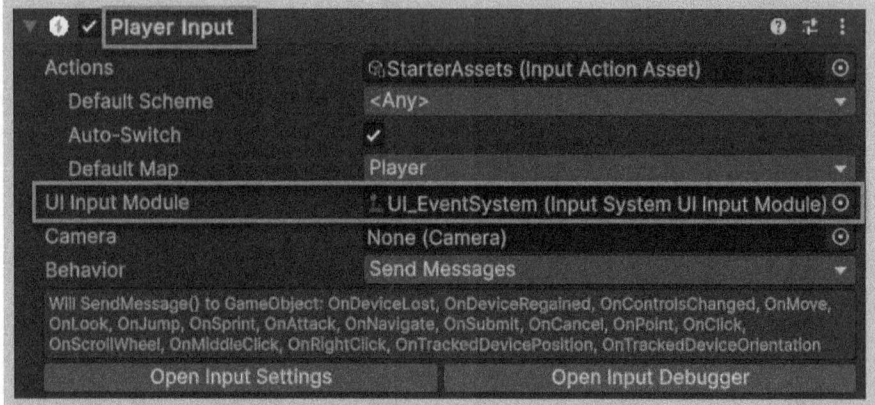

Figure 2-52. *Player Input component with UI Input Module populated*

To address the issue of overlapping inputs, where using the up or down arrow keys, as well as the "W" and "S" keys, results in both player movement and menu navigation, you need to implement a system to disable the Player action map when in UI mode and vice versa. You could utilize the Escape key as a toggle to switch between UI and gameplay modes. To achieve this, you first need to create a new action map dedicated to actions shared across different contexts, such as the UI toggle described here. This shared action map should remain enabled at all times to ensure seamless switching and prevent input conflicts.

1. Open the "StarterAssets" Input Actions Asset where you have defined your "Player" and "UI" action maps.

2. Create a new action map called "Universal" for actions that you would want to be shared across contexts.

3. Create a new action called "ToggleUI."

CHAPTER 2   UNITY'S NEW INPUT SYSTEM

4. Set the Input Binding for this new "ToggleUI" action to the "Escape" key of your Keyboard and ensure that you set its control scheme to KeyboardMouse (Figure 2-53).

5. Ensure that you save the "StarterAssets" and close it.

6. Now, select the "PlayerArmature" game object in the hierarchy, and within the inspector locate the Player Input Component. Set its Default Map property to "Universal" from the drop-down (Figure 2-54).

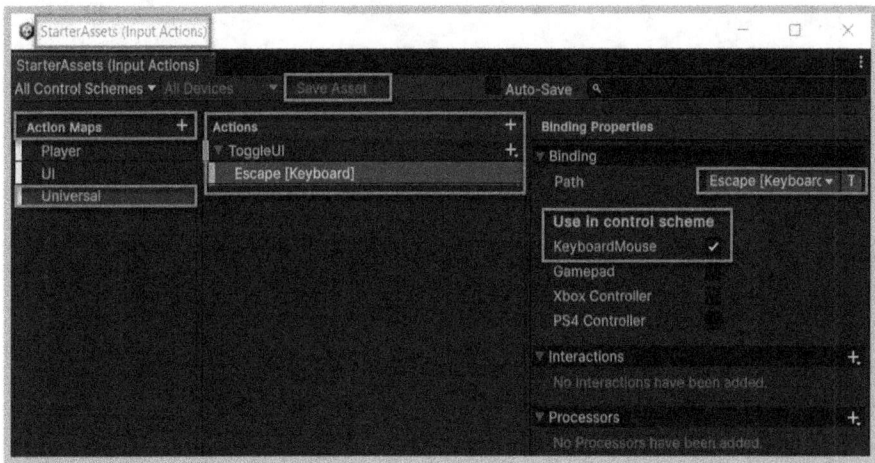

Figure 2-53. *Universal action map with the ToggleUI action and Escape Key binding*

167

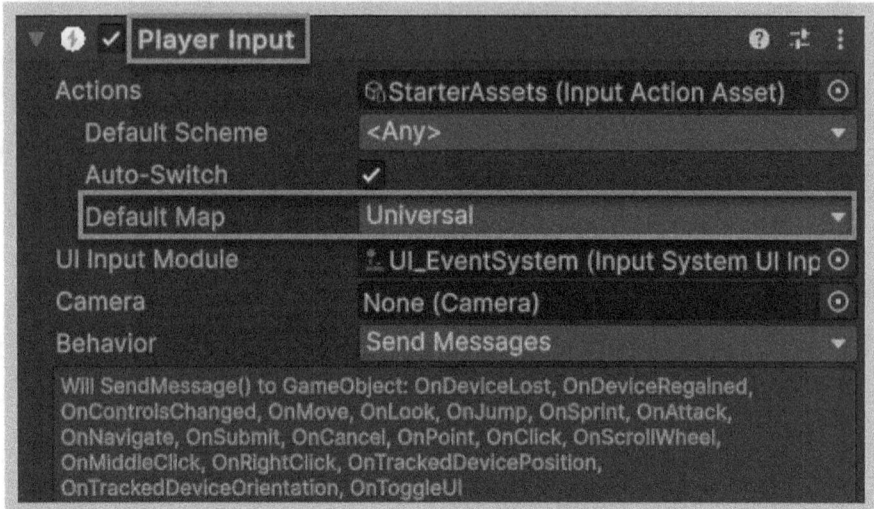

Figure 2-54. Default Map property set to the Universal action map you created

Scripting the ToggleUI Action

Within the Project tab, navigate to the Assets folder and locate the Scripts directory, which houses all C# scripts you create. Find the "ActionMapManager" script designed to control the switching between UI and action maps based on the game's context. Attach this script as a component to the "PlayerArmature" game object by selecting "PlayerArmature" in the hierarchy and dragging the "ActionMapManager" script onto it. Once attached, open this script in your preferred editor of choice (Listing 2-1).

Listing 2-1. ActionMapManager

```
using UnityEngine;
using UnityEngine.InputSystem;
using StarterAssets;
using UnityEngine.EventSystems;
```

```csharp
public class ActionMapManager : MonoBehaviour
{
    public InputActionAsset actionAsset;//Assign in Inspector
    public GameObject gameUICanvas;     //Assign in Inspector
    public GameObject rebindControlsCanvas; //Assign in
                                            //Inspector
    public GameObject gameUIDefaultButton; //Assign in
                                           //Inspector
    private PlayerInput playerInput;
    private InputActionMap playerMap;
    private InputActionMap uiMap;
    private InputActionMap universalMap;
    private bool isActiveGameUICanvas = true;
    private InputAction toggleUIAction;

    private void Awake()
    {
        playerInput = GetComponent<PlayerInput>();

        // Get all three action maps
        playerMap = actionAsset.actionMaps[0];
        uiMap = actionAsset.actionMaps[1];
        universalMap = actionAsset.actionMaps[2];

        //Get the ToggleUI and ToggleRbindControls action
        toggleUIAction = playerInput.actions["ToggleUI"];

    }

    private void OnEnable()
    {
       toggleUIAction.performed += ToggleUIPerformed;

    }
```

```csharp
private void OnDisable()
{
    toggleUIAction.performed -= ToggleUIPerformed;
}

private void ToggleUIPerformed(InputAction.CallbackContext context)
{
  isActiveGameUICanvas = !isActiveGameUICanvas;
  gameUICanvas.SetActive(isActiveGameUICanvas);

  if (!isActiveGameUICanvas)
        playerMap.Enable();
  else
  {         EventSystem.current.SetSelectedGameObject(
            gameUIDefaultButton);
  playerMap.Disable();
  }

 Debug.Log($"PlayerMap Enabled: {playerMap.enabled} ;
 UIMap Enabled: {uiMap.enabled} ; " +
 $"UniversalMap Enabled: {universalMap.enabled}");
   Debug.Log($"Current Action Map is:
   {playerInput.currentActionMap.name}");

  //Universal Map Needs to be enabled at all times as it
  //holds the Esc Key binding
  universalMap.Enable();
  }
}
```

CHAPTER 2   UNITY'S NEW INPUT SYSTEM

The ActionMapManager class provided as part of Listing 2-1 is designed to manage input actions using Unity's new Input System. It specifically handles toggling between different action maps ("Player" and "UI") and controls the visibility of a UI canvas based on user interactions with the "Escape" key. Here's a detailed explanation of its variables and functionality:

Variables:

- **public InputActionAsset actionAsset:** A public variable to be assigned in the Unity Editor that references the "StarterAssets" Input Actoin Asset.

- **public GameObject gameUICanvas:** Another public variable to be assigned in the Unity Editor. It references the UI canvas GameObject that is used to display game interactive UI elements.

- **public GameObject gameUIDefaultButton:** This public variable needs to be assigned in the Unity Editor. It references a button of the game UI Canvas that will be selected as the default button when the game UI Canvas is displayed.

- **private PlayerInput playerInput:** This private variable is cached in the Awake() method. This PlayerInput component is responsible for handling all input-related configurations.

- **private InputActionMap playerMap:** A private variable that stores the "Player" action map, which contains input bindings for general gameplay (like moving, jumping, etc.).

- **private InputActionMap uiMap:** A private variable that stores the "UI" action map, which contains input bindings specific to UI interactions, such as navigating menus, buttons, etc..

171

CHAPTER 2 UNITY'S NEW INPUT SYSTEM

- **private InputActionMap universalMap:** This variable holds a "Universal" action map, designed to contain input actions that should be available at all times, regardless of the current game state (e.g., the "Escape" key binding action).

- **private bool isActiveGameUICanvas = true:** A private boolean variable that is used to keep track of whether the game UI Canvas is active or not.

- **private InputAction toggleUIAction:** A private variable that references the specific action "ToggleUI" which is triggered by pressing the "Esc" key. This action is used to toggle between the player and UI action maps.

Methods:

- **Awake():** Called when the script instance is being loaded. This method caches the playerInput variable with a reference to the PlayerInput component. It initializes the action maps by retrieving them using the Input Action Asset (StarterAssets) using a zero-based index. It then initializes the toggle action by retrieving it from the PlayerInput component. This setup ensures that the action maps and actions are ready before the game starts.

- **OnEnable() and OnDisable():** These methods manage event subscriptions. When the GameObject is enabled, OnEnable() subscribes the ToggleUIPerformed method (event handler) to the performed event of the toggleUIAction. Conversely, OnDisable() unsubscribes from the event to clean up references and prevent potential memory leaks or unwanted behavior when the GameObject is disabled.

- **ToggleUIPerformed(InputAction.CallbackContext context):** Triggered whenever the "ToggleUI" action is performed (i.e., when the "Escape" key is pressed). It is designed to toggle the visibility of the game UI canvas and handle the enabling/disabling of input action maps based on the UI's visibility. The line of code "isActiveGameUICanvas = ! isActiveGameUICanvas;" toggles the boolean variable isActiveGameUICanvas. Initially set to true, indicating that the game UI canvas is active, this line flips its state every time the method is called. If the UI canvas is visible, it becomes hidden, and vice versa. The next line of code "gameUICanvas.SetActive(isActiveGameUICanvas);" sets the active state of the gameUICanvas game object based on the current value of isActiveGameUICanvas. This effectively shows or hides the game UI canvas each time the method is executed. The conditional block "if (!isActiveGameUICanvas)" checks if isActiveGameUICanvas is false, which would mean the UI canvas was just deactivated, in which case the player action map (playerMap) is enabled. This allows player control inputs to be processed, as the player is now interacting with the game environment instead of UI elements. The "else" block executes if the game UI canvas is active (isActiveGameUICanvas is true), meaning the UI canvas was just activated, in which case the SetSelectedGameObject() method for the current event system sets focus to a default button (gameUIDefaultButton) in the game UI. It's important for usability and accessibility, ensuring that when the Game UI becomes active, there is a clear and immediate focus for player input on this UI. Still within the else block, the line of code "playerMap.Disable();" disables the player action map, preventing player control inputs from affecting the game while the Game UI is active. This is crucial to avoid conflicts between UI interactions and game controls. This first "Debug.Log(...)" line of code outputs a log message to the console indicating the enabled/disabled state of all action maps. It's a debugging tool to help track the state of action maps during development or troubleshooting. The second "Debug.Log(...)" logs the name of the currently active action map. This helps verify which map is active and ensures the toggling logic is working as expected. This last line of code "universalMap.Enable();" ensures that the universal action map, which contains critical bindings such as the "Escape" key used to toggle the Game UI, is always enabled. This is necessary because it must be available at all times, regardless of the game or UI state, to handle essential controls like opening and closing the UI.

The "ActionMapManager" class effectively manages to switch between gameplay and Game UI modes in a game using Unity's new Input System. Leveraging action maps and the PlayerInput component allows for a clean and manageable way to handle different input contexts within the game. The use of the universal action map ensures that critical actions like toggling the UI are always available, enhancing the robustness of the input management system.

CHAPTER 2 UNITY'S NEW INPUT SYSTEM

Recipe 2-6: Implementing Rebindable Controls

Problem

Modern games need to cater to a diverse audience with varying preferences and accessibility requirements, necessitating a flexible control system. Implementing a re-bindable controls feature is challenging as it requires a robust system that not only allows players to customize their key bindings easily but also retains these settings between gaming sessions.

Solution

Unity's new Input System provides an efficient framework for integrating re-bindable controls that enhance user accessibility and personalization. Developers can set up a dynamic control scheme that allows players to modify key bindings through a user-friendly interface. This system involves creating a UI that connects with the Input System to display current bindings and gather new user inputs. To ensure persistence, the system saves these settings using Unity's data storage options, allowing players to maintain their customized controls across multiple sessions. By implementing these re-bindable controls, developers can significantly boost player satisfaction and accessibility, making their games more adaptable and inclusive.

How It Works

Let's begin by importing Unity's new Input System "Rebinding UI" sample using the Package Manager that can significantly enhance your project by allowing you to incorporate advanced input rebinding functionalities

CHAPTER 2 UNITY'S NEW INPUT SYSTEM

directly into your game. This sample provides a ready-to-use interface and scripts that can be customized to fit any game's control scheme. Here's a detailed step-by-step guide for this process:

- **Access the Package Manager:** Start by opening the Package Manager in Unity. You can do this by going to Window ▶ Package Manager.

- **Find the Input System Package:** In the Package Manager window, you'll need to find the "Input System" package. You can use the search bar to type "Input System" to find it quickly. Ensure you have selected the "Packages: Unity Registry" option from the dropdown to view all available Unity packages.

- **View Samples:** Once the Input System package is selected, select the "Samples" tab within the pane on the right, and scroll down until you locate the "Rebinding UI" sample (Figure 2-55).

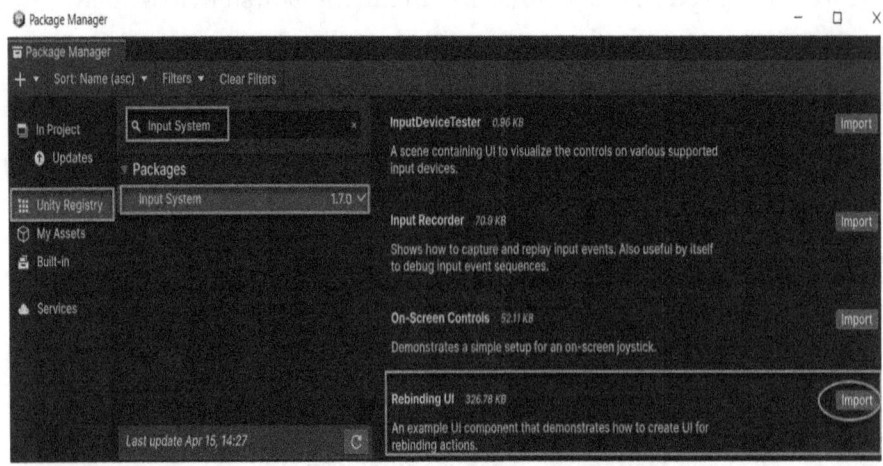

Figure 2-55. *Importing the Rebingind UI Sample*

CHAPTER 2   UNITY'S NEW INPUT SYSTEM

- **Import the Rebinding UI Sample:** Next to the "Rebinding UI" sample, there should be an "Import" button. Click this button to import the sample into your project.

- **Locate the Sample in the Project:** After importing, the "Rebinding UI" sample will appear in your project's Asset folder. Typically, this is placed under Assets/Samples/Input System/<version_number>/Rebinding UI. Open the sample folder to view the contents. It usually includes scenes, scripts, and other assets that demonstrate how to implement rebinding in your game.

- **Open the Sample Scene:** Double-click on the sample scene to open it. This scene contains a setup that demonstrates how input rebinding works.

- **Change Key Bindings:** Experiment with changing key bindings to understand the user experience.

In the Rebinding Controls scene viewed in Game mode, the layout is divided into two sections: one for Keyboard and Mouse actions and another for Gamepad actions, both of which are customizable. While this sample does not utilize Text Mesh Pro, you could modify it to incorporate Text Mesh Pro elements, enhancing the aesthetic appeal of the interface.

Let's change the binding for the Interact action which can be activated by pressing the "E" key on the keyboard. To change this binding to the key "I," follow the steps listed below:

- Click on the button denoted by the "E" key.

- You should see a small overlay prompt appear (Waiting for button input…), indicating that it is waiting for a new key press binding.

CHAPTER 2   UNITY'S NEW INPUT SYSTEM

- Press the "I" key on your keyboard. The Input System will detect this key press and assign it as the new binding for the "Interact" action. The UI will update to reflect that the "Interact" action is now bound to the "I" key instead of "E."

- Pressing the Reset button resets the "Interact" action to utilize the "E" key.

Let's now try changing the bindings for the "Move" action which is a composite, comprising four bindings. To change this binding to the keys "I," "J," "K," and "L," follow the steps listed below:

- Click on the button denoted by the "W/A/S/D" keys.

- You should see a small overlay prompt appear for each binding starting with the binding up, binding down, binding left, and binding right indicating that it is waiting for new key presses for each of these movements.

- For binding up – press the "I" key, binding down – press the "K" key, binding left – press the "J" key, and for binding right – press the "L" key.

- Pressing the Reset button resets the "Move" action to utilize the "W/A/S/D" keys.

You could similarly change gamepad bindings once you have a gamepad connected. If you stop playing the scene and then restart it again, you will note that the new bindings you created continue to persist.

Let's explore the Canvas in the hierarchy that makes up this "Rebind Controls" UI. As children of the canvas, you have several UI elements such as the Background, Title text, Help text, and a Rebind Overlay with a RebindPrompt text (Figure 2-56). You could replace all these text elements using their Text Mesh Pro counterparts to enhance their aesthetic appeal.

CHAPTER 2 UNITY'S NEW INPUT SYSTEM

Within the Keyboard game object, you will find two prefabs: "MoveRebind" and "InteractRebind." Select the "MoveRebind" prefab in the hierarchy and examine the Inspector, where you will see the "Rebind Action UI" component. This component is the core script of the prefab, essential for its functionality (Figure 2-57). Within its Binding section, its Action property provides a reference to an Input Action Asset. Double click this "Gameplay/Move (Input Action Reference" to open up the "Rebind UI sample Actions" Input Actions Asset window (Figure 2-58). Here you see the various actions used by the "Rebind Controls" UI sample. You could either replace the actions here with ones you have created or add on additional actions. The Binding property has been set to a composite value that includes all the Movement bindings. However, you could select individual key bindings too in the event you wanted to display each movement key separately and not as part of a composite binding. Within the UI section, you have references to several of the UI elements that have been used as part of the "Rebind Controls" UI. The Action Label property represents the UI Text element that displays the name label name beside the button, "Move" in this case. The Binding Text property represents the UI Text element that displays the text within the button, which should currently be "I/J/K/L," as you had previously changed the bindings for the "Move" action. The Rebind Overlay property is responsible for ensuring the Overlay is activated upon commencing the rebinding process.

Figure 2-56. *Rebind Controls UI-Canvas*

The Rebind Text property references the text you see when the rebinding process has commenced. Lastly, you will note that this "MoveRebind" prefab also contains a "ResetToDefault" button, which can be used to reset the binding to its default value. Also, note that the "Rebind Action UI" component comprises several events that you could utilize if required.

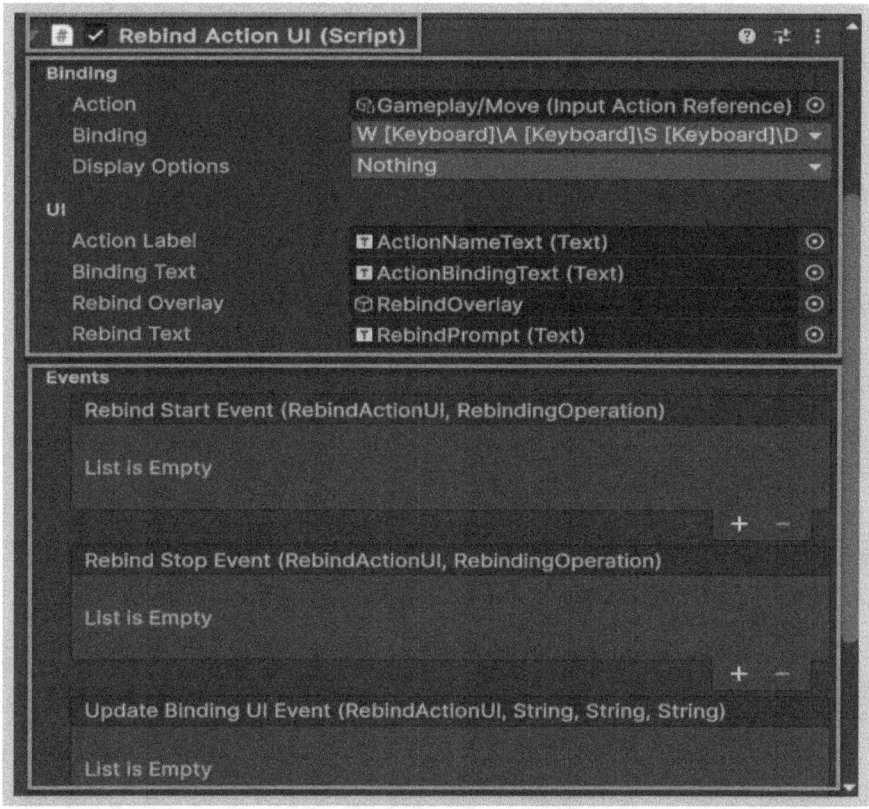

Figure 2-57. Keyboard Rebind Action UI Component for the prefab – MoveRebind

CHAPTER 2   UNITY'S NEW INPUT SYSTEM

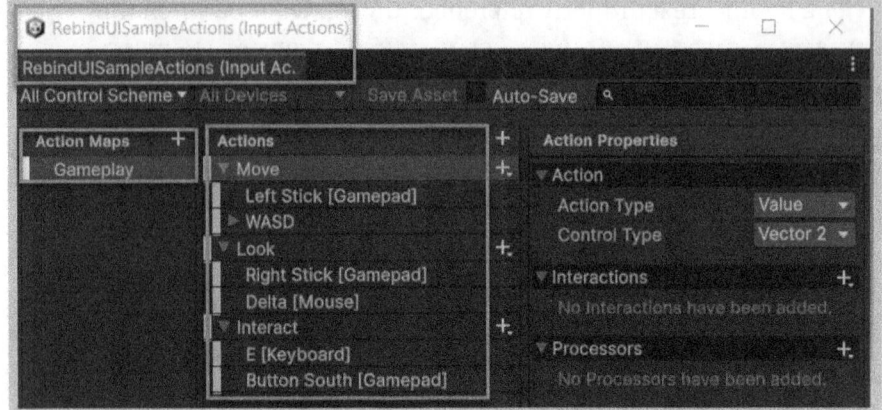

Figure 2-58. *Rebind UI Sample Actions – Input Actions Map*

The "InteractRebind" prefab within the Keyboard game object (Figure 2-56), which enables changing of the binding for the "Interact" action, currently set to the "E" key, uses the same "Rebind Action UI" component with different property values (Figure 2-59).

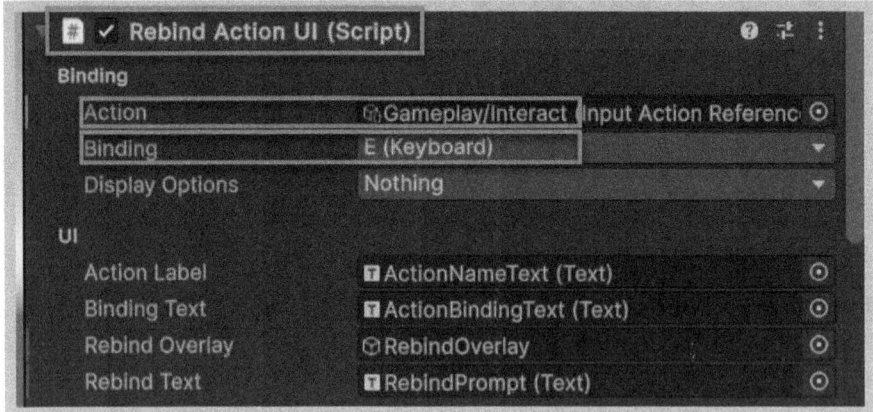

Figure 2-59. *Keyboard Rebind Action UI Component for the prefab – InteractRebind*

CHAPTER 2   UNITY'S NEW INPUT SYSTEM

As you will note from Figure 2-59 for its Action property, it uses "Gameplay/Interact" and for its Binding property it uses the "E" Key. Properties within its UI section reference UI Elements related to this Interact button, except for the Rebind Overlay and Rebind Text properties that utilize the same UI Elements used with the "MoveRebind" prefab.

Now let's look at the Gamepad game object and its prefabs (Figure 2-56). You will note that it has three rebind prefabs, namely, "MoveRebind," "LookRebind," and "InteractRebind" allowing you to change bindings for three different actions. Select the "MoveRebind" prefab in the hierarchy and within the Inspector you will note that it uses the same "Rebind Action UI" component (Figure 2-60).

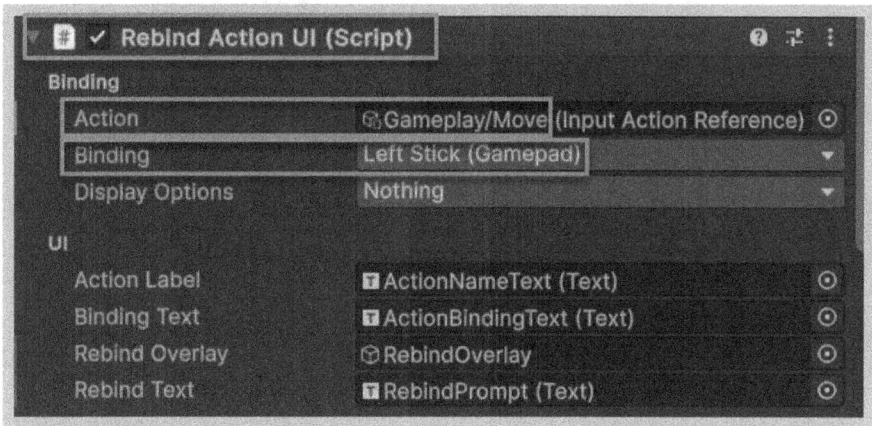

Figure 2-60. *Gamepad Rebind Action UI Component for the prefab – MoveRebind*

You will note that its Action property has been set to "Gameplay/Move," which is the same Input Action Asset used with the Keyboard "Rebind Action UI" components Action property. However, you will note that as we are dealing with gamepad bindings here its Bindig property has been set to Left Stick (Gamepad). Properties within its UI section,

183

CHAPTER 2   UNITY'S NEW INPUT SYSTEM

reference UI Elements related to this Move gamepad button. The Rebind Overlay and Rebind Text properties utilize the commonly available UI Elements used with the previously discussed prefabs.

In the hierarchy if you expand this "MoveRebind" prefab and then further expand its child game object "TriggerRebindButton," you will note that it comprises an additional child game object, namely, "ActionBindingIcon" (Figure 2-61). This is the image used to display gamepad bindings.

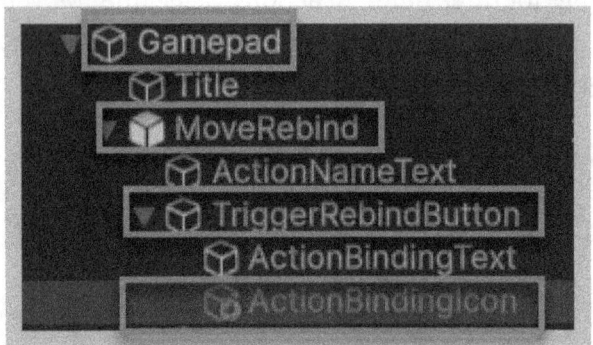

Figure 2-61. *Gamepad Action Binding Icon game object*

In the hierarchy, select the Gamepad game object and within the Inspector you will note that it contains a component "GamepadIconsExample" (Figure 2-62). This script helps enhance the user interface by customizing how gamepad bindings are displayed, by replacing generic text labels with specific, easy-to-understand icons. By default, it comprises icons for the Xbox and Ps4 controllers. Click on any icon to have all available icons displayed in the Project tab.

Next in the hierarchy, select the Canvas game object. You will note that it has been fitted with a "Rebind Save Load" component (Figure 2-63) and has an Actions property that references the "RebindUISamplesActions" Input Action Asset. This script provides a straightforward mechanism

CHAPTER 2 UNITY'S NEW INPUT SYSTEM

that manages the saving and loading of persisting player-customized input bindings across game sessions, enhancing the user experience by maintaining their preferred control setup.

For the Canvas game object modify its properties as follows:

- Set the UI Scale Mode property to Scale With Screen Size.

- Set Reference Resolution for X to 1920 and for Y to 1080

- Set the Match property value to 0.5

- Select the Keyboard game object in the hierarchy and within the Inspector set its anchor point to be Middle Left. Set Pos X to 400, Pos Y to 0, and set its Scale property for X and Y to 1.5.

- Select the Gamepad game object in the hierarchy and within the Inspector set its anchor point to be Middle Right. Set Pos X to -400, Pos Y to 0, and set its Scale property for X and Y to 1.5.

This should make the "Rebind Controls" UI look better than the original. Feel free to play around with the settings to obtain the like and feel you desire.

CHAPTER 2   UNITY'S NEW INPUT SYSTEM

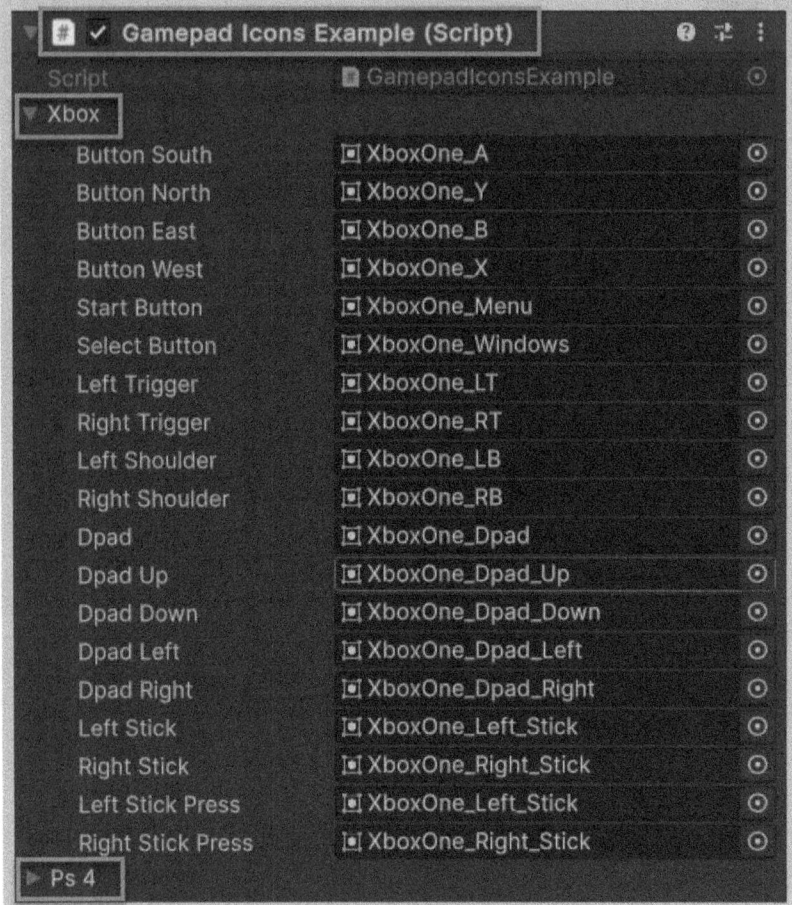

Figure 2-62. *Gamepad Icons Example Component*

Rename the Canvas to "Rebind_Controls_Canvas." Now copy this "Rebind_Controls_Canvas" game object, open up the Playground scene for the Third Person Controller, and paste the "Rebind_Controls_Canvas" game object into the Playground scene.

CHAPTER 2   UNITY'S NEW INPUT SYSTEM

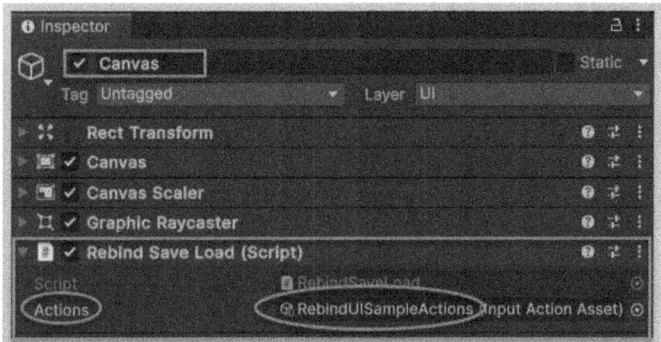

Figure 2-63. *Canvas game object with the Rebind Save Load Component*

Select the UI_EventSystem game object in the hierarchy and observe in the inspector that it references the "Starter Assets" Input Action Asset. Double-click this asset to open it in the Unity Editor. Within the "Universal" action map, create a new action named "ToggleRebindControls." This action utilizes the Tab key on the keyboard to open the Rebind Controls UI, overlaying it above the current game display.

Let's first set up the new action named "ToggleRebindControls."

1. Create a new action called "ToggleRebindControls."

2. Set the Input Binding for this new "ToggleRebindControls" action to the "Tab" key of your Keyboard and ensure that you set its control scheme to KeyboardMouse (Figure 2-64).

3. Ensure that you save the "StarterAssets" and close it.

187

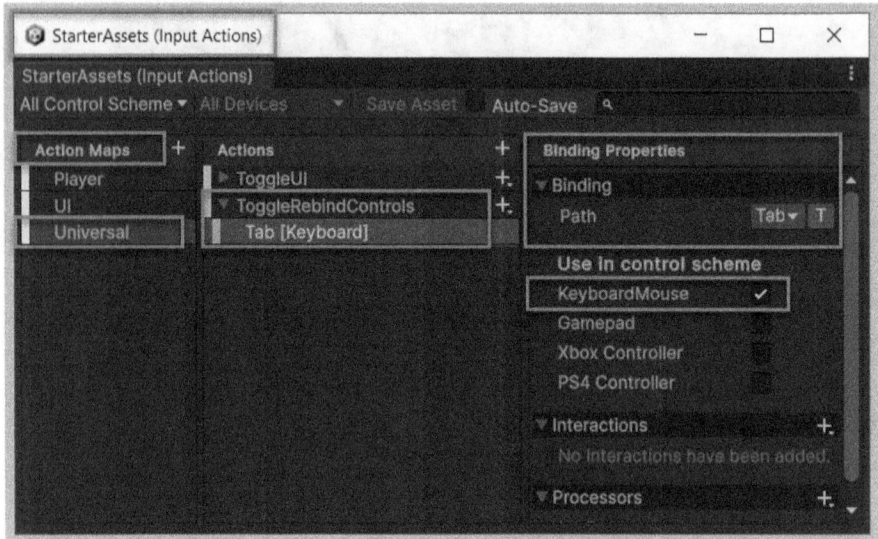

Figure 2-64. *Setting up the Toggle Rebind Controls action*

Let's now work on restructuring the " "Rebind_Controls_Canvas" game object:

1. To restructure the Rebind_Controls_Canvas game object, follow these steps: Begin by selecting and expanding it in the hierarchy. Focus on the Keyboard game object and expand it to access the MoveRebind prefab (refer to Figure 2-65). In the Inspector, under the Binding section, use the target icon next to the Action property to open the Select Input Action Reference window. Type "Move" in the find box and select the "Player/Move" reference from the "Starter Assets" Input Action Asset. Choose the appropriate composite binding from the dropdown menu as shown in Figure 2-65. Optionally, you may create separate buttons for each movement direction with individual bindings.

CHAPTER 2   UNITY'S NEW INPUT SYSTEM

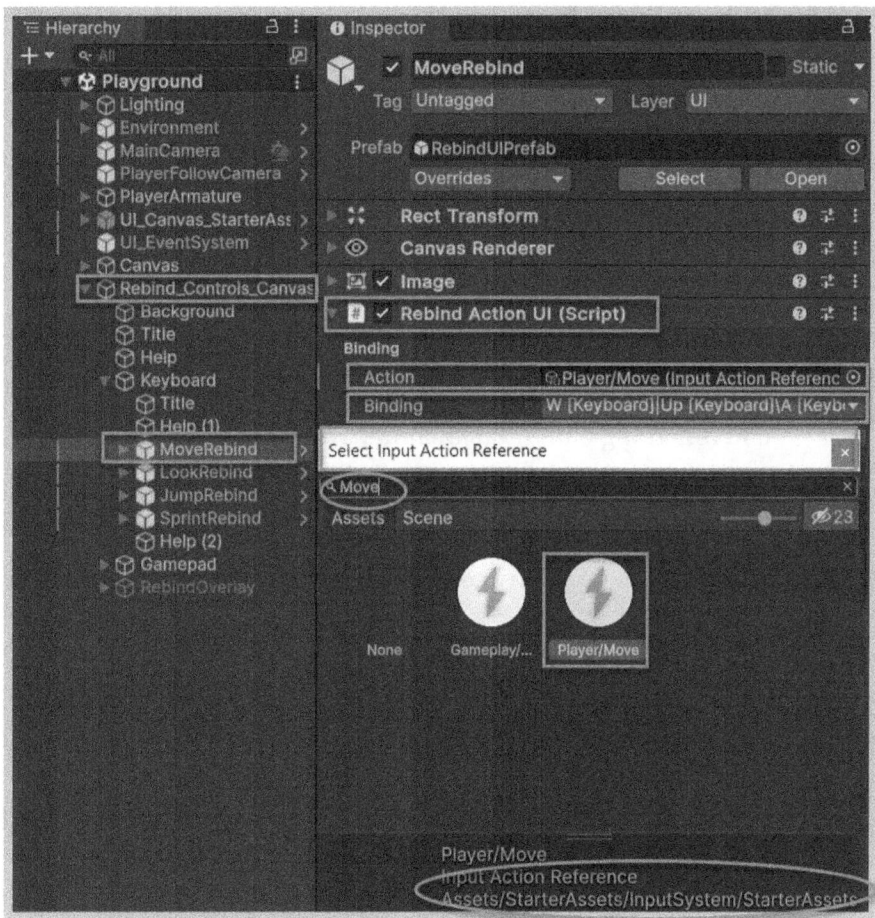

Figure 2-65. *Rebinding Control Buttons*

2. To set up rebinding controls for looking around with the KeyboardMouse scheme, duplicate the "MoveRebind" prefab and rename it "LookRebind." Repeat the setup process from step 1, by selecting "Player/Look" under the Action property. For the Binding property, choose Delta (KeyboardMouse).

189

3. Next, select the "InteractRebind" prefab, rename it "JumpRebind," and assign it to "Player/Jump" from the Action selection. Set its binding to Space (KeyboardMouse).

4. Duplicate the "JumpRebind" prefab, this time renaming it "SprintRebind," and set it to "Player/Sprint" from the Action selection, with the binding as Shift (KeyboardMouse).

5. Continue by duplicating the "SprintRebind" prefab, and renaming it to "AttackRebind." Assign it to "Player/Attack" from the Action selection, with the binding set to 'K' (KeyboardMouse).

Let's now set up the necessary control rebinding actions for the gamepad.

1. Focus on the Gamepad game object and expand it to access its "MoveRebind" prefab In the Inspector, under the Binding section, use the target icon next to the Action property to open the Select Input Action Reference window. Type "Move" in the find box and select the "Player/Move" reference from the "Starter Assets" Input Action Asset. Choose LeftStick (Gamepad) from the dropdown menu.

2. Select the "LookRebind" prefab in the hierarchy. Repeat the setup process from step 1, by selecting "Player/Look" under the Action property, and for the Binding property, choose Right Stick (Gamepad).

3. Select the "InteractRebind" prefab in the hierarchy, and rename it to "JumpRebind." Assign it to "Player/Jump" from the Action selection, and set its binding to Button South (Gamepad).

4. Duplicate the "JumpRebind" prefab and rename it to "SprintRebind." Assign it to "Player/Sprint" from the Action selection and set its binding to Left Trigger (Gamepad).

5. Duplicate the "SprintRebind" prefab and rename it to "AttackRebind." Assign it to "Player/Attack" from the Action selection and set its binding to Button East (Gamepad).

The Rebind Controls UI will function like a Modal window, requiring users to finish interacting with it before they can return to the windows beneath it. Modal windows are commonly used for confirming critical tasks or displaying important information that needs immediate action or acknowledgment and rebinding controls being an important task would fall in this category. This would mean that you need to set up some sort of a close button on the Rebind Controls UI canvas:

1. Expand and select the "Rebind_Controls_Canvas" game object in the hierarchy. Right-click and from the context menu that pops up select UI ➤ Button - TextMeshPro and rename it to "Close."

2. You can anchor the button at the top right corner and set both its width and height to 40 or a value that suits your liking.

3. In the hierarchy expand the "Close" button and you will see its child "Text (TMP)" game object. With this child game object selected, in the Inspector expand its "TextMeshPro - Text (UI)" component and within its Text box type in the value "X." Check the AutoSize checkbox. This "X" now appears within your "Close" button on the "Rebind_Controls_Canvas."

4. When the game is playing and your Rebind Controls UI Modal window is displayed and once you are done binding new controls you would need to click on this "Close" button the Rebind Controls UI Modal window needs to close. To achieve this, you need to set up the OnClick() event for the "Close" button.

5. In the hierarchy select the "Close" button, and within the Inspector scroll down until you see its OnClick() event. Click the "+" icon at the bottom of this event to add a new event listener box.

6. When the "Close" button is clicked, this OnClick() event gets notified and it runs code to handle this event, which needs to deactivate this "Rebind_Controls_Canvas" game object amongst other actions, which are executed upon calling a method within the "ActionMapManager" script, namely, OnrebindControlsCanvasClose(). This method has not yet been written and will be written shortly.

7. You know that the "ActionMapManager" script resides on the "PlayerArmature" game object, so you can partially set up this OnClick() event by dragging the "PlayerArmature" game object into the slot available beneath the "Runtime Only" drop-down as depicted in Figure 2-66. However, the method "OnrebindControlsCanvasClose()" that needs to be selected from within the adjacent drop-down that states "No Function," has not yet been written within the "ActionMapManager" script, so you will set up this final part once the "ActionMapManager" script has this method created.

CHAPTER 2   UNITY'S NEW INPUT SYSTEM

This comprehensive setup enables all controls within the KeyboardMouse and Gamepad schemes to be reconfigured as needed, enhancing the game's customization options. Figure 2-67 illustrates the appearance of the Rebind Controls UI during gameplay. You may refine the alignment and design of the UI elements to improve visual appeal and functionality (by not using composites for Move). Note that the "GamepadIconsExample" component that can be found on the Gamepad game object has assigned icons to the gamepad-related buttons, which can be changed too.

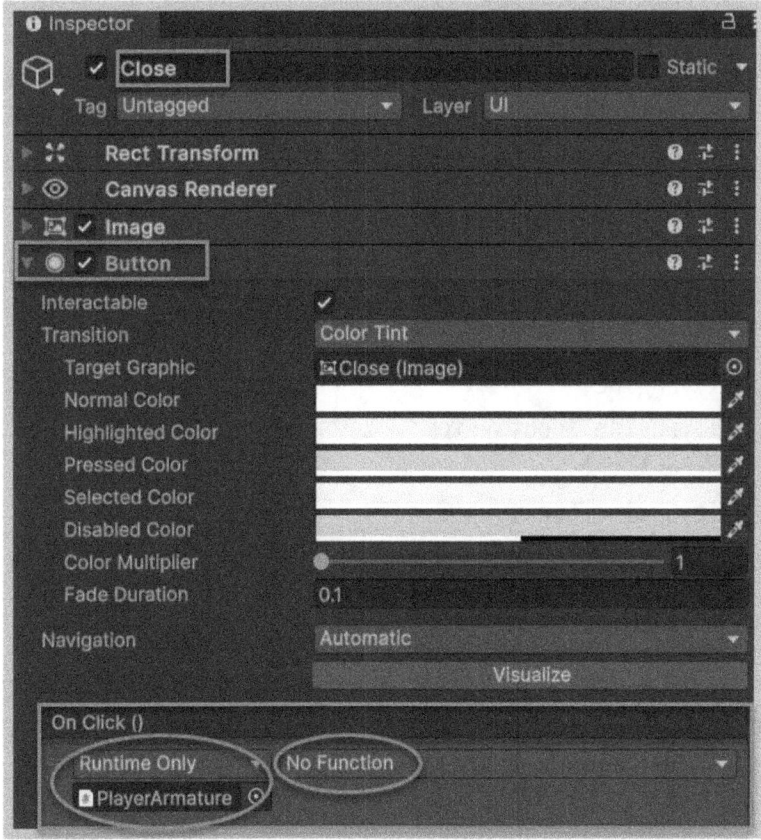

Figure 2-66. *OnClick() event of the Close button*

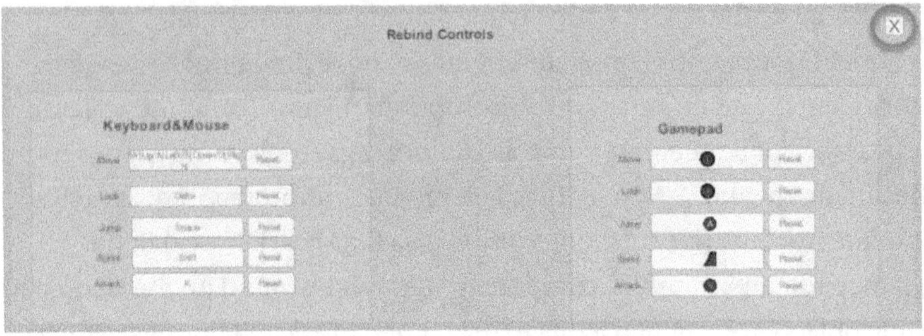

CHAPTER 2   UNITY'S NEW INPUT SYSTEM

Figure 2-67. *Rebind Controls UI during gameplay*

Now that you have a Game UI canvas as well as a Rebind Controls canvas, you need to make some modifications to the "ActionMapManager" script so that it can activate and deactivate the Rebind Controls Canvas when using the Tab key. The script is similar to Listing 2-1, with some additional code that has been tagged with a comment //ACC as depicted in Listing 2-2.

Listing 2-2. Modified ActionMapManager script

```
using UnityEngine;
using UnityEngine.InputSystem;
using StarterAssets;
using UnityEngine.EventSystems;
public class ActionMapManager : MonoBehaviour
{
    public InputActionAsset actionAsset;//Assign in Inspector
    public GameObject gameUICanvas;     //Assign in Inspector
    public GameObject rebindControlsCanvas; //ACC - Assign in
                                            //Inspector
    public GameObject gameUIDefaultButton; //Assign in
                                           //Inspector
    private PlayerInput playerInput;
```

```csharp
 private StarterAssetsInputs starterAssetsInput; //ACC
private InputActionMap playerMap;
private InputActionMap uiMap;
private InputActionMap universalMap;
private bool isActiveGameUICanvas = true;
private InputAction toggleUIAction;
private InputAction toggleRebindControlsAction; //ACC

private void Awake()
{
    playerInput = GetComponent<PlayerInput>();
    starterAssetsInput =
    GetComponent<StarterAssetsInputs>(); //ACC
    //cursorLocked should be false to receive standard
    //input when using Rebind Controls UI.
    starterAssetsInput.cursorLocked = false; //ACC

    // Get all three action maps
    playerMap = actionAsset.actionMaps[0];
    uiMap = actionAsset.actionMaps[1];
    universalMap = actionAsset.actionMaps[2];

    //Get the ToggleUI and ToggleRbindControls action
    toggleUIAction = playerInput.actions["ToggleUI"];
    toggleRebindControlsAction =
    universalMap.actions[1];//ACC
}
private void OnEnable()
{
   toggleUIAction.performed += ToggleUIPerformed;
    toggleRebindControlsAction.performed +=
   ToggleRebindControlsPerformed;   //ACC
}
```

```csharp
    private void OnDisable()
    {
        toggleUIAction.performed -= ToggleUIPerformed;
        toggleRebindControlsAction.performed -=
        ToggleRebindControlsPerformed; //ACC
    }
private void ToggleRebindControlsPerformed(InputAction.
CallbackContext context) // ACC
{
 //Universal Map Needs to be enabled as it holds the Touch Key
 //binding
    universalMap.Enable();

    //Disable playerInput so that Rebind Controls UI can
    //receive standard input.
    playerInput.enabled = false;
    rebindControlsCanvas.SetActive(true);
}
    private void ToggleUIPerformed(InputAction.CallbackContext
    context)
    {
      isActiveGameUICanvas = !isActiveGameUICanvas;
      gameUICanvas.SetActive(isActiveGameUICanvas);

      if (!isActiveGameUICanvas)
          playerMap.Enable();
      else
      {        EventSystem.current.SetSelectedGameObject(gameUID
            efaultButton);
      playerMap.Disable();
      }
```

CHAPTER 2 UNITY'S NEW INPUT SYSTEM

```
    Debug.Log($"PlayerMap Enabled: {playerMap.enabled} ;
    UIMap Enabled: {uiMap.enabled} ; " +
    $"UniversalMap Enabled: {universalMap.enabled}");

    Debug.Log($"Current Action Map is:
    {playerInput.currentActionMap.name}");

    //Universal Map Needs to be enabled at all times as it
    //holds the Esc Key binding
    universalMap.Enable();
    }
    public void OnrebindControlsCanvasClose()//ACC
    {
        rebindControlsCanvas.SetActive(false);
        playerInput.enabled = true;
        if (isActiveGameUICanvas)
        {
          universalMap.Enable();
          playerMap.Disable();
          EventSystem.current.SetSelectedGameObject(
        gameUIDefaultButton);
        }
    }
}
```

Here's a detailed explanation of the modified parts of the ActionMapManager class provided as part of Listing 2-2 that have been tagged with the comment //ACC.

CHAPTER 2   UNITY'S NEW INPUT SYSTEM

Variables:

1. **public GameObject rebindControlsCanvas:** This variable refers to a Canvas element assigned via the Unity Inspector, which is used to display or hide the "Controls Rebind" interface. This is a UI where players can customize their keyboard, gamepad, or other input device bindings.

2. **private StarterAssetsInputs starterAssetsInput:** This variable holds a reference to the StarterAssetsInputs component attached to the same GameObject (PlayerArmature) as this script. StarterAssetsInputs typically handles input states like cursor locking, which are common in Unity's standard asset packages.

3. **private InputAction toggleRebindControlsAction:** This InputAction is part of Unity's Input System – Input Actions Asset (Starter Assets). It is used to toggle the visibility and functionality of the rebindControlsCanvas. It listens for a Tab key press to trigger this functionality.

Methods:

1. **Awake():** Within the Awake() method the line of code "starterAssetsInput = GetComponent<StarterAssetsInputs>();" is responsible for obtaining a reference to the StarterAssetsInputs component attached to the same game object as the ActionMapManager script. Having access to StarterAssetsInputs allows the script to Manipulate cursor behavior, such as locking or unlocking the cursor during gameplay or while interacting with

CHAPTER 2   UNITY'S NEW INPUT SYSTEM

the UI. For example, when opening the Rebind Controls UI, you need to unlock the cursor so that the player can interact with its UI elements, and starterAssetsInput provides the ability to achieve this via code. This is achieved by setting the cursorLocked property of StarterAssetsInputs to false. This ensures that the cursor is not locked and is visible. This is particularly important when the player is interacting with the game's UI, such as menus or control rebinding UI, where the player needs to see the cursor to make selections.
The line toggleRebindControlsAction = universalMap.actions[1]; in the Awake() method of the ActionMapManager class assigns the second action (Tab key) from the universalMap collection to toggleRebindControlsAction. This setup is crucial for handling the user input that triggers the displaying of the Rebind Controls UI. By linking this specific action, the script enables dynamic UI interaction, allowing players to access and customize their control settings seamlessly during gameplay.

2. **OnEnable() and OnDisable():** These methods manage event subscriptions. When the game object is enabled, OnEnable() subscribes the ToggleRebindControlsPerformed method (event handler) to the performed event of the toggleRebindControlsAction. Conversely, OnDisable() unsubscribes from the event to clean up references and prevent potential memory leaks or unwanted behavior when the game object is disabled.

3. **private void ToggleRebindControlsPerformed(InputAction.CallbackContext context):** This method is triggered by the toggleRebindControlsAction. When executed, it toggles the rebindControlsCanvas visibility, enabling it while simultaneously disabling the "playerInput" to prevent gameplay input from interfering with the UI input. This ensures that when players are rebinding their controls, they won't accidentally trigger in-game actions.

4. **public void OnrebindControlsCanvasClose():** This method is called when the close button on the Rebind Controls UI is clicked when the player has finished rebinding controls and wishes to close the Rebind Controls UI. This is the method that needs to be invoked from the OnClick() event of the Close button you created. It resets the visibility of the rebindControlsCanvas, re-enables the playerInput to resume gameplay input handling, and if the game UI canvas is active, it ensures the Universal input map is enabled and the Player input map is disabled. It also sets up a default selected button on the gameUICanvas using the EventSystem.

By toggling the playerInput component and input action maps (playerMap, uiMap, and universalMap), the script dynamically shifts input handling between gameplay and UI contexts. This ensures that input actions do not conflict across different modes (gameplay vs. UI settings).

When toggling UI elements, especially those involved with input rebinding or game settings, managing the focus of UI elements via EventSystem.current.SetSelectedGameObject(gameUIDefaultButton) is crucial for usability. It provides a smoother user experience by automatically selecting default buttons when switching contexts.

CHAPTER 2   UNITY'S NEW INPUT SYSTEM

Before testing the Playground scene, you need to hook up the OnrebindControlsCanvasClose() method to the OnClick() event of the "Close" button. In the hierarchy within the "Rebind_Controls_Canvas" game object, select the "Close" button and locate the OnClick() event within the Inspector. Click the drop-down that states "No Function" and from the context menu that pops up select "ActionMapManager" and then further select the OnrebindControlsCanvasClose() method. Ensure you save the scene.

Execute the Playground scene for the Third Person Controller to evaluate the functionality of the "Tab" and "Escape" keys. Pressing the "Tab" key opens the Rebind Controls UI, which must be manually closed using its designated "Close" button. The "Escape" key switches between gameplay mode and the in-game UI. You have the option to modify the code to tailor these UI interactions according to your requirements. Additionally, you may observe that the Rebind controls are nonfunctional, suggesting that further coding is necessary to enable the full functionality of these controls.

To enable complete functionality for rebinding controls, you will need to make some minor modifications to the "RebindActionUI" script available as part of the various rebind game objects you created for the Keyboard and Gamepad within the "Rebind_Controls_Canvas" game object. In the hierarchy, select and expand the "Rebind_Controls_Canvas" game object and further expand its child game objects Keyboard and Gamepad. You will note that they comprise several rebind game objects (MoveRebind, LookRebind, JumpRebind, SprintRebind, and AttackRebind). Select any one of the rebind game objects in the hierarchy and within the inspector, you will note that they all have the same "RebindActionUI" component (Figure 2-68). It is to this Unity-provided script that you will make a few modifications.

Before making these scripting changes let's explore one of the rebind game objects. Select and rebind the game object in the hierarchy and expand it. You will note that it comprises a "TriggerRebindButton" game object. Select this game object and within the Inspector locate its

201

OnClick() event. Note that this event is tied to the selected rebind objects "RebindActionUI" script and invokes the public StartInteractiveRebind() method within the "RebindActionUI" script (Figure 2-69). It is important to note that it is this method that sets in motion the rebinding process for the selected Action whose control needs rebinding. Similarly the "ResetToDefaultButton" game object's OnClick() event invokes the public ResetToDefault() method (Figure 2-70) within the "RebindActionUI" script.

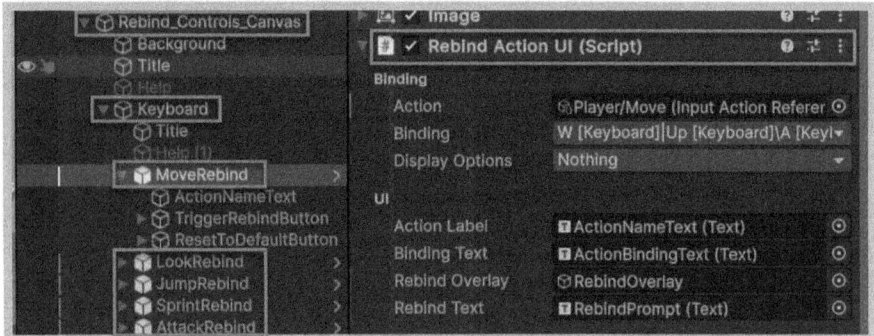

Figure 2-68. Rebind Action UI component

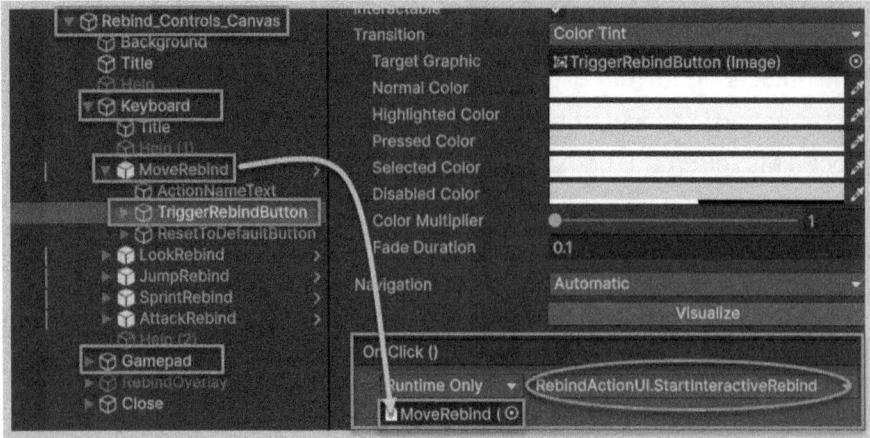

Figure 2-69. StartInteractiveRebind() method within the RebindActionUI script

CHAPTER 2   UNITY'S NEW INPUT SYSTEM

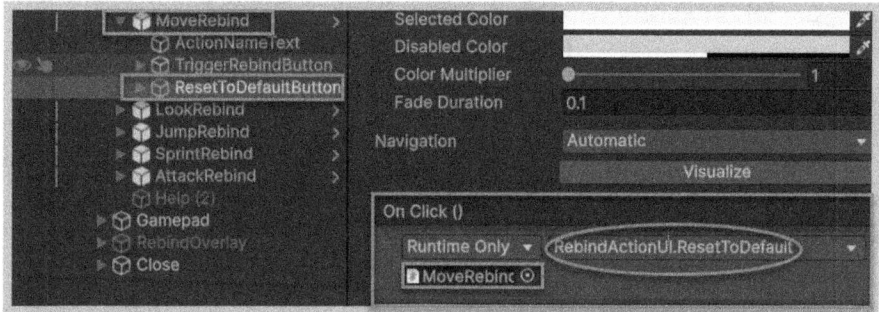

Figure 2-70. *ResetToDefault() method within the RebindActionUI script*

To modify the "RebindActionUI" script, start by selecting a rebind game object in the hierarchy, such as "MoveRebind." In the Inspector, find the Rebind Action UI component, click the vertical ellipses beside it, and choose "Edit Script" from the resulting menu to open the script in your code editor.

The RebindActionUI class is a comprehensive component designed for Unity's new Input System. It facilitates the UI-driven reconfiguration of input bindings, allowing players to customize their control setups within a game. It is a robust solution that encapsulates the complexity of handling different types of bindings and provides a user-friendly interface to facilitate easy customization of controls by end-users. Some of its core features include the following:

1. **Dynamic Binding Reconfiguration:** The class allows players to interactively rebind specific actions to different controls. This is particularly useful for games that want to offer customizable controls to accommodate different player preferences or hardware setups.

2. **UI Integration:** It includes several properties to manage and display UI elements such as labels for action names, current bindings, and prompts during the rebinding process. This integration helps in making the rebinding process intuitive and user-friendly.

3. **Event-Driven Updates:** The class uses a variety of events to manage the state of the UI and the underlying input system. For example, it triggers events when rebinding starts and stops, which can be used to update the UI accordingly or to execute additional custom logic.

4. **Composite Binding Support:** It includes handling for composite bindings (where a single action might be triggered by multiple simultaneous key presses), allowing each part of a composite binding to be rebound individually.

5. **Visual Feedback and Interaction:** Through properties like rebindOverlay and rebindPrompt, it provides visual feedback and prompts to the player during the rebinding process, enhancing the interactivity and clarity of the rebind operation. It uses the Unity Event system extensively to trigger UI updates and custom behaviors.

6. **Fallback and Error Handling:** The class includes error checking and fallback mechanisms, such as logging errors when a binding cannot be found.

7. **Properties and Events:** Properties like actionReference, bindingId, and various text components are used to specify the action to rebind and to display relevant information. Events such

as updateBindingUIEvent, startRebindEvent, and stopRebindEvent allow for customization and extension of the basic rebinding functionality.

8. **Interactive Rebind Process:** The StartInteractiveRebind method (Figure 2-69) initiates the rebind process, handling both simple and composite bindings. This method, along with helper methods like PerformInteractiveRebind, manages the lifecycle of the rebinding operation, ensuring the input system is temporarily disabled during the process to prevent unintended actions.

The two core methods within the RebindActionUI class that you need to focus on are the StartInteractiveRebind() (Figure 2-71), and the PerformInteractiveRebind() (Figure 2-72) methods. Let's briefly discuss these two methods and the modifications you need to make to the PerformInteractiveRebind() method, to have the "Rebind_Controls_Canvas" functional.

```
public void StartInteractiveRebind()
{
    //Debug.Log("Inside Method 'StartInteractiveRebind()'");

    if (!ResolveActionAndBinding(out var action, out var bindingIndex))
        return;

    // If the binding is a composite, we need to rebind each part in turn.
    if (action.bindings[bindingIndex].isComposite)
    {
        var firstPartIndex = bindingIndex + 1;
        if (firstPartIndex < action.bindings.Count && action.bindings[firstPartIndex].isPartOfComposite)
            PerformInteractiveRebind(action, firstPartIndex, allCompositeParts: true);
    }
    else
    {
        PerformInteractiveRebind(action, bindingIndex);
    }

    Debug.Log("Inside Method 'StartInteractiveRebind()'");
}
```

Figure 2-71. StartInteractiveRebind() Method

The StartInteractiveRebind() method is designed to initiate an interactive rebinding session where the player can actuate the desired control or key to set as the new binding for an action, thereby enabling user-driven customization of input bindings in games. It provides the necessary infrastructure to ensure that players can easily and effectively set their preferred controls for various game actions, by accommodating individual preferences and hardware setups. It manages the setup and execution of this rebinding session through several key steps:

1. ResolveActionAndBinding(): This method's primary purpose is to resolve and validate the specific InputAction and its corresponding binding index based on the binding ID provided. This resolution is critical because it determines exactly which binding of which action is going to be modified during the rebinding process.

2. Handling Composite Bindings: If the target binding is a composite, the method iterates through each component of the composite binding. It starts with the first component immediately after the composite's main binding and continues through other components if present.

3. Interactive Rebinding Setup: This is done by invoking action.PerformInteractiveRebinding(), within PerformInteractiveRebind () which prepares the system to listen for the next user input that will define the new binding. The setup includes callbacks for handling cancellation and completion of the rebinding.

CHAPTER 2   UNITY'S NEW INPUT SYSTEM

The PerformInteractiveRebind() method depicted in Figure 2-72 is central to the interactive rebinding process, handling the execution of rebinding an individual binding or a part of a composite binding for an action. Here's a closer look at what the PerformInteractiveRebind() method accomplishes:

1. Cancel Existing Rebind Operation: Before starting a new rebinding session, it cancels any ongoing rebinding operation (m_RebindOperation?.Cancel();). This ensures that there are no conflicting or overlapping rebinding sessions that could cause errors or unexpected behavior.

2. Clean-Up Function: The method defines a local function, CleanUp(), used to dispose of the rebind operation once it is complete or canceled. This function is crucial for ensuring that resources are properly released and that the operation is cleaned up correctly, preventing memory leaks or stale references.

3. Disable the Action: The action is temporarily disabled (action.Disable();). This is important to prevent the action from triggering during the rebinding process, which could interfere with the rebinding or lead to confusing behavior for the user. This line of code is one of the modifications you need to introduce into the script.

CHAPTER 2 UNITY'S NEW INPUT SYSTEM

4. Setup and Start the Rebinding Operation: The rebinding operation is set up through action. PerformInteractiveRebinding(bindingIndex) which prepares the system to detect and register a new control or key press from the user as the new binding for the specified action. The method configures the operation with handlers for cancellation (OnCancel) and completion (OnComplete), ensuring that appropriate actions are taken when the rebinding session ends, regardless of whether it ends successfully or is aborted by the user. With the OnCancel handler, you need to introduce the line of code "action.Enable()," which is responsible for restoring the action to its normal operational state, allowing it to respond to inputs again as defined before the initiation of the rebinding process.

5. Rebind Completion and Continuation Handling: Upon successful completion of a rebind (OnComplete), it checks if there are more parts of a composite binding that need to be rebound. If so, it recursively calls PerformInteractiveRebind for the next part, allowing for sequential rebinding of composite bindings. After handling a part or a full binding, it re-enables the action (action.Enable()), ensuring that the action can be used immediately with the new binding. This line of code is one of the modifications you need to introduce into the script.

CHAPTER 2 UNITY'S NEW INPUT SYSTEM

```
private void PerformInteractiveRebind(InputAction action, int bindingIndex, bool allCompositeParts = false)
{
    m_RebindOperation?.Cancel(); // Will null out m_RebindOperation.

    void CleanUp()
    {
        m_RebindOperation?.Dispose();
        m_RebindOperation = null;
    }

    action.Disable(); // ACC

    // Configure the rebind.
    m_RebindOperation = action.PerformInteractiveRebinding(bindingIndex)
        .OnCancel(
            operation =>
            {
                action.Enable(); // ACC

                m_RebindStopEvent?.Invoke(this, operation);
                m_RebindOverlay?.SetActive(false);
                UpdateBindingDisplay();
                CleanUp();
            })
        .OnComplete(
            operation =>
            {
                m_RebindOverlay?.SetActive(false);
                m_RebindStopEvent?.Invoke(this, operation);
                UpdateBindingDisplay();
                CleanUp();

                // If there's more composite parts we should bind, initiate a rebind
                // for the next part.
                if (allCompositeParts)
                {
                    var nextBindingIndex = bindingIndex + 1;
                    if (nextBindingIndex < action.bindings.Count && action.bindings[nextBindingIndex].isPartOfComposite)
                        PerformInteractiveRebind(action, nextBindingIndex, true);
                }

                action.Enable() ; // ACC
            });
    // If it's a part binding, show the name of the part in the UI.
    var partName = default(string);
    if (action.bindings[bindingIndex].isPartOfComposite)
        partName = $"Binding '{action.bindings[bindingIndex].name}'. ";

    // Bring up rebind overlay, if we have one.
    m_RebindOverlay?.SetActive(true);
    if (m_RebindText != null)
    {
        var text = !string.IsNullOrEmpty(m_RebindOperation.expectedControlType)
            ? $"{partName}Waiting for {m_RebindOperation.expectedControlType} input..."
            : $"{partName}Waiting for input...";
        m_RebindText.text = text;
    }

    // If we have no rebind overlay and no callback but we have a binding text label,
    // temporarily set the binding text label to "<Waiting>".
    if (m_RebindOverlay == null && m_RebindText == null && m_RebindStartEvent == null && m_BindingText != null)
        m_BindingText.text = "<Waiting...>";

    // Give listeners a chance to act on the rebind starting.
    m_RebindStartEvent?.Invoke(this, m_RebindOperation);

    m_RebindOperation.Start();
}
```

Figure 2-72. *PerformInteractiveRebind() Method*

209

CHAPTER 2   UNITY'S NEW INPUT SYSTEM

6. UI Feedback: During the rebind process, if a rebindOverlay is available, it activates this UI element to inform the user that the system is waiting for input. If a rebindPrompt is set, it updates this text to guide the user, typically indicating what type of input is expected.

7. Event Invocation: The method triggers the startRebindEvent with the ongoing rebind operation as a parameter, allowing any external listeners or systems to react to the start of a rebind. Similarly, stopRebindEvent is invoked when the rebind is completed or canceled, which can be used to perform additional cleanup or UI updates externally.

PerformInteractiveRebind() is a comprehensive method that handles the intricacies of initiating, managing, and completing the rebinding of player controls interactively. It ensures that the user can seamlessly assign new keys or buttons to actions, with robust support for handling errors, user cancellation, and sequential rebinding of composite inputs.

Note Additional code has been tagged with a comment // ACC and needs to be introduced into the PerformInteractiveRebind() method as depicted in Figure 2-72.

Run the Playground scene for the Third Person Controller and experiment with rebinding keyboard keys and gamepad inputs. While the game is active, these rebinding changes will persist. However, note that once you exit play mode, all bindings are reset to their original settings. The subsequent recipe will address how to permanently save these rebindings.

Recipe 2-7: Persisting Rebound Controls

Problem

In the current situation, it's possible to temporarily rebind keyboard keys and gamepad inputs to test different control schemes. However, these adjustments only persist during the active game session in play mode, and default settings are restored upon exiting, posing a challenge for evaluating long-term control configurations.

Solution

Implement a permanent saving mechanism where rebound changes continue to persist even when you exit play mode.

How It Works

With the Playground scene for the Third Person Controller open, select the "Rebind_Control_Canvas" in the hierarchy. In the Inspector locate its Rebind Save Load component. Note that for its Actions property, it is currently referencing the Input Action Asset (RebindUISampleActions) (Figure 2-73). Replace it with the Starter Assets Input Action Asset (Figure 2-74).

Figure 2-73. RebindUISampleActions – Input Action Asset

CHAPTER 2 UNITY'S NEW INPUT SYSTEM

Figure 2-74. *StarterAssets – Input Action Asset*

Run the Playground scene for the Third Person Controller and test to ensure that the default bindings are working. Now press the Tab key to launch the Rebind Controls UI. Reset the binding for the Jump action to the "Z" key and close the Rebind Controls UI canvas. While still in gameplay mode test to ensure that pressing the "Z" key causes the player character to jump.

Now exit play mode and then re-enter play mode again. Now again press the "Z" key to check if the player can jump as this was the new binding created for the jump action. You will note that it doesn't work and instead pressing the "Space Bar" key which was the old binding causes the player character to jump.

Now press the Tab key to open the Rebind Controls UI. You will note that for the Jump action, the binding depicted on the button is the "Z" key. Now simply close the Rebind Controls UI to return to gameplay mode and press the "Z" key. You will notice that it now works and the player character can jump. Opening the Canvas reactivated the new "Z" key binding that was set. You will need to write a couple of lines of code within the RebindActionUI script to fix this. The solution is to load the binding that has been saved before the Rebind Controls UI canvas is opened. Let's look at the RebindSaveLoad script that is responsible for saving and loading the bindings, as you will be using the code provided within this script in the RebindActionUI script. Figure 2-75 depicts the code within the RebindSaveLoad script.

CHAPTER 2   UNITY'S NEW INPUT SYSTEM

```
using UnityEngine;
using UnityEngine.InputSystem;

public class RebindSaveLoad : MonoBehaviour
{
    public InputActionAsset actions;

    public void OnEnable()
    {
        var rebinds = PlayerPrefs.GetString("rebinds");
        if (!string.IsNullOrEmpty(rebinds))
            actions.LoadBindingOverridesFromJson(rebinds);
    }

    public void OnDisable()
    {
        var rebinds = actions.SaveBindingOverridesAsJson();
        PlayerPrefs.SetString("rebinds", rebinds);
    }
}
```

Figure 2-75. RebindSaveLoad script

The RebindSaveLoad script uses Unity's PlayerPrefs system and the InputActionAsset to manage and persist custom input bindings across game sessions. It effectively bridges the gap between sessions by saving and loading user-defined input configurations. Here's a concise overview of what the code accomplishes:

1. **Loading Binding Overrides on Enable:** When the script or its GameObject is enabled (i.e., when OnEnable() is called), it checks Unity's PlayerPrefs for a stored string under the key "rebinds." If a stored string is found (indicating that previously saved custom bindings exist), it loads these bindings into

CHAPTER 2   UNITY'S NEW INPUT SYSTEM

the actions (an InputActionAsset (StarterAssets), which contains all input actions for the game) using LoadBindingOverridesFromJson(). This function parses the JSON string and applies the binding overrides to the input actions, thereby customizing the input configuration based on previously saved user preferences.

2. **Saving Binding Overrides on Disable:** When the script or its GameObject is disabled (i.e., when OnDisable() is called), it saves the current binding overrides from the actions asset (StarterAssets) into a JSON string using SaveBindingOverridesAsJson(). This JSON string, which represents the current state of all customized input bindings, is then saved back to PlayerPrefs under the key "rebinds." This ensures that any changes made to the input bindings during the game session are persisted and can be reloaded in future sessions.

You need to copy the lines of code within the OnEnable() method as depicted within the oval border in Figure 2-75. Now select the PlayerArmature game object in the hierarchy and within the inspector locate its Action Map Manager component. Note that the Action Map Manager component references the "StarterAssets" Input Action Asset as part of its Action Asset property.

Launch open the ActionMapManager script within your code editor. Within it find the OnEnable() method and paste in the code you copied from the RebindSaveLoad script. As within the ActionMapManager script, you have a public Input Action Asset variable declared "actionAsset" that references "StarterAssets," use it to replace the "actions" variable. The completed code for the OnEnable() method of the ActionMapManager script is depicted in Figure 2-76.

```
private void OnEnable()
{
    toggleUIAction.performed += ToggleUIPerformed;
    toggleRebindControlsAction.performed += ToggleRebindControlsPerformed;   // ACC

    var rebinds = PlayerPrefs.GetString("rebinds");
    if (!string.IsNullOrEmpty(rebinds))
        actionAsset.LoadBindingOverridesFromJson(rebinds);
}
```

Figure 2-76. *Modified OnEnable() method within the ActionMapManager script*

Now run the Playground scene for the Third Person Controller. The bindings will now be loaded the moment the game starts. You should still have the jump action binding tied down to the "Z" key, so press the "Z" key and you will note that the player's character jumps. Change other bindings and test them to ensure they work.

Recipe 2-8: Dynamic Icons for Gamepad Actions

Problem

Integrating intuitive and visually appealing gamepad control icons into a game's UI can be challenging, especially when supporting multiple types of gamepads like Xbox and PlayStation. Developers need a method to dynamically replace text descriptions with appropriate icons during the control rebinding process, enhancing both the aesthetics and usability of the game's input configuration UI.

Solution

The Gamepad Icons Example component in Unity addresses this challenge by automatically updating the UI with relevant gamepad control icons based on the player's current gamepad type. This script subscribes to UI update events, checks the device type, and uses a structured method to fetch and display the correct icons for different controls. By employing this script, developers can significantly improve the user interface's intuitiveness and visual appeal, making the game more accessible and satisfying for players using various gamepad models.

How It Works

The prefabs for gamepad bindings are slightly different from those available for the Keypad, in that for the gamepad bindings for each rebind prefab (MoveRebind, LookRebind, JumpRebind, SprintRebind, and AttackRebind), there exists an additional child game object "ActionBindingIcon" as depicted in Figure 2-77, which is the image for the icon that gets applied to each action button.

On the Gamepad game object, there exists the Gamepad Icons Example component that is designed to enhance the user interface of a game by replacing text descriptions of gamepad controls with appropriate icons.

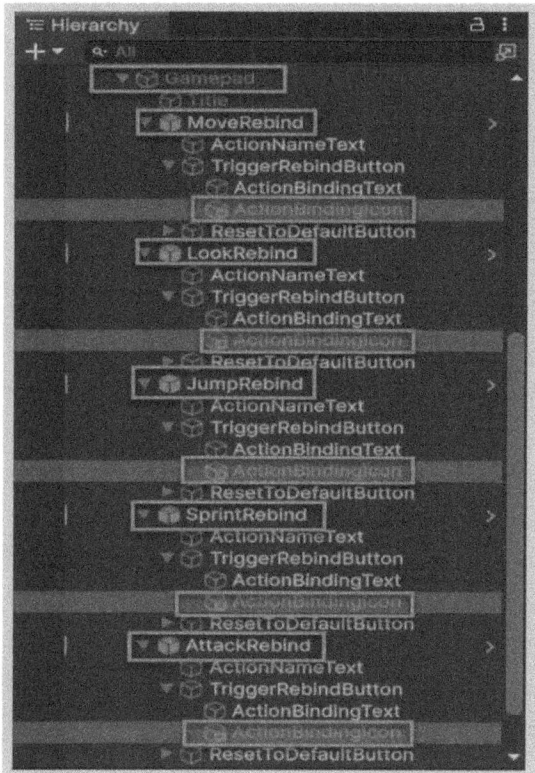

Figure 2-77. *Gamepad bindings*

This approach significantly improves the visual appeal and intuitiveness of the game's input configuration UI, particularly during the rebinding process. This script provides a sophisticated solution for dynamically updating game input configuration UIs, making them more intuitive and visually appealing. By integrating this script, developers can offer a better configuration experience in their games, aligning with modern UI design standards that favor graphical elements over text for enhanced interaction and accessibility.

Here's an overview of what this script accomplishes:

1. **Event Subscription:** On enabling, the script subscribes to the updateBindingUIEvent on all RebindActionUI components found within its hierarchy. This event is triggered whenever the UI display for a binding needs to be refreshed – typically after a binding change.

2. **Dynamic UI Update:** The script listens for updates from the RebindActionUI components and, upon receiving an update, executes the OnUpdateBindingDisplay method. This method determines the appropriate icon based on the current binding and the type of gamepad (e.g., Xbox or PlayStation).

3. **Conditional Icon Replacement:** Within the OnUpdateBindingDisplay method, it checks the deviceLayoutName to identify the type of gamepad being used (like a PlayStation or Xbox controller). Depending on the type, it retrieves the corresponding icon for the specific control from predefined GamepadIcons structures (xbox or ps4).

4. **UI Element Manipulation:** If a suitable icon is found, the script sets this icon in the UI and hides the default text label that would normally display the binding. If no icon is found, it ensures the text label remains visible, allowing for fallback to text if specific control icons are not available.

CHAPTER 2   UNITY'S NEW INPUT SYSTEM

5. **GetSprite() Method:** This method serves a crucial role in mapping control paths from a gamepad to specific sprite assets that visually represent these controls. This method is integral to enhancing the user interface by replacing text labels with intuitive icons for each gamepad button or control.

    - **Control Path Parameter**: This method takes a single parameter, controlPath, which is a string representing the path of the control on the device. This path is used to identify which specific control on the gamepad is being referred to. If you open the "StarterAssets" and select a binding for an action, and within the last pane on the right you click the "T" button the path is revealed to you besides the "Path" property (Figure 2-78).

    - **Switch Statement for Mapping**: This method uses a switch statement to match the controlPath to the corresponding Sprite. Each case in the switch statement handles a different potential controlPath value, each mapping directly to a specific sprite that visually represents that control on the gamepad.

    - **Return the Matching Sprite**: When a match is found in the switch statement, the method returns the sprite associated with that control. This sprite is then used to display the corresponding gamepad button in the UI, allowing for a visual representation that users can easily recognize.

CHAPTER 2   UNITY'S NEW INPUT SYSTEM

- **Fallback for Non-matching Controls**: If the controlPath provided does not match any of the cases in the switch statement, the method returns null. This signifies that there is no specific sprite associated with the given control path, and the default text label or another fallback visual representation should be used.

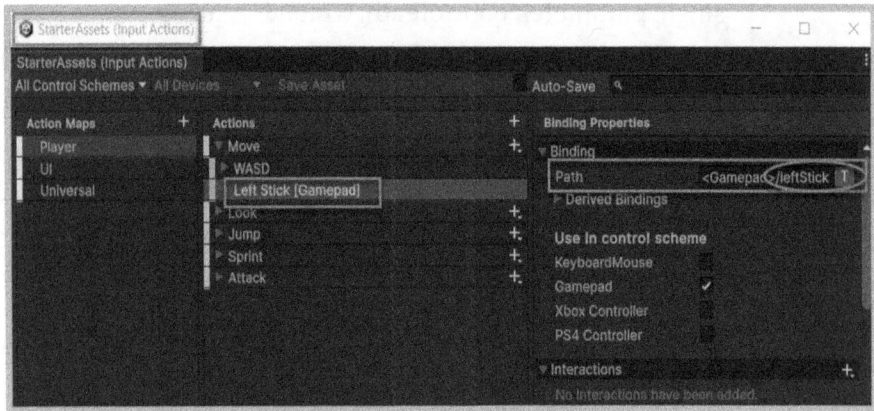

Figure 2-78. Path property revealing the bindings control path

This script supports different gamepad layouts by distinguishing between Xbox and PlayStation controllers. This feature enhances the script's versatility across various platforms and user preferences. The architecture of the script, with its separation of icon retrieval into a struct (GamepadIcons), allows for easy expansion or modification to include more gamepad types or additional icons for new controls. Figure 2-79 illustrates the code for this script.

CHAPTER 2 UNITY'S NEW INPUT SYSTEM

```csharp
public class GamepadIconsExample : MonoBehaviour
{
    public GamepadIcons xbox;
    public GamepadIcons ps4;

    protected void OnEnable()
    {
        // Hook into all updateBindingUIEvents on all RebindActionUI components in our hierarchy.
        var rebindUIComponents = transform.GetComponentsInChildren<RebindActionUI>();
        foreach (var component in rebindUIComponents)
        {
            component.updateBindingUIEvent.AddListener(OnUpdateBindingDisplay);
            component.UpdateBindingDisplay();
        }
    }

    protected void OnUpdateBindingDisplay(RebindActionUI component, string bindingDisplayString,
                            string deviceLayoutName, string controlPath)
    {
        if (string.IsNullOrEmpty(deviceLayoutName) || string.IsNullOrEmpty(controlPath))
            return;

        var icon = default(Sprite);
        if (InputSystem.IsFirstLayoutBasedOnSecond(deviceLayoutName, "DualShockGamepad"))
            icon = ps4.GetSprite(controlPath);
        else if (InputSystem.IsFirstLayoutBasedOnSecond(deviceLayoutName, "Gamepad"))
            icon = xbox.GetSprite(controlPath);

        var textComponent = component.bindingText;

        // Grab Image component.
        var imageGO = textComponent.transform.parent.Find("ActionBindingIcon");
        var imageComponent = imageGO.GetComponent<Image>();

        if (icon != null)
        {
            textComponent.gameObject.SetActive(false);
            imageComponent.sprite = icon;
            imageComponent.gameObject.SetActive(true);
        }
        else
        {
            textComponent.gameObject.SetActive(true);
            imageComponent.gameObject.SetActive(false);
        }
    }

    [Serializable]
    public struct GamepadIcons
    {
        public Sprite buttonSouth;
        public Sprite buttonNorth;
        public Sprite buttonEast;
        public Sprite buttonWest;
        public Sprite startButton;
        public Sprite selectButton;
        public Sprite leftTrigger;
        public Sprite rightTrigger;
        public Sprite leftShoulder;
        public Sprite rightShoulder;
        public Sprite dpad;
        public Sprite dpadUp;
        public Sprite dpadDown;
        public Sprite dpadLeft;
        public Sprite dpadRight;
        public Sprite leftStick;
        public Sprite rightStick;
        public Sprite leftStickPress;
        public Sprite rightStickPress;

        public Sprite GetSprite(string controlPath)
        {
            // From the input system, we get the path of the control on device. So we can just
            // map from that to the sprites we have for gamepads.
            switch (controlPath)
            {
                case "buttonSouth": return buttonSouth;
                case "buttonNorth": return buttonNorth;
                case "buttonEast": return buttonEast;
                case "buttonWest": return buttonWest;
                case "start": return startButton;
                case "select": return selectButton;
                case "leftTrigger": return leftTrigger;
                case "rightTrigger": return rightTrigger;
                case "leftShoulder": return leftShoulder;
                case "rightShoulder": return rightShoulder;
                case "dpad": return dpad;
                case "dpad/up": return dpadUp;
                case "dpad/down": return dpadDown;
                case "dpad/left": return dpadLeft;
                case "dpad/right": return dpadRight;
                case "leftStick": return leftStick;
                case "rightStick": return rightStick;
                case "leftStickPress": return leftStickPress;
                case "rightStickPress": return rightStickPress;
            }
            return null;
        }
    }
}
```

***Figure 2-79.** GamepadIconExample script*

CHAPTER 2 UNITY'S NEW INPUT SYSTEM

Summary

This chapter offered an in-depth exploration of Unity's New Input System, a framework designed to enhance game development through improved control and flexibility over player inputs. This comprehensive chapter not only introduced the fundamental aspects of the new system but also delved into advanced techniques and integration strategies, making it an essential resource for both novice and experienced game developers.

CHAPTER 3

Architecting Enemy AI with Finite State Machines

In the realm of game development, the creation of intelligent and responsive enemy AI is pivotal to crafting engaging and challenging gameplay. This chapter delves into the intricacies of using finite state machines (FSMs) to orchestrate enemy behavior in Unity, offering a structured approach to understanding and implementing this powerful concept. You will focus on establishing finite state machines (FSMs) for enemy AI exclusively via coding your very own FSM. This method offers unparalleled flexibility and precise control, enabling the development of finely tuned AI logic that functions independently of graphical animations. By leveraging this approach, developers can meticulously craft complex AI behaviors, ensuring a seamless integration of strategic decision-making processes within the game environment. Additionally, this chapter will cover the essentials of navigation and pathfinding within Unity's environment, including the setup of a Nav Mesh and configuring NavMesh Agents, ensuring that your AI is not only smart in decision-making but also adept at moving within the game world. By the end of this chapter, you will be equipped with the knowledge to implement sophisticated enemy AI that can navigate, pursue, and interact with the player in a dynamically challenging manner.

CHAPTER 3　ARCHITECTING ENEMY AI WITH FINITE STATE MACHINES

Recipe 3-1: Setting Up a NavMesh

Problem

Navigating characters and agents in a complex game environment can be challenging due to the need for efficient pathfinding and obstacle avoidance. This issue arises from the difficulty of programming AI to dynamically calculate optimal paths in real-time, especially in environments with varying terrain and numerous obstacles, which can lead to performance bottlenecks and less responsive or unrealistic AI behavior.

Solution

Setting up a NavMesh in Unity provides a robust solution for AI navigation in game environments. A NavMesh is a simplified representation of the game's playable area that AI agents use to determine walkable surfaces and obstacles. By baking a NavMesh into your scene, you enable AI characters to use Unity's built-in pathfinding algorithms to find efficient paths to their destinations while automatically avoiding obstacles. This approach not only simplifies the development process but also enhances the performance and realism of AI agent movements, making it easier to create complex and dynamic interactions in the game world.

How It Works

Make a copy of the final downloadable resource provided as part of Chapter 2. Start by opening the Playground scene for the ThirdPersonController that is available within Assets/StarterAssets/ThirdPersonController/Scenes. To install Unity's AI Navigation package, follow the steps listed below:

CHAPTER 3   ARCHITECTING ENEMY AI WITH FINITE STATE MACHINES

1. Go to the Window menu in the Unity Editor and select Package Manager.

2. In the Package Manager, switch to the Unity Registry from the top-left dropdown to view all available Unity packages.

3. Search for "AI Navigation" in the search bar.

4. Select the AI Navigation package from the list and click the Install button to add it to your project.

Create a new "Player" Layer using the Layer drop-down available at the top of the Inspector. Select the PlayerArmature game object in the hierarchy and set its layer to "Player." You don't need to apply this layer to the PlayerArmature child game objects.

With the Playground scene open, expand the Environment game object in the hierarchy. To configure the NavMesh, you will include only the ground plane, walls, and boxes within the Playground scene. Other objects such as the Cylinder, Stairs, Ramp Mesh, and Tunnel prefab need to be disabled. This approach simplifies the focus on the Enemy AI FSM, avoiding the complexities of Unity's NavMesh with offmesh links, etc., which would warrant a dedicated chapter.

Figure 3-1 (excluding the patrol point indicators) illustrates the expected appearance of your un-baked NavMesh, which includes only the ground plane, walls, and boxes, with all other objects disabled. Refer to the downloadable resource accompanying this chapter to configure the Environment objects as depicted. Ensure that each of the enabled Environment objects has their NavigationStatic property checked, which should be the default (Figure 3-2).

225

CHAPTER 3 ARCHITECTING ENEMY AI WITH FINITE STATE MACHINES

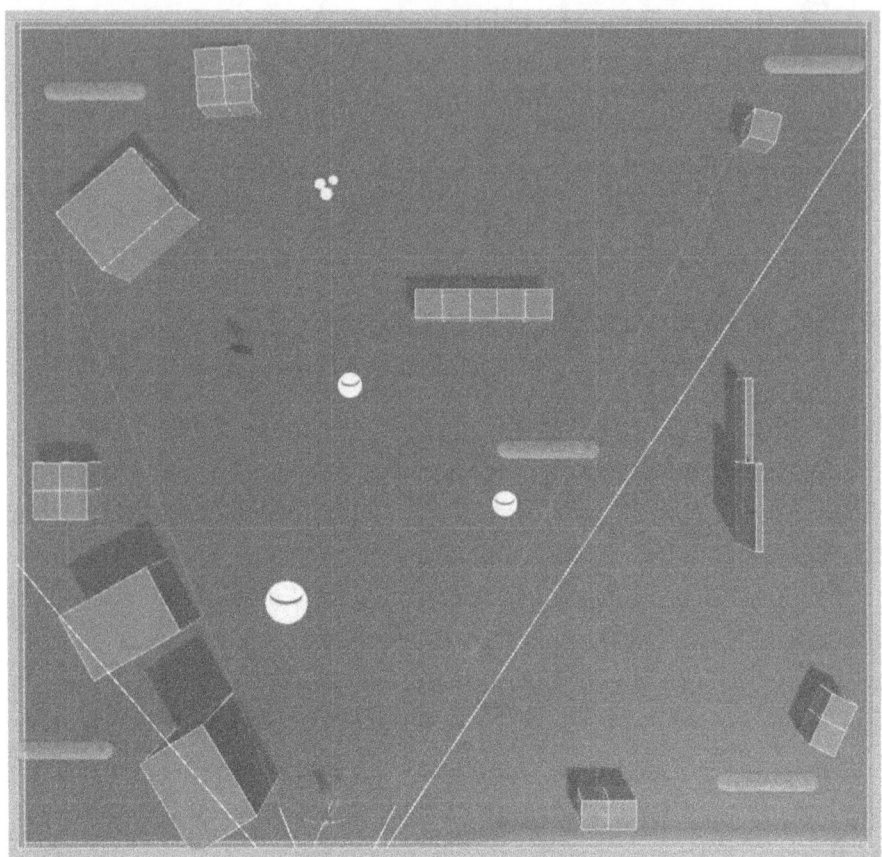

Figure 3-1. Un-baked NavMesh

CHAPTER 3   ARCHITECTING ENEMY AI WITH FINITE STATE MACHINES

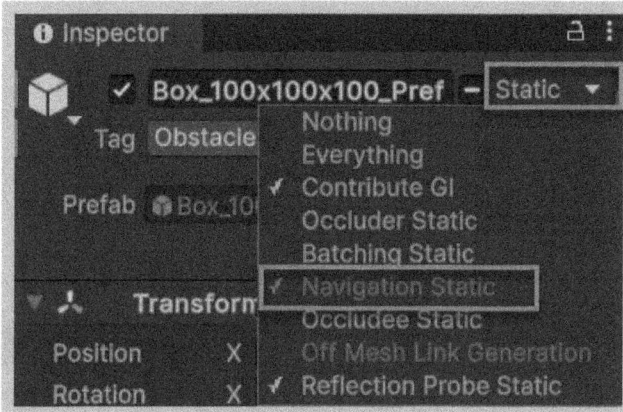

Figure 3-2. *Object setup as Navigation Static*

In the hierarchy, with the Environment game object expanded, select the Greybox object. In the Inspector, add a NavMeshSurface component as shown in Figure 3-3. This component generates the navigation mesh for your scene. In the Include Layers property dropdown, uncheck the Pushable and Player layers. This ensures that when the NavMesh is baked, objects on these layers will not be marked as navigation static, allowing your player and pushable objects to remain dynamic. Additionally, ensure that the static property for your PlayerArmature game object in the Inspector is unchecked.

CHAPTER 3   ARCHITECTING ENEMY AI WITH FINITE STATE MACHINES

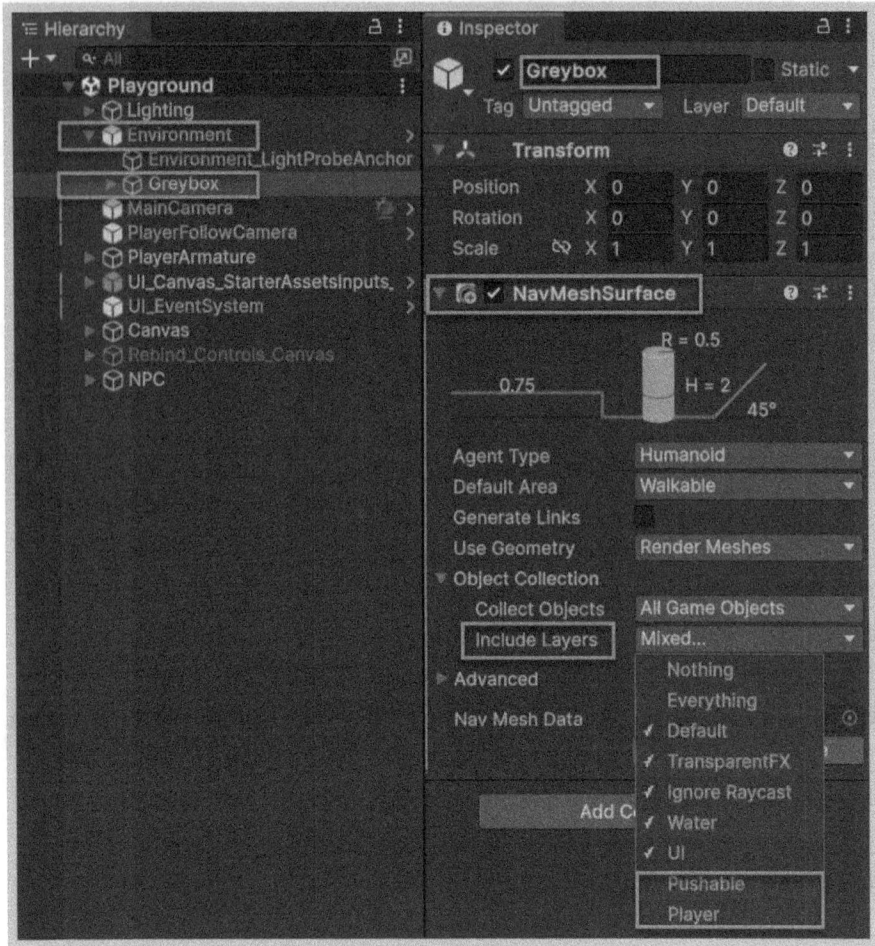

***Figure 3-3.** NavMeshSurface component setup*

With the Greybox game object still selected in the hierarchy and with the NavMeshSurface component visible in the Inspector, locate and click the Bake button. A small window should pop up indicating that your NavMesh is being baked. Unity calculates and displays a bluish navigation

CHAPTER 3 ARCHITECTING ENEMY AI WITH FINITE STATE MACHINES

mesh over your scene geometry. Each time you add a new obstacle be it a wall, a box, or some other type of object to your scene, you need to ensure that you re-bake your NavMesh by clicking the Bake button. Figure 3-4 depicts the bluish-baked NavMesh.

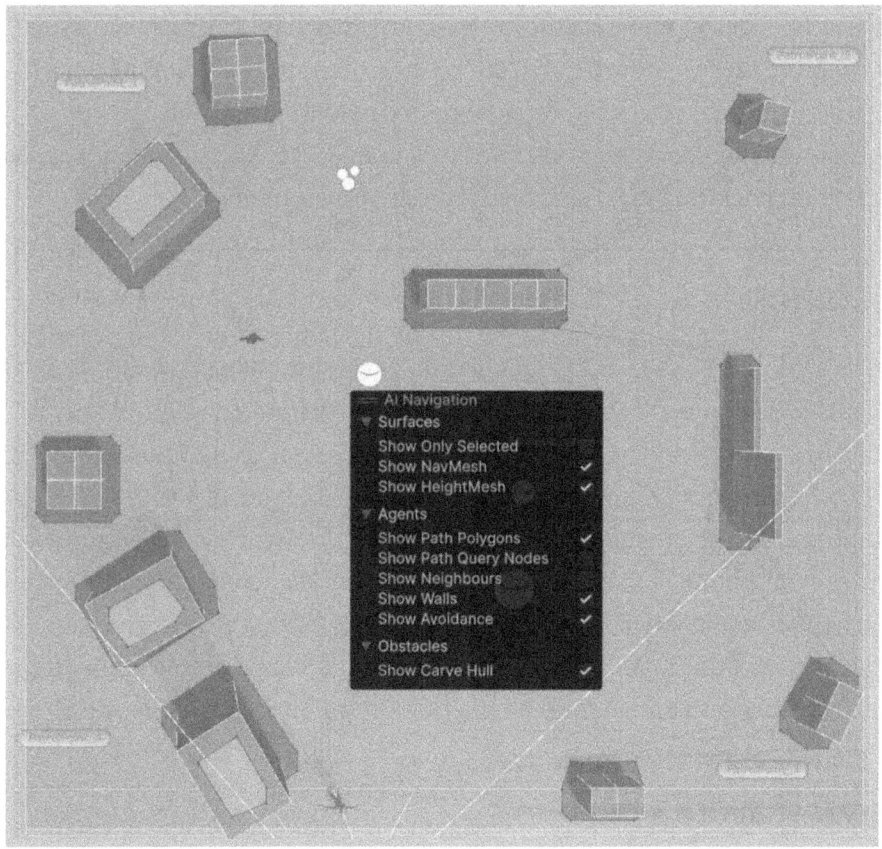

Figure 3-4. Baked NavMesh

CHAPTER 3   ARCHITECTING ENEMY AI WITH FINITE STATE MACHINES

Recipe 3-2: Setting Up a NavMesh Agent

Problem

In dynamic game environments, AI NPCs (non-player characters) often face challenges in moving efficiently and realistically. The primary issue is enabling these agents to navigate complex terrains and interact with changing obstacles without manual path calculations, which can be computationally intensive and hard to manage, especially in larger scenes or where precise, context-aware movement is essential for gameplay.

Solution

By setting up a NavMesh Agent in Unity, developers can empower AI NPC agents to navigate automatically within the environment defined by a NavMesh. This involves attaching a NavMesh Agent component to your AI NPC character and configuring its parameters like speed, acceleration, and stopping distance to match the desired behavior. The NavMesh Agent uses the precomputed NavMesh to determine paths, avoid obstacles, and adapt to changes in the environment. This setup simplifies AI programming, allowing for smooth and realistic NPC agent movement while optimizing performance and enhancing the interactive quality of the game world.

How It Works

In this recipe, I will demonstrate how to configure a NavMesh agent and setup a Capsule collider for it. Begin by downloading the Chapter 3 resource and open the Playground scene found in Assets/StarterAssets/ThirdPersonController/Scenes. This resource includes the completed setup for this chapter, allowing you to examine how various game objects are equipped with components that contribute to the complex operation of the Enemy AI system.

CHAPTER 3   ARCHITECTING ENEMY AI WITH FINITE STATE MACHINES

Within the hierarchy, observe that an empty NPC game object has been created, encompassing two child game objects: AllPatrolPoints and Soldier_0. The AllPatrolPoints game object includes five child patrol points, each representing a location on the NavMesh where the NPC soldier can patrol. Each patrol point consists solely of a transform component, specifying its position within the game environment's NavMesh (Figure 3-5).

The NPC setup here has just one NPC soldier and the five patrol points listed are the patrol points that this NPC soldier will patrol. You could have five or even more NPC soldiers within your scene and accordingly setup more patrol points, perhaps five for each NPC soldier in which case you would end up with a total of twenty-five patrol points. All these patrol points would need to be created as children of the AllPatrolPoints game object and they could then be numbered sequentially. This would enable you to assign patrol points one through five to the first NPC soldier, patrol points six through ten to the second NPC soldier, and so on, enabling your NPC soldiers to have distinct patrol zones.

The Soldier_0 child game object comprises all the functionality required by this NPC soldier to patrol, chase, attack, wander, take cover, receive damage, and die. Thus if you need more than one NPC soldier all you need to do is duplicate this Soldier_0 game object several times, ensuring they are children of the NPC game object, reposition them at different locations within your game environment, and assign them the appropriate patrol points. As shown in Figure 3-5, you will note that this NPC Soldier_0 has been fitted with a capsule collider.

CHAPTER 3   ARCHITECTING ENEMY AI WITH FINITE STATE MACHINES

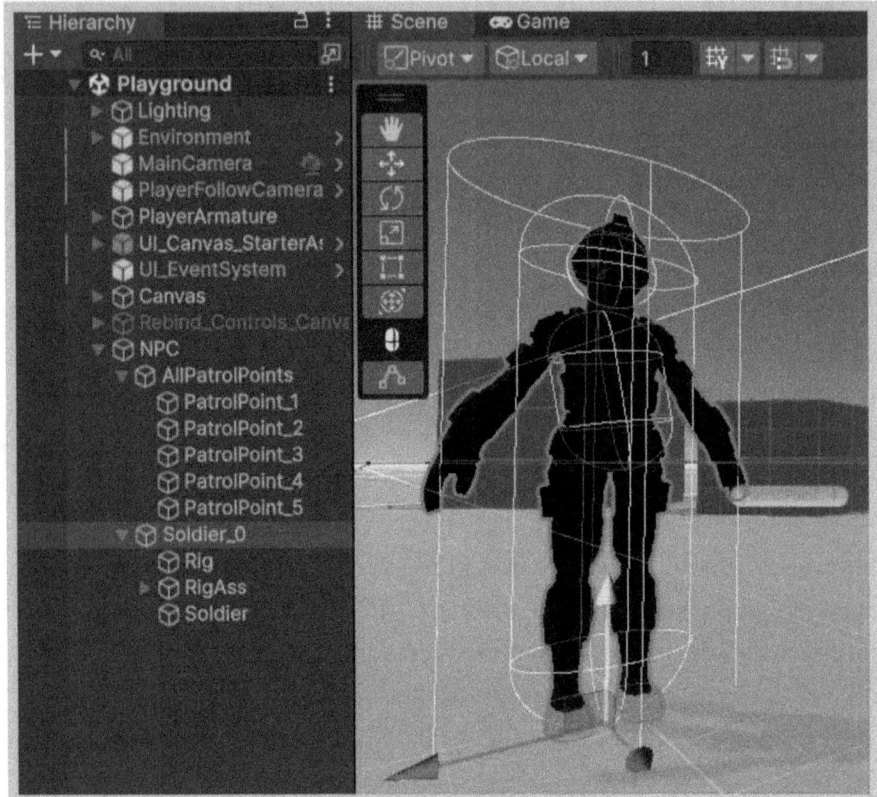

Figure 3-5. *Structure of the NPCs game object*

In the hierarchy, select the Soldier_0 game object and observe in the Inspector that it is equipped with multiple components essential for the Enemy AI system. This recipe will specifically detail the setup of the NavMeshAgent component and the capsule collider.

The capsule collider, with its IsTrigger property enabled, allows the use of the OnTriggerEnter, OnTriggerStay, and OnTriggerExit methods to detect if objects enter the NPC's trigger collider. Although not utilized in this specific setup, this functionality can be valuable for scenarios such as

CHAPTER 3 ARCHITECTING ENEMY AI WITH FINITE STATE MACHINES

detecting player proximity or interacting with other game objects within the NPC's range. Note that its Center property for the Y axis has been set to 0.5, its Radius to 0.15, and its Height to 1, which encompasses NPC Soldier_0 well enough. The Direction property has been set to Y-Axis (Figure 3-6).

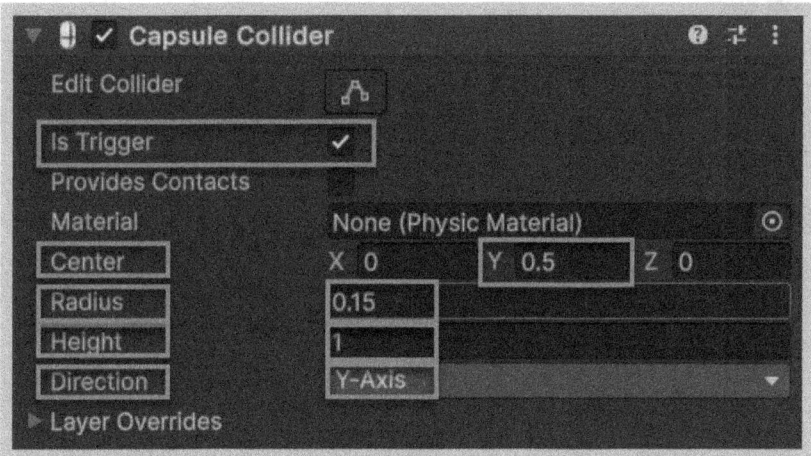

Figure 3-6. *Capsule Collider setup*

CHAPTER 3   ARCHITECTING ENEMY AI WITH FINITE STATE MACHINES

Figure 3-7. NavMesh Agent component

Most properties of the NavMesh agent have retained their default values, except for the Stopping Distance, which is set to 0.15. You may adjust this based on your requirements. Figure 3-7 displays the properties and their respective values for the NavMesh agent component. This component is essential for controlling the movement behavior and pathfinding capabilities of the NPC, allowing it to navigate the game environment effectively.

To enable NPC Soldier_0 to patrol the configured NavMesh, patrol points are linked to the NPC through the PatrolState component. With Soldier_0 selected in the hierarchy, expand and observe the PatrolState component, where the patrol points are assigned to a "wayPoints" array. This array has been populated within the Unity Editor with patrol points one through five. The functionality and implementation of the PatrolState script will be discussed in a subsequent recipe of this chapter. This setup allows for systematic NPC movement along predefined paths in the game environment.

Recipe 3-3: Managing NPC Behavior and Weapon Arsenal

Problem

A system is required that facilitates the dynamic assignment and management of weapons for a Non-Player Character (NPC). This system must ensure that upon initialization, the NPC selects a weapon at random from a predefined arsenal, thereby avoiding being in an unarmed state. Furthermore, the system needs to facilitate seamless transitions between weapons and their respective animations to suit various gameplay scenarios. This requires a robust and flexible approach to weapon handling and visualization, ensuring that the NPC's interactions remain consistent and immersive throughout the game.

Solution

The NPCController class tackles the problem by leveraging an arsenal array to hold various weapon options and corresponding animations. On initialization, the NPC randomly selects a weapon (excluding the default empty state) from the arsenal. The class manages weapon instantiation by attaching the selected weapons to the specified bones of the NPC model and setting the appropriate animator controller. This approach not only achieves a dynamic and visually accurate representation of the NPC with its weapon but also ensures that the NPC is ready with operational weaponry and animations right from the start, enhancing the gameplay experience.

CHAPTER 3   ARCHITECTING ENEMY AI WITH FINITE STATE MACHINES

How It Works

Select the NPC Soldier_0 game object in the hierarchy and add an Animator component, maintaining its default property values. This step is essential for controlling the NPC's animations within the Unity environment.

Add the NPCController component to the NPC Soldier_0 game object. This component is essential for equipping the NPC with weapons and specifying the body part from which the NPC will wield these weapons, typically the hands. Figure 3-8 shows the setup of the NPCController, which includes a sniper rifle and an AK-47 in the NPC's weapon arsenal. The figure also indicates the positions at which these weapons will be held by the NPC, specifically within the right and left hands.

Figure 3-8. *NPC Controller setup*

CHAPTER 3 ARCHITECTING ENEMY AI WITH FINITE STATE MACHINES

To populate the NPC Controller component follow the steps listed below:

1. Navigate the hierarchy from Soldier_0 by expanding game object RigAss, then sequentially through RigSpine1, RigSpine2, RigSpine3, RightArmRightCollarBone, RigArmRight1, RigArmRight2, and RigArmRight3 to locate RigPistolRight. Drag RigPistolRight from the hierarchy to the RightGunBone property in the NPC Controller component in the Inspector (Figure 3-9).

2. Next beneath RigSpine3 sequentially expand game objects RigArmLeftCollarbone, RigArmLeft1, RigArmLeft2, and RigArmLeft3 to locate RigLeftPistol. Drag RigLeftPistol from the hierarchy to the LeftGunBone property in the NPC Controller component in the Inspector (Figure 3-9).

3. Ensure that the Arsenal array size has been set to three so that you are provided with three Arsenal slots. For the first slot name property type in Empty. Likewise, name the second slot SniperRifle, and the third slot AK47 (Figure 3-9).

4. Within the Project tab navigate to Assets/Enemy_AI/Enemy/Controllers where you have been provided with two animator controllers, namely, FreeHandController and SniperRifleController.

5. From within the Project tab drag and drop the FreeHandController onto the Controller property of the Empty Arsenal array slot (Figure 3-9).

237

CHAPTER 3   ARCHITECTING ENEMY AI WITH FINITE STATE MACHINES

6. Next, from within the Project tab drag and drop the SniperRifleController onto the Controller property of the SniperRifle Arsenal array slot (Figure 3-9).

7. Lastly, from within the Project tab drag and drop the SniperRifleController onto the Controller property of the AK47 Arsenal array slot (Figure 3-9).

8. For the Empty Arsenal array slot leave the Right Gun and Left Gun property values at their default values of None (Figure 3-9).

9. Within the Project tab navigate to Assets/Enemy_AI/Enemy/Weapons where you have been provided with two weapon prefabs, namely, AutomaticRifle and SniperGun.

10. From within the Project tab drag and drop the SniperGun prefab onto the RightGun property of the SniperRifle Arsenal array slot (Figure 3-9). This ensures that when the NPC is initialized in the game, it would start with the weapon held in its right hand. Should you want it to start with the weapon in its left hand, then populate the LeftGun property instead.

11. Next, from within the Project tab drag and drop the AutomaticRifle prefab onto the RightGun property of the AK47 Arsenal array slot (Figure 3-9).

For weapons like handguns or revolvers that don't require a secondary supporting hand, you can equip an NPC with two such weapons, one in each hand, by adding an extra Arsenal element. This isn't necessary for larger weapons like Sniper guns and Automatic rifles, which need support.

CHAPTER 3   ARCHITECTING ENEMY AI WITH FINITE STATE MACHINES

Now that the NPC Controller component is set up in the Inspector, let's explore the NPCController script (Listing 3-1). This script manages weapon options in its arsenal, facilitates random weapon selection, and handles weapon instantiation by attaching the chosen weapons to the specified bones of the NPC model.

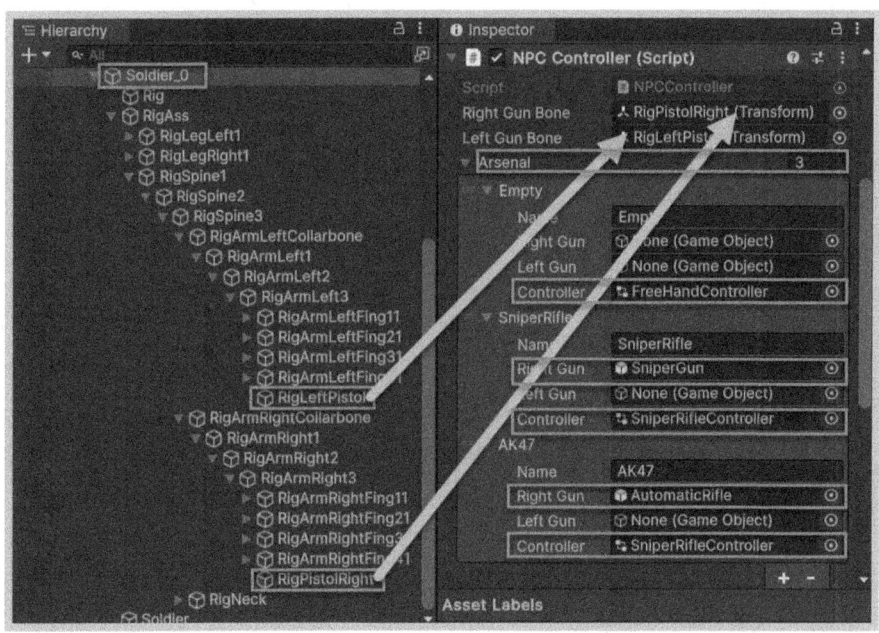

Figure 3-9. Populating NPC Controller properties

Listing 3-1. NPCController script

```
using UnityEngine;
using Random = UnityEngine.Random;

[RequireComponent (typeof (Animator))]
public class NPCController : MonoBehaviour {

    [System.Serializable]
    public struct Arsenal
```

CHAPTER 3 ARCHITECTING ENEMY AI WITH FINITE STATE MACHINES

```
{
    public string name;
    public GameObject rightGun;
    public GameObject leftGun;
    public RuntimeAnimatorController controller;
}
[SerializeField] private Transform rightGunBone;
[SerializeField] private Transform leftGunBone;
[SerializeField] private Arsenal[] arsenal;

private Animator animator;

void Awake()
{
    animator = GetComponent<Animator> ();

    int index = Random.Range(1, arsenal.Length);
    if (arsenal.Length > 0)
        SetArsenal (arsenal[index].name); //Setup NPC to be
        //holding a randomly selected weapon from the
        //arsenal array other than 'Empty' at startup.
}
public void SetArsenal(string name) {
    foreach (Arsenal hand in arsenal) {
        if (hand.name == name) {
            if (rightGunBone.childCount > 0)
            Destroy(rightGunBone.GetChild(0).gameObject);
            if (leftGunBone.childCount > 0)
            Destroy(leftGunBone.GetChild(0).gameObject);
            if (hand.rightGun != null) {
                GameObject newRightGun = (GameObject)
                    Instantiate(hand.rightGun);
```

```
            newRightGun.transform.parent =
              rightGunBone;
            newRightGun.transform.localPosition =
              Vector3.zero;
            newRightGun.transform.localRotation =
              Quaternion.Euler(90, 0, 0);
        }
        if (hand.leftGun != null) {
            GameObject newLeftGun = (GameObject)
              Instantiate(hand.leftGun);
            newLeftGun.transform.parent =
              leftGunBone;
            newLeftGun.transform.localPosition =
              Vector3.zero;
            newLeftGun.transform.localRotation =
              Quaternion.Euler(90, 0, 0);
        }
        animator.runtimeAnimatorController =
        hand.controller;
        return;
            }
          }
        }
}
```

This NPCController script is a robust component designed for setting up a non-player character (NPC) within a game environment. It manages the NPC's arsenal of weapons and its animations through a structured approach. This class is primarily responsible for equipping an NPC with weapons and setting the corresponding animations based on the weapon selection. It leverages Unity's Animator component to achieve dynamic and context-specific animations. Let's break down the class and its elements to understand its functionality in detail.

CHAPTER 3   ARCHITECTING ENEMY AI WITH FINITE STATE MACHINES

1. public struct Arsenal: It holds details about the weapon assigned to the NPC and the corresponding animation controller. The field name is a string identifier for an Arsenal element. The field rightGun represents a weapon game object to be equipped in the NPC's right hand, while the field leftGun represents a weapon game object to be equipped in the NPC's left hand. The field controller is an AnimatorController to be used when this arsenal element is equipped, ensuring the correct animations play for the specific weapon.

2. rightGunBone and leftGunBone: These are Transform references where the respective weapons will be attached. They ensure the weapons are positioned correctly in the NPC's hands.

3. arsenal: An array of Arsenal structures to define all possible weapon combinations and their respective animations that the NPC can use.

4. animator: A private Animator reference used to control the NPC's animations dynamically based on the equipped weapons.

5. Awake(): It begins by caching the Animator component. It then initializes the NPC's weapon setup by randomly selecting a weapon from the arsenal (excluding the first item which is assumed to be an empty or default setup) and applying it by invoking the SetArsenal() method.

CHAPTER 3   ARCHITECTING ENEMY AI WITH FINITE STATE MACHINES

6. SetArsenal(): This method accepts a string (i.e. arsenal name), and configures the NPC's weapons and animations based on the specified arsenal name. The foreach loop then iterates through each arsenal configuration and checks if the current arsenal matches the specified name. Existing weapons, if any are then cleared from the NPC's right and left hands. If a right-hand weapon was specified in the Inspector, that weapon is instantiated as the weapon for the right-hand. This weapon's parent is then set to the right-hand bone and the local position for this right-hand weapon is reset. The local rotation for this right-hand weapon is then set to 90 about the X-axis. The same logic applies to setting up the left-hand weapon. Lastly, the runtimeAnimatorController property is set based on the selected arsenal element, which populates the Animator component at runtime. Now that the correct arsenal has been found and applied, the return statement exits the loop.

This class offers a versatile approach to managing weapon configurations and animations for NPCs, enabling straightforward customization and dynamic behavior adjustments. With minor code modifications, it can also be adapted for player use, allowing a similar setup of weapons and animations.

CHAPTER 3   ARCHITECTING ENEMY AI WITH FINITE STATE MACHINES

Recipe 3-4: Integrating the Actions Class with the SniperRifleController Animator

Problem

Managing and coordinating a diverse set of Non-Player Character (NPC) animations and states within a game environment is a complex challenge that necessitates the use of an independent class. The primary challenge involves ensuring seamless transitions between various states—such as idle, walk, run, attack, and more—based on game events while maintaining an accurate correspondence between each animation and the NPC's actual behavior. Furthermore, the class must prevent repetitive or conflicting animations, especially in the context of damage sequences, and effectively manage nuanced states like squatting and aiming to ensure a coherent and realistic NPC experience.

Solution

The Actions class effectively addresses these challenges by using a central Animator component and subscribing to various NPC state events like idle, patrol, chase, attack, and more. It dynamically sets animation parameters and triggers in response to these events, ensuring that the NPC's visual behavior matches its game logic state. The class uses randomness and tracking to prevent repeating damage animations, thereby enhancing realism. Additionally, it incorporates functionality to adjust NPC postures, like crouching and aiming, providing a comprehensive and flexible solution to NPC animation management.

CHAPTER 3   ARCHITECTING ENEMY AI WITH FINITE STATE MACHINES

How It Works

In the Unity Project tab, navigate to Assets/Enemy_AI/Enemy/Controllers and open the SniperRifleController in the Animator tab. This controller contains multiple NPC states with transitions, each with modular animations. Rather than embedding complex parameter combinations in each state's script, you use the Actions script to manage these parameters. This script defines methods corresponding to each state, controlling animations based on real-time game logic. These methods are invoked from their respective states to streamline animation management.

The SniperRifleController Animator features multiple parameters and two layers: Base Layer and Damage Layer, with the latter's blending set to Additive. The Base Layer and its parameters are shown in Figure 3-10, while the Damage Layer, depicted in Figure 3-11, includes three types of damage animations triggered randomly in the code. Review the transitions between states in both layers and identify the parameters influencing these transitions.

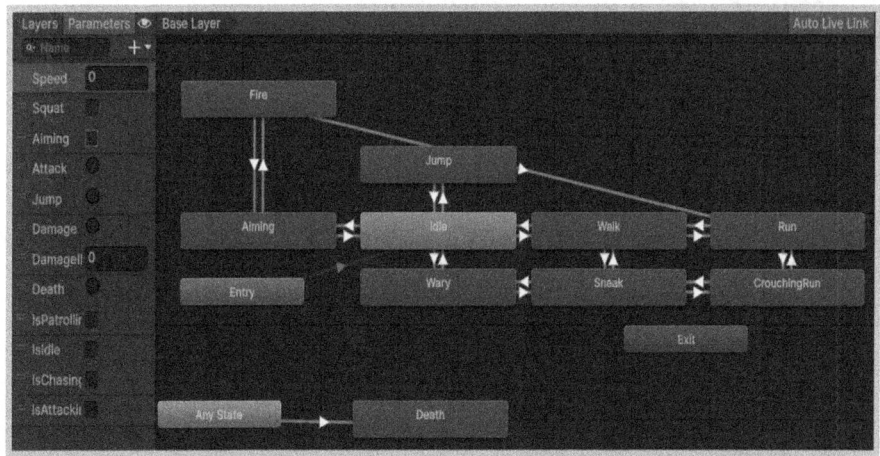

Figure 3-10. *SniperRifleController Base Layer and parameters*

245

CHAPTER 3 ARCHITECTING ENEMY AI WITH FINITE STATE MACHINES

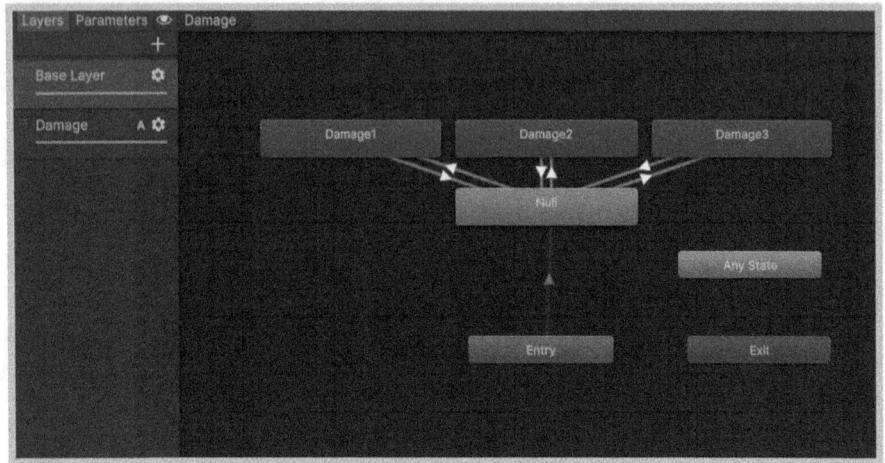

Figure 3-11. *SniperRifleController Damage Layer*

Listing 3-2. Actions script

```
using UnityEngine;
[RequireComponent (typeof (Animator))]
[RequireComponent(typeof(Health))]

public class Actions : MonoBehaviour {

    private Animator animator;

    const int countOfDamageAnimations = 3;
    int lastDamageAnimation = -1;

    private void OnEnable()
    {
        GetComponent<IdleState>().OnNpcIdle += Idle;
        GetComponent<PatrolState>().OnNpcPatrol += Walk;
        GetComponent<ChaseState>().OnNpcChase += Run;
        GetComponent<AttackState>().OnNpcAttack += Attack;
        GetComponent<DeathState>().PlayNpcDeadAnim += Death;
```

246

CHAPTER 3　ARCHITECTING ENEMY AI WITH FINITE STATE MACHINES

```csharp
        GetComponent<HitState>().PlayNpcHitAnim += Damage;
        GetComponent<WanderState>().OnNpcWander += Walk;
        GetComponent<CoverState>().OnNpcTakeCover +=
        CrouchingRun;
        GetComponent<CoverState>().OnNPCSquat += Squat;
    }
    private void OnDisable()
    {
        GetComponent<IdleState>().OnNpcIdle -= Idle;
        GetComponent<PatrolState>().OnNpcPatrol -= Walk;
        GetComponent<ChaseState>().OnNpcChase -= Run;
        GetComponent<AttackState>().OnNpcAttack -= Attack;
        GetComponent<DeathState>().PlayNpcDeadAnim -= Death;
        GetComponent<HitState>().PlayNpcHitAnim -= Damage;
        GetComponent<WanderState>().OnNpcWander -= Walk;
        GetComponent<CoverState>().OnNpcTakeCover -=
        CrouchingRun;
        GetComponent<CoverState>().OnNPCSquat -= Squat;
    }
    void Awake () {
        animator = GetComponent<Animator> ();
    }

    //Invoked from the IdleState script
    private void Idle () {
        animator.SetBool("Aiming", false);
        animator.SetFloat ("Speed", 0f);
    }

    //Invoked from the Patrol state script
    private void Walk () {
        animator.SetBool("Aiming", false);
```

CHAPTER 3   ARCHITECTING ENEMY AI WITH FINITE STATE MACHINES

```csharp
        animator.SetBool("Squat", false);
        animator.SetFloat ("Speed", 0.5f);
    }

    //Invoked from the Chase state script
    private void Run () {
        animator.SetBool("Aiming", false);
        animator.SetBool("Squat", false);
        animator.SetFloat ("Speed", 0.7f);
    }

    private void CrouchingRun()
    {
        animator.SetBool("Squat", true);
        animator.SetFloat("Speed", 0.7f);
    }

    //Invoked from the Attack state script
    private void Attack () {
        Aiming ();
        animator.SetTrigger ("Attack");
    }

    //Invoked from the Death state script
    private void Death () {
        animator.SetFloat("Speed", 0f);
        animator.SetTrigger ("Death");
    }

    //Invoked from the HitState script.
    private void Damage () {
        if (animator.GetCurrentAnimatorStateInfo (0).IsName
          ("Death")) return;
```

CHAPTER 3 ARCHITECTING ENEMY AI WITH FINITE STATE MACHINES

```
    // Randomly choose a damage animation to play, ensuring
    // it's different from the last one played
        int id = Random.Range(0, countOfDamageAnimations);
        while (countOfDamageAnimations > 1 && id ==
        lastDamageAnimation)
            id = Random.Range(0, countOfDamageAnimations);

        lastDamageAnimation = id;
        animator.SetInteger("DamageID", id);
        animator.SetTrigger("Damage");
   }

   //Can be invoked from a state that requires the NPC to Jump
    public void Jump () {
        animator.SetBool ("Squat", false);
        animator.SetFloat ("Speed", 0f);
        animator.SetBool("Aiming", false);
        animator.SetTrigger ("Jump");
    }

    //Invoked from the Attack() method above.
    private void Aiming () {
        animator.SetBool ("Squat", false);
        animator.SetFloat ("Speed", 0f);
        animator.SetBool("Aiming", true);
    }

    //Can be utilized when NPC hiding from the Player
    public void Squat () {
        animator.SetBool("Squat", true);
        animator.SetBool("Aiming", false);
        animator.SetFloat("Speed", 0f);
    }
}
```

CHAPTER 3   ARCHITECTING ENEMY AI WITH FINITE STATE MACHINES

The Actions class is a comprehensive Unity script that facilitates the control and transition of animations for a non-player character (NPC) based on its current state. It primarily uses Unity's Animator component to switch animations according to various game states like idle, patrol, chase, attack, and others. This class is highly integral to the dynamic and reactive behavior of NPCs in the game. Let's proceed with analyzing this Actions class whose main purpose is to manage and trigger different animations for an NPC based on its state changes communicated via various state components like IdleState, PatrolState, ChaseState, etc., ensuring smooth and contextually appropriate animation transitions to reflect the NPC's current activities or reactions.

1. RequiredComponent: These attributes ensure that the NPC has the Animator and Health component attached.

2. animator: This private Animator field reference is used to control the animation of the NPC. It directly manipulates the NPC's animation state machine based on the different states the NPC could be in.

3. countOfDamageAnimations: An integer constant that holds the number of different damage animations available. This helps in cycling through various damage animations for variety. The Damage Layer comprises three different damage animations that are randomly selected.

4. lastDamageAnimation: This integer keeps track of the last played damage animation index. It ensures that the same damage animation is not repeated consecutively if there are multiple options.

CHAPTER 3   ARCHITECTING ENEMY AI WITH FINITE STATE MACHINES

5. OnEnable(): This method establishes event subscriptions with various state scripts to handle transitions into corresponding animations. Each GetComponent<*SomeState*>().*OnNpcEvent* += *Method*; lines register the *Method* to be called when the *OnNpcEvent* is triggered from the *SomeState* script, linking game state changes with animation changes.

6. OnDisable(): This method cleans up event subscriptions to avoid memory leaks and potential errors when the object is disabled. Each GetComponent<*SomeState*>().*OnNpcEvent* -= *Method*; lines unregister the *Method* from the *OnNpcEvent* in the *SomeState* script, ensuring clean transitions out of states.

7. Awake(): It initializes the animator field by fetching the Animator component from the same game object (i.e. Soldier_0).

8. Animation State Methods: The methods Idle(), Walk(), Run(), CrouchingRun(), Attack(), Death(), Damage(), Jump(), Aiming(), Squat() are designed to transition the NPC's animator parameters based on different game states the NPC could be in. The methods Idle(), Walk(), Run(), and CrouchingRun() adjust the Aiming, Squat, and Speed animator parameters to reflect movement states. The method Attack() sets the NPC in an aiming state, before triggering the attack animation. The method Death() stops all movement and triggers the death animation. It is important to note

that this death animation can be invoked while the NPC is in any state, be it patrolling, attacking, chasing, or taking cover. This is depicted within the SniperRifleController where the transition to the death state happens from AnyState. The method Damage() avoids playing damage animations if in the "Death" state, otherwise it randomly selects a damage animation different from the last one, updating the animator with the new damage ID. The methods Jump(), Aiming(), and Squat() handle specific actions like jumping or crouching, adjusting Aiming, Squat, and Speed parameters accordingly.

This class structure ensures that the NPC animations are dynamically and appropriately set based on their interactions and current state within the game, enhancing the realism and responsiveness of the NPC character.

Recipe 3-5: Configuring NPC Health Management

Problem

Managing the health system of NPCs within the game environment necessitates the requirement for a dedicated Health class whose primary challenge is to ensure precise tracking and updating of health levels, initiating suitable animations and responses when damage is taken, and accurately processing death events on the NPC. Additionally, this system needs to seamlessly integrate with the broader game logic, especially the NPC state machine, to appropriately modify NPC behavior in response to health-related changes.

CHAPTER 3   ARCHITECTING ENEMY AI WITH FINITE STATE MACHINES

Solution

The Health class implements a robust health management system. It initializes health at a predefined maximum and decreases it upon taking damage, invoking specific actions and animations through events. The class differentiates between NPCs and the player, invoking distinct death-handling procedures for each. For NPCs, it signals the depletion of health and death through events monitored by the NPC state machine, influencing their behavior. For the player, it sets up the potential for unique UI updates or game state changes upon death with some minor code modifications. The class also includes a testing mechanism to simulate health reduction on the NPC, via mouse clicks in a development environment.

How It Works

The Health component, attached to the NPC Soldier_0 game object, ideally exposes only the Max Health field to set the NPC's maximum health. However, as shown in Figure 3-12, the currentHealth value can also be made visible in the Inspector for testing purposes. Once testing is complete, this variable should be set to private.

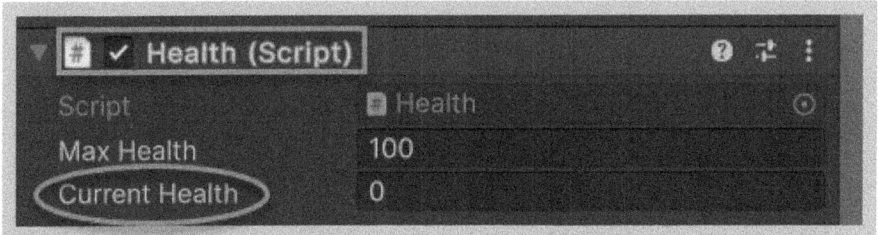

Figure 3-12. Health Component on NPC Soldier_0

253

Listing 3-3. Health script

```csharp
using UnityEngine;
using UnityEngine.InputSystem;
using System;

//Attach this Health script to your NPCs-Soldier game object
public class Health : MonoBehaviour, IHealth
{
    public event Action<string> OnHealthDepleted; //C# Event
        //invoked from TakeHealth() and listened for in
        //NPCStateMachine script.
    public event Action OnPlayerDeath; //C# Event invoked from
            //Die() and listened for in NPCStateMachine script.
    public event Action OnNpcDeath; //Being listened for in
                                    //NPCStateMachine script.

    [SerializeField] private int maxHealth = 100;

    private int currentHealth;
    private bool isDead = false;
    private Animator animator;

    public int CurrentHealth { get { return currentHealth; }
                    private set { currentHealth = value; } }

    private void Awake()
    {
        animator = GetComponent<Animator>();

    }
    private void Start()
    {
        currentHealth = maxHealth;
    }
```

CHAPTER 3   ARCHITECTING ENEMY AI WITH FINITE STATE MACHINES

```csharp
public void TakeHealth(int amount)
{
    if (!isDead)
    {
        currentHealth -= amount;
        Debug.Log($"Health is now : {currentHealth}");

        if (currentHealth <= 0)
            Die();
        else
            OnHealthDepleted?.Invoke(gameObject.tag);
   //Event being listened for in NPCStateMachine script
    }
}
public void Die()
{
    if (isDead)
        return;

    isDead = true;

    if (!gameObject.CompareTag("Player"))
    {
            OnNpcDeath?.Invoke(); //Being listened for in
                                  //NPCStateMachine script
    }
    else
    {
   //Handle player death logic here. Show Death screen etc
   //Ensure NPC goes back to Patrolling.
        Debug.Log("Player is Dead");
     //Event being listened for in NPCStateMachine.Ensures
     //that the NPC that finally killed the player stops
```

CHAPTER 3   ARCHITECTING ENEMY AI WITH FINITE STATE MACHINES

```
            //attacking and continues patrolling
                OnPlayerDeath?.Invoke();
            }
        }

        private void Update() //For Testing purposes only.
        {
            Mouse myMouse = Mouse.current ;

          //Example of triggering firing of a weapon, e.g. when the
          //player fires the weapon by clicking the left Mouse
          //Button
            if (myMouse != null)
            {
                if (myMouse.leftButton.wasPressedThisFrame)
                {
                    if (gameObject.CompareTag("NPC"))
                        TakeHealth(10); //Simulates Player
                  //shooting NPC demonstrating the Damage and Death
                  //animations on NPC.
                }
            }
        }

}
```

The Health class is a critical component in a game that manages the health of game objects, such as NPCs and the player. It defines the life management system, dictating when a character is alive, damaged, or dead. Below is a detailed analysis of this class, including its fields, properties, and methods, along with their significance and operational logic in relation to the NPC. Note that this class inherits from Monobehaviour and implements the IHealth interface.

CHAPTER 3   ARCHITECTING ENEMY AI WITH FINITE STATE MACHINES

1. Events: The class begins by declaring three C# Action events:

   - OnHealthDepleted: Triggered when the NPC's health decreases but hasn't reached zero. This event is being listened to within the NPCStateMachine class. It results in the NPC either playing a damage animation or taking cover if its health is less than 50.

   - OnPlayerDeath: Invoked when the player's health reaches zero, influencing game flow like showing a death screen or resetting the game. This has not been setup as the goal of this chapter and its recipes are about the Enemy AI system. However, it could be set up easily with minor code modifications.

   - OnNpcDeath: Triggered when an NPC's health reaches zero and is used to switch the NPC's state to "dead." This event is being listened for within the NPCStateMachine class and switches the SateMachine to the DeathState resulting in the Death() method within the Actions script being invoked.

2. maxHealth (Serialized Field): Defines the maximum health with which an NPC begins, and this value is adjustable in the Inspector for various game objects. Beyond its application to NPCs, this component is versatile enough to be utilized on the player and inanimate game objects, such as explodable crates and barrels.

CHAPTER 3   ARCHITECTING ENEMY AI WITH FINITE STATE MACHINES

3. currentHealth: It keeps track of the NPC's current health. Changes in this value affect the game's visual and logical response to NPC damage.

4. isDead: This boolean flag indicates whether the NPC is dead. This prevents redundant logic from executing once the NPC has died. If the Health component were attached to the Player, then this flag would indicate whether the Player was dead.

5. CurrentHealth property: Allows controlled access to currentHealth, ensuring that only internal logic can modify this vital game statistic.

6. Start(): This method sets the initial currentHealth to maxHealth when the game object is activated, preparing the NPC for gameplay.

7. TakeHealth(int amount): Decreases the NPC health by the specified amount and triggers events or death logic based on the resultant health. It ensures no action is taken if the NPC is already dead. However, In the event the NPC is not dead, the NPC's health is reduced and the new health value is logged. if reducing the health results in the NPC health reaching zero or less, the Die() method is invoked, otherwise, the OnHealthDepleted event is invoked, notifying the NPCStateMachine component that it eventually needs to invoke either the HitState or the CoverState for the NPC.

8. Die(): Finalizes the death of the NPC by setting the isDead flag to true, marking the NPC as dead and triggering appropriate events. If isDead is true the method is exited, preventing re-entry or

redundant execution when the NPC is already dead. It then goes on to check the character type (Player or NPC) and triggers the corresponding event, managing different logic paths for each character type. In the case of the NPC death, the OnNpcDeath event is invoked which is being listened for within the NPCStateMachine component, which in turn ensures that the NPC transitions into the DeathState.

9. Update(): This method, designed for testing purposes only, simulates NPC damage upon a left mouse button click using Unity's new Input System. It checks the mouse state and, if the left button is clicked and the object is an NPC, deducts ten health points to simulate the NPC being shot at. This method can be adapted or removed based on production requirements.

This class structure ensures that the character's (NPC or Player) health is not only a numeric value but also a trigger for various game dynamics, enhancing the interactivity and realism of the game environment.

Recipe 3-6: Coding the NPC State Machine

Problem

Setting up complex NPC behavior, such as patrolling, chasing the player when sighted, attacking when within range, seeking cover when hit, dying when health reaches zero, returning to chasing after fleeing, and resuming patrolling when the player is lost, can be challenging to code without a state machine, as each NPC behavior must be manually handled with extensive conditional logic, making the code difficult to understand, maintain, and debug. Also, adding new behaviors or modifying existing ones can become cumbersome and error-prone. This can result in unintended interactions between states, inefficient performance, and a higher likelihood of bugs.

Solution

Utilizing a state machine to manage NPC behavior significantly simplifies the development process. A state machine allows for a clear definition and organization of various NPC states, such as patrolling, chasing, attacking, seeking cover, and dying. It ensures that the NPC can only be in one state at a time, with well-defined transitions between states based on specific conditions. This approach reduces the need for extensive conditional logic, making the code more readable, maintainable, and less prone to errors. Additionally, a state machine facilitates the addition of new behaviors and modification of existing ones without introducing unintended interactions or performance inefficiencies. By structuring NPC behavior through a state machine, developers can create more robust and responsive game entities, enhancing the overall gameplay experience.

How It Works

Finite state machines (FSMs) have been fundamental to computer game programming since its inception. An FSM is an abstract computational model that can exist in one of several defined states at any given time, specifying conditions that dictate transitions between these states. The current state determines the machine's behavior and outputs.

In the game Super Mario, for example, Mario is controlled by an FSM. He can be in states such as running, jumping, swimming, or invincible. Each state dictates its behavior, like defeating enemies or interacting with the environment. For instance, when Mario collects a Super Star, he transitions to the invincible state, allowing him to defeat

CHAPTER 3   ARCHITECTING ENEMY AI WITH FINITE STATE MACHINES

enemies on contact. Transition conditions, such as collecting items or player input, define how and when these states change.

Anyone familiar with Unity's Animator is acquainted with state machines. The Animator comprises states like Idle, Walk, Run, JumpStart, JumpLand, InAir, and Attack, each with its animation. A character can only be in one state at a time, with transitions triggered by inputs or interactions with the game environment.

FSMs provide a robust framework for modeling complex behaviors in systems with a finite number of states. Their simplicity and versatility make them indispensable in game development, enabling developers to create sophisticated and responsive behaviors for game entities.

The state machine created in this recipe can be utilized not only for NPCs as part of the Enemy AI system but also for the player character. Figure 3-13 illustrates the NPC state machine, detailing the various states and possible transitions between them.

The NPC starts in the Idle state and has an equal probability of transitioning into either the Patrol or Wander state. In both the Patrol and Wander states, if the NPC spots the player, it transitions to the Chase state and pursues the player. Once within attacking range, the NPC enters the Attack state and begins shooting at the player. As shown in Figure 3-13, the double-sided arrows indicate that these state transitions can flow bidirectionally.

The state transitions depicted in Figure 3-13 from the Hit state to the Cover state and from the Hit state to the Death state are one-way transitions. Upon being hit, the NPC transitions to the Hit state, where its health is assessed. If the health reaches zero, the NPC transitions to the Death state, triggering the death animation and subsequently destroying the NPC after a predefined delay. If the health is not zero and is above fifty, a random damage animation is played to indicate the NPC was hit. However, if the health is below fifty but not zero, the NPC transitions to the Cover state, where it searches for the nearest or furthest location to hide from the player. The AnyState in the diagram does not represent a specific

CHAPTER 3 ARCHITECTING ENEMY AI WITH FINITE STATE MACHINES

state within the state machine; instead, it signifies that the NPC can transition into the Hit state from any of the existing states, namely, Idle, Patrol, Wander, Chase, Attack, and Cover.

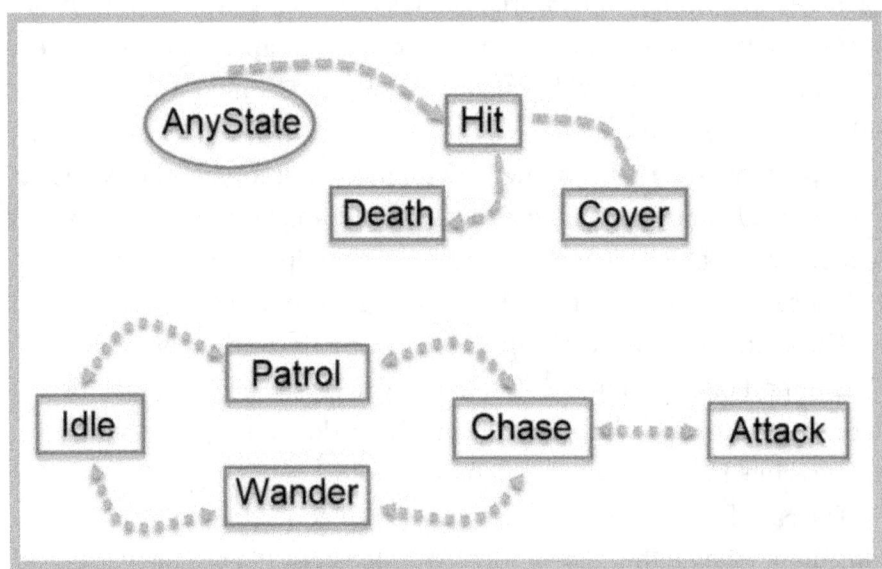

Figure 3-13. *NPC state machine*

Figure 3-14 depicts two core classes that form the foundation of an NPC state machine system: StateMachine and NPCStateMachine. The StateMachine class is an abstract base class that manages the current and previous states of an NPC, providing methods for state transitions and state updates. It ensures that each state is entered and exited properly, maintaining a smooth flow of state transitions. The NPCStateMachine class, which inherits from StateMachine, is tailored specifically for NPCs. It includes properties and methods relevant to NPC behavior, such as detecting the player's visibility, determining attack range, and rotating to face the player. Additionally, it encapsulates commonly used methods, providing a centralized and efficient way to manage complex NPC behaviors. The depicted states—Idle, Patrol, Wander, Chase, and

CHAPTER 3 ARCHITECTING ENEMY AI WITH FINITE STATE MACHINES

Attack—represent the specific behaviors an NPC can adopt at any given time, with transitions between them managed by the StateMachine. The NPCStateMachine class, as illustrated, effectively manages these states and transitions, ensuring that NPC behavior is both dynamic and responsive. Similarly, a PlayerStateMachine can be created to manage the various states of a player's character. By leveraging a finite state machine, both NPC and player behaviors can be controlled with precision, enhancing the overall gameplay experience. This structured approach is particularly beneficial in providing a clear and maintainable framework for complex state management.

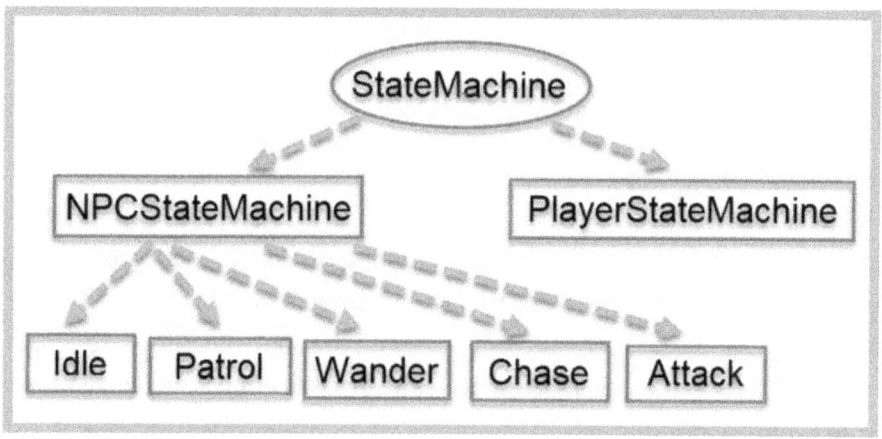

Figure 3-14. *State inheritance*

Listing 3-4. StateMachine abstract class

```
using UnityEngine;
public abstract class StateMachine : MonoBehaviour
{
    private IState currentState;
    private IState previousState;  //Track the previous state
```

```
    public IState PreviousState => previousState;
    public void SwitchState(IState newState)
    {
        currentState?.OnStateExit();
        previousState = currentState;
        currentState = newState;
        currentState?.OnStateEnter();
    }
    private void Update()
    {
        currentState?.OnStateUpdate(Time.deltaTime);
    }
}
```

The abstract StateMachine class provided as part of Listing 3-4 leverages the concept of a state machine by handling different states and the smooth and logical transitions between them. Let's proceed with analyzing this class whose purpose is to manage the current and previous states of an NPC or Player game object using the state machine pattern. It allows for dynamic transitions between behaviors or actions based on game events or conditions.

1. The StateMachine class extends MonoBehaviour, enabling derived classes to be attached as components to game objects in Unity.

2. currentState: This private field of type IState holds a reference to the current state of the NPC. It defines the active behavior or action the NPC is performing.

3. previousState: This private field of type IState keeps track of the state the NPC was in just before the current state. It is essential for situations where the NPC needs to revert to its immediate last state, such

CHAPTER 3 ARCHITECTING ENEMY AI WITH FINITE STATE MACHINES

as after being hit and then recovering. Consider an NPC that can be in various states like Chasing, Attacking, Patrolling, or Wandering. When the NPC is hit, you want it to temporarily switch to the Hit state, where it plays its taking damage (being hit) animation, and then have it immediately revert to whatever it was doing before being hit, which could be either chasing or attacking the player or simply patrolling or wandering. Thus if the NPC is in one of its usual states, say Patrolling state, and then receives damage (shot at), it needs to transition to the Hit state to play a hit reaction animation or effect. After the hit reaction, the NPC should return to the Patrolling state and not to any other random state.

4. PreviousState: A read-only property of type IState that provides external access to the previousState field, allowing other parts of the game logic to reference or use the last state information if needed.

5. SwitchState(IState newState): This method enables transitioning from the current state to a new state as follows:

    - currentState?.OnStateExit(): Invokes the OnStateExit() method of the current state if it exists, performing any necessary cleanup or transition effects.

    - previousState = currentState: Updates the previousState with the current state before it changes, preserving the last state for potential future use.

    - currentState = newState: Sets the new state as the current state.

- currentState?.OnStateEnter(): Invokes the OnStateEnter() method of the newly set state to initialize or set up any necessary behavior or conditions.

6. Update(): The Update() method continuously updates the current state as part of the game loop. The statement currentState?.OnStateUpdate(Time.deltaTime); - invokes the OnStateUpdate() method of the current state, passing in the time elapsed since the last frame, which allows the current state to perform its ongoing actions or checks, until some condition within it forces it to break out from within its OnStateUpdate() method.

Here's how this StateMachine functions using a simple example of when the NPC is not engaged in any specific action and is just idle. Here's a simplified explanation of how the StateMachine class would process the Idle state:

1. The StateMachine will call the OnStateEnter() method on the Idle state class when the NPC transitions into this state. This is typically triggered by the StateMachine using its SwitchState() method to change the current state to the Idle state.

2. Next, the OnStateUpdate() method is called continuously (every frame in the Update() method of StateMachine). This method checks the NPC's surroundings or other conditions to determine the next state. In the event the NPC detects the Player, the state machine switches to the Chase state using the SwitchState() method.

CHAPTER 3   ARCHITECTING ENEMY AI WITH FINITE STATE MACHINES

3. Finally, the OnStateExit() method is called when the NPC is about to leave the Idle state on account of spotting the Player and transitioning into the Chase state.

Throughout this process, the StateMachine class is responsible for managing these transitions by invoking the OnStateEnter(), OnStateUpdate(), and OnStateExit() methods at the appropriate times based on the game's logic and events. The StateMachine essentially orchestrates when to enter, update, and exit each state based on the NPC's interactions and the game environment.

Listing 3-5. StateMachine abstract class

```
public interface IState
{
    public void OnStateEnter();
    public void OnStateUpdate(float deltaTime);
    public void OnStateExit();
}
```

The IState interface provided as part of Listing 3-5 plays a crucial role in defining a common structure for all states that can be managed by the StateMachine class. The IState interface defines three essential methods: OnStateEnter(), OnStateUpdate(), and OnStateExit(). These methods provide a uniform way to interact with different states, ensuring that any class implementing IState will have these methods implemented. This standardization means that the StateMachine can manage any state implementing IState without needing to know the specific details of each state. It can call these methods on any state object, allowing for a flexible and extensible system where new states can be added easily.

CHAPTER 3   ARCHITECTING ENEMY AI WITH FINITE STATE MACHINES

The StateMachine holds a reference to the current state as an IState. This allows the StateMachine to invoke OnStateEnter(), OnStateUpdate(), and OnStateExit() on whichever state is currently active. When transitioning between states, the StateMachine uses these methods to ensure that each state correctly initializes itself (OnStateEnter()), performs its logic during each frame (OnStateUpdate()), and cleans up when exiting (OnStateExit()). You will explore several states that implement the IState interface in upcoming recipes.

In summary, the IState interface acts as a contract that ensures consistency and predictability in how states are managed within the StateMachine. It allows the StateMachine to remain decoupled from the specifics of each state, promoting a modular and maintainable design in the game's architecture.

Listing 3-6. NPCStateMachine class

```
using System.Collections.Generic;
using System.Linq;
using UnityEngine;

public class NPCStateMachine : StateMachine
{
    [Tooltip("NPC's distance from Player to begin Chase.")]
    [SerializeField] private float visibleChaseDistance = 15f;
    [Tooltip("NPC's visibility angle for initiating chase")]
    [SerializeField] private float visibleChaseAngle = 70f;
    [Tooltip("NPC's visibility angle for initiating chase")]
    [SerializeField] private float attackDistance = 3f;
    [Tooltip("NPC's stopping distance from Player whilst
             Chasing it")]

    public List<IState> states = new List<IState>();
    private IState startingState;
```

CHAPTER 3   ARCHITECTING ENEMY AI WITH FINITE STATE MACHINES

```
private Transform player;//Reference to the Player
                        //transform
private float rotSpeed = 1.5f;
private bool  isPlayerDead;

//Properties
public Transform Player => player;

void OnEnable()
{
  GetComponent<Health>().OnNpcDeath += NpcDead;
  GetComponent<Health>().OnHealthDepleted += TakeDamage;

}

void OnDisable()
{
    GetComponent<Health>().OnNpcDeath -= NpcDead;
GetComponent<Health>().OnHealthDepleted -= TakeDamage;

}

private void Awake()
{
    states = GetComponents<IState>().ToList();
    if (states.Count == 0)
    {
        Debug.LogError($"[NPCStateMachine -
        {gameObject.name}] : No NPC States found.");
        return;
    }
```

CHAPTER 3 ARCHITECTING ENEMY AI WITH FINITE STATE MACHINES

```
        player = GameObject.FindWithTag("Player").transform;
        if (player == null)
        {
            Debug.LogError($"[NPCStateMachine - 
            {gameObject.name}] : Player not found.");
            return;
        }
    }
    void Start()
    {
        //Selects Idle state as default starting state
        startingState = states.Find(s => s.GetType() == 
        typeof(IdleState));
        if (!isPlayerDead)
            SwitchState(startingState);
    }

    /*** Commonly used Methods that can be accessed from any 
        State ***/
    public bool IsPlayerVisible()
    {
        Vector3 npcToPlayerDir = player.transform.position - 
        this.transform.position;
        float angle = Vector3.Angle(npcToPlayerDir, 
        this.transform.forward);

        if(npcToPlayerDir.magnitude < visibleChaseDistance && 
        angle < visibleChaseAngle)
            return true;
        else
            return false;
    }
```

CHAPTER 3 ARCHITECTING ENEMY AI WITH FINITE STATE MACHINES

```
public bool IsPlayerAttackable()
{
        Vector3 npcToPlayerDir = player.transform.position -
        this.transform.position;

        if (npcToPlayerDir.magnitude < attackDistance)
            return true;
        else
            return false;
}

    //Have NPC Rotate to face the player.
    public void RotateToFacePlayer()
    {
        Vector3 npcToPlayerDir = player.transform.position -
        this.transform.position;
        npcToPlayerDir.y = 0;
        this.transform.rotation =
        Quaternion.Slerp(this.transform.rotation,Quaternion.
        LookRotation(npcToPlayerDir),Time.deltaTime *
        rotSpeed);
    }

    private void NpcDead()
    {
        IState death = states.Find(s => s.GetType() ==
        typeof(DeathState));
        SwitchState(death);
    }

    private void TakeDamage(string objTag)
    {
      if(objTag == "NPC")
```

CHAPTER 3   ARCHITECTING ENEMY AI WITH FINITE STATE MACHINES

```
        {
            if ((GetComponent<Health>().CurrentHealth < 50))
            {
                Debug.Log("NPC Health < 50% - Taking Cover");
                IState takeCover = states.Find(s => s.GetType() ==
                typeof(CoverState));
                SwitchState(takeCover);
                return;
            }
            Debug.Log("NPC Has been Hit");
            IState hit = states.Find(s => s.GetType() ==
            typeof(HitState));
            SwitchState(hit);
        }
    else if (objTag == "Player")
    {
            //Deal with Player Health damage response.
    }
}
```

The NPCStateMachine class provided as part of Listing 3-6 is a specialized implementation of a StateMachine designed to manage the various states and behaviors of a non-player character (NPC) in a game. This class orchestrates transitions between states based on game conditions and player interactions, ensuring the NPC reacts intelligently to its environment.

The NPCStateMachine serves as a centralized control point that is ideally positioned to manage all state transitions because it holds references to all states within its states list and other crucial game parameters like player position, attacking distance, visible chase distance, visible chase angle, etc. It facilitates efficient event management by having

CHAPTER 3   ARCHITECTING ENEMY AI WITH FINITE STATE MACHINES

event handlers like NpcDead and NpcHit within the NPCStateMachine class that ensure that state transitions based on these events are managed centrally, avoiding redundancy and ensuring consistency across different states.

Placing commonly used methods such as IsPlayerVisible(), IsPlayerAttackable(), and RotateToFacePlayer() in NPCStateMachine allows all states to access these behaviors without duplicating code, leading to cleaner, more maintainable code.

This centralized approach allows for a modular yet cohesive behavior management system, where each state can focus on specific actions while the state machine handles the broader logic of state transitions and shared actions.

Let's break down this class and its elements to understand its functionality in detail.

1. visibleChaseDistance, visibleChaseAngle, attackDistance: These fields define the NPC's sensory parameters for detecting and responding to the player. They determine how far and at what angle the NPC can start chasing the player and the distance within which it can attack.

2. states: This list which is of type IState holds all the states the NPC can transition into. Each state is an implementation of the IState interface, enabling polymorphic behavior handling. Each of the states you will go on to create in upcoming recipes extends MonoBehaviour and implements the IState interface. This allows you to attach each state to your NPC game object as a component, and you must do so.

CHAPTER 3   ARCHITECTING ENEMY AI WITH FINITE STATE MACHINES

3. startingState: The initial state of the NPC, usually IdleState. It's where the NPC starts its behavior cycle.

4. player: A reference to the player's transform, used to calculate distances, angles, and directions for various state transitions.

5. rotSpeed: Determines how quickly the NPC rotates to face the player, enhancing realism in movements, especially during interactions like chasing or attacking.

6. isPlayerDead: A flag indicating the player's status, which could influence the NPC's behavior (not actively used in the provided code but essential for potential extensions).

7. OnEnable() and OnDisable(): Enable subscribing and unsubscribing from NPC health-related events (OnNpcDeath, OnHealthDepleted) that ensure appropriate state transitions upon health events occurring.

8. Awake(): Here you initialize the states list and validate the presence of required components and the player. You fetch all attached state behaviors (GetComponents<IState>().ToList()) and store a reference to them within the state's list. If no states are found or the player transform is missing, you log appropriate errors and halt further setup to prevent runtime errors.

CHAPTER 3   ARCHITECTING ENEMY AI WITH FINITE STATE MACHINES

9. Start(): Here you set the NPC's initial state. You find the IdleState in the state's list and switch to it unless isPlayerDead is true.

10. IsPlayerVisible(): Here you determine if the player is within the NPC's field of view and chase distance. You calculate the direction, angle, and distance to the player and check against visibleChaseDistance and visibleChaseAngle to decide on visibility. This method is invoked by several states, namely, Idle, Patrol, and Wander, as will be explored in later recipes.

11. IsPlayerAttackable(): Here you check if the player is within the NPC's attack range, by calculating the distance to the player and comparing it with attackDistance. This method is invoked from within the Chase state.

12. RotateToFacePlayer(): Here you gradually rotate the NPC to face the player, enhancing visual realism. You compute the direction to the player and adjust rotation using Quaternion.Slerp(), and apply it, considering rotSpeed. Setting npcToPlayerDir.y to zero is a common technique used in 3D games to ensure that the rotation of the NPC focuses solely on the horizontal (XZ) plane. By setting npcToPlayerDir.y to zero, you effectively ignore any vertical difference between the NPC and the player. This adjustment ensures that the NPC rotates to face the player horizontally without tilting upward or downward, regardless of any elevation differences between them.

13. NpcDead(): When this event handler is triggered in response to the OnNpcDeath event being invoked, you transition the NPC to its DeathState. You find the DeathState from the state's list and switch to it.

14. TakeDamage(): When this event handler is triggered in response to the OnHealthDepleted event being invoked, you transition the NPC to either its HitState or the CoverState based on the health threshold. If health falls below 50%, switch to CoverState; otherwise, switch to HitState. In the CoverState the NPC looks for a hiding spot that could be either closest or farthest from the player. In the HitState the NPC plays a damage animation and returns to its immediate last (previous) state. You will be exploring these states in upcoming recipes.

Note Quaternion.Slerp(from, to, t) interpolates between two quaternion rotations "from" and "to" by a fraction "t," where "t" is a value between 0 and 1. The interpolation is spherical, meaning it follows the shortest path on the quaternion's four-dimensional sphere, resulting in a smooth and constant-speed rotation.

The parameter "from" is this.transform.rotation, which represents the current rotation of the NPC.

The parameter "to" is Quaternion.LookRotation(npcToPlayerDir), which creates a quaternion looking in the direction of npcToPlayerDir, where npcToPlayerDir has been adjusted to ignore vertical differences (npcToPlayerDir.y = 0). This ensures the target rotation is strictly in the horizontal plane (XZ).

CHAPTER 3 ARCHITECTING ENEMY AI WITH FINITE STATE MACHINES

The parameter "t" is Time.deltaTime * rotSpeed, which scales the interpolation fraction by the time passed since the last frame and a rotation speed factor (rotSpeed). This means that the rotation adjustment is frame-rate independent and can be adjusted for speed using rotSpeed.

At each frame, Quaternion.Slerp() calculates an intermediate rotation from the current rotation (from) towards the target rotation (to). The amount of rotation applied in each frame is controlled by (t), ensuring the NPC turns towards the player gradually.

The use of Slerp (Spherical Linear Interpolation) ensures the rotation transition is smooth and avoids abrupt changes. It also ensures the rotation is done over the shortest path on the unit quaternion sphere, which is the most direct rotational path in 3D space.

By multiplying Time.deltaTime by rotSpeed, the rotation speed remains consistent across different frame rates. A higher rotSpeed results in a faster turn towards the player, while a lower value results in a slower, more gradual turn.

Note IState death = states.Find(s => s.GetType() == typeof(DeathState));

The above statement is used to search through a list of IState objects, each representing a different state that an NPC can be in, such as Idle, Patrol, Chase, Hit, Cover, Death, etc.

Here, states is a List<IState> referencing various NPC states. The Find() method searches this list for the first state that matches a specified condition, provided as a lambda expression "s => s.GetType() == typeof(DeathState)." In this expression, "s" represents each state in the list, and the condition checks if the type of "s" is DeathState.

The Find() method iterates over the state's list, evaluating s.GetType() == typeof(DeathState) for each state "s." It returns the first state that meets this condition, or null if no such state is found. This approach efficiently identifies the DeathState instance for the NPC to transition into upon death.

Recipe 3-7: Implementing Enemy AI Idle State

Problem

The NPC state machine needs to be initialized with an appropriate state to start with, apart from having a Non-Player Character (NPC) during periods of inactivity and having a default behavior to transition to.

Solution

The IdleState class, as part of the NPC's state machine, initializes the NPC in an idle state and monitors for conditions to transition to other states like Chase, Patrol, or Wander. It leverages the NavMeshAgent for movement controls and employs a state machine pattern to dynamically switch states based on game events and randomness. This approach ensures that the NPC behaves intelligently and responsively in the game environment, enhancing the player's experience.

How It Works

The IdleState class is a specific state in the state machine architecture of an NPC. It represents the state where the NPC is not actively engaging in any specific activity, such as chasing or attacking, but is instead idling, waiting for a trigger to change its behavior. This state monitors the environment and decides the next state based on certain conditions being met, such as the player coming into view, and then transitioning to the appropriate state like chasing, patrolling, or wandering.

Listing 3-7. IdleState class

```
using System;
using UnityEngine;
using UnityEngine.AI;
using Random = UnityEngine.Random;

//States have access to MonoBehaviour methods too.
//All States must be added as components to the NPC game
//object.
public class IdleState : MonoBehaviour, IState
{
    public event Action OnNpcIdle; //Being listened for in
                                   //Actions script.

    private NPCStateMachine stateMachine;
    private NavMeshAgent agent; // Reference to the soldier
                            //NPC Agent

    void Awake()
    {
        stateMachine = GetComponent<NPCStateMachine>();
        if (stateMachine == null)
```

CHAPTER 3   ARCHITECTING ENEMY AI WITH FINITE STATE MACHINES

```
        {
            Debug.LogError($"[IdleState - {gameObject.name}] : 
            NPCStateMachine not found.");
            return;
        }

         agent = GetComponent<NavMeshAgent>();
         if (agent == null)
         {
             Debug.LogError($"[IdleState - {gameObject.name}] : 
             No NavMesh Agent found.");
             return;
         }
    }

    void IState.OnStateEnter()
    {
        if(agent.enabled)
            agent.isStopped = true;
        else
            return;

        OnNpcIdle?.Invoke(); //Being listened for in Actions
                            //script.

        Debug.Log("IdleState: Enter");
    }

    void IState.OnStateUpdate(float deltaTime)
    {
        if (stateMachine.IsPlayerVisible())
        {
            IState chase = stateMachine.states.Find(s =>
            s.GetType() == typeof(ChaseState));
```

```
            stateMachine.SwitchState(chase);
        }
        else //Player not visible - provide 50% chance of
            //entering either Wander or Patrol states
        {
            if (Random.Range(0, 100) < 50)
            {
                IState patrol = stateMachine.states.Find(s =>
                s.GetType() == typeof(PatrolState));
                Debug.Log("IdleState: Switching to Patrol
                State");
                stateMachine.SwitchState(patrol);
            }
            else
            {
                IState wander = stateMachine.states.Find(s =>
                s.GetType() == typeof(WanderState));
                Debug.Log("IdleState: Switching to Wander
                State");
                stateMachine.SwitchState(wander);
            }
        }
    }

    void IState.OnStateExit()
    {
        Debug.Log("IdleState: Exit");
    }
}
```

CHAPTER 3 ARCHITECTING ENEMY AI WITH FINITE STATE MACHINES

This class inherits from MonoBehaviour and implements the IHealth interface, allowing it to be attached to the NPC game object and access MonoBehaviour methods. Ensure this script is a component of the NPC game object. This analysis will delve into the class's code functionality in detail.

1. OnNpcIdle: An action event that is triggered when the NPC enters the idle state. This event is being listened for in the Actions script and invokes the Idle() method therein, triggering the NPC's idle animation.

2. stateMachine: A reference to the NPCStateMachine component attached to the same NPC GameObject. This allows the IdleState to request state transitions based on game logic, accessing other states and invoking SwitchState() as needed.

3. agent: A reference to the NavMeshAgent component of the NPC. This is crucial for controlling the NPC's movement, particularly to stop it when the NPC is in an idle state.

4. Awake(): Here you initialize the class by setting up the necessary references. It retrieves the NPCStateMachine attached to the NPC, allowing for state control. It then obtains the NavMeshAgent to manage movement. In the event a NaMeshAgent component is not available an error is logged to the console.

5. IState.OnStateEnter(): This method is activated when the NPC transitions into the idle state. It checks to ensure that the agent is enabled and then stops the NPC's movement by halting the

CHAPTER 3   ARCHITECTING ENEMY AI WITH FINITE STATE MACHINES

NavMeshAgent. The event OnNpcIdle is then invoked which triggers subscribed actions (within the Actions script) ensuring the NPC becomes idle.

6. IState.OnStateUpdate(float deltaTime): This method is executed each frame, and checks if the player is visible, in which case it transitions to the ChaseState using the SwitchState() method of the state machine. If the player is not visible, it randomly decides whether to switch to the PatrolState or WanderState, enabling dynamic behavior based on a simple probability.

7. IState.OnStateExit(): This method is activated when the NPC is leaving the idle state. It simply logs a message to the console to assist in debugging by showing when the NPC moves out of the idle state.

The IdleState heavily relies on the NPCStateMachine for its operation. It uses "stateMachine" to transition to other states based on the NPC's perception of the player and randomized behavior choices.

The use of "stateMachine.states.Find(s => s.GetType() == typeof(ChaseState))" and similar lines of code allows for dynamic lookup of states to transition into, ensuring that the NPC can respond to changes in its environment by moving to the most appropriate state.

This structure allows the IdleState to serve as a foundational behavior where the NPC can assess its surroundings and decide on the next course of action, maintaining the flexibility and responsiveness needed for realistic NPC behavior in a game.

Recipe 3-8: Implementing Enemy AI Patrol State

Problem

An essential game mechanic is required for automating NPC patrol behavior within the gaming environment, transitioning NPCs from the IdleState to navigate predefined waypoints autonomously. A class that ensures seamless transitions to a chase state upon player detection and manages pathfinding and waypoint selection to prevent repetitive or stagnant NPC movement, would help enhance gameplay engagement.

Solution

A Patrol state that leverages Unity's NavMeshAgent to direct NPC movement along a series of predefined waypoints, enhancing the game's realism and dynamism. Upon entering the PatrolState, the NPC's speed is set, and it moves towards the next waypoint. If the player becomes visible during the patrol, the NPC switches to the ChaseState. The FindNextPoint() method ensures diverse patrol paths by selecting a random waypoint that is different from the last, preventing repetitive movement patterns.

How It Works

The PatrolState class is a state component for the NPCStateMachine, managing the patrol behavior where the NPC moves between predefined randomized waypoints. This state ensures the NPC keeps moving along a set path of waypoints unless interrupted by the player's appearance, prompting a transition to a chase state.

CHAPTER 3 ARCHITECTING ENEMY AI WITH FINITE STATE MACHINES

Listing 3-8. PatrolState class

```
using System;
using UnityEngine;
using UnityEngine.AI;
using Random = UnityEngine.Random;

//States have access to MonoBheaviour methods too.
//All States must be added as components to the NPC
game object.
public class PatrolState : MonoBehaviour, IState
{
    public event Action OnNpcPatrol; //Being listened for in
                                     //Actions script.
    [Tooltip("Patrol points assigned to this NPC")]
    [SerializeField] private Transform[] wayPoints;

    [Tooltip("Speed at which NavMeshAgent moves")]
    [SerializeField] private float npcSpeed = 1.5f;

    private NPCStateMachine stateMachine;
    private NavMeshAgent agent; //Reference to the soldier NPC
                                //Agent
    private Vector3 target; //target is the Patrol point
    private int lastWaypointIndex = -1; //Initialize to an
                                        //impossible index

    void Awake()
    {
        stateMachine = GetComponent<NPCStateMachine>();
        if (stateMachine == null)
```

```csharp
    {
        Debug.LogError($"[PatrolState - {gameObject.name}] :
        NPCStateMachine not found.");
        return;
    }

    agent = GetComponent<NavMeshAgent>();
    if (agent == null)
    {
        Debug.LogError($"[PatrolState-{gameObject.name}] :
        No NavMesh Agent found.");
        return;
    }
}

void IState.OnStateEnter()
{
    if (agent.enabled)
    {
        agent.speed = npcSpeed;
        agent.isStopped = false;
        target = FindNextPoint();
        agent.SetDestination(target);
    }
    else
        return;

    OnNpcPatrol?.Invoke(); //Being listened for in Actions
                          //script.
    Debug.Log("PatrolState: Enter");
}
```

CHAPTER 3   ARCHITECTING ENEMY AI WITH FINITE STATE MACHINES

```
void IState.OnStateUpdate(float deltaTime)
{
    if (agent.enabled)
    {
     //Check if the agent has reached its current
    //destination
        if (agent.remainingDistance <=
           agent.stoppingDistance)
        {
            if (!agent.hasPath ||
            agent.velocity.sqrMagnitude == 0f)
            {
                target = FindNextPoint();
                agent.SetDestination(target);
            }
        }
    }

    if (stateMachine.IsPlayerVisible())
    {
        IState chase = stateMachine.states.Find(s =>
        s.GetType() == typeof(ChaseState));
        stateMachine.SwitchState(chase);
    }

}
void IState.OnStateExit()
{
    Debug.Log("PatrolState: Exit");
}
```

CHAPTER 3   ARCHITECTING ENEMY AI WITH FINITE STATE MACHINES

```
    private Vector3 FindNextPoint()//Find the next random
                                  //patrol point
{
        if (wayPoints.Length == 0)
        {
            Debug.LogError("No waypoints assigned to Patrol
            behavior.");
            return transform.position; //Return current
                                      //position if no waypoints.
        }
        int rndIndex;
        do
        {
            rndIndex = Random.Range(0, wayPoints.Length);
        } while (wayPoints.Length > 1 && rndIndex ==
          lastWaypointIndex);//Ensure it's not the same if
                            //there's more than one point

        lastWaypointIndex = rndIndex;//Store the index of the
                                    //chosen waypoint
        return wayPoints[rndIndex].position;
    }
}
```

Ensure this script is a component of the NPC game object. Let's delve into this class's code in detail.

1. OnNpcPatrol: An event triggered when the NPC transitions to the patrol state. This event is being listened for in the Actions script and invokes the Walk() method therein, triggering the NPC's walk/patrol animation.

CHAPTER 3   ARCHITECTING ENEMY AI WITH FINITE STATE MACHINES

2. wayPoints: An array of Transform objects that mark the patrol path for the NPC. The NPC navigates from one waypoint to the next randomly. You need to populate these patrol points via the Inspector.

3. NPCSpeed: Here you set the movement speed of the NPC when patrolling, controlling how fast the NPC moves towards its targets.

4. stateMachine: A reference to the NPCStateMachine component attached to the same NPC GameObject. This allows the PatrolState to request state transitions based on game logic, accessing other states and invoking SwitchState() as needed.

5. agent: A reference to the NavMeshAgent component of the NPC. This is crucial for controlling the NPC's movement, particularly to set it in motion when the NPC is in the patrol state.

6. target: Represents the current waypoint target the NPC needs to move towards.

7. lastWaypointIndex: Tracks the index of the last waypoint visited to avoid revisiting the same point consecutively.

8. Awake(): Here you initialize "stateMachine" and "agent" by fetching them from the same NPC GameObject this script is attached to. if an agent is not found, you log an error, ensuring the state can't operate without this essential component.

9. IState.OnStateEnter(): Here you activate the NavMeshAgent and set its speed, ensuring it is not stopped upon entering this state. You then find

CHAPTER 3 ARCHITECTING ENEMY AI WITH FINITE STATE MACHINES

its very first waypoint using FindNextPoint() and set it as the agent's destination. You then invoke the OnNpcPatrol event that triggers subscribed actions (within the Actions script) ensuring the NPC begins patrolling the environment. You finally log a message to the console stating that you have entered the Patrol state.

10. IState.OnStateUpdate(float deltaTime): This method is executed each frame, and checks if the NPC has reached its current target. If so, it finds the next point and updates the agent destination. You also check to see if the player is visible (stateMachine.IsPlayerVisible()), and if so transition to the ChaseState.

11. IState.OnStateExit(): This method is activated when the NPC is leaving the patrol state. It simply logs a message to the console to assist in debugging by showing when the NPC moves out of the patrol state.

12. FindNextPoint(): This method determines the next waypoint for the NPC. It ensures the new waypoint is not the same as the last one by selecting randomly from the wayPoints array. It returns either the newly selected waypoint or the NPC's current position if no waypoints are defined, thereby avoiding errors and ensuring the NPC remains functional.

This design ensures that the PatrolState is both autonomous in handling routine navigation and integrated with the broader NPC logic to respond to player actions, maintaining gameplay engagement and NPC realism.

CHAPTER 3   ARCHITECTING ENEMY AI WITH FINITE STATE MACHINES

Recipe 3-9: Implementing Enemy AI Wander State

Problem

Apart from the NPC's predictable patrolling movement, it would be a lot more engaging if the Non-Player Characters (NPCs) exhibited unpredictable and dynamic movements within the game environment.

Solution

This can be achieved by autonomously guiding NPCs to explore within a predefined radius, while also facilitating smooth transitions to other behavioral states, such as chasing, as required by game conditions. This ability to generate random, yet accessible, navigation points will ensure that NPCs behave realistically, avoiding repetitive or static patterns that could detract from the game's immersion. The WanderState class enables NPCs to navigate randomly within a specified radius, using Unity's NavMesh system for pathfinding. The state recalculates random destinations as needed, transitioning seamlessly to a chase state if the player becomes visible. This approach further enhances NPC dynamism and realism in the game environment.

How It Works

The WanderState class manages the behavior of an NPC in a "wander" mode, using the NavMeshAgent to randomly move around within a specified radius. This state allows the NPC to roam freely until it spots the player, triggering a transition to a more interactive state like chasing. It controls the NPC's wandering behavior ensuring the NPC roams within a defined radius, simulating a random exploration or patrol without a fixed path.

CHAPTER 3   ARCHITECTING ENEMY AI WITH FINITE STATE MACHINES

Listing 3-9. WanderState class

```
using System;
using UnityEngine;
using UnityEngine.AI;
using Random = UnityEngine.Random;

//States have access to MonoBehaviour methods too.
//All States must be added as components to the NPC game
//object.
public class WanderState : MonoBehaviour, IState
{
    public event Action OnNpcWander; //Being listened for in
                                      //Actions script.
    [Tooltip("Speed at which NavMeshAgent moves")]
    [SerializeField] private float npcSpeed = 1.5f;

    [Tooltip("Area around NPC where it can Wander to")]
    [SerializeField] private float navigationRadius = 7.0f;

    private NPCStateMachine stateMachine;
    private NavMeshAgent agent; // Reference to the soldier
                                //NPC Agent
    private Vector3 target; //target is the random Wander
                            //location for NPC Agent
    private bool isTargetSet;

    void Awake()
    {
        stateMachine = GetComponent<NPCStateMachine>();
        if (stateMachine == null)
        {
```

CHAPTER 3 ARCHITECTING ENEMY AI WITH FINITE STATE MACHINES

```csharp
        Debug.LogError($"[WanderState - {gameObject.name}] : 
        NPCStateMachine not found.");
        return;
    }

    agent = GetComponent<NavMeshAgent>();
    if (agent == null)
    {
        Debug.LogError($"[WanderState - {gameObject.name}] 
        : No NavMesh Agent found.");
        return;
    }
}

void IState.OnStateEnter()
{
    if (agent.enabled)
    {
        agent.speed = npcSpeed;
        agent.isStopped = false;
        isTargetSet = false; // Reset target selection on
                            //state enter
    }
    else
        return;

    OnNpcWander?.Invoke(); //Being listened for in Actions
                        //script.
    Debug.Log("WanderState: Enter");
}
```

Chapter 3   Architecting Enemy AI with Finite State Machines

```
void IState.OnStateUpdate(float deltaTime)
{
    if (agent.enabled)
    {
        // Check if the agent has reached its wander
        //target or if no target is set
        if (!isTargetSet || agent.remainingDistance <
            agent.stoppingDistance)
        {
            // Calculate a new random target
            Vector3 randomDirection =
            Random.insideUnitSphere * navigationRadius;
            randomDirection += agent.transform.position;

            NavMeshHit hit;
            if (NavMesh.SamplePosition(randomDirection,
            out hit, navigationRadius, NavMesh.AllAreas))
            {
                target = hit.position;
                agent.SetDestination(target);
                isTargetSet = true; //Mark target as set
            }
        }
    }
    else
        return;

    if (stateMachine.IsPlayerVisible())
    {
        IState chase = stateMachine.states.Find(s =>
        s.GetType() == typeof(ChaseState));
        stateMachine.SwitchState(chase);
```

CHAPTER 3 ARCHITECTING ENEMY AI WITH FINITE STATE MACHINES

```
        }
    }
    void IState.OnStateExit()
    {
        Debug.Log("WanderState: Exit");
    }
}
```

Ensure this script is a component of the NPC game object. Let's analyze this class's code functionality in detail.

1. OnNpcWander: An event triggered when the NPC transitions to the wander state. This event is being listened for in the Actions script and invokes the Walk() method therein, triggering the NPC's walk/wandering animation.

2. NPCSpeed: Here you set the movement speed of the NPC when wandering, controlling how fast the NPC moves towards its wander target.

3. navigationRadius: Here you define the radius within which the NPC can randomly choose new locations to wander to. This controls the scope of the NPC's exploration area.

4. stateMachine: A reference to the NPCStateMachine component attached to the same NPC GameObject. This allows the WanderState to request state transitions based on game logic, accessing other states and invoking SwitchState() as needed.

CHAPTER 3   ARCHITECTING ENEMY AI WITH FINITE STATE MACHINES

5. agent: A reference to the NavMeshAgent component of the NPC used for pathfinding and moving the NPC on the mesh. This is crucial for controlling the NPC's movement, particularly to set it in motion when the NPC is wandering.

6. target: It represents the currently selected random location within the navigation radius where the NPC aims to move.

7. isTargetSet: Indicates whether a valid wander target has been set for the NPC, helping manage when to seek out a new target.

8. Awake(): Here you initialize "stateMachine" and "agent" by fetching them from the same NPC GameObject this script is attached to. if an agent is not found, you log an error, ensuring the state can't operate without this essential component.

9. IState.OnStateEnter(): Here you activate the NavMeshAgent and set its speed, ensuring it is not stopped upon entering this state. You then reset "isTargetSet" to false, forcing a new target selection. You then invoke the OnNpcWander event that triggers subscribed actions (within the Actions script) ensuring the NPC begins wandering about the environment. You finally log a message to the console stating that you have entered the Wander state.

10. IState.OnStateUpdate(float deltaTime): This method is executed every frame, and checks if the NPC has a set target and if it has reached its current target. If no target is set or the target is reached, it computes

CHAPTER 3   ARCHITECTING ENEMY AI WITH FINITE STATE MACHINES

a new random target within the navigationRadius. It uses Random.insideUnitSphere() to compute a new direction. It then uses NavMesh.SamplePosition() to ensure the target is on the navigable mesh, in which case it sets the target to the position on the NavMesh that was hit and sets the agent destination to this new target location. It finally sets the variable "isTargetSet" to true, indicating that a valid wander target has been set for the NPC.

You also check to see if the player is visible (stateMachine.IsPlayerVisible()), and if so transition to the ChaseState.

11. IState.OnStateExit(): This method is activated when the NPC is leaving the wandering state. It simply logs a message to the console to assist in debugging by showing when the NPC moves out of the wandering state.

This design ensures that the WanderState keeps the NPC autonomously exploring its environment while staying ready to engage with the player when necessary, supporting a dynamic and interactive game world.

Note NavMesh.SamplePosition(randomDirection, out hit, navigationRadius, NavMesh.AllAreas)

The NavMesh.SamplePosition() method is used to find the nearest valid point on the navigation mesh (NavMesh) with reference to a specified position. This is particularly useful in AI navigation to ensure that agents like NPCs are given valid and reachable destinations.

This method attempts to locate the closest point on the NavMesh to the randomDirection, within the specified navigationRadius. If a suitable point is found, it populates the hit structure with details about this point and returns true. This allows your game logic to proceed, typically setting this point as a new destination for your NPC. If no suitable point is found within the specified radius and areas, the method returns false, indicating that the operation failed to find a valid navigation point. In this case, the NPC might need to try again with a different random direction or handle the failure in some other way.

Recipe 3-10: Implementing Enemy AI Chase State

Problem

The Non-Player Characters (NPCs) need to dynamically and realistically pursue the player within the game environment. A game mechanic is required that focuses on guiding NPCs to transition seamlessly from states like Patrol or Wander to Chase upon detecting the player, and back again when the player is no longer visible. This game mechanic also needs to manage the NPC's transition to the Attack state when the player is within attack range, ensuring efficient pathfinding and maintaining gameplay fluidity through responsive state transitions based on the player's actions and the evolving game context.

Solution

The ChaseState class effectively manages the NPC's transition into an aggressive pursuit mode by increasing the NPC's speed and guiding it toward the player's position. It utilizes the NavMeshAgent to ensure pathfinding is efficient and maintains state integrity by remembering the NPC's previous state. This approach allows for a seamless switch back to Patrol or Wander when the player is no longer visible. Additionally, the class ensures a smooth transition to the Attack state when the player is within attack range, enhancing the NPC's responsiveness and realism in the game.

How It Works

The ChaseState class manages the behavior of an NPC while it is in chase mode, specifically designed to pursue the player when detected. It uses the NavMeshAgent to dynamically navigate towards the player and transitions to other states like attack or previous states like patrol or wander, based on the player's visibility and proximity.

Listing 3-10. ChaseState class

```
using System;
using UnityEngine;
using UnityEngine.AI;

//States have access to MonoBheaviour methods too.
//All States must be added as components to the NPC game
// object.
public class ChaseState : MonoBehaviour, IState
{
    public event Action OnNpcChase;//Being listened for in
                                    //Actions script.
```

CHAPTER 3 ARCHITECTING ENEMY AI WITH FINITE STATE MACHINES

```csharp
[Tooltip("Speed at which NavMeshAgent moves while
Chasing")]
[SerializeField] private float npcSpeed = 4f;

private NPCStateMachine stateMachine;
private NavMeshAgent agent; //Reference to the soldier NPC
                            //Agent
private IState previousState;

void Awake()
{
   stateMachine = GetComponent<NPCStateMachine>();
   if (stateMachine == null)
   {
      Debug.LogError($"[ChaseState - {gameObject.name}] :
      NPCStateMachine not found.");
      return;
   }

    agent = GetComponent<NavMeshAgent>();
    if (agent == null)
    {
        Debug.LogError($"[ChaseState - {gameObject.name}]
        : No NavMesh Agent found.");
        return;
    }
}
void IState.OnStateEnter()
{
    if (agent.enabled)
    {
```

CHAPTER 3 ARCHITECTING ENEMY AI WITH FINITE STATE MACHINES

```
        agent.speed = npcSpeed;
        agent.isStopped = false;
    }
    else
        return;

    OnNpcChase?.Invoke(); //Being listened for in Actions
                          //script.
    Debug.Log("ChaseState: Enter");
}
void IState.OnStateUpdate(float deltaTime)
{
 //Check if the previous state is not of type
//ChaseState as NPC could continuously chase the player
    if (stateMachine.PreviousState.GetType() !=
    typeof(ChaseState)) //ACC
    {
        //previous state can be either Patrol or Wander
        previousState = stateMachine.PreviousState;
    }

    if (!stateMachine.IsPlayerVisible())
    {
     //If coming from Patrol to Chase state, switch back
     //to Patrol
     //If coming from Wander to Chase state, switch back
     //to Wander
        stateMachine.SwitchState(previousState);
        return;
    }
```

CHAPTER 3 ARCHITECTING ENEMY AI WITH FINITE STATE MACHINES

```
            //if Player is visible to NPC
            if(agent.enabled)
                agent.SetDestination(stateMachine.Player.position);

if(agent.enabled && agent.hasPath)
{
  if (stateMachine.IsPlayerAttackable())
  {
      Debug.Log("ChaseState: Player in Attackable Range");
      IState attack = stateMachine.states.Find(s =>
      s.GetType() == typeof(AttackState));
      stateMachine.SwitchState(attack);
  }
}
}

void IState.OnStateExit()
{
    Debug.Log("ChaseState: Exit");
}
}
```

Ensure this script is a component of the NPC game object. Let's analyze this class's code functionality in detail.

1. OnNpcChase: An event triggered when the NPC transitions to the chase state. This event is being listened for in the Actions script and invokes the Run() method therein, triggering the NPC's chasing animation.

2. NPCSpeed: Here you set the movement speed of the NPC while chasing the player, setting the urgency of the pursuit.

CHAPTER 3   ARCHITECTING ENEMY AI WITH FINITE STATE MACHINES

3. stateMachine: A reference to the NPCStateMachine component attached to the same NPC GameObject. This allows the ChaseState to request state transitions based on game logic, accessing other states and invoking SwitchState() as needed.

4. agent: A reference to the NavMeshAgent component of the NPC used for pathfinding and moving the NPC on the mesh, ensuring it can navigate toward the player.

5. previousState: Required to keep track of the state from which the NPC transitioned into the chase, enabling a return to that state if the player is no longer visible.

6. Awake(): Here you initialize "stateMachine" and "agent" by fetching them from the same NPC GameObject this script is attached to. If an agent is not found, you log an error, ensuring the state can't operate without this essential component.

7. IState.OnStateEnter(): Here you activate the NavMeshAgent and set its speed, ensuring it is not stopped upon entering this state. You then invoke the OnNpcChase event that triggers subscribed actions (within the Actions script) ensuring the NPC begins chasing the player. You finally log a message to the console stating that you have entered the Chase state.

8. IState.OnStateUpdate(float deltaTime): This method is executed every frame, and checks if the player is still visible (IsPlayerVisible()). If not, it switches the NPC back to its previous state (either patrol

CHAPTER 3   ARCHITECTING ENEMY AI WITH FINITE STATE MACHINES

or wander). if the player is visible, it continues to update the NPC's destination to the player's current position. It goes on to check if the player is within attackable range (IsPlayerAttackable()), and if so, transitions the NPC to the attack state.

9. IState.OnStateExit(): This method is activated when the NPC is leaving the chase state. It simply logs a message to the console to assist in debugging by showing when the NPC moves out of the chase state.

The ChaseState uses the stateMachine to monitor the player's visibility and manage transitions between states based on the NPC's perception and proximity to the player. By keeping a reference to the previousState, the ChaseState ensures that the NPC can return to its normal behavior (patrol or wander) if the player is lost, maintaining a fluid and realistic NPC behavior pattern.

Recipe 3-11: Implementing Enemy AI Attack State

Problem

Managing Non-Player Characters (NPCs) in combat scenarios within a game environment is a complex challenge. It must ensure NPCs cease movement while attacking, maintain focus on the player, and transition seamlessly between combat and other behaviors such as chasing, patrolling, or wandering. This is crucial for maintaining a fluid and realistic NPC response when the player moves into or out of attack range or is no longer visible.

CHAPTER 3   ARCHITECTING ENEMY AI WITH FINITE STATE MACHINES

Solution

The AttackState class ensures that the NPC halts movement and focuses on attacking when the player is within range, using the NavMeshAgent to manage positioning. It triggers the attack animation and handles transitions back to chase if the player moves out of range but remains visible or to patrol or wander if the player is no longer visible. This approach facilitates a responsive and immersive combat experience, dynamically adjusting NPC behavior based on the player's actions and the evolving game context.

How It Works

The AttackState class manages the behavior of an NPC when it is in an attacking mode. It utilizes the NavMeshAgent for positioning and stopping the NPC and leverages the NPCStateMachine to manage transitions between different states based on conditions like player visibility and proximity.

Listing 3-11. AttackState class

```
using System;
using UnityEngine;
using UnityEngine.AI;
using Random = UnityEngine.Random;

//States have access to MonoBheaviour methods too.
//All States must be added as components to the NPC game
//object.
public class AttackState : MonoBehaviour, IState
{
    public event Action OnNpcAttack;//Being listened for in
                                    //Actions script.
```

CHAPTER 3   ARCHITECTING ENEMY AI WITH FINITE STATE MACHINES

```csharp
[Tooltip("Speed at which NavMeshAgent moves while
 Attacking")]
[SerializeField] private float npcSpeed = 0f;

private NPCStateMachine stateMachine;
private NavMeshAgent agent; //Reference to the soldier NPC
                            //Agent

void Awake()
{
    stateMachine = GetComponent<NPCStateMachine>();
    if (stateMachine == null)
    {
        Debug.LogError($"[AttackState - {gameObject.name}] :
        NPCStateMachine not found.");
        return;
    }

     agent = GetComponent<NavMeshAgent>();
     if (agent == null)
     {
         Debug.LogError($"[AttackState - {gameObject.name}]
         : No NavMesh Agent found.");
         return;
     }
}

void IState.OnStateEnter()
{
  //Exit early if the agent is not enabled
     if(!agent.enabled)
         return;
```

CHAPTER 3 ARCHITECTING ENEMY AI WITH FINITE STATE MACHINES

```
        agent.speed = npcSpeed;
        agent.isStopped = true;
        OnNpcAttack?.Invoke(); //Being listened for in Actions
                          //script.
        Debug.Log("AttackState: Enter");
    }

    void IState.OnStateUpdate(float deltaTime)
    {
        stateMachine.RotateToFacePlayer();
        OnNpcAttack?.Invoke();//provides visual of NPC firing
                          //weapon.

        if (!stateMachine.IsPlayerAttackable())
        {
            if (stateMachine.IsPlayerVisible())
            {
                IState chase = stateMachine.states.Find(s =>
                s.GetType() == typeof(ChaseState));
                stateMachine.SwitchState(chase);
            }
            else//Player not visible got to either Patrol or
              //Wander State with 50% chance for either state.
            {
                if (Random.Range(0, 100) < 50)
                {
                    IState patrol = stateMachine.states.Find(s
                    => s.GetType() == typeof(PatrolState));
                    stateMachine.SwitchState(patrol);
                    Debug.Log("AttackState: Switching to
                    Patrol State");
                }
```

CHAPTER 3　ARCHITECTING ENEMY AI WITH FINITE STATE MACHINES

```
            else
            {
                IState wander = stateMachine.states.Find(s
                => s.GetType() == typeof(WanderState));
                stateMachine.SwitchState(wander);
                Debug.Log("AttackState: Switching to
                Wander State");
            }
        }
    }
    Debug.Log("AttackState: Update");
    }
    void IState.OnStateExit()
    {
        Debug.Log("AttackState: Exit");
    }
}
```

Ensure this script is attached as a component of the NPC game object. Let's explore this class in detail.

1. OnNpcAttack: An event triggered when the NPC transitions to the attack state. This event is being listened for in the Actions script and invokes the Attack() method therein, triggering the NPC's attacking animation.

2. NPCSpeed: Here you set the movement speed of the NPC while attacking the player. It is set to 0 to ensure the NPC stops moving while attacking.

CHAPTER 3   ARCHITECTING ENEMY AI WITH FINITE STATE MACHINES

3. stateMachine: A reference to the NPCStateMachine component attached to the same NPC GameObject. This allows the AttackState to request state transitions based on game logic, accessing other states and invoking SwitchState() as needed.

4. agent: A reference to the NavMeshAgent component of the NPC used for pathfinding and moving the NPC on the mesh. It is used to stop the NPC and manage its positioning during the attack.

5. Awake(): Here you initialize "stateMachine" and "agent" by fetching them from the same NPC GameObject this script is attached to. if an agent is not found, you log an error, ensuring the Attack behavior can't proceed without this essential component.

6. IState.OnStateEnter(): Here you set the NPC's speed to 0 and stop it from moving. You then invoke the OnNpcCAttack event that triggers subscribed actions (within the Actions script) ensuring the NPC begins attacking the player. You finally log a message to the console stating that you have entered the Attack state.

7. IState.OnStateUpdate(float deltaTime): This method is executed every frame. It ensures that the NPC is continuously facing the player using stateMachine.RotateToFacePlayer(). It invokes the OnNpcAttack event to simulate the NPC continuously firing its weapon. It checks to see if the player is still attackable. If not, it transitions to chase state if the player is still visible, or randomly selects the patrol or wander state if the player is not visible.

CHAPTER 3   ARCHITECTING ENEMY AI WITH FINITE STATE MACHINES

8. IState.OnStateExit(): This method is activated when the NPC is leaving the attack state. It simply logs a message to the console to assist in debugging by showing when the NPC moves out of the attack state.

The AttackState uses the stateMachine to monitor and react to the player's visibility and proximity. When the player is no longer in attackable range, it decides whether to transition back to chase, patrol, or wander states based on the current conditions. The AttackState ensures that the NPC can dynamically respond to changes in the player's position and visibility, maintaining a fluid and realistic combat behavior pattern.

Recipe 3-12: Implementing Enemy AI Hit State

Problem

The Enemy AI system needs to manage the response of Non-Player Characters (NPCs) when they are hit in various states such as Patrol, Idle, Attack, or Chase. It needs to ensure a smooth transition into the HitState to trigger a hit animation, and then seamlessly return the NPC to its previous behavior. The challenge lies in maintaining continuous and realistic NPC reactions, particularly in preventing repetitive or stuck states due to consecutive hits, while preserving the integrity of the game's logic and flow.

Solution

The HitState class ensures that when an NPC is hit, its movement halts, and it enters a state where a hit animation is triggered. Upon entering this state, the NPC's speed is set to zero, and it stops navigating to reflect the

CHAPTER 3 ARCHITECTING ENEMY AI WITH FINITE STATE MACHINES

impact of being hit. The class then transitions the NPC back to its previous state, avoiding continuous hits by checking the type of the previous state. This approach provides a responsive and realistic reaction to being hit, enhancing the NPC's behavior dynamics in the game.

How It Works

The HitState class manages the behavior of an NPC when it is hit, typically by a player attack. It transitions the NPC into a state where it plays a hit animation, temporarily stops its movement, and then reverts to its immediate previous state. The HitState uses the stateMachine to monitor and manage the NPC's state transitions. When the NPC is hit, it temporarily enters the hit state and then uses stateMachine.PreviousState to return to the state it was in before being hit, ensuring that the NPC can dynamically respond to being hit by stopping its movement, playing the appropriate animation, and then resuming its previous behavior, maintaining a seamless and realistic NPC behavior pattern.

Listing 3-12. HitState class

```
using UnityEngine;
using UnityEngine.AI;
using System;

/***
Whilst in any State (i.e. Patrol, Idle, Attack, Chase) NPC can be Hit (i.e. shot at)
and will need to enter the HitState, playing a Hit animation.
*****
States have access to MonoBheaviour methods too.
All States must be added as components to the NPC game object.
***/
```

CHAPTER 3   ARCHITECTING ENEMY AI WITH FINITE STATE MACHINES

```csharp
public class HitState : MonoBehaviour, IState
{
    public event Action PlayNpcHitAnim;//Being listened for in
                                      //Actions script.
    private NPCStateMachine stateMachine;
    private NavMeshAgent agent; // Reference to the soldier
                                //NPC Agent
    private bool isNpcHit;
    private IState previousState;

    void Awake()
    {
       stateMachine = GetComponent<NPCStateMachine>();
       if (stateMachine == null)
       {
          Debug.LogError($"[HitState - {gameObject.name}] :
          NPCStateMachine not found.");
          return;
       }

        agent = GetComponent<NavMeshAgent>();
        if (agent == null)
        {
            Debug.LogError($"[HitState - {gameObject.name}] :
            No NavMesh Agent found.");
            return;
        }
    }

    void IState.OnStateEnter()
    {
        //Exit early if the agent is not enabled
        if(!agent.enabled)
            return;
```

CHAPTER 3 ARCHITECTING ENEMY AI WITH FINITE STATE MACHINES

```
        agent.speed = 0f;
        agent.isStopped = true;
        isNpcHit = true;
        PlayNpcHitAnim?.Invoke();//Plays NPC Hit Animation.
        Debug.Log("HitState: Enter");
    }

    void IState.OnStateUpdate(float deltaTime)
    {
        if (isNpcHit)//switch to the immediate previous state
                    //before the HitState
        {
        //Check if the previous state is not of type HitState
        //as NPC could be hit several times in succession.
            if (stateMachine.PreviousState.GetType() !=
            typeof(HitState))
            {
                previousState = stateMachine.PreviousState;
            }

            IState prevState = stateMachine.states.Find(s =>
            s.GetType() == previousState.GetType());
            stateMachine.SwitchState(prevState);
        }

        Debug.Log("HitState: Update");
    }

    void IState.OnStateExit()
    {
        Debug.Log("HitState: Exit");
        isNpcHit = false;
    }
}
```

CHAPTER 3   ARCHITECTING ENEMY AI WITH FINITE STATE MACHINES

Ensure this script is attached as a component of the NPC game object. Let's explore this script in detail.

1. PlayNpcHitAnim: An event triggered when the NPC transitions to the hit state. This event is being listened for in the Actions script and invokes the Damage() method therein, triggering the NPC's taking damage animation.

2. stateMachine: A reference to the NPCStateMachine component attached to the same NPC GameObject. This allows the HitState to request state transitions based on game logic, accessing other states and invoking SwitchState() as needed.

3. agent: A reference to the NavMeshAgent component of the NPC used for pathfinding and moving the NPC on the mesh. It is used to stop the NPC during the hit state to simulate the NPC being staggered or immobilized.

4. isNpcHit: A boolean flag indicating whether the NPC is currently in the hit state. It is used to control the transition back to the previous state.

5. previousState: It stores the state from which the NPC transitioned into the hit state, allowing it to return to that state after handling the hit.

6. Awake(): Here you initialize "stateMachine" and "agent" by fetching them from the same NPC GameObject this script is attached to. if an agent is not found, you log an error, ensuring the Hit behavior can't proceed further.

CHAPTER 3   ARCHITECTING ENEMY AI WITH FINITE STATE MACHINES

7. IState.OnStateEnter(): Here you stop the NPC's movement and set its speed to zero. You set isNpcHit to true, indicating that the NPC has been hit. You then invoke the PlayNpcHitAnim event that triggers subscribed actions (within the Actions script) ensuring the NPC's damage animation plays. You finally log a message to the console stating that you have entered the Hit state.

8. IState.OnStateUpdate(float deltaTime): This method is executed every frame. It checks to see if the NPC is in the hit state and not transitioning back from a previous hit state, on account of possible consecutive hits. It then finds the previous state stored in stateMachine.PreviousState and switches back to it.

9. IState.OnStateExit(): This method is activated when the NPC is leaving the hit state. It resets isNpcHit to false and logs a message to the console to assist in debugging by declaring that the NPC is exiting the hit state.

This setup ensures that the HitState handles the NPC's reaction to being hit effectively, providing visual feedback and maintaining logical state transitions.

CHAPTER 3   ARCHITECTING ENEMY AI WITH FINITE STATE MACHINES

Recipe 3-13: Implementing Enemy AI Cover State

Problem

The Enemy AI system needs to address the challenge of enabling Non-Player Characters (NPCs) to execute realistic defensive maneuvers within a dynamic game environment. The primary issue involves guiding NPCs to strategically select and navigate to hiding spots, either closest or farthest from the player, based on random probability. Additionally, the system must ensure NPCs maintain realistic behavior by squatting upon reaching cover and adaptively transitioning back to other states depending on the player's visibility and the NPC's health status.

Solution

The CoverState class ensures that NPCs navigate to hiding spots using the NavMeshAgent, where they choose between the closest or farthest cover based on a 50% probability. Upon reaching the hiding spot, NPCs squat to simulate taking cover, enhancing realism. The class also manages transitions back to chase, patrol, or wander states based on the player's visibility and NPC health, maintaining dynamic and responsive NPC behavior in the game.

How It Works

The CoverState class manages the behavior of an NPC when it needs to seek cover, typically when under attack or in danger. It directs the NPC to move to either the closest or farthest hiding spot and squat behind it., providing realistic and strategic behavior in combat situations. The class uses the NavMeshAgent for navigation and the NPCStateMachine for state transitions.

CHAPTER 3   ARCHITECTING ENEMY AI WITH FINITE STATE MACHINES

Listing 3-13. CoverState class

```
using System;
using UnityEngine;
using UnityEngine.AI;
using Random = UnityEngine.Random;

//States have access to MonoBheaviour methods too.
//All States must be added as components to the NPC game
//object.
public class CoverState : MonoBehaviour, IState
{
    public event Action OnNpcTakeCover; //Being listened for
                                        //in Actions script.
    public event Action OnNPCSquat; //Being listened for in
                                    //Actions script.

    private GameObject[] coverSpots;

    [Tooltip("Speed at which NavMeshAgent moves while seeking
    Cover")]
    [SerializeField] private float npcSpeed = 2.5f;

    private NPCStateMachine stateMachine;
    private NavMeshAgent agent; //Reference to the soldier
                                //NPC Agent
    private Transform player; //Reference to the Player
                              //transform
    private Vector3 target; //target is the Hiding spot
    private float offset = 1.5f;

    void Awake()
    {
        stateMachine = GetComponent<NPCStateMachine>();
```

CHAPTER 3   ARCHITECTING ENEMY AI WITH FINITE STATE MACHINES

```
        if (stateMachine == null)
        {
            Debug.LogError($"[CoverState - {gameObject.name}] : 
            NPCStateMachine not found.");
            return;
        }

        agent = GetComponent<NavMeshAgent>();
        if (agent == null)
        {
            Debug.LogError($"[CoverState- {gameObject.name}] : 
            No NavMesh Agent found.");
            return;
        }
        player = GameObject.FindWithTag("Player").transform;
        if (player == null)
        {
            Debug.LogError("Couldn't find Player with tag 
            'Player'");
            return;
        }

        coverSpots = 
        GameObject.FindGameObjectsWithTag("Obstacle");
    }

    void IState.OnStateEnter()
    {
        if (agent.enabled)
        {
            agent.speed = npcSpeed;
            agent.isStopped = false;
```

CHAPTER 3 ARCHITECTING ENEMY AI WITH FINITE STATE MACHINES

```
    //provide a 50% chance of NPC moving to either closest
     //or farthest hiding spot for Cover
        if (Random.Range(0, 100) < 50)
            target = FindClosestCover();
        else
            target = FindFarthestCover();

        agent.SetDestination(target);
    }
    else
        return;

    OnNpcTakeCover?.Invoke(); //Being listened for in
                              //Actions script.

    Debug.Log("CoverState: Enter");
}

void IState.OnStateUpdate(float deltaTime)
{

//Check if the agent has reached its currentdestination
    if (agent.enabled && agent.remainingDistance <=
    agent.stoppingDistance)
    {
        //NPC reached a hiding spot so let him squat.
        agent.isStopped = true;
        OnNPCSquat?.Invoke();
    }

    if (stateMachine.IsPlayerVisible() &&
    GetComponent<Health>().CurrentHealth >= 50)
    {
        IState chase = stateMachine.states.Find(s =>
        s.GetType() == typeof(ChaseState));
```

CHAPTER 3   ARCHITECTING ENEMY AI WITH FINITE STATE MACHINES

```
                stateMachine.SwitchState(chase);
        }
        else if(GetComponent<Health>().CurrentHealth >= 50 &&
        !stateMachine.IsPlayerVisible())
        {
            //provide a 50% chance of entering into either
            //Wander or Patrol states
            if (Random.Range(0, 100) < 50)
            {
                IState patrol = stateMachine.states.Find(s =>
                s.GetType() == typeof(PatrolState));
                Debug.Log("CoverState: Switching to Patrol
                State");
                stateMachine.SwitchState(patrol);
            }
            else
            {
                IState wander = stateMachine.states.Find(s =>
                s.GetType() == typeof(WanderState));
                Debug.Log("CoverState: Switching to Wander
                State");
                stateMachine.SwitchState(wander);
            }
        }
    }

    void IState.OnStateExit()
    {
        Debug.Log("CoverState: Exit");
    }
```

CHAPTER 3   ARCHITECTING ENEMY AI WITH FINITE STATE MACHINES

```csharp
private Vector3 FindClosestCover()
{
    // Check if there are any cover spots available
    if (coverSpots.Length == 0)
    {
        Debug.LogError("No Obstacles found for NPC to hide
        behind.");
        return transform.position;   //Return current NPC
                    //position if no covers are found
    }

    float minDistance = Mathf.Infinity;
    Vector3 bestHidingSpot = transform.position;
    GameObject closestHidingSpot = null;

    foreach (GameObject coverSpot in coverSpots)
    {
    //Calculate the distance from the current cover spot
    //to the player
        float distanceToPlayer =
        Vector3.Distance(player.position,
        coverSpot.transform.position);

        if (distanceToPlayer < minDistance)
        {
            minDistance = distanceToPlayer;
            closestHidingSpot = coverSpot;
        }
    }

    // Calculate the direction from the closest cover spot
    //obtained to player
    Vector3 coverToPlayer = player.position -
    closestHidingSpot.transform.position;
```

321

```csharp
//Get the Collider component to determine size
Collider obstacleCollider =
closestHidingSpot.GetComponent<Collider>();
if (obstacleCollider == null)
{
    Debug.LogError($"CoverState: Obstacle:
    '{closestHidingSpot.name}' not fitted with a
    Collider");
    return Vector3.zero;
}
else
{
// Compute an appropriate offset based on the
//obstacle's collider size
    float obstacleOffset =
    Mathf.Max(obstacleCollider.bounds.size.x,
    obstacleCollider.bounds.size.z) / 2.0f + offset;

  //Find a potential hiding spot behind the cover spot
  //with the adjusted offset
    Vector3 potentialHidingSpot =
    closestHidingSpot.transform.position -
    coverToPlayer.normalized * obstacleOffset;

    NavMeshHit hit;
    if (NavMesh.SamplePosition(potentialHidingSpot,
    out hit, obstacleOffset, NavMesh.AllAreas))
        bestHidingSpot = hit.position;
    else
    {
        bestHidingSpot = Vector3.zero;
        Debug.LogError($"CoverState: NPC cannot be
```

CHAPTER 3 ARCHITECTING ENEMY AI WITH FINITE STATE MACHINES

```
            positioned behind Hiding Spot:
            '{closestHidingSpot.name}'");
        }
        return bestHidingSpot;
    }
}

private Vector3 FindFarthestCover()
{
    // Check if there are any cover spots available
    if (coverSpots.Length == 0)
    {
        Debug.LogError("No Obstacles found for NPC to hide
        behind.");
        return transform.position;//Return current NPC
                    //position if no covers are found
    }

    float maxDistance = Mathf.NegativeInfinity;
    Vector3 bestHidingSpot = transform.position;
    GameObject farthestHidingSpot = null;

    foreach (GameObject coverSpot in coverSpots)
    {
     //Calculate the distance from the current cover spot
     //to the player
        float distanceToPlayer =
        Vector3.Distance(player.position,
        coverSpot.transform.position);

        if (distanceToPlayer > maxDistance)
        {
            maxDistance = distanceToPlayer;
```

CHAPTER 3   ARCHITECTING ENEMY AI WITH FINITE STATE MACHINES

```
            farthestHidingSpot = coverSpot;
    }
}

//Calculate the direction from the farthest cover
//spot obtained to player
Vector3 coverToPlayer = player.position -
farthestHidingSpot.transform.position;

//Get the Collider component to determine size
Collider obstacleCollider =
farthestHidingSpot.GetComponent<Collider>();
if (obstacleCollider == null)
{
    Debug.LogError($"CoverState: Obstacle:
    '{farthestHidingSpot.name}' not fitted with a
    Collider");
    return Vector3.zero;
}
else
{
//Compute an appropriate offset based on the
//obstacle's collider size
    float obstacleOffset =
    Mathf.Max(obstacleCollider.bounds.size.x,
    obstacleCollider.bounds.size.z) / 2.0f + offset;

//Find a potential hiding spot behind the cover spot
//with the adjusted offset
    Vector3 potentialHidingSpot =
    farthestHidingSpot.transform.position -
    coverToPlayer.normalized * obstacleOffset;
```

CHAPTER 3   ARCHITECTING ENEMY AI WITH FINITE STATE MACHINES

```
            NavMeshHit hit;
            if (NavMesh.SamplePosition(potentialHidingSpot,
            out hit, obstacleOffset, NavMesh.AllAreas))
                bestHidingSpot = hit.position;
            else
            {
                bestHidingSpot = Vector3.zero;
                Debug.LogError($"CoverState: NPC cannot be
                positioned behind Hiding Spot:
                '{farthestHidingSpot.name}'");
            }
            return bestHidingSpot;
        }
    }
}
```

Ensure this script is attached as a component of the NPC game object. Let's explore this class in detail.

1. OnNpcTakeCover: An event triggered when the NPC transitions to the Cover state. This event is being listened for in the Actions script and invokes the CrouchingRun() method therein, triggering the NPC's fleeing animation.

2. OnNPCSquat: An event triggered when the NPC reaches its hiding spot. This event is being listened for in the Actions script and invokes the Squat() method therein, triggering an animation that ensures the NPC stops and squats.

3. coverSpots: An array of game objects representing potential hiding spots for the NPC. These hiding spots have been tagged as "Obstacle" in the game environment.

325

4. NPCSpeed: Sets the movement speed of the NPC while seeking cover, ensuring it moves at an appropriate speed when navigating to hiding spots.

5. stateMachine: A reference to the NPCStateMachine component attached to the same NPC GameObject. This allows the CoverState to request state transitions based on game logic, accessing other states and invoking SwitchState() as needed.

6. Agent: A reference to the NavMeshAgent component of the NPC used for pathfinding and moving the NPC on the mesh, allowing it to navigate to hiding spots.

7. Player: A reference to the player's transform, used to calculate distances and directions for finding hiding spots.

8. Target: The currently selected hiding spot where the NPC aims to move to and take cover.

9. Offset: A small distance added to ensure the NPC hides properly behind the cover, avoiding the direct line of sight with threats (i.e., the player).

10. Awake(): Here you initialize "stateMachine" and "agent" by fetching them from the same NPC GameObject this script is attached to. You then locate the player using the tag "Player." if any of these components are missing, you log an error, ensuring the take cover behavior can't proceed further. Lastly, you initialize the coverSpots array by locating all game objects within the scene that have been tagged as "Obstacle."

CHAPTER 3 ARCHITECTING ENEMY AI WITH FINITE STATE MACHINES

11. IState.OnStateEnter(): Here you set the NPC speed for seeking cover and start its movement. You then randomly choose between the closest and farthest cover spot and set it as the agent's destination. You then invoke the OnNpcTakeCover event that triggers subscribed actions (within the Actions script) ensuring the NPC begins moving to the selected hiding spot. You finally log a message to the console stating that you have entered the Cover state.

12. IState.OnStateUpdate(float deltaTime): This method is executed every frame. It checks to see if the NPC has reached its cover spot and invokes the OnNPCSquat event. It then checks to see if the player is visible and its health is at least fifty or above, in which case it begins chasing the player. In the event, that the player is not visible and its health is at least fifty or above, it switches to either the patrol or the wander state.

13. IState.OnStateExit(): This method is activated when the NPC is leaving the cover state. It logs a message to the console to assist in debugging by declaring that the NPC is exiting the cover state.

14. FindClosestCover(): This method aims to locate the nearest suitable cover spot for the NPC to hide behind when in the CoverState. This involves evaluating potential cover spots, calculating distances, and ensuring the chosen spot is navigable.

    - Check if there are any cover spots available: First check to ensure that there are cover spots available. If no cover spots are found, the NPC cannot hide and should remain in its current position.

CHAPTER 3   ARCHITECTING ENEMY AI WITH FINITE STATE MACHINES

- Initialize minDistance to a very large value: minDistance is initialized to a very large value to ensure that any actual distance measured will be smaller. It serves as the initial comparison value to find the smallest distance to a cover spot.

- Initialize bestHidingSpot: bestHidingSpot is initialized to the NPC's current position. This will be updated to the best hiding spot found eventually. It ensures the method has a valid return value even if no better hiding spot is found.

- Initialize closestHidingSpot: closestHidingSpot is initialized to null. It stores the closest cover spot found during the iteration over coverSpots. It keeps track of the best cover spot based on distance to the player.

- Iterate through each cover spot in coverSpots: The foreach loop iterates through each cover spot available to the NPC, allowing the method to evaluate all potential cover spots and determine the closest one.

- Calculate the distance from the player to the current cover spot: Within the foreach loop, the distance from the player to the current cover spot is calculated, providing the necessary metric to compare cover spots and determine the closest one.

- Update minDistance and closestHidingSpot: The if(...) condition then checks to see if the current cover spot is closer to the player than the previously found closest spot and updates minDistance and closestHidingSpot if the current spot is closer, ensuring the closest spot is found.

- Calculate the direction vector from the closest cover spot to the player: You then calculate a direction vector from the closest cover spot to the player. This vector is used to determine the NPC's hiding position relative to the cover spot and the player.

- Retrieve the collider component of the closest cover spot: You then retrieve the collider component of the closest cover spot. This collider is necessary to determine the size and bounds of the cover spot, ensuring the NPC can hide appropriately behind it.

- Missing collider: You then ensure that this closest cover spot has a collider, and if not, you log an error, returning an invalid position if no collider is found, preventing the NPC from hiding behind an object without defined bounds.

- Calculate an appropriate offset based on collider size: If a collider is present, you calculate an offset based on the size of the collider, ensuring the NPC hides properly behind the cover. Here the variable "offset" adjusts the hiding position to be sufficiently behind the cover spot, avoiding direct line of sight with threats (i.e., the player).

- Compute a potential hiding spot: You then calculate a potential hiding position by offsetting from the cover spot along the direction to the player, ensuring the NPC hides behind the cover spot at a safe distance, utilizing the calculated "obstacleOffset."

CHAPTER 3 ARCHITECTING ENEMY AI WITH FINITE STATE MACHINES

- Use NavMesh.SamplePosition to validate the potential hiding spot: The if(…) condition uses NavMesh.SamplePosition() to validate and adjust the potential hiding spot to ensure it's on the navigable mesh, ensuring the NPC can navigate to the hiding spot, adjusting the position if necessary to fit the NavMesh.

- Update bestHidingSpot: The variable bestHidingSpot is then updated to the validated position returned by NavMesh.SamplePosition(), ensuring the NPC has a valid and reachable hiding spot on the NavMesh.

- No valid position found: If NavMesh.SamplePosition() fails to find a valid position, you log an error and set bestHidingSpot to an invalid position, preventing the NPC from hiding at an unreachable spot.

- Return bestHidingSpot: Finally you return the variable bestHidingSpot.

15. FindFarthestCover(): This method aims to locate the farthest suitable cover spot for the NPC to hide behind when in the CoverState. This involves evaluating potential cover spots, calculating distances, and ensuring the chosen spot is navigable. The code here is a replica of the code used within the FindClosestCover() method, except for the fact that its computations have been altered to find the farthest distance.

CHAPTER 3 ARCHITECTING ENEMY AI WITH FINITE STATE MACHINES

By combining the above fields and methods, the CoverState class effectively manages the NPC's behavior when it needs to seek cover, providing a dynamic and realistic response to in-game threats.

Recipe 3-14: Implementing Enemy AI Death State

Problem

The Enemy AI system needs to handle the conclusion of non-player characters (NPCs) within a game by stopping their movements, deactivating their navigation systems, and visually representing their death. The challenge lies in smoothly transitioning NPCs out of active gameplay, triggering appropriate animations, and removing them from the game environment after a delay, ensuring the integrity and realism of the game are maintained.

Solution

The DeathState class effectively manages the termination of NPC activities by stopping the NavMeshAgent and disabling its pathfinding capabilities upon entering the state. It ensures that the NPC's death is visually represented by invoking a death animation and subsequently destroys the NPC game object after a predefined delay. This approach provides a seamless and realistic end to the NPC's participation in the game, enhancing the overall player experience by properly concluding the NPC's lifecycle.

CHAPTER 3   ARCHITECTING ENEMY AI WITH FINITE STATE MACHINES

How It Works

The DeathState class manages the behavior of an NPC when it dies. It stops the NPC's movement, plays a death animation, and eventually removes the NPC from the game. This class uses the NavMeshAgent to control movement and the NPCStateMachine to manage state transitions.

Listing 3-14. DeathState class

```
using UnityEngine;
using UnityEngine.AI;
using System;

//States have access to MonoBheaviour methods too.
//All States must be added as components to the NPC game
//object.
public class DeathState : MonoBehaviour, IState
{
    public event Action PlayNpcDeadAnim;//Being listened for
                                        //in Actions script.

    private NPCStateMachine stateMachine;
    private NavMeshAgent agent; // Reference to the soldier
                                //NPC Agent
    private float destroyDelay = 5f;
    private bool isNpcDead;

    void Awake()
    {
        stateMachine = GetComponent<NPCStateMachine>();
        if (stateMachine == null)
        {
            Debug.LogError($"[DeathState - {gameObject.name}] : 
            NPCStateMachine not found.");
```

CHAPTER 3 ARCHITECTING ENEMY AI WITH FINITE STATE MACHINES

```csharp
            return;
        }

        agent = GetComponent<NavMeshAgent>();
        if (agent == null)
        {
            Debug.LogError($"[DeathState - {gameObject.name}]
            : No NavMesh Agent found.");
            return;
        }
    }

    void IState.OnStateEnter()
    {
        //Exit early if the agent is not enabled
        if(!agent.enabled)
            return;
        agent.isStopped = true;
        agent.ResetPath();
        agent.enabled = false;
        isNpcDead = true;
        PlayNpcDeadAnim?.Invoke();//Plays NPC Death Animation.
        Debug.Log("DeathState: Enter");
    }

    void IState.OnStateUpdate(float deltaTime)
    {
        if (isNpcDead)
        {
            IState Idle = stateMachine.states.Find(s =>
            s.GetType() == typeof(IdleState));
            stateMachine.SwitchState(Idle);
        }
```

CHAPTER 3 ARCHITECTING ENEMY AI WITH FINITE STATE MACHINES

```
        Debug.Log("DeathState: Update");
    }

    void IState.OnStateExit()
    {
        Debug.Log("DeathState: Exit");
        Destroy(gameObject, destroyDelay);
    }
}
```

Ensure this script is attached as a component of the NPC game object. Let's explore this class in detail.

1. PlayNpcDeadAnim: An event triggered when the NPC transitions to the Death state. This event is being listened for in the Actions script and invokes the Death() method therein, triggering the NPC's dying animation.

2. stateMachine: A reference to the NPCStateMachine component attached to the same NPC GameObject. This allows the DeathState to request state transitions based on game logic, accessing other states and invoking SwitchState() as needed.

3. agent: A reference to the NavMeshAgent component of the NPC used for pathfinding and moving the NPC on the mesh. It is stopped and reset upon entering the death state.

4. destroyDelay: The delay before destroying the NPC GameObject, allowing time for the death animation to play.

CHAPTER 3   ARCHITECTING ENEMY AI WITH FINITE STATE MACHINES

5. isNpcDead: A boolean flag indicating whether the NPC is in the death state.

6. Awake(): Here you initialize "stateMachine" and "agent" by fetching them from the same NPC GameObject this script is attached to. If an agent is not found, you log an error, ensuring the Death behavior can't proceed further.

7. IState.OnStateEnter(): You stop the NPC's movement and reset its path. You also disable the NavMeshAgent and set isNpcDead to true. You then invoke the PlayNpcDeadAnim event that triggers subscribed actions (within the Actions script), ensuring the NPC death animation plays. You finally log a message to the console stating that you have entered the Death state.

8. IState.OnStateUpdate(float deltaTime): This method is executed every frame. It checks if the NPC is in the death state, and if so, it finds the IdleState from the state machine and switches to it.

9. IState.OnStateExit(): This method is activated when the NPC is leaving the death state. It logs a message to the console to assist in debugging by stating that the NPC is exiting the death state and schedules the destruction of the NPC game object after a delay.

The DeathState handles the NPC's death by stopping movement, playing the appropriate animations, using the stateMachine to switch to the IdleState after the NPC is considered dead, ensuring a smooth transition out of the death state, and eventually removing the NPC from the game world, maintaining a consistent and immersive gameplay experience.

CHAPTER 3   ARCHITECTING ENEMY AI WITH FINITE STATE MACHINES

Summary

This chapter focuses on creating intelligent and responsive enemy AI using finite state machines (FSMs) in Unity. It emphasizes coding FSMs for enemy AI, offering flexibility and precise control. This approach allows for the development of complex AI behaviors independent of graphical animations, ensuring seamless integration of strategic decision-making processes within the game environment. The chapter also covered essential navigation and pathfinding setup, ensuring AI agents are adept at moving within the game world. It comprehensively guides the reader through setting up and managing intelligent enemy AI using FSMs, providing detailed steps and explanations for implementing various NPC behaviors and states.

CHAPTER 4

Architecting Melee Combat: Building the Core Framework

This heavy but vital chapter is dedicated to crafting sophisticated melee combat systems akin to those found in today's most immersive action games. This chapter serves as your gateway into designing a dynamic and fluid combat system that enhances gameplay through strategic enemy interactions and customizable combat mechanics.

In this chapter, you embark on constructing a free-flow combat system, a design choice inspired by the exhilarating confrontations seen in titles like Assassin's Creed, Batman Arkham series, and Marvel's Spider-Man. Unlike conventional combat systems where foes may charge at the player relentlessly and somewhat predictably, the system we aim to develop will feature enemies that engage the player in a more calculated and harmonious manner. They will encircle the player, taking turns to attack, thereby creating a tactical challenge that requires players to think on their feet and prioritize threats in real-time.

This combat framework is designed with flexibility at its core. Whether your game's universe calls for bare-knuckled brawls or elegant swordplay, the system will accommodate a wide range of combat styles without the

CHAPTER 4   ARCHITECTING MELEE COMBAT: BUILDING THE CORE FRAMEWORK

need for extensive rewrites in your codebase. This adaptability ensures that game developers can tailor the combat experience to meet specific narrative or gameplay requirements.

Central to your melee combat system is the implementation of a robust Finite-State Machine (FSM) for enemy AI. The FSM is a tried-and-true method for structuring game AI, having been utilized in many renowned games over the past two decades, including Last of Us and the Batman Arkham series. By utilizing the very same FSM you created from the ground up in Chapter 3, each recipe in this chapter will guide you through setting up various basic AI states, such as Idle, Chase, etc., and progress toward implementing more complex strategies, such as the coordinated circling and attacking maneuvers that define your free-flow combat system.

By the end of this chapter, you will not only have laid down the architectural groundwork for a cutting-edge melee combat system but also gained insights into enhancing player engagement through intelligent enemy behavior design and customizable combat mechanics. Let's begin this journey into the art and science of combat system design in Unity, crafting memorable combat experiences that resonate with players and elevate your game to new heights.

Note   The animations provided as part of this chapter download are those that have been made freely available for educational use. Consequently, these animations lack the fluidity characteristic of high-budget "AAA" games. Achieving the level of finesse required for such fluid animations extends beyond the scope of this chapter, as it necessitates professional design and meticulous refinement. The focus of the recipes in this chapter is on building the core Melee combat framework.

CHAPTER 4 ARCHITECTING MELEE COMBAT: BUILDING THE CORE FRAMEWORK

To fully engage with the recipes in Chapter 4, please ensure you download the completed Unity project available for this chapter. This will enable you to directly apply the concepts discussed and effectively explore the intricacies of the melee combat system within a functioning Unity environment.

Recipe 4-1: Exploring the Warrior Game Object

Problem

In the context of developing a melee combat system, a significant challenge lies in crafting a Warrior NPC AI that behaves intelligently and dynamically during encounters. The Warrior must navigate the game environment, recognize and react to player actions, and execute combat strategies that are believable and engaging. It must effectively utilize AI patterns to create a realistic and challenging experience for players, adapting to different combat situations while maintaining a cohesive behavior model.

Solution

The recipe for the Warrior NPC AI addresses these challenges by implementing a robust finite-state machine to manage its various states, including idling, chasing, attacking, circling, etc. By exploring the Warrior GameObject setup, you learn how to integrate AI behaviors that allow the NPC to engage in combat effectively, utilize the environment for strategic advantages, and respond to player actions. This approach not only enhances the realism of the combat interactions but also ensures that the NPC can adapt its strategy based on the dynamics of each encounter.

How It Works

Begin by downloading the resource provided as part of Chapter 4. Start by opening the Playground scene for the ThirdPersonController that is available within Assets/StarterAssets/ThirdPersonController/Scenes.

Open the Playground scene and navigate to the hierarchy. Expand the Warrior game object, which incorporates the Paladin model sourced from Mixamo. The child object named mixamorig:Hips contains the model's skeletal structure. Another child, the Paladin Helmet, has its Transform Position Y value set to 1.6, positioning it at approximately eye level for raycasting purposes. Adjust this value as necessary to align with your specific game requirements.

The Player Detection Sphere is another crucial game object, configured as a child object with a sphere collider set to trigger mode. It has a radius of nine units, forming a detection zone around the player. This setup is crucial for triggering player detection when they enter the collider's bounds, facilitating an immediate Warrior response to player proximity within the game. It has also been fitted with a Player Detector component that facilitates the detection of the player. You will explore this script within this recipe.

Select the Warrior game object in the hierarchy, and within the Inspector, you will note that it has been fitted with several components that make up your Warrior NPC:

1. Animator: The Animator component includes a basic animator controller named "Warrior Controller," which is used for managing the animations of the Warrior character. This controller features two layers: the default Base Layer and an Override Layer. Both layers contain all the animations essential for demonstrating the core functionality of the Melee Combat system.

CHAPTER 4   ARCHITECTING MELEE COMBAT: BUILDING THE CORE FRAMEWORK

Currently, these animations are set without transitions to focus solely on showcasing the fundamental operations of the system.

2. Character Controller: This component is Unity's standard Character Controller, configured with its default settings. The Character Controller facilitates efficient handling of character movement and interactions with the game environment, providing built-in methods for collision detection and character dynamics, essential for realistic and responsive NPC control.

3. Nav Mesh Agent: This component is Unity's standard Nav Mesh Agent, configured with its default settings except for the Angular Speed, which has been set to 540, to facilitate more rapid turning. The Nav Mesh Agent enables automated navigation of game objects across complex environments, efficiently handling pathfinding and obstacle avoidance. This component is integral for AI characters that need to move.

4. Warrior State Machine: This component mirrors the implementation detailed in Recipe 3-6, where you developed your NPC State Machine. Although it utilizes the same fundamental state machine architecture, it has been specifically adapted for melee combat scenarios.

5. Idle State: This component is similar to the implementation detailed in Recipe 3-7 on Implementing the Enemy AI Idle State, specifically adapted for a melee combat scenario.

6. Chase State: This component is akin to the implementation outlined in Recipe 3-10, "Implementing the Enemy AI Chase State," but has been specifically tailored for melee combat scenarios.

7. Circling State: This is a new component specially designed for melee combat scenarios. It is designed to control the behavior of an NPC when it is circling the player. It manages the transition into and out of this state, handles the circling logic and animations, checks for collisions with obstacles, and transitions to other states like attacking or wandering based on various conditions. This ensures that the warrior's behavior is dynamic and responsive to the player's actions and the game environment.

8. Attack State: This component closely resembles the system described in Recipe 3-11, "Implementing the Enemy AI Attack State," yet it has been specifically modified to suit melee combat scenarios.

9. Retreat State: This new component is specifically designed for managing NPC behavior in melee combat scenarios, particularly focusing on retreat actions post-attack. When activated, the NPC disengages its weapon collider and initiates a backward walking animation. The retreat behavior is programmed to maintain the warrior's orientation toward the player as it moves to a predefined distance, after which it seamlessly transitions back into a circling state. This integration ensures fluid and dynamic warrior behavior within the combat system.

CHAPTER 4   ARCHITECTING MELEE COMBAT: BUILDING THE CORE FRAMEWORK

10. Hit State: This component is similar to the implementation detailed in Recipe 3-12 on Implementing the Enemy AI Hit State, with animations adapted for a melee combat scenario.

11. Cover State: This component is akin to the implementation outlined in Recipe 3-13, "Implementing the Enemy AI Cover State."

12. Death State: This component mirrors the structure outlined in Recipe 3-14, "Implementing the Enemy AI Death State," while featuring animations adapted for melee combat scenarios.

13. Wander State: This component is akin to the implementation outlined in Recipe 3-9, "Implementing the Enemy AI Wander State."

14. Health: This is the same component devised as part of Recipe 3-5.

15. Warrior Animation Events: This component is tailored specifically to manage the activation and deactivation of the sword's collider via animation events. It includes proxy methods that adjust the collider's state, ensuring accurate timing for hit detection synchronized with the warrior's animations.

16. Rigidbody: The warrior GameObject is equipped with a Rigidbody component with both the "Use Gravity" and "Is Kinematic" properties disabled. This setup allows the Rigidbody to be influenced by physics calculations without being affected by gravitational forces, and it does not respond to physics-based movement unless directly manipulated through scripts.

CHAPTER 4   ARCHITECTING MELEE COMBAT: BUILDING THE CORE FRAMEWORK

Let's examine the Player Detector script, which is attached to the Player Detection Sphere, a child object of the Warrior GameObject. This child object features a sphere collider configured as a Trigger, designed to detect the player's presence within a defined proximity.

Listing 4-1. PlayerDetector script

```
using UnityEngine;
using System.Collections;

public class PlayerDetector : MonoBehaviour
{
    private WarriorStateMachine stateMachine;
    private Coroutine visibilityCoroutine;

    void Awake()
    {
        stateMachine =
        GetComponentInParent<WarriorStateMachine>();
        if (stateMachine == null)
        {
        Debug.LogError($"[PlayerDetector - {gameObject.name}] : WarriorStateMachine not found.");
        return;
        }
    }

    private void OnTriggerEnter(Collider other)
    {
        if (other.CompareTag("Player"))
        {
          Debug.Log($"[PlayerDetector - {gameObject.name}] : Player Entered NPCs Trigger");
```

CHAPTER 4   ARCHITECTING MELEE COMBAT: BUILDING THE CORE FRAMEWORK

```csharp
        // Start the coroutine to continuously check for
        //player visibility
            if (visibilityCoroutine == null)
            {
                visibilityCoroutine =
                StartCoroutine(CheckPlayerVisibility());
            }
        }
    }

    private void OnTriggerExit(Collider other)
    {
        if (other.CompareTag("Player"))
        {
          Debug.Log($"[PlayerDetector - {gameObject.name}] :
          Player Exited NPCs Trigger");

    NPCManager.Instance.UnregisterOutOfRangeNpc(stateMachine);

    //Stop the coroutine when the player exits the trigger
            if (visibilityCoroutine != null)
            {
                StopCoroutine(visibilityCoroutine);
                visibilityCoroutine = null;
            }
        }
    }
    private IEnumerator CheckPlayerVisibility()
    {
        while (true)
        {
            if (stateMachine.IsPlayerVisible())
```

CHAPTER 4   ARCHITECTING MELEE COMBAT: BUILDING THE CORE FRAMEWORK

```
        {
            IState chase =
            stateMachine.FindState<W_ChaseState>();
            if (chase != null)
            {
    NPCManager.Instance.RegisterInRangeNpc(stateMachine);
            Debug.Log($"[PlayerDetector -
            {gameObject.name}] : Player Visible -
              Switching to Chase State");
              stateMachine.AlertNearbyNPCs();//Alert NPCs
              //within range to join the attack on Player
              stateMachine.SwitchState(chase);
            }
            yield break; //Exit the coroutine once the
            //player becomes visible and state is switched
        }
        else
        {
          Debug.Log($"[PlayerDetector - {gameObject.name}]
          : Player Not in Visible Range");
        }
        yield return new WaitForSeconds(0.1f); //Check
        //every 0.1 seconds
    }
  }
}
```

The PlayerDetector class is designed to detect when the player enters or exits a trigger collider associated with the warrior and subsequently manage the warrior's behavior based on the player's visibility. This includes starting a coroutine to continuously check if the player is visible

CHAPTER 4   ARCHITECTING MELEE COMBAT: BUILDING THE CORE FRAMEWORK

and switching the warrior to a chase state if the player is detected. Additionally, it alerts nearby warriors to join the attack on the player.

1. WarriorStateMachine stateMachine: A reference to the WarriorStateMachine component, which manages the warrior's state transitions. It is essential for accessing and modifying the warrior's current state and behavior based on player detection.

2. Coroutine visibilityCoroutine: A reference to the coroutine that checks for player visibility. It allows for starting and stopping the coroutine as the player enters or exits the warrior's trigger area.

3. Awake(): Initializes the stateMachine field by finding the WarriorStateMachine component in the parent object. If the stateMachine is not found, it logs an error message.

4. OnTriggerEnter(): Here you start the visibility checking coroutine when the player enters the warrior's trigger collider. You go on to check if the collider that entered the trigger has the tag "Player," and if so, log a message indicating that the player entered the warrior's trigger area. Finally, you check if the visibility coroutine is already running, and if not, you start the visibility checking coroutine.

5. OnTriggerExit(): It is triggered when another collider exits the warrior's trigger collider. It stops the player visibility monitoring and unregisters the warrior if the player exits its trigger. It unregisters the warrior from being considered in chasing range. It stops the visibility checking coroutine and nullifies the coroutine reference.

CHAPTER 4   ARCHITECTING MELEE COMBAT: BUILDING THE CORE FRAMEWORK

6. CheckPlayerVisibility(): This coroutine continuously checks if the player remains visible to the warrior. If so, it triggers a state change to chase the player and notifies other warriors to possibly join the chase. A while loop that runs indefinitely commences until manually stopped. It checks if the player is currently visible, in which case it retrieves a chase state instance from the state machine. It then registers the warrior as being in range for potential interaction with the player and signals nearby warriors to potentially respond to the player's presence. It then switches to the Chase state, effectively allowing the warrior to begin the chase sequence. The statement yield break exits the coroutine if the player is visible and the state has been changed. The statement yield return new WaitForSeconds(0.1f): pauses the coroutine for a brief period before rechecking, thus optimizing performance by not continuously running the logic.

This script effectively manages detection and state transitions for warriors based on the player's presence, leveraging Unity's component-based architecture and coroutine system for responsive and efficient behavior control. Additionally, this detection system, which utilizes a trigger, is presented as an alternative to the method introduced in Chapter 3, showcasing a different approach to player detection in Unity.

CHAPTER 4 ARCHITECTING MELEE COMBAT: BUILDING THE CORE FRAMEWORK

Recipe 4-2: Implementing the NPC Manager

Problem

You need a way to handle complex interactions between NPCs (warriors) and the player within a game environment. This includes managing how NPCs detect the player, respond to their presence, and coordinate attacks. The challenge lies in dynamically managing NPC states from detection through various responses based on proximity and ensuring that NPC behaviors are both realistic and synchronized. The class you create must efficiently manage lists of NPCs who are both aware and unaware of the player, orchestrate timed attacks, and maintain global access to NPC management functions without duplicating resources or efforts.

Solution

The NPCManager class provides a centralized solution to orchestrate NPC behaviors relating to player interaction within the scene. It uses a Singleton pattern to ensure a single global point of access while managing two lists of NPCs: those within alert range and all NPCs in the level. Through event-driven programming, it responds to player detection, initializes NPC attacks based on a timing system, and maintains state coherence among the NPCs. This setup allows for dynamic and responsive NPC behavior, from alerting nearby NPCs to managing attack sequences, thus enhancing the overall interactivity and realism of the game environment.

How It Works

The NPCManager class provided as part of Listing 4-2 serves as a centralized manager for handling NPC behaviors and interactions in the game environment, particularly concerning player detection, NPC

CHAPTER 4   ARCHITECTING MELEE COMBAT: BUILDING THE CORE FRAMEWORK

alerting, and attacking mechanics. This class orchestrates multiple NPC actions, ensuring their coordinated response to the player's presence and managing attack sequences among NPCs within a defined alert range.

Listing 4-2. NPCManager script

```
using System.Collections.Generic;
using UnityEngine;
//Attached to the NPCManager game object in the hierarchy that
//contains Patrol Points

public class NPCManager : MonoBehaviour
{
    [Tooltip("Range within which NPCs will be alerted")]
    [SerializeField] private float alertRange = 15f;

    [Tooltip("Time in seconds that needs to elapse  before NPC attacks Player")]
    [SerializeField] private Vector2 attackTimeRange = new
     Vector2(2.0f, 4.0f);

    //Represents NPCs for whom the Player has entered within
    //the bounds of their trigger collider.
    public List<WarriorStateMachine> npcsInRange = new
    List<WarriorStateMachine>();

    //Represents all the NPCs available in the current level
    public List<WarriorStateMachine> npcsInLevel = new
    List<WarriorStateMachine>();
    private static NPCManager instance;
    private WarriorStateMachine currentAttackingNPC;
    private float attackTimer = 2.0f;
```

CHAPTER 4   ARCHITECTING MELEE COMBAT: BUILDING THE CORE FRAMEWORK

```csharp
void Awake()
{
    if (instance == null)
        instance = this;
    else
        Destroy(gameObject);
}

private void Start()
{
 //Populate the npcsInLevel list with all NPCs available
 //within the level.
    PopulateNpcsInLevel();
}

private void OnEnable()
{
    WarriorStateMachine.OnPlayerSpotted +=
    HandlePlayerSpotted;
}

private void OnDisable()
{
    WarriorStateMachine.OnPlayerSpotted -=
    HandlePlayerSpotted;
}

public static NPCManager Instance
{
    get
    {
        if (instance == null)
```

CHAPTER 4   ARCHITECTING MELEE COMBAT: BUILDING THE CORE FRAMEWORK

```csharp
            {
                GameObject go = new GameObject("NPCManager");
                instance = go.AddComponent<NPCManager>();
            }
            return instance;
        }
    }

    private void Update()
    {
        if (npcsInRange.Count > 0)
        {
            if (!IsAnyNPCAttacking())
            {
                if (attackTimer > 0)//wait attackTimer seconds
                        //before having an NPC attack Player.
                {
                    attackTimer -= Time.deltaTime;
                }
                else //select an NPC to attack player
                {
                    //Randomly select NPC to perform an Attack.
                    currentAttackingNPC =
                  npcsInRange[Random.Range(0, npcsInRange.Count)];

                    attackTimer =
                Random.Range(attackTimeRange.x, attackTimeRange.y);
                        if(currentAttackingNPC != null)
                            Debug.Log($"[NPCManager]
                {currentAttackingNPC.name} -  has been selected to
                attack");
                    }
```

CHAPTER 4   ARCHITECTING MELEE COMBAT: BUILDING THE CORE FRAMEWORK

```
            }
        }
        else
            return;
    }

    private void HandlePlayerSpotted(Vector3 alertPosition)
    {
        foreach (WarriorStateMachine npc in npcsInLevel)
        {
            if (Vector3.Distance(npc.transform.position,
        alertPosition) <= alertRange && !npc.HasSpottedPlayer)
            {
                npc.InitiateAttackOnPlayer(npc); //Method to
                    //get NPC to chase and attack player
            }
        }
    }

    private void PopulateNpcsInLevel()
    {
        GameObject[] npcs =
        GameObject.FindGameObjectsWithTag("NPC");
        foreach (GameObject npc in npcs)
        {
            WarriorStateMachine warrior =
            npc.GetComponent<WarriorStateMachine>();
            if (warrior != null)
            {
                npcsInLevel.Add(warrior);
            }
        }
    }
```

CHAPTER 4　ARCHITECTING MELEE COMBAT: BUILDING THE CORE FRAMEWORK

```
//Method below invoked from PlayerDetector class.
public void RegisterInRangeNpc(WarriorStateMachine npc)
{
    if(!npcsInRange.Contains(npc))
    {
        npcsInRange.Add(npc);
        npc.HasSpottedPlayer = true;
    }
}

//Method below invoked from PlayerDetector class.
public void UnregisterOutOfRangeNpc(WarriorStateMachine
                                   npc)
{
    npcsInRange.Remove(npc);
    npc.HasSpottedPlayer = false;
}

 public bool IsAnyNPCAttacking()
{
    return currentAttackingNPC != null;
}

public void SetAttackingNPC(WarriorStateMachine npc)
{
    currentAttackingNPC = npc;
}

public WarriorStateMachine GetAttackingNPC()
{
    return currentAttackingNPC;
}
```

CHAPTER 4 ARCHITECTING MELEE COMBAT: BUILDING THE CORE FRAMEWORK

```
public void ClearAttackingNPC(WarriorStateMachine npc)
{
    if (currentAttackingNPC == npc)
    {
        currentAttackingNPC = null;
    }
}
}
```

1. float alertRange: Specifies the distance within which NPCs are alerted to the player's presence. It is used to determine which NPCs should react to certain player-related events.

2. Vector2 attackTimeRange: Defines the minimum and maximum time intervals between possible attacks by NPCs on the player. This variability adds unpredictability to NPC attacks.

3. List<WarriorStateMachine> npcsInRange: A list of NPCs that have detected the player within their proximity. These NPCs are candidates for initiating an attack or other interaction.

4. List<WarriorStateMachine> npcsInLevel: Contains all NPCs present in the current level, allowing the NPCManager to easily access and manipulate any NPC's state as needed.

5. static NPCManager instance: Implements the Singleton pattern to ensure that there is only one instance of NPCManager throughout the game. This instance can be accessed globally.

CHAPTER 4   ARCHITECTING MELEE COMBAT: BUILDING THE CORE FRAMEWORK

6. WarriorStateMachine currentAttackingNPC: Keeps track of the NPC currently engaged in an attack, ensuring that no other NPC initiates an attack simultaneously.

7. float attackTimer: A countdown timer used to manage the delay before an NPC initiates an attack, providing a cooldown period between attacks.

8. Awake(): This method ensures that the singleton pattern is maintained, destroying any new instances that are created if one already exists.

9. Start(): The Start() method populates the npcsInLevel list with all NPCs present in the level by finding all game objects tagged as "NPC" and adding their WarriorStateMachine component to the list. You will note that each Warrior game object within the scene has been tagged as "NPC."

10. OnEnable() and OnDisable(): Here you subscribe and unsubscribe the HandlePlayerSpotted() event handler method to the OnPlayerSpotted event in the WarriorStateMachine. This ensures that the HandlePlayerSpotted() method is called whenever an NPC spots the player.

11. Instance Property: Provides a safe way to access the Singleton instance of NPCManager. If the instance does not exist, a new one is created.

12. Update(): It manages the attack timing and selection of an NPC to attack the player. If no NPC is currently attacking and the attack timer has elapsed, it selects a random NPC from npcsInRange to initiate an attack.

CHAPTER 4   ARCHITECTING MELEE COMBAT: BUILDING THE CORE FRAMEWORK

13. HandlePlayerSpotted(): Responds to the OnPlayerSpotted event by checking the distance of each NPC from the alert position. If the NPC is within alertRange and has not already spotted the player, it initiates an attack.

14. PopulateNpcsInLevel(): Retrieves and stores all NPCs available in the level to allow for easy access and manipulation throughout the game.

15. RegisterInRangeNpc() and UnregisterOutOfRangeNpc(): Add or remove NPCs to/from the npcsInRange list when the player enters or exits their detection range, respectively. It also updates the HasSpottedPlayer property of the NPCs.

16. IsAnyNPCAttacking(), SetAttackingNPC(), GetAttackingNPC(), and ClearAttackingNPC(): These methods manage the state of the currently attacking NPC, allowing other parts of the system or other NPCs to adjust their behavior based on whether an NPC is currently engaged in an attack.

Recipe 4-3: Implementing the Warrior State Machine

Problem

The Melee Combat System needs to manage complex behaviors of non-player characters (NPCs) in a dynamic game environment. The challenge lies in orchestrating various NPC states, such as Idle, Chase, Attack, Circling, etc., and ensuring these states react appropriately to player interactions. This involves leveraging Unity's NavMeshAgent for seamless

CHAPTER 4　ARCHITECTING MELEE COMBAT: BUILDING THE CORE FRAMEWORK

movement, an Animator for animations, and a state machine architecture to handle state transitions based on gameplay events such as spotting the player, taking damage, etc.

Solution

The WarriorStateMachine utilizes a modular approach to control an NPC's behavior by integrating Unity's component system, including NavMeshAgent for navigation and Animator for animation control. It manages a list of states the NPC (Warrior) can transition between, reacting dynamically to changes in the game environment such as player visibility, health status, etc. The system enhances gameplay by providing NPCs with the ability to detect the player, initiate attacks, or retreat based on strategic decisions, making the interactions more immersive and realistic.

How It Works

The WarriorStateMachine class initializes by setting up references to essential Unity components and subscribing to relevant events that affect NPC behavior, such as player death or NPC health depletion. It uses a list of states to manage the NPC's current behavior, which includes wandering, chasing, attacking, etc., based on the player's actions and the game's evolving context. Each state is defined as a separate component that implements the IState interface, allowing for easy management and transition of states. The class methods such as IsPlayerVisible() and RotateToFacePlayer() handle real-time decision-making and movement adjustments to maintain engagement with the player. Event-driven methods like AlertNearbyNPCs() ensure that NPC reactions are synchronized across the game environment, providing a cohesive and responsive AI system. The architecture not only supports complex behavior patterns but also adheres to principles of modularity and reusability, enhancing the maintainability and scalability of the game's AI systems.

Listing 4-3. WarriorStateMachine script

```
using System;
using System.Collections.Generic;
using System.Linq;
using UnityEngine;
using UnityEngine.AI;

public class WarriorStateMachine : StateMachine
{
    //Events
    public static event Action<Vector3> OnPlayerSpotted;

    [Tooltip("Warriors Field Of View for initiating chase")]
    [SerializeField] private float visibleChaseAngle = 180f;

    public List<IState> states = new List<IState>();
    public Transform Player { get; private set; }//Reference
                                    //to the Player transform
    public NavMeshAgent Agent { get; private set; }//Reference
                                    //to the warrior Agent
    public Animator Anim { get; private set; } //Reference to
                                                //the Animator
    public float CirclingTime { get; set; } //Circling time of
                            //each NPC - used within NPCManager
    public bool HasSpottedPlayer { get; set; } //Determines if
    //Player has been spotted by NPC i.e. Player entered
    into NPCs
    //trigger zone.
    public bool IsPlayerDead { get; set; } //Keeps track of
                        //whether the Player is dead or alive

    private IState startingState;
    private float rotSpeed = 2f;
```

CHAPTER 4   ARCHITECTING MELEE COMBAT: BUILDING THE CORE FRAMEWORK

```csharp
void OnEnable()
{
    Health health = GetComponent<Health>();
    if (health != null)
    {
        health.OnNpcDeath += NpcDead;
        health.OnHealthDepleted += TakeDamage;
    }
}

void OnDisable()
{
    Health health = GetComponent<Health>();
    if (health != null)
    {
        health.OnNpcDeath -= NpcDead;
        health.OnHealthDepleted -= TakeDamage;
    }

    if(Player != null)
        Player.GetComponent<Health>().OnPlayerDeath -=
        PlayerDead;

}

private void Awake()
{
    states = GetComponents<IState>().ToList();
    if (states == null || states.Count == 0)
    {
        Debug.LogError($"[WarriorStateMachine - 
        {gameObject.name}] : No NPC States found.");
        return;
    }
```

CHAPTER 4   ARCHITECTING MELEE COMBAT: BUILDING THE CORE FRAMEWORK

```
        Player = GameObject.FindWithTag("Player").transform;
        if (Player == null)
        {
            Debug.LogError($"[WarriorStateMachine -
            {gameObject.name}] : Player not found.");
            return;
        }
        else
            Player.GetComponent<Health>().OnPlayerDeath +=
            PlayerDead;

        Anim = GetComponent<Animator>();
        if(Anim == null)
        {
            Debug.LogError($"[WarriorStateMachine -
            {gameObject.name}] : Animator not found.");
            return;
        }

        Agent = GetComponent<NavMeshAgent>();
        if (Agent == null)
        {
            Debug.LogError($"[WarriorStateMachine -
            {gameObject.name}] : No NavMesh Agent found.");
            return;
        }
    }

    void Start()
    {
      //Selects Warriow Idle state as a default starting state
        startingState = states.Find(s => s.GetType() ==
        typeof(W_IdleState));
```

CHAPTER 4 ARCHITECTING MELEE COMBAT: BUILDING THE CORE FRAMEWORK

```csharp
        if (!IsPlayerDead)
            SwitchState(startingState);
    }

    /*** Commonly used Methods that can be accessed from any 
        State ***/

    public void InitiateAttackOnPlayer(WarriorStateMachine 
                                    npc)
    {
        Debug.Log($"[WarriorStateMachine - {gameObject.name}]
        : Initiating NPC - {npc.name} to chase down Player");
        IState chase = FindState<W_ChaseState>();
        if (chase != null)
        {
            SwitchState(chase);
        }
    }

    public bool IsPlayerVisible()
    {
        Vector3 npcToPlayerDir = Player.transform.position - 
        transform.position;
        float angle = Vector3.Angle(npcToPlayerDir, 
        transform.forward);

        if (angle < visibleChaseAngle/2)
            return true;
        else
            return false;
    }
```

CHAPTER 4 ARCHITECTING MELEE COMBAT: BUILDING THE CORE FRAMEWORK

```
//Alert nearby NPCs when an NPC detects the Player
public void AlertNearbyNPCs()//Invoked from PlayerDetector
                            //class
{
    //Event being listened for within the NPCManager class
    OnPlayerSpotted?.Invoke(transform.position);
}
//Have NPC Rotate to face the player.
public void RotateToFacePlayer()
{
    Vector3 npcToPlayerDir = Player.transform.position -
    this.transform.position;
    npcToPlayerDir.y = 0;
    this.transform.rotation =
    Quaternion.Slerp(this.transform.rotation,
    Quaternion.LookRotation(npcToPlayerDir),
    Time.deltaTime * rotSpeed);
}

private void NpcDead()
{
    IState death = FindState<W_DeathState>();
    if (death != null)
        SwitchState(death);
    else
    {
     Debug.LogError($"[WarriorStateMachine -
     gameObject.name}] : W_DeathState component not
     attached to the game object.");
        return;
    }
}
```

CHAPTER 4　ARCHITECTING MELEE COMBAT: BUILDING THE CORE FRAMEWORK

```csharp
private void PlayerDead()
{
        IsPlayerDead = true;//Being polled in Warriors
                           //CirclingState.
        Debug.Log("WarriorStateMachine: Player is Dead");
}
private void TakeDamage(string objTag)
{
  if (objTag == "NPC")
  {
    Health health = GetComponent<Health>();
    if (health != null && health.CurrentHealth < 50)
    {
      Debug.Log("NPC Health < 50% - Taking Cover");
      IState takeCover = FindState<W_CoverState>();
      if (takeCover != null)
      {
        SwitchState(takeCover);
        return;
      }
      else
      {
        Debug.LogError($"[WarriorStateMachine - 
        {gameObject.name}] : W_CoverState component not 
        attached to the game object.");
        return;
      }
    }

    Debug.Log("NPC Has been Hit");
    IState hit = FindState<W_HitState>();
```

CHAPTER 4   ARCHITECTING MELEE COMBAT: BUILDING THE CORE FRAMEWORK

```
      if (hit != null)
       SwitchState(hit);
      else
      {
        Debug.LogError($"[WarriorStateMachine -
        {gameObject.name}] : W_HitState component not attached
        to game object.");
        return;
      }
    }
    else if (objTag == "Player")
    {
            // Deal with Player Health damage response.
    }
  }
//A way to refactor logic for finding states into a helper
//method

    //Made public to be invokable from different States.
     public IState FindState<T>() where T : IState
     {
         return states.Find(s => s.GetType() == typeof(T));
     }

     public IState FindState(IState stateInstance)
     {
         return states.Find(s => s.GetType() ==
         stateInstance.GetType());
     }
}
```

1. OnPlayerSpotted: The OnPlayerSpotted event, triggered by the AlertNearbyNPCs() method within this class, is central to NPC coordination, as detailed in Recipe 4-2. This event informs NPCs within the NPCManager class about player detection. NPCs within the specified alert range then collectively engage the player, enhancing the game's interactive dynamics.

2. float visibleChaseAngle: The visibleChaseAngle property, settable via the Inspector with a default value of 180 degrees, defines the NPC's field of view angle for initiating pursuits. It allows for a 90-degree vision to both the left and right, thereby determining the NPC's visibility range. It is critical to determine if the NPC can see the player based on their relative positions and orientations.

3. List<IState> states: This property represents a list of all state instances (IState interface implementations) associated with the NPC. This list essentially stores all states the NPC can be in and is used for managing the different behaviors the NPC can exhibit, such as idling, chasing, wandering, etc.

4. Transform Player: This public property holds a reference to the player's transform, allowing the NPC to orient toward or move relative to the player. It is utilized by several of the individual states an NPC could be in and is used frequently to calculate distances and directions relative to the NPC. You will see this in action in upcoming recipes.

CHAPTER 4   ARCHITECTING MELEE COMBAT: BUILDING THE CORE FRAMEWORK

5. NavMeshAgent Agent: A reference to the NPC's NavMeshAgent, which handles pathfinding and movement within the game world.

6. Animator Anim: A reference to the NPC's Animator component, which controls animations based on the NPC's state and actions.

7. float CirclingTime: A float used to determine how long an NPC circles the player before engaging in an attack on it. This property is set from within the W_CirclingState class and can be referenced from this central location whenever required.

8. bool HasSpottedPlayer: A boolean flag indicating whether the NPC has spotted the player, influencing the NPC's state transitions. Its value is set from the NPCManager class discussed in Recipe 4-2.

9. bool IsPlayerDead: The IsPlayerDead boolean flag tracks the player's status, influencing NPC behavior to cease attacks and transition to wandering once the player is deceased.

10. IState: The initial state of the NPC when the game starts, typically set to the Idle state.

11. float rotSpeed: A private float that determines the speed at which the NPC rotates to face the player, used in the RotateToFacePlayer() method available in this class.

12. OnEnable(): Here you first retrieve the Health component attached to the same GameObject as this script. If the Health component exists, the script subscribes to the Health component's events,

namely, OnNpcDeath and OnHealthDepleted. The OnNpcDeath event is triggered when the NPC's health reaches zero, indicating that the NPC has died. The OnHealthDepleted event is triggered any time the NPC takes damage.

13. OnDisable(): Similarly to OnEnable(), the OnDisable() method retrieves the Health component of the NPC. If the component exists, the method unsubscribes from the events, OnNpcDeath and OnHealthDepleted to prevent the script from reacting to changes when it is not active. You will also note that the player's OnPlayerDeath event is being unsubscribed here. It is important to note that, as seen in Chapter 3, Recipe 3-5 the Health script is common to both the NPC and the Player. In the case of the NPC (warrior), it exists on the Warrior game object and the same script has been placed on the PlayerArmature game object too. Thus, the Player Health component and consequently its OnPlayerDeath event need to be referenced separately. Also, the subscription of the Player–OnPlayerDeath event is done within the Awake() method as described next.

14. Awake(): This method begins by retrieving all components on the GameObject that implement the IState interface. This is done using GetComponents<IState>(), which collects every component that matches the IState type. The array returned by GetComponents<IState>() is immediately converted to a list using.ToList(). This conversion facilitates easier manipulation of the

CHAPTER 4 ARCHITECTING MELEE COMBAT: BUILDING THE CORE FRAMEWORK

states, such as adding, removing, or iterating over items. It then checks whether the state's list is either null or empty. The list being null is theoretically unlikely given the method used, but checking for an empty list is critical because it ensures there are behavior states attached to the NPC. If no states are found, it logs an error with a specific message indicating that no NPC states were found and terminates further execution of the method with a return. This prevents the state machine from proceeding without any states to manage.

Next, you search for the GameObject tagged as "Player" using GameObject.FindWithTag("Player"). This is a common technique to locate important game objects like the player. If no player object is found (i.e., if Player is null), it logs an error stating the player was not found and stops further execution. If the player is found, it then subscribes to the OnPlayerDeath event of the player's Health component. This subscription allows the state machine to react appropriately if the player dies, such as by stopping any NPC attack behavior.

Next, you attempt to get the Animator component attached to the same GameObject. The Animator is crucial for controlling NPC animations based on state changes. If no Animator is found, it logs an error and returns early. This is crucial because, without an Animator, the NPC cannot display animations, which are typically integral to the gameplay experience.

Lastly, you retrieve the NavMeshAgent component, which is essential for handling navigation and movement within a scene. If no NavMeshAgent is found, it logs an error and exits. The NavMeshAgent is fundamental for the NPC to move according to AI pathfinding, making it critical for NPCs that need to chase or evade the player.

15. Start(): Here you set the initial state of the NPC from the list of states, focusing on finding a W_IdleState as the starting state and triggering a state transition to this state if the player isn't dead.

16. InitiateAttackOnPlayer(WarriorStateMachine npc): This method is invoked from within the NPCManager class (Recipe 4-2) via its HandlePlayerSpotted() method. It directly transitions to W_ChaseState if available, resulting in the NPC chasing down the player.

17. IsPlayerVisible(): Computes the visibility of the player based on the angle between the NPC's forward direction and the direction of the player.

18. AlertNearbyNPCs(): This method is invoked from within the PlayerDetector class (Recipe 4-1). It triggers the static event OnPlayerSpotted, which is being listened for within the NPCManager class (Recipe 4-2), which informs other NPCs that the player has been detected so that those NPCs that are within the alert range can then initiate an attack on the player.

CHAPTER 4　ARCHITECTING MELEE COMBAT: BUILDING THE CORE FRAMEWORK

19. RotateToFacePlayer(): Gradually rotates the NPC to face the player, using spherical interpolation for smooth rotation.

20. NpcDead(): This event handler invoked upon the OnNpCDeath event being triggered, transitions the NPC to a death state when it dies.

21. PlayerDead(): The PlayerDead() method, triggered by the OnPlayerDeath event, sets the IsPlayerDead property to true, influencing subsequent NPC behavior. Currently, it logs a message to the console, with no player death animations implemented; these could be added as needed. Importantly, this property is checked in the W_CirclingState; if true, indicating the player's death, it triggers NPCs to switch to the wander state, reflecting the end of active gameplay.

22. TakeDamage(): The TakeDamage() method in the WarriorStateMachine class is a nuanced and critical function that manages the response of an NPC when it takes damage. This method employs a conditional approach based on the source of the damage (identified through the objTag parameter) and implements state transitions according to the NPC's health status and the type of attacker. "objTag" that represents a string indicates the tag of the object causing the damage, which is used to tailor the NPC's response based on whether the damage comes from an NPC or the player. The method first checks if the objTag matches "NPC,"

indicating the damage is inflicted by the player or its ally. Here the Health component is retreived from the NPC itself using GetComponent<Health>(). This component manages the health-related data and behaviors such as the current health level. The method checks if the NPC's current health is below 50, in which case a message is logged to the console indicating "NPC Health < 50% - Taking Cover." It then attempts to find a cover state (W_CoverState) using FindState<W_CoverState>(). If the state is found, it transitions to this state using SwitchState(takeCover). If the W_CoverState is not found, an error is logged indicating that the necessary state component is not attached, which aids in debugging issues related to state management. If a state transition occurs (either to the cover state or upon an error in finding the state), the method returns early to prevent further execution.

If the NPC's health is not below 50, a general hit response is processed, logging the message "NPC Has Been Hit" to indicate a hit has been taken, which is useful for debugging and gameplay feedback. It then searches for a hit state (W_HitState) and transitions to this state if found (where a hit animation for the NPC is played). If no hit state (W_HitState) is found, it logs an error indicating the missing W_HitState.

The method also includes a conditional block for when the damage source is the player (else if (objtag == "Player")), which is currently empty. This block

CHAPTER 4   ARCHITECTING MELEE COMBAT: BUILDING THE CORE FRAMEWORK

is intended to handle specific reactions when the player is hit by an NPC, such as triggering different behaviors or animations that are specific to player interactions.

23. FindState<T>() and FindState(IState stateInstance): The FindState<T>() and FindState(IState stateInstance) overloaded methods in the WarriorStateMachine class are crucial for facilitating state management within the NPC's state machine. These methods are designed to search for and retrieve specific state objects from a list of states associated with the NPC based on different criteria.

    The generic method FindState<T>() is intended to find and return a state of a specific type from the state's list. It is generic, which allows it to be flexible and reusable for any state type that implements the IState interface. It utilizes a generic type parameter <T>, which must be a class that implements the IState interface. This method uses the List<T>.Find() method on the states list to search for the first state that matches the specified type <T>. The Lambda expression: s => s.GetType() == typeof(T) is used as the predicate for the Find() method. This expression checks each state in the list to see if its runtime type matches the type T specified in the method call.

    The overloaded method FindState(IState stateInstance) accepts a parameter as an instance of a class implementing the IState interface. The method uses this instance to determine the type

CHAPTER 4   ARCHITECTING MELEE COMBAT: BUILDING THE CORE FRAMEWORK

to search for within the state's list. Like its generic method, this method also uses List<T>.Find() on the state's list. The Lambda Expression: s => s.GetType() == stateInstance.GetType() is used as the predicate that checks each state in the list to see if its runtime type matches the runtime type of the state instance provided.

Recipe 4-4: Implementing the Chase State

Problem

To get the NPC (Warrior) moving, you need to create a class that defines the behavior of a non-playable character (NPC) when it is in the chase phase. This state is part of the finite state machine managing the NPC's actions based on game dynamics. The primary challenge addressed by this class is to enable realistic NPC behavior that dynamically adjusts between chasing the player and transitioning to other states like circling or idling based on the proximity to the player.

Solution

To tackle the problem, the W_ChaseState class implements the IState interface, allowing it to be controlled by the WarriorStateMachine. The class manages navigation and animation based on the NPC's distance from the player, employing Unity's NavMeshAgent for movement and Animator for animations. Critical elements like stopping distance, collision handling, and state transitions are configured to make the NPC's behavior appear more lifelike and responsive to player movements.

How It Works

The W_ChaseState class provided as part of Listing 4-4 manages an NPC's behavior when chasing the player, utilizing the WarriorStateMachine for state control and the NavMeshAgent for navigation. Upon initialization, the class establishes essential component references and ensures all necessary elements are present. When the NPC enters the chase state, its path is reset, its navigation stopping distance is set, and its weapon collider is disabled to enhance realism, with the running animation triggered to depict the chase visually. During the state update, the NPC constantly adjusts its orientation and position relative to the player, checking proximity to potentially transition to a circling state with a delayed switch to maintain fluidity in movement.

Listing 4-4. W_ChaseState script

```
using UnityEngine;

//States have access to MonoBheaviour methods too.
//All States must be added as components to the NPC game
//object.
public class W_ChaseState : MonoBehaviour, IState
{
    [Tooltip("Stopping Distance from Player at which NPC
      begins Circling Player after Chasing it down")]
    [SerializeField] private float stopDist = 4.75f;

    //Properties
    public float StopDist => stopDist;

    private WarriorStateMachine stateMachine;
    private IState previousState;
    private float playerDetectionSphereRadius;
    private float stopDistBuffer = 1.0f;
```

CHAPTER 4   ARCHITECTING MELEE COMBAT: BUILDING THE CORE FRAMEWORK

```csharp
    private static readonly int ChaseHash =
    Animator.StringToHash("Run");
    private static readonly int IdleHash =
    Animator.StringToHash("Idle");

    void Awake()
    {
        stateMachine = GetComponent<WarriorStateMachine>();
        if (stateMachine == null)
        {
         Debug.LogError($"[ChaseState - {gameObject.name}] :
         WarriorStateMachine not found.");
         return;
        }

        GameObject pds = GameObject.FindGameObjectWithTag
                    ("PlayerDetectionSphere");
        if (pds == null)
        {
         Debug.LogError($"[CirclingState - {gameObject.name}]
         : PlayerDetectionSphere Game Object not found.");
         return;
        }
        else
            playerDetectionSphereRadius =
            pds.GetComponent<SphereCollider>().radius;
    }

    void IState.OnStateEnter()
    {
        if (stateMachine.Agent.enabled)
        {
            stateMachine.Agent.ResetPath();
```

CHAPTER 4   ARCHITECTING MELEE COMBAT: BUILDING THE CORE FRAMEWORK

```
        stateMachine.Agent.stoppingDistance = stopDist;
        stateMachine.Agent.isStopped = false;
    }
    else
    return;

    GameObject meleeWeapon =
    GameObject.FindGameObjectWithTag("MeleeWeapon");
    //Deactivate the Swords collider in Chase state
    meleeWeapon.GetComponent<Collider>().enabled = false;

    stateMachine.Anim.CrossFade(ChaseHash, 0.1f);

    Debug.Log("ChaseState: Enter");
}

void IState.OnStateUpdate(float deltaTime)
{
    stateMachine.RotateToFacePlayer();
    stateMachine.Agent.SetDestination
    (stateMachine.Player.position);//Could use
     //MoveTowardsPlayer() available in W_AttackState
      // Preserve the previous state if not chase state
    if (stateMachine.PreviousState.GetType() !=
        typeof(W_ChaseState))
    {
        previousState = stateMachine.PreviousState;
    }
    // If agent has reached stopping distance from player,
    //have agent circle Player
    if (Vector3.Distance(stateMachine.Player.position,
        transform.position) <= StopDist + stopDistBuffer)
```

377

```csharp
            {
                stateMachine.Anim.CrossFade(IdleHash, 0.1f);
                stateMachine.RotateToFacePlayer();
                Debug.Log($"[ChaseState - {gameObject.name}]
                :Agent has reached stopping distance from Player");

                IState circling =
                stateMachine.FindState<W_CirclingState>();
                if (circling != null)
                {
                 Debug.Log($"[ChaseState - {gameObject.name}] :
                 Switching to Circling State");
                 Utils.Wait(1.0f, this, () =>
                 stateMachine.SwitchState(circling));
                }
            }
            /***
            else if(Vector3.Distance(stateMachine.Player.position,
                transform.position) > playerDetectionSphereRadius)
            {
                //Player is outside bounds of the NPC Collider,
                //then switch to Idle State
                IState idle =
                stateMachine.FindState<W_IdleState>();
                if (idle != null)
                {
                 Debug.Log($"[ChaseState - {gameObject.name}] :
                 Player Escaped NPC Collider - Switching to Idle
                 State");
                 stateMachine.SwitchState(idle);
                }
            }
```

CHAPTER 4   ARCHITECTING MELEE COMBAT: BUILDING THE CORE FRAMEWORK

```
    ***/
}

void IState.OnStateExit()
{
    Debug.Log("ChaseState: Exit");
    stateMachine.Agent.isStopped = false;
}
}
```

1. float stopDist: This serialized field specifies the distance at which the NPC should stop chasing and transition to circling the player. This is critical for maintaining a realistic interaction, preventing the NPC from colliding directly with the player.

2. float StopDist: This is a public property that exposes the stopDist backing field as read-only, ensuring that other classes can read but not modify the distance at which chasing stops.

3. WarriorStateMachine stateMachine: A reference to the WarriorStateMachine attached to the same GameObject. This is crucial for accessing other components and states managed by the state machine.

4. IState previousState: Tracks the state from which the NPC transitioned into the current chase state. This is ideally used for returning to a prior state or for decision-making in complex state transitions.

CHAPTER 4   ARCHITECTING MELEE COMBAT: BUILDING THE CORE FRAMEWORK

5. float playerDetectionSphereRadius: Holds the radius of a sphere (trigger collider) that determines the range at which the NPC can detect the player. This helps in managing the chase logic, particularly in determining when the player is out of detection range.

6. float stopDistBuffer: Adds a buffer to the stopping distance, providing a margin to prevent abrupt state transitions due to minor fluctuations in distance measurements.

7. int ChaseHash and IdleHash: Static fields initialized with hashes of animation states. Using hashes improves performance over using string names directly with the animation system.

8. Awake(): Initializes the stateMachine by attempting to get the WarriorStateMachine component. It also finds the GameObject tagged "PlayerDetectionSphere" and retrieves its radius. If either the state machine or the player detection sphere is not found, an error is logged and further execution is stopped.

9. IState.OnStateEnter(): Here you reset the NPC's navigation agent path and set its stopping distance. You also ensure that the NPC's navigation is not stopped (isStopped = false). You then cache the melee weapon (sword) game object and deactivate its collider, assuming a non-combat physical interaction during the chase. You finally initiate the run animation using a cross-fade for a smooth transition. Note that the sword (melee weapon) carried by the warrior NPC has been tagged as "MeleeWeapon."

CHAPTER 4   ARCHITECTING MELEE COMBAT: BUILDING THE CORE FRAMEWORK

10. IState.OnStateUpdate(float deltaTime): This method that runs every frame consistently rotates the NPC to face the player, keeping the player targeted. It sets the NPC's destination to the player's position, effectively continuing the chase. It then goes on to cache the previous state so long as it was not the chase state, in the event it needs to be used to revert to that previous state. It then checks if the NPC is within the stopping plus buffer distance from the player, in which case it transitions to the circling state after a delay, using a utility Wait() method for delayed execution.

11. The else if block of code that has been commented out can be used to handle a scenario where the player escapes the detection range, in which case the NPC can switch to the Idle state or possibly to the Wander state. Currently, the warrior NPC has been setup to continuously chase down the player.

12. IState.OnStateExit(): Logs exiting the chase state and ensures the NPC's navigation is not forcibly stopped, allowing for continued movement in the subsequent circling state.

Each method in this class is structured to perform specific tasks essential for the chase behavior, with careful management of state transitions based on proximity to the player and other game logic conditions. This setup not only maintains the modular design of NPC behaviors but also facilitates easy adjustments and additions to the NPC's chase behavior logic.

Recipe 4-5: Implementing the Circling State

Problem

Developing a circling mechanic as seen in titles like Assassin's Creed, Batman Arkham series, and Marvel's Spider-Man requires a warrior NPC to execute a circling movement around the player with varying durations and random directions, while also responding to changes in the game environment and player actions. This involves handling state transitions, timing, and environmental interactions, ensuring the NPC's behavior is both challenging and unpredictable.

Solution

The solution involves implementing a state machine pattern using the W_CirclingState class, which allows an NPC to circle the player for a configurable duration and direction. The class integrates with the animation system and pathfinding capabilities to manage NPC movements smoothly and responsively. Key features include randomized circling durations and directions, pause intervals between circling actions, and transitions to other states based on distance checks and environmental triggers like obstacles.

How It Works

The W_CirclingState class provided as part of Listing 4-5 controls an NPC's behavior, allowing it to circle the player with dynamic, configurable durations and directions. Initialization involves setting up the state machine and related components, such as distance and detection parameters. Upon entering the circling state, NPC movement is configured, including direction and circling duration with associated animations. The update routine continually assesses player proximity and

CHAPTER 4 ARCHITECTING MELEE COMBAT: BUILDING THE CORE FRAMEWORK

life status to adjust NPC actions or switch states as needed. If an obstacle is encountered, the circling is interrupted, prompting an immediate state transition, typically to an attack mode. Finally, on exiting the circling state, the NPC resets its movement and animation to a default idle state, ensuring readiness for subsequent actions. This system enhances the interactivity and realism of NPC behavior in-game scenarios.

Listing 4-5. W_CirclingState script

```
using UnityEngine;
using Random = UnityEngine.Random;

//States have access to MonoBheaviour methods too.
//All States must be added as components to the NPC game
//object.

public class W_CirclingState : MonoBehaviour, IState
{
    [Tooltip("A range of seconds for which the NPC Circles
      around the Player")]
    [SerializeField] private Vector2 circlingTime = new
      Vector2(5.0f, 7.0f);
    [Tooltip("NPC's angular circling speed around Player")]
    [SerializeField] private float circlingSpeed = 30f;
    [Tooltip("NPC's pause time after circling time ends before
      restarting Circling")]

    private WarriorStateMachine stateMachine;
    private float circlingTimer;
    private int circlingDir;//Circling direction  of NPC -
            //Left represented by -1 & Right represented by +1
    private float circlingDist;//Distance from Player at which
                        //NPC circles around it.
```

```csharp
private float playerDetectionSphereRadius;
private float stopDistBuffer = 1.0f;

private static readonly int StrafeLeftHash =
Animator.StringToHash("StrafeLeft");
private static readonly int StrafeRightHash =
Animator.StringToHash("StrafeRight");
private static readonly int IdleHash =
Animator.StringToHash("Idle");

void Awake()
{
    stateMachine = GetComponent<WarriorStateMachine>();
    if (stateMachine == null)
    {
    Debug.LogError($"[CirclingState - 
    {gameObject.name}] : WarriorStateMachine not found.");
    return;
    }

    GameObject pds = GameObject.
            FindGameObjectWithTag("PlayerDetectionSphere");
    if ( pds == null)
    {
     Debug.LogError($"[CirclingState - {gameObject.name}] 
     : PlayerDetectionSphere Game Object not found.");
     return;
    }
    else
        playerDetectionSphereRadius =
        pds.GetComponent<SphereCollider>().radius;
```

CHAPTER 4   ARCHITECTING MELEE COMBAT: BUILDING THE CORE FRAMEWORK

```
    //Distance at which NPC circles the Player after
    //having chased it down.
    circlingDist = GetComponent<W_ChaseState>().StopDist;
}
void IState.OnStateEnter()
{
    if (stateMachine.Agent.enabled)
    {
        stateMachine.Agent.isStopped = false;
        stateMachine.Agent.ResetPath();
    }
    else
        return;

    GameObject meleeWeapon =
    GameObject.FindGameObjectWithTag("MeleeWeapon");
    //Deactivate the Swords collider in Idle state
    meleeWeapon.GetComponent<Collider>().enabled = false;

    circlingTimer = Random.Range(circlingTime.x,
                    circlingTime.y);
    stateMachine.CirclingTime = circlingTimer;
    circlingDir = Random.Range(0, 2) == 0 ? -1 : 1;

    if (circlingDir == -1)
    {
     stateMachine.Anim.CrossFade(StrafeLeftHash, 0.1f);
    }
    else
    {
     stateMachine.Anim.CrossFade(StrafeRightHash, 0.1f);
    }
```

CHAPTER 4   ARCHITECTING MELEE COMBAT: BUILDING THE CORE FRAMEWORK

```csharp
        Debug.Log("CirclingState: Enter");
    }

    void IState.OnStateUpdate(float deltaTime)
    {
        if(stateMachine.IsPlayerDead)
        {
         Debug.Log("CirclingState: Player is Dead - Switching
         to Wandering state");
         IState wander =
         stateMachine.FindState<W_WanderState>();
            if (wander != null)
                stateMachine.SwitchState(wander);
        }

        Debug.Log($"[CirclingState - {gameObject.name}] :
        CirclingTimer: {circlingTimer} - Dist NPC To Player:
        {Vector3.Distance(stateMachine.Player.position,
        transform.position)} - Circling Dist: {circlingDist+
        stopDistBuffer}");

        if (circlingTimer > 0 && Vector3.Distance(
            stateMachine.Player.position, transform.position)
            <= (circlingDist + stopDistBuffer))
        {
         Debug.Log($"[CirclingState - {gameObject.name}] :
         Circling Player");
         circlingTimer -= deltaTime;
         transform.RotateAround(stateMachine.Player.position,
         Vector3.up, circlingSpeed * circlingDir * deltaTime);
         stateMachine.RotateToFacePlayer();
        }
```

```
else if (circlingTimer <= 0 ||
        Vector3.Distance(stateMachine.Player.position,
        transform.position) >
        (circlingDist + stopDistBuffer))
{
 Debug.Log($"[CirclingState - {gameObject.name}] :
 Switch to Attacking State");

 if (NPCManager.Instance.GetAttackingNPC() ==
    stateMachine)
    {
    IState attack =
    stateMachine.FindState<W_AttackState>();
        if (attack != null)
        {
         Debug.Log($"[CirclingState -
         {gameObject.name}] : Switching to Attack
          State having completed Circling");
         Utils.Wait(1.0f, this, () =>
         stateMachine.SwitchState(attack));
        }
    }
    else
    {
     // Reset timers to start circling again
     circlingTimer = Random.Range(circlingTime.x,
     circlingTime.y);
    }
}
```

```csharp
        if(Vector3.Distance(stateMachine.Player.position,
           transform.position) >
           (circlingDist + stopDistBuffer) &&
           Vector3.Distance(stateMachine.Player.position,
           transform.position) <= playerDetectionSphereRadius)
        {
         Debug.Log($"[CirclingState - {gameObject.name}] :
         Stop Dist : {circlingDist + stopDistBuffer} - Sphere
         Radius: {playerDetectionSphereRadius} - Enemy To
         Player Distance:
         {Vector3.Distance(stateMachine.Player.position,
          transform.position)}");
         //Can still Chase Player as it's within NPC collider
         //radius.
            IState chase =
            stateMachine.FindState<W_ChaseState>();
            if (chase != null)
            {
              Debug.Log($"[CirclingState - {gameObject.name}] :
              Chasing Escaping Player who is still within NPC
              Collider Radius - Switching to Chase State");
              Utils.Wait(1.0f, this, () =>
              stateMachine.SwitchState(chase));
            }
        }
    }

    private void OnTriggerEnter(Collider other)
    {
        if (other.CompareTag("Obstacle"))
```

CHAPTER 4 ARCHITECTING MELEE COMBAT: BUILDING THE CORE FRAMEWORK

```
    {
      /***
        If NPC stopping distance (radius) is not large
        enough to allow it to circle the Obstacle
        then when it collides with the Obstacle, set
        circlingTime to zero to stop circling and enter
        Attacking state. ***/
      //Ensure CapsuleCollider radius is at least 0.75

      Debug.Log($"CirclingState - {gameObject.name}] :
      Collided with Obstacle");
      circlingTimer = 0;
    }
  }

  void IState.OnStateExit()
  {
      Debug.Log("CirclingState: Exit");
      stateMachine.Agent.ResetPath();
      stateMachine.Anim.CrossFade(IdleHash, 0.1f);
  }
}
```

1. Vecto2 circlingTime: This serialized field defines a range of time in seconds that the NPC will circle the player. It introduces variability to the NPC behavior, making it less predictable.

2. float circlingSpeed: Determines how fast the NPC circles the player, affecting the dynamics of the encounter.

CHAPTER 4   ARCHITECTING MELEE COMBAT: BUILDING THE CORE FRAMEWORK

3. WarriorStateMachine stateMachine: Reference to the WarriorStateMachine component on the same GameObject, central to managing state transitions and accessing shared properties.

4. float circlingTimer: Keeps track of the remaining time for which the NPC will continue to circle the player during its current circling phase.

5. int circlingDir: Indicates the direction of circling; -1 for left and +1 for right. This is randomly set each time circling starts, enhancing NPC behavior's unpredictability.

6. float circlingDist: The radial distance from the player at which the NPC maintains its circling. This is set to the stopping distance defined in the chase state (Recipe 4-4).

7. float playerDetectionSphereRadius: Represents the radius within which the player is detectable by the NPC, crucial for decision-making about when to engage or disengage from circling.

8. float stopDistBuffer: A buffer added to the circling distance to provide leeway in stopping distance calculations, helping prevent abrupt transitions due to minor position errors that could occur.

9. int StrafeLeftHash, StrafeRightHash, IdleHash: Animation parameter hashes used to switch between animations efficiently.

CHAPTER 4 ARCHITECTING MELEE COMBAT: BUILDING THE CORE FRAMEWORK

10. Awake(): Initializes the stateMachine and retrieves the radius from the "PlayerDetectionSphere." It also sets the circlingDist from the W_ChaseState component on the same GameObject, which sets up initial conditions for the NPCs circling behavior.

11. IState.OnStateEnter(): Here you stop the NPC agent movement and reset its path. You then disable the collider for its melee weapon to indicate non-combat motion. You then randomly determine the circling time and direction and choose the appropriate strafing animation based on the circling direction selected.

12. IState.OnStateUpdate(float deltaTime): This method is called every frame and begins by checking if the player is dead and if true, switches to a wandering state, signaling disengagement with the player. The very first if() condition checks if the timer that tracks the duration for which the NPC should circle the player is still greater than zero. If true, it indicates that the NPC should continue circling the player. The second condition within this if() statement ensures that the NPC is within a specific distance from the player (defined by circlingDist plus a buffer stopDistBuffer). This distance check confirms that the NPC is close enough to the player to validly perform circling maneuvers. Upon both these conditions evaluating to true, the circlingTimer is decreased by the delta time (deltaTime), which represents the elapsed time since the last frame

update, effectively counting down the circling duration. Transform.RotateAround() is then used to orbit the player at a specified circlingSpeed, adjusted by the circling direction (circlingDir which can be -1 or +1 for left or right circling) and the frame time delta to ensure smooth motion. The call to stateMachine.RotateToFacePlayer() ensures the NPC continually faces the player while circling, maintaining a logical orientation toward the player.

The else if() condition checks if the circling timer has run out, indicating that the scheduled circling time has been completed. It also verifies if the NPC has drifted or moved beyond the maximum allowed circling distance from the player, possibly due to external forces or player movement. If any of these conditions evaluate to true, it indicates a potential switch to the attacking state. The nested if() condition checks to see if the current NPC is the designated attacker (NPCManager.Instance.GetAttachingNPC() == stateMachine), and if true, it attempts to switch to an attack state. The NPCManager class (Recipe 4-2) randomly selects the designated attacker. If the attack state is found, it schedules a state transition to the W_AttackState after a 1-second delay using Utils.Wait(), providing a brief pause before initiating the attack. This delay can serve as a transition buffer to make the NPC's behavior appear more fluid and natural.

CHAPTER 4   ARCHITECTING MELEE COMBAT: BUILDING THE CORE FRAMEWORK

In the event the NPC is not the designated attacker (as selected within the NPCManager class), it resets the NPC circling timer to have it circle the player again instead of attacking, as this NPC has not yet been selected by the NPCManager to perform an attack on the player. This prepares the NPC to begin a new cycle of circling, maintaining continuous behavior dynamics around the player. The final if() condition within this OnStateUpdate() method addresses the scenario where the NPC finds itself outside of the ideal circling range but still within a broader detection sphere. The first part of this if() condition checks if the NPC is further away from the player than the maximum desired circling distance (circlingDist) plus a buffer (stopDistBuffer). This part of the condition is true if the NPC has drifted or been pushed beyond the intended circling boundary, possibly due to player movement, obstacles, or other in-game dynamics. The second part of this if() condition confirms that despite being out of the circling range, the player is still within the radius of the NPC player detection sphere, which defines how far the NPC can detect the player. This ensures that the player is not too far to be engaged by the NPC again. If the condition evaluates to true, the code attempts to retrieve the W_ChaseState from the state machine's list of states. If the W_ChaseState is found, the utility function, Utils.Wait(), delays the state transition by 1 second, before the NPC resumes active pursuit of the player.

13. OnTriggerEnter(Collider other): Responds to collisions with obstacles by setting the circling timer to zero, thus prompting a state change to an attack state, reflecting an interruption in circling due to environmental factors.

14. IState.OnStateExit(): Here the NPC's path is reset and fades to an idle animation, thereby cleaning up and preparing for the next state.

The W_CirclingState class encapsulates the logic for an NPC circling the player with dynamic behaviors influenced by timers, distances, and environmental interactions. It utilizes Unity's animation system to visually represent the NPC's actions and handles transitions between states based on conditions like timing, player actions, and collision events, showcasing a sophisticated use of state machines in-game AI design. This implementation not only contributes to creating a challenging and engaging player-NPC interaction but also maintains robust and manageable code through clear state management and responsive NPC behavior adjustments.

Recipe 4-6: Implementing the Attack State Problem

NPCs (non-player characters) require dynamic interaction systems to engage players effectively. The challenge is to develop a system where NPCs can detect, approach, and attack the player based on specific conditions, such as proximity and line-of-sight, without overwhelming or underchallenging the player. This system must handle state transitions smoothly to maintain immersion and gameplay flow.

CHAPTER 4   ARCHITECTING MELEE COMBAT: BUILDING THE CORE FRAMEWORK

Solution

The W_AttackState class addresses this challenge by encapsulating the attack behavior of an NPC within a game. By implementing the IState interface, this class manages the NPC's actions during its attack phase, such as moving toward the player, checking for obstacles, initiating an attack when conditions are met, and handling transitions between animations and other states. This solution leverages Unity's animation and navigation systems, ensuring that the NPC's behavior is both realistic and responsive to the player's actions.

How It Works

The W_AttackState class manages an NPC's attack behavior by leveraging the IState interface to control actions like movement toward the player, obstacle detection, and attack initiation based on specific gameplay conditions. Upon entering the attack state, the NPC prepares for movement and engagement, activating necessary components like weapon colliders. During the state, it continuously evaluates its proximity to the player and the presence of obstacles, triggering an attack sequence if conditions are favorable, or transitioning to a retreat state otherwise. The attack process is managed through careful control of animations, ensuring that actions are synchronized with the game state. Upon exiting the attack state, the class ensures all actions are cleanly terminated, resetting navigation and state flags to maintain smooth gameplay transitions.

Listing 4-6. W_AttackState script

```
using System.Collections;
using UnityEngine;
//States have access to MonoBheaviour methods too.
//All States must be added as components to the NPC game
//object.
```

CHAPTER 4   ARCHITECTING MELEE COMBAT: BUILDING THE CORE FRAMEWORK

```csharp
public class W_AttackState : MonoBehaviour, IState
{
    [Tooltip("A child object of the NPC that indicates its Eye
     Level")]
    [SerializeField] private GameObject npcEyes; //Object that
                                    //indicates eye level of NPC
    [Tooltip("NPC can attack Player only when within this
     distance")]
    [SerializeField] private float attackDistance =
      1f;  //Distance from Player at which NPC launches a sword
           //attack.
    private WarriorStateMachine stateMachine;
    private bool isAttacking;

    private readonly int attackHash =
    Animator.StringToHash("SwordSlash");
    private readonly int walkHash =
    Animator.StringToHash("Walk");
    private readonly int idleHash =
    Animator.StringToHash("Idle");

    private const float crossFadeTime = 0.1f;

    void Awake()
    {
        stateMachine = GetComponent<WarriorStateMachine>();
        if (stateMachine == null)
        {
            Debug.LogError($"[AttackState - {gameObject.name}]
             : WarriorStateMachine not found.");
            return;
        }
    }
```

CHAPTER 4   ARCHITECTING MELEE COMBAT: BUILDING THE CORE FRAMEWORK

```
void IState.OnStateEnter()
{
    if (stateMachine.Agent.enabled)
    {
        stateMachine.Agent.isStopped = false;
    }
    else
        return;

    GameObject meleeWeapon =
    GameObject.FindGameObjectWithTag("MeleeWeapon");
    //Activate the Swords collider in the Attack state
    meleeWeapon.GetComponent<Collider>().enabled = true;

    stateMachine.RotateToFacePlayer();

      //Let the NPCManager Singleton know an Attack is
    //underway.
    NPCManager.Instance.SetAttackingNPC(stateMachine);

    stateMachine.Anim.CrossFadeInFixedTime(walkHash,
    crossFadeTime);//walk to attack Player.

    Debug.Log("AttackState: Enter");
}
void IState.OnStateUpdate(float deltaTime)
{
    if (isAttacking)
        return;

    MoveTowardsPlayer();
```

CHAPTER 4   ARCHITECTING MELEE COMBAT: BUILDING THE CORE FRAMEWORK

```
if(Vector3.Distance(stateMachine.Player.position, 
transform.position) <= (attackDistance + 0.25f))
{
    if (!IsObstacleInPath())
    {
        stateMachine.Anim.CrossFadeInFixedTime(
        attackHash,crossFadeTime);
        StartCoroutine(AttackPlayer());
    }
    else
    {
      //You can't attack a Player if he is behind an
      //Obstacle

      //Give other NPCs a chance to Attack
      NPCManager.Instance.
      ClearAttackingNPC(stateMachine);

      //Retreat from the Player.
      IState retreat =
      stateMachine.FindState<W_RetreatState>();
      if (retreat != null)
      {
       Debug.Log($"[AttackState - {gameObject.name}] : 
       Switching to Retreat State having completed an 
       Attack on Player");
       Utils.Wait(1.0f, this, () =>
       stateMachine.SwitchState(retreat));
      }
    }
  }
}
```

CHAPTER 4   ARCHITECTING MELEE COMBAT: BUILDING THE CORE FRAMEWORK

```
private void MoveTowardsPlayer()
{
    if (stateMachine == null) return;

    Vector3 directionToPlayer =
    (stateMachine.Player.position -
    transform.position).normalized;
    directionToPlayer.y = 0; //Ensure movement is only
                             //on the horizontal plane
    float distanceToPlayer =
    Vector3.Distance(stateMachine.Player.position,
    transform.position);

    if (distanceToPlayer > attackDistance)
    {
        // Calculate the desired movement vector
        Vector3 moveVector = directionToPlayer *
        stateMachine.Agent.speed * Time.deltaTime;
        stateMachine.Agent.Move(moveVector);

        // Rotate to face the player
        Quaternion lookRotation =
        Quaternion.LookRotation(directionToPlayer);
        transform.rotation =
        Quaternion.Slerp(transform.rotation,
        lookRotation,stateMachine.Agent.angularSpeed *
        Time.deltaTime);
    }
    else
    {
        // Stop movement if within stopping distance
        stateMachine.Agent.Move(Vector3.zero);
```

CHAPTER 4   ARCHITECTING MELEE COMBAT: BUILDING THE CORE FRAMEWORK

```
            // Rotate to face the player
            Quaternion lookRotation =
            Quaternion.LookRotation(directionToPlayer);
            transform.rotation =
            Quaternion.Slerp(transform.rotation, lookRotation,
            stateMachine.Agent.angularSpeed * Time.deltaTime);
        }
    }

    void IState.OnStateExit()
    {
        Debug.Log("AttackState: Exit");

        // Clear the attacking NPC if this NPC was attacking
        if (NPCManager.Instance.IsAnyNPCAttacking() &&
        NPCManager.Instance.GetAttackingNPC() == stateMachine)
        {
           NPCManager.Instance.
           ClearAttackingNPC(stateMachine);
        }
        stateMachine.Agent.ResetPath();
        isAttacking = false;
    }

    private bool IsObstacleInPath()
    {
        int layerMask = LayerMask.GetMask("Obstacle");
        // Use a simple Raycast to detect obstacles
        RaycastHit hit;
        if(Physics.Raycast(npcEyes.transform.position,
          transform.forward,out hit,attackDistance,layerMask))
        {
            if (hit.collider.CompareTag("Obstacle"))
```

CHAPTER 4   ARCHITECTING MELEE COMBAT: BUILDING THE CORE FRAMEWORK

```
        {
            Debug.Log($"[CirclingState -
            {gameObject.name}] : Obstacle Encountered :
            {hit.collider.gameObject.name}");
            return true;
        }
    }
    return false;
}

IEnumerator AttackPlayer()
{
    isAttacking = true;

    // Wait until the 'RightHandAttack' animation is
    //nearly completed
    yield return new WaitUntil(() =>
    IsAnimationNearlyComplete("SwordSlash", 0.99f));
    stateMachine.Anim.CrossFadeInFixedTime(idleHash,
    crossFadeTime);//stop walking.

    //Retreat from the Player.
    IState retreat =
    stateMachine.FindState<W_RetreatState>();
    if (retreat != null)
    {
     Debug.Log($"[AttackState - {gameObject.name}] :
     Switching to Retreat State having completed an Attack
     on Player");
     Utils.Wait(1.0f, this, () =>
     stateMachine.SwitchState(retreat));
    }
}
```

CHAPTER 4   ARCHITECTING MELEE COMBAT: BUILDING THE CORE FRAMEWORK

```
    private bool IsAnimationNearlyComplete(string stateName,
                                        float threshold)
{
        //Using layer 1
        AnimatorStateInfo stateInfo =
        stateMachine.Anim.GetCurrentAnimatorStateInfo(1);

        return stateInfo.IsName(stateName) &&
        stateInfo.normalizedTime >= threshold;
    }
}
```

1. GameObject npcEyes: Represents the eye level of the NPC. It is used as the starting point of line-of-sight checks (via a Raycast()) for detecting obstacles between the NPC and the player.

2. float attackDistance: Defines the maximum distance from which the NPC can initiate an attack on the player. It's crucial for gameplay balance, ensuring the NPC doesn't initiate attacks from an unrealistically long range.

3. WarriorStateMachine stateMachine: A reference to the WarriorStateMachine component on the NPC, crucial for state management and accessing shared NPC properties and methods.

4. bool isAttacking: A boolean flag indicating whether the NPC is currently in the process of executing an attack. This prevents executing the entire logic within the OnStateUpdate() method if an attack is already in progress. Note that OnStateUpdate() is invoked every frame.

CHAPTER 4   ARCHITECTING MELEE COMBAT: BUILDING THE CORE FRAMEWORK

5. int attackHash, walkHash, idleHash: Animator parameter hashes used to efficiently manage transitions between animations for attacking, walking, and idling.

6. const float crossFadeTime: The duration of the cross-fade for animation transitions, enhancing the visual smoothness of state changes.

7. Awake(): Initializes the stateMachine and logs an error if it's not found. This setup is critical for the subsequent operations of the attack state.

8. IState.OnStateEnter(): Here you set the NPC's navigation agent's "isStopped" property to false, preparing it for movement. You then activate the melee weapon collider, making the NPC ready to physically attack the player and deal it damage. The NPC is then rotated to face the player, and the NPCManager is notified that this NPC is now the attacking unit. Lastly, you play the Walk animation to get the NPC to walk toward the player to engage in combat.

9. IState.OnStateUpdate(float deltaTime): This core method plays a crucial role in handling the NPC's behavior when it is in the attack state. This method is called every frame while the NPC is in this state, allowing the NPC to update its behavior based on its proximity to the player, the presence of obstacles, and other factors. If the NPC is currently in the process of attacking (isAttacking is true), the method returns early, skipping the subsequent code. This prevents the NPC from moving toward the player

while an attack is already underway, ensuring that each attack sequence is completed before another begins.

Next, the MoveTowardsPlayer() method is invoked, which handles the logic for moving the NPC toward the player. This method calculates the direction of the player and commands the NPC's navigation agent to keep moving toward the player until it reaches the defined attackDistance.

The first If() statement encountered, determines if the NPC is close enough to initiate an attack sequence. It checks if the NPC is within a small margin of the attackDistance.The addition of 0.25f acts as a buffer to account for minor discrepancies in distance calculations due to frame rates or NPC movement speeds. If the NPC is within this range, it proceeds to check for obstacles before attacking.

The nested if() statement invokes the IsObstacleInPath() method, which uses a raycast from the NPC's "eyes" to check for any obstacles directly in the line of sight to the player. If there are no physical barriers (like walls or other environmental obstacles) between the NPC and the player that would realistically prevent an attack from connecting, the NPC launches its attack on the player by initiating a cross-fade to the attack animation using the attackHash. The AttackPlayer() coroutine is also invoked, managing the attack logic, which includes animation handling and subsequently retreating after the attack, allowing for controlled attack behavior.

In the event an obstacle is detected, the NPC informs the NPCManager to clear its attacking status, allowing other NPCs the opportunity to attack. This is crucial in scenarios where multiple NPCs are engaging the player, maintaining a dynamic and fluid combat situation. The NPC then looks for a W_RetreatState within its state machine. If found, it uses the Wait() utility method to delay the state transition by one second and then invokes the retreat state, which provides a brief respite in the action, adding to the realism and giving the player a short breather.

10. MoveTowardsPlayer(): This method is responsible for controlling the NPC's movement toward the player until it reaches the defined attack distance. This method determines the direction and amount of movement required in each frame.

    You begin by calculating the vector pointing from the NPC to the player by subtracting the NPC's position (transform.position) from the player's position (stateMachine.Player.position). The resulting vector represents the direction from the NPC to the player in 3D space. The .normalized property converts this vector into a unit vector (length of 1) while maintaining its direction. Normalization is crucial as it allows consistent movement regardless of distance. Setting the y component of the direction vector to zero ensures that the NPC moves strictly in the horizontal (XZ) plane, avoiding any vertical movement that is typical for walking characters on flat terrain.

CHAPTER 4   ARCHITECTING MELEE COMBAT: BUILDING THE CORE FRAMEWORK

You now proceed to calculate the straight-line distance between the NPC and the player using Vector3.Distance(), which essentially computes the magnitude of the vector difference between the two points.

The If() statement then checks to see if the distance to the player computed earlier is greater than the defined attack distance, and if true, you calculate a new moveVector by multiplying the normalized direction vector (directionToPlayer) by the NPC's movement speed (stateMachine.Agent.speed) and the time elapsed since the last frame (Time.deltaTime), which yields a vector that ensures smooth and frame-rate independent movement.

You then use the NavMeshAgent.Move() method to move the NPC along the calculated vector. This method is used for manual movement control, applying the movement vector directly to the NPC's position. The reason you are using NavMeshAgent.Move() instead of simply setting the NavMeshAgent destination via the stateMachine.Agent.SetDestination() method is because the movements involved within this Attack state could be extremely small, in which case the SetDestination() method fails to work well enough given my testing experiences. You then proceed to create a rotation that looks along the directionToPlayer vector, orienting the NPC so that its forward direction points toward the player. Quaternion.Slerp() then interpolates smoothly between the NPC's current rotation and the target rotation (lookRotation).

CHAPTER 4   ARCHITECTING MELEE COMBAT: BUILDING THE CORE FRAMEWORK

The interpolation is scaled by the NPC's angular speed (stateMachine.Agent.angularSpeed) and Time.deltaTime, which ensures that the rotation is smooth and consistent over time, regardless of frame rate.

The else condition checks to see if the NPC is closer to the player than the attackDistance, in which case it stops it from moving by setting its movement vector to Vector3.zero and has it rotate to face the player.

11. IsObstacleInPath(): This method is designed to determine whether there is an obstacle between the NPC and its target (the player) within the specified attack range. This is crucial for ensuring that the NPC does not attempt to attack through walls or other solid objects.

    You begin by defining a layer mask for a ray cast to interact only with objects that are in the "Obstacle" layer. This is a filtering step that optimizes the ray cast by ignoring other types of objects that the NPC should not consider as obstacles (like other NPCs, the ground, etc.).

    You then use Physics.Raycast() to perform a ray cast from the NPC's "eyes" position (npcEyes.transform.position). This starting point is chosen because it represents a logical point on the NPC's body to check the line of sight. The ray is cast in the direction the NPC is currently facing (transform.forward), which is the forward direction relative to the NPC's current orientation. The out parameter "hit" captures information about what the ray hits. This includes the point of collision, the distance, the object hit, and more. The ray extends up to the attackDistance, which is the defined range at which the NPC is programmed to initiate an attack. This ensures the obstacle check is relevant to the NPC's current combat context. The raycast only interacts with objects that are on the "Obstacle" layer, ensuring the check is focused and efficient.

A successful raycast hit results in the if() statement evaluating to true, in which case you check if the object hit by the ray cast is tagged as an "Obstacle." This is an additional verification step to ensure that the object is indeed considered an obstacle within the game logic. If an obstacle is confirmed, the method returns true, indicating that there is an obstacle in the NPC's attack path. If the ray cast does not hit an obstacle, or if the object hit is not tagged as an "Obstacle," the method returns false, indicating that the path is clear for the NPC to proceed with its intended action of attacking.

12. IsAnimationNearlyComplete(): This method is designed to determine if a specific animation state in the Animator component of a GameObject is approaching completion. This is crucial for scenarios where game logic needs to synchronize with animations, such as ending an action, transitioning states, or triggering events at precise moments in an animation's playback.

CHAPTER 4 ARCHITECTING MELEE COMBAT: BUILDING THE CORE FRAMEWORK

The method checks if an animation state specified by its animation name ("SwordSlash" in this case) on a particular layer of the Animator (layer 1 in this case) has progressed to or beyond a specified threshold (99 %) of its total duration, in which case you retrieve the AnimatorStateInfo for the animation state currently playing on layer 1 of the Animator. Layer indices start at 0, so 1 typically refers to a secondary layer that might be used for more specific or overriding animations. AnimatorStateInfo is a struct provided by Unity that contains information about the current state of an animation playing on an Animator component.

Within the "return" statement that returns a boolean value, this method checks if the name of the current animation state matches the stateName parameter, which is crucial to ensure that the progress check is being made against the correct animation. The following condition checks if the normalizedTime of the animation has reached or exceeded the threshold value provided. The threshold is expected to be a float typically between 0 and 1, where 1 would mean 100% completed. "stateInfo.normalizedTime" represents the progress of the animation as a value between 0 (start) and 1 (end). For example, a normalizedTime of 0.5 means the animation is halfway completed.

Within the attack state here, this method is being used as a conditional check before changing the state in the state machine to the retreat state, by only allowing an NPC to leave the attack state

CHAPTER 4   ARCHITECTING MELEE COMBAT: BUILDING THE CORE FRAMEWORK

and transition into the retreat state once its attack animation is nearly complete (99%), thus maintaining fluidity and realism in its behavior.

13. AttackPlayer(): This coroutine orchestrates a sequence of actions that comprise an NPC's attack on a player followed by a subsequent retreat. It is designed to manage the attack by timing animations precisely and then transitioning the NPC to the retreat state once the attack completes.

    At the beginning of the coroutine, "isAttacking" is set to true. This flag is used to prevent the NPC from initiating another attack while already in the process of attacking.

    The coroutine uses yield return new WaitUntil(...) to pause its execution until a certain condition is met. The condition is that the "SwordSlash" animation is nearly complete.

    The IsAnimationNearlyComplete("SwordSlash," 0.99f) method checks if the specified animation ("SwordSlash") has reached or exceeded 99% (0.99) of its playback. A threshold of 0.99 ensures that the method waits until the animation is just about to finish, which is crucial for timing effects, damage application, and transitions that need to happen right at the end of the attack animation.

    After the attack animation nears completion, the NPC's animator is instructed to transition to an idle animation using CrossFadeInFixedTime(). This method is used to smoothly blend into the idle animation over a period defined by crossFadeTime.

After the animation transition, the coroutine attempts to find a "retreat" state using stateMachine. FindState<W_RetreatState>(), which when found results in the Utils.Wait() method is invoked, which delays the actual state transition by 1.0 seconds. This delay can be useful to provide a brief pause or cooldown after attacking, simulating recovery, or reevaluation by the NPC before changing its behavior. The Utils.Wait() method schedules the SwitchState() call to occur after the specified delay, ensuring that the gameplay feels responsive yet realistic.

After setting up the transition to the retreat state, the coroutine effectively ends. If the retreat state was not found, the coroutine would also end, but without attempting to change the NPC's state; hence, you need to ensure that every state that could be invoked by the NPC has been attached to it.

14. OnStateExit(): Here you clear this NPC as the attacking unit if it was the attacker and reset its attack flag. You also reset the NPC's navigation path to prevent any residual movement commands from affecting future states.

Recipe 4-7: Implementing the Retreat State

Problem

A new state is required to manage the "retreat" behavior of a non-player character (NPC), particularly after the NPC has engaged in an attack. This class is integral to a larger state machine that governs various NPC behaviors. The key challenge addressed by this class is to enable the NPC to retreat efficiently to a predetermined safe distance after an attack interaction, ensuring strategic repositioning away from the player.

Solution

To solve the problem of managing the NPC's retreat behavior, the W_RetreatState class implements several methods and fields that facilitate this process. Key functionalities include calculating the direction and distance to retreat, handling animation transitions to visually represent the retreat, and managing transitions to other states like "circling" once the retreat is complete. The class also integrates with Unity's pathfinding and animation systems to ensure smooth movement and responsiveness.

How It Works

The W_RetreatState class manages an NPC's retreat behavior post-attack through several key processes. During initialization, it ensures necessary components are present and sets the retreat distance. The OnStateEnter() method activates when the NPC enters the retreat state, handling the calculation of the retreat direction, deactivation of the weapon's collider, and the initiation of a retreat animation. The OnStateUpdate() method continuously evaluates the NPC's position relative to the player, managing the movement and eventual state transition once the retreat is complete. The retreat mechanics are handled by the RetreatFromPlayer() method, which calculates the movement vectors and orientation adjustment. Lastly, OnStateExit() logs the state change and transitions the NPC's animation back to idle, signaling the end of the retreat. This structured approach within the state machine framework ensures strategic and realistic NPC behavior management.

CHAPTER 4 ARCHITECTING MELEE COMBAT: BUILDING THE CORE FRAMEWORK

Listing 4-7. W_RetreatState script

```
using UnityEngine;

//States have access to MonoBheaviour methods too.
//All States must be added as components to the NPC game
//object.

public class W_RetreatState : MonoBehaviour, IState
{
    //Distance to which NPC should retreat after an Attack
    //on Player
    private float retreatDistance;
    private WarriorStateMachine stateMachine;

    private static readonly int WalkBackwardHash =
    Animator.StringToHash("WalkBackward");
    private static readonly int IdleHash =
    Animator.StringToHash("Idle");

    void Awake()
    {
        stateMachine = GetComponent<WarriorStateMachine>();
        if (stateMachine == null)
        {
         Debug.LogError($"[RetreatState -
         {gameObject.name}] : WarriorStateMachine not found.");
         return;
        }

      //After an Attack on the Player NPC retreats only to its
      //circling Distance.
        retreatDistance =
        GetComponent<W_ChaseState>().StopDist;
    }
```

```csharp
void IState.OnStateEnter()
{
    if (stateMachine.Agent.enabled)
    {
        stateMachine.Agent.isStopped = false;
    }
    else
        return;

    GameObject meleeWeapon =
    GameObject.FindGameObjectWithTag("MeleeWeapon");

    //Deactivate the Swords collider in Retreat state
    meleeWeapon.GetComponent<Collider>().enabled = false;

    stateMachine.Anim.CrossFade(WalkBackwardHash, 0.1f);

    Debug.Log("RetreatState: Enter");
}

void IState.OnStateUpdate(float deltaTime)
{
    RetreatFromPlayer(retreatDistance, deltaTime);

    // Check if the NPC has reached its destination to
    // transition back to circling
    if (stateMachine.Agent.remainingDistance <=
        stateMachine.Agent.stoppingDistance &&
        !stateMachine.Agent.pathPending)
    {
      Debug.Log($"[RetreatState: {gameObject.name}]
      Retreated to its original Circling Distance");

        IState circling =
        stateMachine.FindState<W_CirclingState>();
```

```
            if (circling != null)
            {
              Debug.Log($"[RetreatState - {gameObject.name}] :
              Switching to Circling State having completed
              Retreat");
              Utils.Wait(1.0f, this, () =>
              stateMachine.SwitchState(circling));
            }
        }
    }

    private void RetreatFromPlayer(float retreatDistance,
                                   float deltaTime)
    {
     // Calculate the direction from the NPC to the player
     Vector3 directionToPlayer = (stateMachine.Player.position
     - transform.position).normalized;
     directionToPlayer.y = 0; //Ensure movement is only on the
                              //horizontal plane
     float distanceFromPlayer =
     Vector3.Distance(stateMachine.Player.position,
     transform.position);

        if (distanceFromPlayer < retreatDistance)//you could
                                 //provide a buffer here.
        {
         // Calculate the retreat direction and the movement
         //vector
         Vector3 retreatDirection = -directionToPlayer;
         Vector3 moveVector = retreatDirection *
         stateMachine.Agent.speed * deltaTime;
```

```csharp
        // Move the agent
        stateMachine.Agent.Move(moveVector);

        // Rotate to face the player
        Quaternion lookRotation =
        Quaternion.LookRotation(directionToPlayer);
         transform.rotation =
         Quaternion.Slerp(transform.rotation, lookRotation,
         stateMachine.Agent.angularSpeed * deltaTime);
        }
        else
        {
          // Stop movement if the NPC has reached the retreat
          //distance
          stateMachine.Agent.Move(Vector3.zero);

          // Rotate to face the player
          Quaternion lookRotation =
          Quaternion.LookRotation(directionToPlayer);
          transform.rotation =
          Quaternion.Slerp(transform.rotation, lookRotation,
          stateMachine.Agent.angularSpeed * deltaTime);
        }
    }

    void IState.OnStateExit()
    {
        Debug.Log("RetreatState: Exit");
        stateMachine.Anim.CrossFade(IdleHash, 0.1f);
    }
}
```

CHAPTER 4   ARCHITECTING MELEE COMBAT: BUILDING THE CORE FRAMEWORK

1. float retreatDistance: This private float variable represents the distance to which the NPC should retreat relative to the player. It's set to match the stopping distance of the chase state, ensuring the NPC retreats only far enough to maintain strategic positioning.

2. WarriorStateMachine stateMachine: This private variable of type WarriorStateMachine references the state machine controlling the NPC, allowing the state class to request state transitions and access shared components, properties, and methods.

3. int WalkBackwardHash and IdleHash: These are static read-only integers obtained from Animator. StringToHash(). They represent cached hashes of the animator states, making the transition between animations more efficient by avoiding string lookups at runtime.

4. Awake(): This method first ensures the WarriorStateMachine component is present and then sets the retreatDistance to the StopDist of the W_ChaseState.

5. OnStateEnter(): Here you check to ensure that the NPC's navigation agent is enabled, and set its "isStopped" property to false, allowing it freedom of movement. You then find the NPC's melee weapon by tag and disable its collider to prevent it from dealing damage while retreating. Finally, the CrossFade() method is used to blend into the "WalkBackward" animation, indicating a retreat movement.

CHAPTER 4   ARCHITECTING MELEE COMBAT: BUILDING THE CORE FRAMEWORK

6. OnStateUpdate(): This method is called repeatedly every frame and manages the retreat actions as well as the transition back to the circling state once the conditions are met.

    The method starts by calling RetreatFromPlayer(retreatDistance, deltaTime). This method is responsible for calculating and executing the actual retreat motion of the NPC away from the player. It uses the retreatDistance to determine how far back the NPC should move and deltaTime to factor in frame rate independence.

    The If() statement then checks to ensure that both its conditions are met. The first condition checks to ensure that the NPC is close enough to its intended stopping point, suggesting that the retreat action has sufficiently been executed. It then also checks to ensure that there are no pending path calculations for the NPC. If true, it means that the NPC's path to its retreat destination has been fully computed and the NPC is not waiting on further path updates, which can affect the movement or next state transition. If both conditions mentioned are satisfied, indicating that the NPC has successfully retreated to the distance required to return to a circling behavior around the player, it proceeds to find the circling state using stateMaster.FindState<W_CirclingState>(). This method retrieves the state instance for circling, and if not null, indicating that the state was successfully found, it executes the Utils.Wait() method to delay the state transition by 1 second before moving the NPC back to the circling state.

CHAPTER 4   ARCHITECTING MELEE COMBAT: BUILDING THE CORE FRAMEWORK

7. RetreatFromPlayer(): This method manages the physical movement and orientation of the NPC during its retreat behavior. This method utilizes Unity's Transform and NavMeshAgent components to calculate and execute the NPC's movements away from the player based on specific conditions and parameters.

    The first line computes the direction from the NPC to the player using stateMachine.Player.position - transform.position, resulting in a vector pointing from the NPC to the player. This vector is then normalized (.normalized) to ensure it has a unit length, making it suitable for further calculations that do not depend on the distance magnitude. The statement "directionToPlayer.y = 0" ensures that the movement calculation is constrained to the horizontal (XZ) plane. By setting the y-component of the direction vector to zero, vertical movement is eliminated, which is typical in many games where the NPC should only move along the ground. The next line of code calculates the actual distance from the NPC to the player using the Vector3.Distance() method, providing the scalar distance between the two points in 3D space. The If() statement then checks if the current "distanceFromPlayer" is less than the specified "retreatDistance." If the NPC is closer to the player than this distance, it means the NPC needs to increase this distance by moving backward. If this is the case, it calculates the opposite direction of directionToPlayer, effectively determining the direction to move away from the player. It then computes a new movement vector by multiplying the retreat direction by the NPC's speed and the frame's delta time. The NPC is then moved using its NavMeshAgent. The Move() method applies the calculated vector to the NPC's position, facilitating continuous and direct control over the NPC's movement. It then creates a "lookRotation" Quaternion that makes the NPC face toward the player by gradually rotating the NPC from its current rotation toward the newly created "lookRotation" at a rate determined by the agent's angular speed, smoothed over time with deltaTime.

If the NPC has reached the appropriate retreat distance, its movement is stopped by passing a zero vector to the Move method. The rotation logic is repeated here, ensuring that even when the NPC stops moving, it continues to face the player, maintaining engagement and readiness for subsequent actions.

8. OnStateExit(): When exiting the retreat state, you have the animation transitions to "Idle" using CrossFade().

This class effectively encapsulates the behavior of an NPC in retreat, handling both the movement away from threats and the subsequent transition to other behaviors based on the game's logic and the distance to the player. Each method and field serves to maintain the cohesion and necessary operations within this specific state of the NPC's behavior management.

Recipe 4-8: Implementing the Warrior Animation Events Class

Problem

An important challenge that needs to be addressed is that of synchronizing the collision capabilities of a warrior's sword with the corresponding "SwordSlash" animation available within Unity's Animator. This synchronization needs to ensure that the sword's collider is active only during the specific frames of this animation where the sword is meant to impact the player, preventing unrealistic interactions outside of these frames.

Solution

To manage this challenge, the WarriorAnimationEvents class utilizes proxy methods to control the activation and deactivation of the sword's collider based on animation cues. It leverages the MeleeWeaponDamage component, which is attached to the sword – a direct child of the warrior GameObject. This MeleeWeaponDamage class discussed in the next recipe ensures that the collider is enabled during attack animations and disabled afterward, maintaining consistency between visual cues and gameplay mechanics.

How It Works

The WarriorAnimationEvents class serves as a mediator between the animation system and the game mechanics, specifically focusing on managing the collider of a warrior's sword during animations. This is commonly used in games to ensure that collision checks (like hits and damage detection) only occur during the active frames of an

CHAPTER 4 ARCHITECTING MELEE COMBAT: BUILDING THE CORE FRAMEWORK

animation where a weapon is supposed to impact another object or character. This class is designed to synchronize the active state of a warrior's sword collider with its animation frames, ensuring realistic gameplay interactions. This class features two main proxy methods: EnableSwordCollider() and DisableSwordCollider(). These are invoked at specific points in the sword's animations to enable or disable the collider, corresponding to the visual attack movements. This mechanism ensures that the sword only causes damage when it's supposed to, based on the visible animations, enhancing both the realism and fairness of the game.

Listing 4-8. WarrriorAnimationEvents script

```
using UnityEngine;

public class WarriorAnimationEvents : MonoBehaviour
{
    private MeleeWeaponDamage swordDamage;

    private void Awake()
    {
        //Assuming the sword is a direct child of the warrior
        swordDamage =
        GetComponentInChildren<MeleeWeaponDamage>();
        if (swordDamage == null)
        {
            Debug.LogError("MeleeWeaponDamage component not
            found on sword child object.");
        }
    }

    // Proxy method to enable the sword's collider
    public void EnableSwordCollider()
```

```
    {
        if (swordDamage != null)
        {
            swordDamage.EnableCollider();
        }
    }
    // Proxy method to disable the sword's collider
    public void DisableSwordCollider()
    {
        if (swordDamage != null)
        {
            swordDamage.DisableCollider();
        }
    }
}
```

1. MeleeWeaponDamage swordDamage: This private field of type MeleeWeaponDamage holds a reference to the MeleeWeaponDamage component attached to the warrior's sword. This component manages the logic for when the sword deals damage, checks for collision, etc.

2. Awake(): Here you obtain the MeleeWeaponDamage component on any child objects of the GameObject this script is attached to. The sword is a nested child of the warrior GameObject and has the MeleeWeaponDamage component attached. The sword has been attached to the warrior's right hand, as depicted in Figure 4-1.

CHAPTER 4 ARCHITECTING MELEE COMBAT: BUILDING THE CORE FRAMEWORK

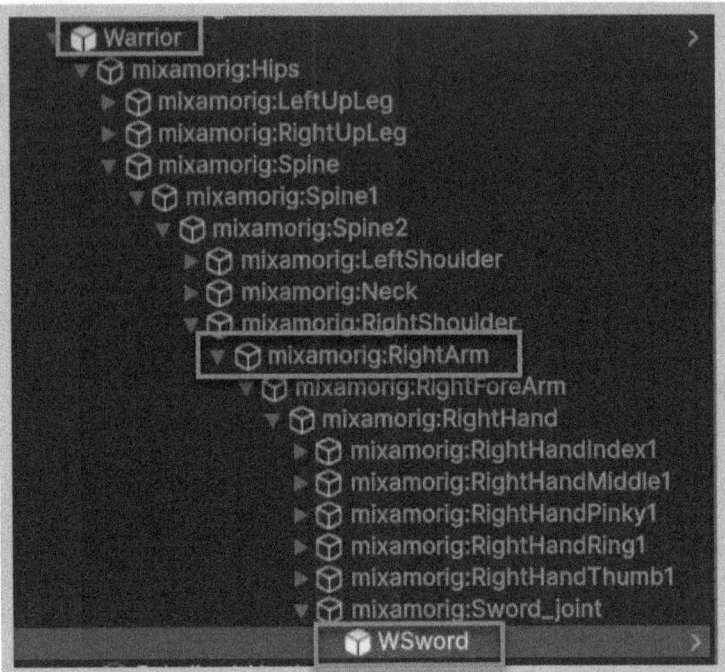

Figure 4-1. *The WSword prefab as a child of the Warrior game object*

3. EnableSwordCollider(): This is a proxy method used to enable the sword's collider during specific animation frames where the sword is supposed to be able to hit and cause damage. If swordDamage is not null, the method "swordDamage. EnableCollider()" is called to enable the collider of the sword, to have it start detecting collisions.

4. DisableSwordCollider(): This method serves as the counterpart to the EnableSwordcollider() method and is used to disable the sword's collider when it should not be interacting with other objects (like when at the beginning or end of a sword swing

CHAPTER 4 ARCHITECTING MELEE COMBAT: BUILDING THE CORE FRAMEWORK

animation). If swordDamage is not null, the method "swordDamage.DisableCollider()" is called to disable the collider of the sword, to have it stop detecting collisions.

To guarantee that these proxy methods are triggered at the correct moments during the "SwordSlash" animation, you must configure two events for this animation in the Animation Window. To open and set up Unity's Animation window, follow these steps:

- Navigate to the main menu in the Unity editor and select Window ➤ Animation ➤
- Animation to open the Animation window.
- Dock the Animation tab next to the Console tab for convenient access.
- Ensure the Scene view is active. Within the hierarchy, select and focus on the Warrior game object as illustrated in Figure 4-2.

CHAPTER 4   ARCHITECTING MELEE COMBAT: BUILDING THE CORE FRAMEWORK

Figure 4-2. *The animation, scene, and hierarchy windows – Setting up animation events*

To effectively manage animation events within the Unity Animation window for the "SwordSlash" animation, follow these steps to ensure proper collider management during animation playback:

- Select the Animation: From the dropdown menu in the Animation window, choose the "SwordSlash" animation.

- Position the Scrubber Head: In the textbox next to the timeline at the top, enter the number 18. This positions the scrubber head at the first animation event, as illustrated in Figure 4-2.

CHAPTER 4   ARCHITECTING MELEE COMBAT: BUILDING THE CORE FRAMEWORK

- Adding Animation Events: Position the scrubber head at the desired frame on the timeline where you wish to add an event. Click the "Add Event" button (highlighted in Figure 4-2) to create an animation event in that frame.

- Review Animation Events: Below the timeline, the created animation events are marked (as shown in Figure 4-2). Hovering over these events will display the name of the method that will be invoked when the animation reaches these frames.

- Enable the Sword's Collider: At frame 18, when the first animation event is triggered, it invokes the EnableSwordCollider() method within the WarriorAnimationEvents script. This action enables the collider for the sword, allowing it to interact with and deal damage to the player.

- View Animation Playback: Move the scrubber head along the timeline to see the animation play through in the Scene view. Observe the position of the sword in frame 18 to understand when the collider is activated.

- Disable the Sword's Collider: When the animation reaches frame 45, at the second animation event (located at the end of the animation), invoke the DisableSwordCollider() method within the WarriorAnimationEvents script. This disables the sword's collider, preventing further contact and damage to the player.

- Set Animation Event Methods: Select the desired animation event, then in the Inspector's "Function" section, choose WarriorAnimationEvents ➤ Methods from the drop-down and select the specific method to be triggered during playback for the selected animation event.

Recipe 4-9: Implementing the Melee Weapon Damage Behavior

Problem

You need a system for handling melee weapon damage for a player or warrior character. This involves managing the activation of the weapon's collider during attacks, ensuring that damage is applied only once per attack, and interacting correctly with other game objects and health systems. Achieving this requires a robust and efficient approach to collider management and collision detection.

Solution

The MeleeWeaponDamage class addresses this problem by implementing a system that activates the weapon's collider only during attacks, checks collisions to prevent self-damage or damage to non-player characters (NPCs), and applies damage to objects with a health component. This class includes methods to enable and disable the collider, manage the state of damage application, and handle collision events appropriately.

CHAPTER 4   ARCHITECTING MELEE COMBAT: BUILDING THE CORE FRAMEWORK

How It Works

The MeleeWeaponDamage class manages melee weapon damage by enabling the weapon's collider only during attacks and ensuring damage is applied once per attack. It initializes the weapon's collider in the Awake() method, enabling it with EnableCollider() and disabling it with DisableCollider(). The OnTriggerEnter() method handles collision detection, checks for valid targets, applies damage if a health component is present, and sets a flag to prevent multiple damage applications. The OnDisable() method resets the collider state and damage flag when the weapon is disabled, ensuring readiness for the next attack.

Listing 4-9. MeleeWeaponDamage script

```
using UnityEngine;

public class MeleeWeaponDamage : MonoBehaviour
{
    [Tooltip("The amount of damage to deal to the Hit
    Object")]
    [SerializeField] private int damageAmount = 10;

    private Collider swordCollider;
    private bool hasDealtDamage;
    private string topMostParentTag;

    private void Awake()
    {
        swordCollider = gameObject.GetComponent<Collider>();
        if (swordCollider == null)
        {
            Debug.LogError($"[MeleeWeaponDamage -
            {gameObject.name}] : No Collider found on the
             sword object.");
```

CHAPTER 4 ARCHITECTING MELEE COMBAT: BUILDING THE CORE FRAMEWORK

```
        return;
    }
    else
    {
        topMostParentTag =
        swordCollider.GetComponentInParent<Transform>()
        .root.tag;
        DisableCollider(); //Ensure collider is initially
                        //disabled
    }
}

// Function to enable the collider at the start of a new
//attack
public void EnableCollider()
{
    swordCollider.enabled = true; // Enable sword collider
    hasDealtDamage = false; // Reset damage flag
}

// Function to disable the collider at the end of the
//attack
public void DisableCollider()
{
    swordCollider.enabled = false;//Disable sword collider
}

// Function to handle collision detection when the
//collider is enabled
private void OnTriggerEnter(Collider other)
{
    if (hasDealtDamage)
        return;
```

```csharp
        //Ensure that the warrior/player wielding the sword
        //has not hit itself and one warrior has not hit
        //another warrior

        //Player has hit itself.
        if (topMostParentTag == "Player" &&
            other.CompareTag("Player"))
            return;
        //NPC has hit itself or another NPC
        else if (topMostParentTag == "NPC" &&
                other.CompareTag("NPC"))
            return;

        if (other.TryGetComponent<Health>(out Health health))
        {
            health.TakeHealth(damageAmount);
            Debug.Log($"Melee Weapon: ({gameObject.name})
                interacted with: {other.name} - Its Health is now:
                {health.CurrentHealth}");
            hasDealtDamage = true; //Set damage flag
        }
        else
        {
            Debug.LogWarning($"[MeleeWeaponDamage -
            {gameObject.name}] : No Health component found.");
        }
    }

    private void OnDisable()
    {
        DisableCollider(); // Reset collider state
        hasDealtDamage = false; // Reset damage flag
    }
}
```

CHAPTER 4 ARCHITECTING MELEE COMBAT: BUILDING THE CORE FRAMEWORK

1. int damageAmount: This field specifies the amount of damage the weapon deals upon hitting another object. It defines the impact strength of the weapon, essential for applying damage to other game objects.

2. Collider swordCollider: This field stores the reference to the collider component attached to the melee weapon itself. It is used to detect collisions with other game objects during an attack.

3. bool hasDealtDamage: This boolean flag tracks whether damage has already been dealt with during the current attack. It prevents dealing multiple damage in a single attack, ensuring fair gameplay mechanics.

4. topMostParentTag: Obtains the tag of the root parent object, of the current object (melee weapon) that this script is attached to.

5. Awake(): Here you set the necessary references and initial states. You begin by retrieving the collider component attached to the melee weapon game object and assigning it to the swordCollider. If the weapon has a collider component, you first obtain its top most parent (root) object tag. You then disable the collider to ensure it is not active when it shouldn't be.

6. EnableCollider(): Activates the weapon's collider at the start of an attack and resets the damage flag. Resetting the "hasDealtDamage" flag allows damage to be dealt with in a new attack.

CHAPTER 4   ARCHITECTING MELEE COMBAT: BUILDING THE CORE FRAMEWORK

7. DisableCollider(): Deactivates the weapon's collider at the end of an attack, thereby stopping collision detection.

8. OnTriggerEnter(): Here you handle collision detection and damage application when the weapon's collider interacts with another collider. You check to see if damage has already been dealt with in the current attack, in which case the method is exited. The conditional if() and else if() statements ensure that the player weapon, if hit against itself, is not registered to take damage, as well as NPC weapon hits against themselves or other NPCs are not registered to take damage. An attempt is then made to get the Health component from the other collider, and if successful, the health of the hit object is reduced by damageAmount. It then sets the hasDealtDamage flag to true, indicating that damage has been dealt. If no Health component is found on the hit object, a warning is logged to the console.

9. OnDisable(): Ensures the collider is disabled and the damage flag is reset when the weapon is disabled, ensuring the melee weapon is ready for the next attack.

The MeleeWeaponDamage class is designed to manage the damage mechanics of a melee weapon. It ensures that the weapon's collider is only active during attacks, prevents the weapon from damaging the wielder, and ensures that damage is only applied once per attack. The class interacts with other game objects through their health components, allowing for

CHAPTER 4   ARCHITECTING MELEE COMBAT: BUILDING THE CORE FRAMEWORK

dynamic and interactive gameplay. Each method and field within the class plays a crucial role in maintaining these functionalities, ensuring a smooth and realistic combat system.

Recipe 4-10: Implementing the Health Script

Problem

Managing the health of NPCs and player characters is crucial for gameplay mechanics, including damage handling, health depletion, and death events. A well-crafted class that provides a structured way to handle these functionalities, ensuring that other game components can react appropriately to changes in health status, is a definitive requirement.

Solution

The Health class manages the health system for both NPCs and player characters. It handles damage application, health depletion, and the triggering of death events. The class includes events that notify other scripts when health is depleted or when a character dies. It also includes a testing function to simulate damage using mouse input, aiding in development and debugging.

How It Works

The Health class manages the health system for NPCs and player characters, initializing health at the start and dynamically tracking it during gameplay. The TakeHealth() method reduces health and triggers appropriate events if health depletes or if the character dies. The Die() method handles death logic, setting the death state and triggering specific

CHAPTER 4 ARCHITECTING MELEE COMBAT: BUILDING THE CORE FRAMEWORK

events for NPCs and players. The Update() method, used for testing, simulates damage to NPCs through mouse input. This class ensures a structured approach to health management, enabling other game components to react to health changes and death events effectively.

Listing 4-10. Health script

```
using UnityEngine;
using UnityEngine.InputSystem;
using System;

//Attach this Health script to your NPCs-Soldier game object
//and the PlayerArmature game object.
public class Health : MonoBehaviour, IHealth
{
    public event Action<string> OnHealthDepleted;//C# Event
    //invoked from TakeHealth() and listened for in
    //WarriorStateMachine script.
    public event Action OnPlayerDeath;//C# Event invoked from
    //Die() and listened for in WarriorStateMachine script.
    public event Action OnNpcDeath;//Being listened for in
    //WarriorStateMachine script.

    [SerializeField] private int maxHealth = 100;

    private int currentHealth;
    private bool isDead = false;

    public int CurrentHealth { get { return currentHealth; }
    private set { currentHealth = value; } }

    private void Start()
    {
        currentHealth = maxHealth;
    }
```

CHAPTER 4   ARCHITECTING MELEE COMBAT: BUILDING THE CORE FRAMEWORK

```
public void TakeHealth(int amount)
{
    if (!isDead)
    {
        currentHealth -= amount;
        Debug.Log($"Health is now : {currentHealth}");

        if (currentHealth <= 0)
            Die();
        else
            OnHealthDepleted?.Invoke(gameObject.tag);
   //Event being listened for in WarriorStateMachine script
    }
}
public void Die()
{
    if (isDead)
        return;

    isDead = true;

    if (!gameObject.CompareTag("Player"))
    {
            OnNpcDeath?.Invoke();//Being listened for in
                                //WarriorStateMachine script
    }
    else
    {
      //Handle player death logic here - Show Death screen
      // Ensure NPC goes back to Wandering.
         Debug.Log("Health: Player is Dead");
      //Event being listened for in WarriorStateMachine,
      //Ensures that the NPCs stop attacking and continue
```

CHAPTER 4 ARCHITECTING MELEE COMBAT: BUILDING THE CORE FRAMEWORK

```
        //Wandering
            OnPlayerDeath?.Invoke();
        }
    }

    private void Update() //For Testing purposes only.
    {
        Mouse myMouse = Mouse.current ;

        //Example of triggering firing of weapon, e.g., when
        //the player fires the weapon by clicking the left
        //Mouse Button
        if (myMouse != null)
        {
            if (myMouse.leftButton.wasPressedThisFrame)
            {
                if (gameObject.CompareTag("NPC"))
                    TakeHealth(10); //Simulates Player
                //shooting NPC demonstrating the Damage and
                //Death animations on NPC.
            }
        }
    }

}
```

1. Events: The class begins by declaring three C# Action events:

    - OnHealthDepleted: Triggered when the NPC's health decreases but hasn't reached zero. This event is being listened to within the WarriorStateMachine class. It results in the NPC either playing a damage animation or taking cover if its health is less than 50.

CHAPTER 4   ARCHITECTING MELEE COMBAT: BUILDING THE CORE FRAMEWORK

- OnPlayerDeath: Invoked when the player's health reaches zero, influencing game flow like showing a death screen or resetting the game. This event is being listened to within the WarriorStateMachine class.

- OnNpcDeath: Triggered when an NPC's health reaches zero and is used to switch the NPC's state to "dead." This event is being listened for within the WarriorStateMachine class and switches the SateMachine to the DeathState.

2. maxHealth (Serialized Field): Defines the maximum health with which an NPC begins, and this value is adjustable in the Inspector for various game objects. Beyond its application to NPCs, this component is versatile enough to be utilized on the player and inanimate game objects, such as explodable crates and barrels.

3. currentHealth: It keeps track of the NPC's/players current health. Changes in this value affect the game's visual and logical response to NPC/player damage.

4. isDead: This boolean flag indicates whether the NPC/player is dead. This prevents redundant logic from executing once the NPC/player has died.

5. CurrentHealth property: Allows controlled access to currentHealth, ensuring that only internal logic can modify this vital game statistic.

6. Start(): This method sets the initial currentHealth to maxHealth when the game object is activated, preparing the NPC/player for gameplay.

CHAPTER 4   ARCHITECTING MELEE COMBAT: BUILDING THE CORE FRAMEWORK

7. TakeHealth(int amount): Decreases the NPC/player health by the specified amount and triggers events or death logic based on the resultant health. It ensures no action is taken if the NPC/player is already dead. However, in the event the NPC/player is not dead, the NPC's/player's health is reduced and the new health value is logged. If reducing the health results in the NPC/player health reaching zero or less, the Die() method is invoked; otherwise, the OnHealthDepleted event is invoked, notifying the WarriorStateMachine component that it eventually needs to invoke either the HitState or the CoverState for the NPC/player.

8. Die(): Finalizes the death of the NPC/player by setting the isDead flag to true, marking the NPC/player as dead, and triggering appropriate events. If isDead is true, the method is exited, preventing re-entry or redundant execution when the NPC/player is already dead. It then goes on to check the character type (Player or NPC) and triggers the corresponding event, managing different logic paths for each character type. In the case of the NPC death, the OnNpcDeath event is invoked, which is being listened for within the WarriorStateMachine component, which in turn ensures that the NPC transitions into the DeathState. In the case of the player's death, the OnPlayerDeath event is invoked, which is being listened for within the WarriorStateMachine component.

Update(): This method, designed for testing purposes only, simulates NPC damage upon a left mouse button click using Unity's new Input System. It checks the mouse state and, if the left button is clicked and the object is an NPC, deducts ten health points to simulate the NPC being hit. This method can be adapted or removed based on production requirements.

Recipe 4-11: Implementing the Hit State

Problem

You need a class that tackles the challenge of managing an NPC's reaction when hit by the player. This class is crucial within the context of a state machine for smoothly transitioning the NPC into a hit state, ensuring a realistic response to combat interactions, and facilitating a return to normal activities after the hit.

Solution

The solution involves implementing the W_HitState class to handle the NPC's behavior during and after being hit. Key features include deactivating the NPC's weapon, playing a hit animation to visualize the impact, and managing state transitions to return the NPC to its previous state, ensuring continuity and realism in NPC behavior.

How It Works

The W_HitState class manages an NPC's reaction when hit by the player. Upon activation, the class ensures all necessary components are present and logs errors if not. The process involves deactivating the NPC's weapon, triggering a hit animation for visual feedback, and checking for the

CHAPTER 4   ARCHITECTING MELEE COMBAT: BUILDING THE CORE FRAMEWORK

previous state to avoid immediate re-entry into the hit state. After a brief delay of allowing the animation to play out, the NPC transitions back to a valid prior state, ensuring continuity in behavior. The class finally resets the NPC's stance to idle upon exiting the hit state, readying it for further actions.

Listing 4-11. W_HitState script

```
using UnityEngine;

/***
Whilst in any State (i.e. Idle, Attack, Wander, Chase) an NPC can be Hit
and will need to enter the HitState, playing a Hit animation.
*****
States have access to MonoBheaviour methods too.
All States must be added as components to the NPC game object.
***/

public class W_HitState : MonoBehaviour, IState
{
    private WarriorStateMachine stateMachine;
    private IState previousState;
    private static readonly int HitHash =
    Animator.StringToHash("HitImpact");
    private static readonly int IdleHash =
    Animator.StringToHash("Idle");

    void Awake()
    {
        stateMachine = GetComponent<WarriorStateMachine>();
        if (stateMachine == null)
```

CHAPTER 4 ARCHITECTING MELEE COMBAT: BUILDING THE CORE FRAMEWORK

```csharp
    {
        Debug.LogError($"[HitState - {gameObject.name}] : 
        WarriorStateMachine not found.");
        return;
    }
}

void IState.OnStateEnter()
{
    if (!stateMachine.Agent.enabled)
        return;

    GameObject meleeWeapon = 
    GameObject.FindGameObjectWithTag("MeleeWeapon");
    //Deactivate the Swords collider in Hit state
    meleeWeapon.GetComponent<Collider>().enabled = false;

    stateMachine.Anim.CrossFade(HitHash, 0.1f);

    Debug.Log("HitState: Enter");
}

void IState.OnStateUpdate(float deltaTime)
{
  //switch to the immediate previous state before the
  //HitState, which should either be Attack or Retreat
 //as NPC needs to be close to the player to get hit,
  //however you can set previousState to Idle if you just
  //want to hit the NPC and see the HitImpact animation play.

 //Check if the previous state is not of type HitState as NPC
 //could be hit several times in succession.
            if (stateMachine.PreviousState.GetType() !=
                typeof(W_HitState))
```

CHAPTER 4　ARCHITECTING MELEE COMBAT: BUILDING THE CORE FRAMEWORK

```
            {
                previousState = stateMachine.PreviousState;
            }

            IState prevState =
            stateMachine.FindState(previousState);
            if (prevState != null)
            {
              Debug.Log($"HitState: Switching to immediate
              Previous State: {prevState.GetType()}. Pausing
              briefly to see Hit Animation Play");

              Utils.Wait(1f, this, () =>
              stateMachine.SwitchState(prevState));
            }

        Debug.Log("HitState: Update");
    }

    void IState.OnStateExit()
    {
        Debug.Log("HitState: Exit");
        stateMachine.Anim.CrossFade(IdleHash, 0.1f);
    }
}
```

1. WarriorStateMachine stateMachine: This is a reference to the WarriorStateMachine component attached to the same GameObject. This field provides access to the NPC's state management system, allowing transitions between different states.

CHAPTER 4   ARCHITECTING MELEE COMBAT: BUILDING THE CORE FRAMEWORK

2. IState previousState: Stores a reference to the state from which the NPC transitioned into the hit state. This allows the NPC to return to its prior activity after reacting to the hit, maintaining continuity in behavior.

3. int HitHash and IdleHash: These static read-only integers are hashes generated from animation state names. Using hashes instead of strings for animation triggers enhances performance as it avoids string comparison operations within the Unity engine.

4. Awake(): This method ensures that the WarriorStateMachine component is present on the NPC. If stateMachine is null, it logs an error indicating the component was not found.

5. OnStateEnter(): Upon the NPC entering the hit state, it ensures that the NPC's navigation agent (Agent) is enabled. If not, the method returns early without further execution, preventing actions on a disabled component. It then finds the GameObject tagged as "MeleeWeapon" and disables its Collider. This is to prevent the NPC from dealing damage to the player as well as receiving additional interactions during the hit reaction. It then transitions the NPC's animation to the hit reaction using CrossFade() with the HitHash, providing a visual cue of the hit, and enhancing the game's responsiveness and realism.

6. OnStateUpdate(): This method is called repeatedly every frame and manages the state behavior during its execution. First, it checks if the previous

CHAPTER 4   ARCHITECTING MELEE COMBAT: BUILDING THE CORE FRAMEWORK

state stored in the stateMachine is not of type W_HitState to prevent looping back into another hit reaction immediately, which would be unrealistic. However, this could be changed should you want to. If a valid previous state is found that is not W_HitState, it retrieves this state using stateMachine.FindState(previousState). This is necessary to transition the NPC back to its previous activity. If a previous state is found (prevState is not null), it uses the utility function Utils.Wait() to delay the transition back to the previous state by 1 second. This delay allows the hit animation to complete and be visible to the player.

7. OnStateExit(): This method undertakes actions required when exiting the hit state. Here it transitions the NPC's animation back to "Idle" using CrossFade(). This returns the NPC to a neutral stance, ready for further actions or reactions.

The W_HitState class effectively encapsulates the behavior expected of an NPC when it receives a hit, including showing a hit reaction and ensuring that the NPC can resume its previous activities smoothly. This setup is essential for creating a dynamic and responsive gameplay experience where player actions (like hitting an NPC) have immediate and noticeable consequences.

As the player is not setup to attack the NPC, to effectively simulate combat interactions within the game, it's crucial to establish a mechanism for the player to trigger a hit against an NPC. As detailed in Recipe 3-5, the Update() method within the Health class has been tailored for testing hit reactions through mouse interactions – specifically, a left mouse button click. Additionally, the player character is equipped with an Attack animation that can be initiated by pressing the "k" key on the

CHAPTER 4   ARCHITECTING MELEE COMBAT: BUILDING THE CORE FRAMEWORK

keyboard. To integrate this capability seamlessly into gameplay, a sword or similar melee weapon should be attached to the player's right hand. This setup involves the activation and deactivation of the weapon's colliders in a manner analogous to the NPC's weapon management. Such a configuration will enable the player to engage NPCs in melee combat effectively within the game environment. This approach will not only enhance the interactivity of the game but also contribute to a more immersive and realistic player experience.

Recipe 4-12: Implementing the Wander State

Problem

A class is required to control the wandering behavior of an NPC. This state, which is part of the NPC's state machine, is required to enable the NPC to move to random points within a defined radius. The class also needs to manage transitions between states, update animations, and ensure that the NPC's melee weapon collider is disabled during wandering.

Solution

The W_WanderState class implements the IState interface and uses Unity's NavMesh system to navigate the NPC to random locations within a specified radius. It contains fields for managing the state machine, target positions, animation transitions, and the navigation radius. Methods within the class need to handle entering and exiting the state, updating the NPC's position, and setting new random targets.

CHAPTER 4   ARCHITECTING MELEE COMBAT: BUILDING THE CORE FRAMEWORK

How It Works

The W_WanderState class controls an NPC's wandering behavior by setting random targets within a defined radius. Upon entering the state, it enables the NavMesh agent, deactivates the melee weapon's collider, and transitions to the walking animation. The OnStateUpdate method checks if the NPC has reached its target and sets a new one if necessary. The SetNewWanderTarget() method calculates a random direction, ensures the target is on the NavMesh, and sets it as the new destination. This process ensures the NPC moves smoothly and dynamically within the game environment.

Listing 4-12. W_WanderState script

```
using UnityEngine;
using UnityEngine.AI;
using Random = UnityEngine.Random;

//States have access to MonoBheaviour methods too.
//All States must be added as components to the NPC game
//object.
public class W_WanderState : MonoBehaviour, IState
{

    [Tooltip("Area around NPC where it can Wander to")]
    [SerializeField] private float navigationRadius = 7.0f;

    private WarriorStateMachine stateMachine;
    private Vector3 target; //target is the random Wander
                            //location for NPC Agent
    private bool isTargetSet;

    private const float crossFadeTime = 0.1f;
    private readonly int walkHash =
    Animator.StringToHash("Walk");
```

CHAPTER 4   ARCHITECTING MELEE COMBAT: BUILDING THE CORE FRAMEWORK

```csharp
void Awake()
{
    stateMachine = GetComponent<WarriorStateMachine>();
    if (stateMachine == null)
    {
        Debug.LogError($"[WanderState - {gameObject.name}]
        : WarriorStateMachine not found.");
        return;
    }
}

void IState.OnStateEnter()
{
    if (stateMachine.Agent.enabled)
    {
        stateMachine.Agent.isStopped = false;
        isTargetSet = false; //Reset target selection on
                             //state enter
        SetNewWanderTarget(); //Set the initial wander
                              //target
    }
    else
        return;

    GameObject meleeWeapon =
    GameObject.FindGameObjectWithTag("MeleeWeapon");
    //Deactivate the Swords collider in Wander state
    meleeWeapon.GetComponent<Collider>().enabled = false;

    stateMachine.Anim.CrossFadeInFixedTime(walkHash,
    crossFadeTime);
    Debug.Log("WanderState: Enter");
}
```

CHAPTER 4 ARCHITECTING MELEE COMBAT: BUILDING THE CORE FRAMEWORK

```
void IState.OnStateUpdate(float deltaTime)
{
    // Check if the agent has reached its wander target
    if (isTargetSet &&
        stateMachine.Agent.remainingDistance <=
        stateMachine.Agent.stoppingDistance)
    {
        // Reset target selection
        isTargetSet = false;
        SetNewWanderTarget();
    }
}
void IState.OnStateExit()
{
    Debug.Log("WanderState: Exit");
}

private void SetNewWanderTarget()
{
    Vector3 randomDirection = Random.insideUnitSphere *
    navigationRadius;
    randomDirection +=
    stateMachine.Agent.transform.position;

    if (NavMesh.SamplePosition(randomDirection, out
    NavMeshHit hit, navigationRadius, NavMesh.AllAreas))
    {
        target = hit.position;
        stateMachine.Agent.SetDestination(target);
        isTargetSet = true; // Mark target as set
        Debug.Log("New wander target set: " + target);
    }
}
}
```

CHAPTER 4   ARCHITECTING MELEE COMBAT: BUILDING THE CORE FRAMEWORK

1. float navigationRadius: Defines the radius within which the NPC can randomly wander. Sets the bounds for the NPC's wander area, controlling the extent of its movement.

2. WarriorStateMachine stateMachine: Holds a reference to the NPC's state machine. Enables interaction with the state machine for transitioning states and accessing the NavMesh agent and animator.

3. Vector3 target: Stores the current random target location for the NPC to move toward. Provides the destination point for the NPC's wandering movement.

4. isTargetSet: Indicates whether a new wander target has been set. Ensures that the NPC continues to wander by checking if a target needs to be set.

5. crossFadeTime: Duration for cross-fading animations. Ensures smooth transitions between animations, enhancing the visual experience.

6. walkHash: Stores the hash value for the "Walk" animation state. Optimizes animation transitions by using hashed values instead of strings.

7. Awake(): Initializes the stateMachine reference. Retrieves the WarriorStateMachine component attached to the same game object and assigns it to stateMachine. It checks if the stateMachine component was found, and if not found, it logs an error.

CHAPTER 4   ARCHITECTING MELEE COMBAT: BUILDING THE CORE FRAMEWORK

8. OnStateEnter(): This method executes when the NPC enters the wandering state, setting initial conditions and deactivating the weapon collider. If the NavMesh agent is enabled, it ensures the agent is not stopped, allowing it to move. The target flag is reset to indicate a new target needs to be set, invoking the SetNewWanderTarget() method to set a new random wander target. If the agent is not enabled, the method returns without further execution. It then finds the melee weapon game object using its tag and disables the collider on the melee weapon to prevent unintended interactions. Finally, it crossfades to the walking animation.

9. OnStateUpdate(): This method updates the NPC's state during each frame, checking if a new wander target needs to be set. Here you check to see if the target is set and the agent has reached its target or is within the stopping distance. If these conditions are met, the target flag is reset to indicate that a new target needs to be set. It then calls the SetNewWanderTarget() method to set a new random wander target.

10. OnStateExit(): This method executes when the NPC exits the wandering state, logging its state exit.

11. SetNewWanderTarget(): This method sets a new random wander target for the NPC within the specified navigation radius. It generates a random direction vector within a unit sphere scaled by the navigation radius. It offsets the random direction by the current position of the agent to get a new potential target position. It then checks if the

random position is on the NavMesh, storing the result in the variable hit. It sets the target to the valid position found on the NavMesh, followed by setting the agent's destination to the new target. The target is then marked as set, followed by logging the new target position for debugging purposes.

The W_WanderState class implements a wandering behavior for an NPC using the NavMesh system for navigation. It handles the logic for transitioning into and out of the wandering state, setting random targets within a defined radius, and ensuring the NPC properly animates and disables its weapon collider during wandering. Each field and method is designed to support these functionalities, creating a cohesive wandering behavior that interacts seamlessly with the state machine and other game components.

Recipe 4-13: Implementing the Cover State

Problem

In action or combat-based games, NPCs (non-player characters) need to exhibit intelligent behaviors such as seeking cover when under threat. A class designed to handle this specific behavior for a warrior NPC is required. This class needs to be part of a state machine that enables the NPC to dynamically find and move to cover spots when needed, enhancing the realism and challenge of the game.

Solution

The W_CoverState class implements the IState interface, making it a state within the state machine for the NPC. When the NPC enters this state, it will identify and move to a suitable cover spot to avoid the player or other

CHAPTER 4   ARCHITECTING MELEE COMBAT: BUILDING THE CORE FRAMEWORK

dangers. The class manages the NPC's movement toward cover spots, taking into account factors such as proximity to the player and the NPC's health. The class also handles animation transitions and ensures that the NPC does not repeatedly select the same cover spot.

How It Works

The W_CoverState class initializes necessary references and potential cover spots during the Awake() method. Upon entering the state, it sets the NPC's movement speed, randomly selects a cover spot, disables the melee weapon's collider, and sets the destination to the chosen cover spot while triggering the run animation. During the state update, the NPC's health and proximity to the destination are checked to determine whether to stop, continue running, or switch states based on the visibility of the player and health status. The class includes methods to find the closest and farthest cover spots, adjusting the NPC's position behind obstacles using their collider sizes.

Listing 4-13. W_CoverState script

```
using UnityEngine;
using UnityEngine.AI;
using Random = UnityEngine.Random;

//States have access to MonoBheaviour methods too.
//All States must be added as components to the NPC game
//object.
public class W_CoverState : MonoBehaviour, IState
{
    private GameObject[] coverSpots;

    [Tooltip("Speed at which NavMeshAgent moves while seeking Cover")]
    [SerializeField] private float npcSpeed = 2.5f;
```

```csharp
    private WarriorStateMachine stateMachine;
    private Transform player; // Reference to the Player
                              //transform
    private Vector3 target; //target is the selected hiding
                            //spot
    private float offset = 1.5f;
    private GameObject lastHidingSpot;//Avoid repeatedly
                              //finding the same hiding spot.

    private const float crossFadeTime = 0.1f;
    private readonly int movementHash =
    Animator.StringToHash("Run");
    private readonly int idleHash =
    Animator.StringToHash("Idle");

void Awake()
{
    stateMachine = GetComponent<WarriorStateMachine>();
    if (stateMachine == null)
    {
        Debug.LogError($"[CoverState - {gameObject.name}]
        : WarriorStateMachine not found.");
        return;
    }

    player = GameObject.FindWithTag("Player").transform;
    if (player == null)
    {
        Debug.LogError($"[CoverState - {gameObject.name}]
        : Couldn't find player with tag Player");
        return;
    }
```

CHAPTER 4   ARCHITECTING MELEE COMBAT: BUILDING THE CORE FRAMEWORK

```
    coverSpots =
    GameObject.FindGameObjectsWithTag("Obstacle");
}

void IState.OnStateEnter()
{
    if (stateMachine.Agent.enabled)
    {
        stateMachine.Agent.speed = npcSpeed;
        stateMachine.Agent.isStopped = false;

        //provide 50% chance of NPC moving to either the
        //closest or farthest hiding spot for Cover
        if (Random.Range(0, 100) < 50)
            target = FindClosestCover();
        else
            target = FindFarthestCover();

        GameObject meleeWeapon =
        GameObject.FindGameObjectWithTag("MeleeWeapon");

        //Deactivate the Swords collider in Cover state
        meleeWeapon.GetComponent<Collider>().enabled =
        false;

        stateMachine.Agent.ResetPath();
        stateMachine.Agent.SetDestination(target);
    }
    else
        return;

    stateMachine.Anim.CrossFadeInFixedTime(movementHash,
    crossFadeTime);
```

```
    Debug.Log("CoverState: Enter");
}

void IState.OnStateUpdate(float deltaTime)
{
    Health health = GetComponent<Health>();

    if (health == null)
        return;

    // Check if the agent has reached its current
    // destination
    if (stateMachine.Agent.remainingDistance <=
        stateMachine.Agent.stoppingDistance ||
        !stateMachine.Agent.hasPath)
    {
        //NPC reached hiding spot so let him stop.
        stateMachine.Agent.isStopped = true;
        stateMachine.Anim.CrossFadeInFixedTime(idleHash,
        crossFadeTime);//Play Idle animation
    }
    else if(stateMachine.Agent.remainingDistance >
            stateMachine.Agent.stoppingDistance &&
            health.CurrentHealth < 50 )
    {
        stateMachine.Agent.isStopped = false;
        stateMachine.Anim.CrossFadeInFixedTime(
        movementHash, crossFadeTime);//Continue run
                                     //animation
    }

    if (stateMachine.IsPlayerVisible() &&
        health.CurrentHealth >= 50)
```

CHAPTER 4   ARCHITECTING MELEE COMBAT: BUILDING THE CORE FRAMEWORK

```
    {
        IState chase =
        stateMachine.FindState<W_ChaseState>();
        if (chase != null)
            stateMachine.SwitchState(chase);
    }
    else if(health.CurrentHealth >= 50 &&
            !stateMachine.IsPlayerVisible())
    {
            IState wander =
            stateMachine.FindState<W_WanderState>();
            if (wander != null)
            {
                Debug.Log("CoverState: Switching to Wander
                State");
                stateMachine.SwitchState(wander);
            }
    }

    Debug.Log("CoverState: Update");
}

void IState.OnStateExit()
{
    Debug.Log("CoverState: Exit");
}

private Vector3 FindClosestCover()
{
    // Check if there are any cover spots available
    if (coverSpots.Length == 0)
```

CHAPTER 4   ARCHITECTING MELEE COMBAT: BUILDING THE CORE FRAMEWORK

```csharp
    {
        Debug.LogError("No Obstacles found for NPC to hide
        behind.");
        return transform.position; //Return current NPC
                    //position if no covers are found
    }

    float minDistance = Mathf.Infinity;
    Vector3 bestHidingSpot = transform.position;
    GameObject closestHidingSpot = null;

    foreach (GameObject coverSpot in coverSpots)
    {
        //Exclude the last hiding spot from consideration
        if (coverSpot == lastHidingSpot)
        {
           //Debug.Log($"FindClosestCover(): Most recent
           //hiding spot:   {lastHidingSpot.name}");
            continue;
        }

        //Calculate the distance from the current cover
        //spot to the player
        float distanceToPlayer =
        Vector3.Distance(player.position,
        coverSpot.transform.position);

        if (distanceToPlayer < minDistance)
        {
            minDistance = distanceToPlayer;
            closestHidingSpot = coverSpot;
        }
    }
```

CHAPTER 4   ARCHITECTING MELEE COMBAT: BUILDING THE CORE FRAMEWORK

```
// Calculate the direction from the closest cover spot
//obtained to player
Vector3 coverToPlayer = player.position -
closestHidingSpot.transform.position;

//Get the Collider component to determine size
Collider obstacleCollider =
closestHidingSpot.GetComponent<Collider>();
if (obstacleCollider == null)
{
    Debug.LogError($"CoverState: Obstacle:
    '{closestHidingSpot.name}' not fitted with a
      Collider");
    return Vector3.zero;
}
else
{
    // Compute an appropriate offset based on the
    //obstacle's collider size
    float obstacleOffset =
    Mathf.Max(obstacleCollider.bounds.size.x,
    obstacleCollider.bounds.size.z) / 2.0f + offset;

    //Find a potential hiding spot behind the cover
   //spot with the adjusted offset
    Vector3 potentialHidingSpot =
    closestHidingSpot.transform.position -
    coverToPlayer.normalized * obstacleOffset;

    if (NavMesh.SamplePosition(potentialHidingSpot,
        out NavMeshHit hit, obstacleOffset,
        NavMesh.AllAreas))
```

CHAPTER 4   ARCHITECTING MELEE COMBAT: BUILDING THE CORE FRAMEWORK

```csharp
            {
                bestHidingSpot = hit.position;
                lastHidingSpot = closestHidingSpot; //Update
                                            //last hiding spot
            }
            else
            {
                bestHidingSpot = Vector3.zero;
                Debug.LogError($"CoverState: NPC cannot be
                positioned behind Hiding Spot:
                '{closestHidingSpot.name}'");
            }
            return bestHidingSpot;
        }
    }

    private Vector3 FindFarthestCover()
    {
        // Check if there are any cover spots available
        if (coverSpots.Length == 0)
        {
            Debug.LogError("No Obstacles found for NPC to hide
            behind.");
            return transform.position;   //Return current NPC
                            //position if no covers are found
        }

        float maxDistance = Mathf.NegativeInfinity;
        Vector3 bestHidingSpot = transform.position;
        GameObject farthestHidingSpot = null;
```

CHAPTER 4   ARCHITECTING MELEE COMBAT: BUILDING THE CORE FRAMEWORK

```
foreach (GameObject coverSpot in coverSpots)
{
    // Exclude the last hiding spot from consideration
    if (coverSpot == lastHidingSpot)
    {
        //Debug.Log($"FindFarthestCover(): Most recent
        //hiding spot: {lastHidingSpot.name}");
        continue;
    }

    //Calculate the distance from the current cover
    //spot to the player
    float distanceToPlayer =
    Vector3.Distance(player.position,
    coverSpot.transform.position);

    if (distanceToPlayer > maxDistance)
    {
        maxDistance = distanceToPlayer;
        farthestHidingSpot = coverSpot;
    }
}

//Calculate the direction from the farthest cover
//spot obtained to player
Vector3 coverToPlayer = player.position -
farthestHidingSpot.transform.position;

//Get the Collider component to determine size
Collider obstacleCollider =
farthestHidingSpot.GetComponent<Collider>();
```

461

```
if (obstacleCollider == null)
{
    Debug.LogError($"CoverState: Obstacle:
    '{farthestHidingSpot.name}' not fitted with a
       Collider");
    return Vector3.zero;
}
else
{
    //Compute an appropriate offset based on the
    //obstacle's collider size
    float obstacleOffset =
    Mathf.Max(obstacleCollider.bounds.size.x,
    obstacleCollider.bounds.size.z) / 2.0f + offset;

    //Find a potential hiding spot behind the cover
    //spot with the adjusted offset
    Vector3 potentialHidingSpot =
    farthestHidingSpot.transform.position -
    coverToPlayer.normalized * obstacleOffset;

    if (NavMesh.SamplePosition(potentialHidingSpot,
        out NavMeshHit hit, obstacleOffset,
        NavMesh.AllAreas))
    {
        bestHidingSpot = hit.position;
        lastHidingSpot = farthestHidingSpot; //Update
                                  //last hiding spot
    }
    else
    {
        bestHidingSpot = Vector3.zero;
        Debug.LogError($"CoverState: NPC cannot be
```

CHAPTER 4   ARCHITECTING MELEE COMBAT: BUILDING THE CORE FRAMEWORK

```
                positioned behind Hiding Spot:
                '{farthestHidingSpot.name}'");
        }
        return bestHidingSpot;
    }
}
}
```

1. GameObject[] coverSpots: An array of GameObjects representing potential cover spots in the game. These spots are identified by the tag "Obstacle."

2. float npcSpeed: A serialized field specifying the speed at which the NPC's NavMeshAgent moves while seeking cover. This can be adjusted in the Unity Inspector.

3. WarriorStateMachine stateMachine: A reference to the WarriorStateMachine component attached to the NPC. This manages the overall state transitions of the NPC.

4. Transform player: A reference to the player's transform. This is used to determine the player's position relative to the NPC and the cover spots.

5. Vector3 target: The target represents the selected hiding spot for the NPC to move to.

6. float offset: A float is used to adjust the NPC's final position when hiding behind an obstacle, ensuring it is sufficiently covered.

7. GameObject lastHidingSpot: A GameObject representing the last hiding spot used by the NPC to avoid selecting it again immediately.

CHAPTER 4   ARCHITECTING MELEE COMBAT: BUILDING THE CORE FRAMEWORK

8. const float crossFadeTime: A constant float defining the duration of animation transitions.

9. int movementHash: A read-only integer hash for the "Run" animation state.

10. int idleHash: A read-only integer hash for the "Idle" animation state.

11. Awake(): This method initializes essential references and data for the NPC's cover-seeking behavior. It first retrieves the WarriorStateMachine component attached to the NPC and logs an error if not found. Next, it obtains the player's transform using the "Player" tag, logging an error if unsuccessful. Finally, it populates the coverSpots array with all game objects tagged "Obstacle," which will serve as potential cover spots for the NPC. This setup ensures that the state has all necessary references and data when the NPC needs to seek cover.

12. OnStateEnter(): This method is responsible for initiating the NPC's transition into the cover-seeking state. When the state is entered, it checks if the NavMeshAgent is enabled, then sets its speed and sets its "isStopped" property to false to get it moving. The method randomly decides whether to find the closest or farthest cover spot and sets the target variable accordingly. It also deactivates the melee weapon's collider to prevent it from being active while the NPC is in cover. The NPC's current path is reset, and the new destination is set. Finally, the NPC's animation transitions to a running state

CHAPTER 4   ARCHITECTING MELEE COMBAT: BUILDING THE CORE FRAMEWORK

using a crossfade animation. This method ensures that the NPC begins moving toward an appropriate cover spot.

13. OnStateUpdate(): This method manages the NPC's actions and decisions while in the cover-seeking state. It first checks if the NPC has a health component. It then checks if the NPC has reached its cover destination or has no path, in which case the agent is stopped and the idle animation is triggered. If the NPC has not yet reached its cover destination and its health is below fifty, it continues the run animation. This method also checks the visibility of the player and the NPC's health to determine if it should switch to a chase state or a wander state. This update loop ensures the NPC's behavior dynamically responds to its environment and health conditions, maintaining realistic and tactical movements.

14. OnStateExit(): This method is executed when the NPC exits the cover state.

15. FindClosestCover(): This method aims to locate the nearest suitable cover spot for the NPC to hide behind when in the CoverState. This involves evaluating potential cover spots, calculating distances, and ensuring the chosen spot is navigable.

    - Check if there are any cover spots available: First check to ensure that there are cover spots available. If no cover spots are found, the NPC cannot hide and should remain in its current position.

CHAPTER 4   ARCHITECTING MELEE COMBAT: BUILDING THE CORE FRAMEWORK

- Initialize minDistance to a very large value: minDistance is initialized to a very large value to ensure that any actual distance measured will be smaller. It serves as the initial comparison value to find the smallest distance to a cover spot.

- Initialize bestHidingSpot: bestHidingSpot is initialized to the NPC's current position. This will be updated to the best hiding spot found eventually. It ensures the method has a valid return value even if no better hiding spot is found.

- Initialize closestHidingSpot: closestHidingSpot is initialized to null. It stores the closest cover spot found during the iteration over coverSpots. It keeps track of the best cover spot based on distance to the player.

- Iterate through each cover spot in coverSpots: The foreach loop iterates through each cover spot available to the NPC, allowing the method to evaluate all potential cover spots and determine the closest one.

- Calculate the distance from the player to the current cover spot: Within the foreach loop, the distance from the player to the current cover spot is calculated, providing the necessary metric to compare cover spots and determine the closest one.

- Update minDistance and closestHidingSpot: The if(...) condition then checks to see if the current cover spot is closer to the player than the previously found closest spot, and updates minDistance and closestHidingSpot if the current spot is closer, ensuring the closest spot is found.

CHAPTER 4 ARCHITECTING MELEE COMBAT: BUILDING THE CORE FRAMEWORK

- Calculate the direction vector from the closest cover spot to the player: You then calculate a direction vector from the closest cover spot to the player. This vector is used to determine the NPC's hiding position relative to the cover spot and the player.

- Retrieve the collider component of the closest cover spot: You then retrieve the collider component of the closest cover spot. This collider is necessary to determine the size and bounds of the cover spot, ensuring the NPC can hide appropriately behind it.

- Missing collider: You then ensure that this closest cover spot has a collider, and if not, you log an error, returning an invalid position if no collider is found, preventing the NPC from hiding behind an object without defined bounds.

- Calculate an appropriate offset based on collider size: If a collider is present, you calculate an offset based on the size of the collider, ensuring the NPC hides properly behind the cover. Here the variable "offset" adjusts the hiding position to be sufficiently behind the cover spot, avoiding direct line of sight with threats (i.e., the player).

- Compute a potential hiding spot: You then calculate a potential hiding position by offsetting from the cover spot along the direction to the player, ensuring the NPC hides behind the cover spot at a safe distance, utilizing the calculated "obstacleOffset."

- Use NavMesh.SamplePosition to validate the potential hiding spot: The if(…) condition uses NavMesh.SamplePosition() to validate and adjust the potential hiding spot to ensure it's on the navigable mesh, ensuring the NPC can navigate to the hiding spot, adjusting the position if necessary to fit the NavMesh.

- Update bestHidingSpot: The variable bestHidingSpot is then updated to the validated position returned by NavMesh.SamplePosition(), ensuring the NPC has a valid and reachable hiding spot on the NavMesh.

- No valid position found: If NavMesh.SamplePosition() fails to find a valid position, an error is logged and bestHidingSpot is set to an invalid position, preventing the NPC from hiding at an unreachable spot.

- Return bestHidingSpot: Finally you return the variable bestHidingSpot.

16. FindFarthestCover(): This method aims to locate the farthest suitable cover spot for the NPC to hide behind when in the CoverState. This involves evaluating potential cover spots, calculating distances, and ensuring the chosen spot is navigable. The code here is a replica of the code used within the FindClosestCover() method, except for the fact that its computations have been altered to find the farthest distance.

CHAPTER 4　ARCHITECTING MELEE COMBAT: BUILDING THE CORE FRAMEWORK

The W_CoverState class is an essential part of an NPC's state machine, responsible for dynamically finding and moving to cover spots based on the NPC's current situation. The class uses Unity's NavMesh system to navigate to cover spots and makes decisions based on the NPC's health and the visibility of the player. This behavior enhances the NPC's AI, making it more realistic and challenging for players.

Recipe 4-14: Implementing the Death State

Problem

Managing the states of non-playable characters (NPCs) is essential for smooth gameplay. Specifically, handling the death state of an NPC involves stopping its movements, disabling its abilities, playing a death animation, and eventually removing it from the game. The challenge is to implement this behavior efficiently within a state machine framework.

Solution

The W_DeathState class is designed to manage the death state of a warrior NPC within the state machine. Implementing the IState interface ensures the NPC transitions smoothly into the death state, stops its movements, disables its melee weapon, triggers the death animation, and eventually destroys the NPC game object after a delay. This class utilizes Unity's Animator component for animations and ensures state transitions are managed effectively.

How It Works

The W_DeathState class handles the NPC's death state by stopping its movements, disabling its pathfinding agent, and deactivating its melee weapon. Upon entering the state, it triggers a death animation and sets a flag to indicate the NPC is dead. During the state, it continuously checks

CHAPTER 4 ARCHITECTING MELEE COMBAT: BUILDING THE CORE FRAMEWORK

if it should transition to the idle state. When exiting, the class logs the exit and destroys the NPC game object after a delay, ensuring a smooth transition and appropriate handling of the NPC's death within the state machine.

Listing 4-14. W_DeathState script

```
using UnityEngine;

//States have access to MonoBheaviour methods too.
//All States must be added as components to the NPC game
//object.
public class W_DeathState : MonoBehaviour, IState
{
    private WarriorStateMachine stateMachine;
    private float destroyDelay = 3f;
    private bool isNpcDead;

    private const float crossFadeTime = 0.1f;
    private readonly int deathHash =
    Animator.StringToHash("Death");

    void Awake()
    {
        stateMachine = GetComponent<WarriorStateMachine>();
        if(stateMachine == null)
        {
            Debug.LogError($"[DeathState - {gameObject.name}]
            : WarriorStateMachine not found.");
            return;
        }

        Debug.Log("In W_DeathState");
    }
```

```csharp
void IState.OnStateEnter()
{
    if (!stateMachine.Agent.enabled)
        return;

    stateMachine.Agent.isStopped = true;
    stateMachine.Agent.ResetPath();
    stateMachine.Agent.enabled = false;
    isNpcDead = true;

    GameObject meleeWeapon =
    GameObject.FindGameObjectWithTag("MeleeWeapon");
    //Deactivate the Swords collider in Death state.
    meleeWeapon.GetComponent<Collider>().enabled = false;

    stateMachine.Anim.CrossFadeInFixedTime(deathHash,
    crossFadeTime);

    Debug.Log("DeathState: Enter");
}
void IState.OnStateUpdate(float deltaTime)
{
    if (isNpcDead)
    {
        IState idle =
        stateMachine.FindState<W_IdleState>();
        if (idle != null)
        {
            Debug.Log("DeathState: Switching to Idle
            State");
            stateMachine.SwitchState(idle);
        }
    }
}
```

```
    void IState.OnStateExit()
    {
        Debug.Log("DeathState: Exit");
        Destroy(gameObject, destroyDelay);
    }
}
```

1. WarriorStateMachine stateMachine: This field stores a reference to the WarriorStateMachine component attached to the NPC. It is essential for transitioning between different states and controlling the NPC's behavior.

2. float destroyDelay: This field sets a delay before the game object is destroyed after the NPC dies. In this case, the delay is set to 3 seconds.

3. bool isNpcDead: This boolean flag indicates whether the NPC is dead. It helps to ensure that certain actions are only performed once when the NPC enters the death state.

4. const float crossFadeTime: This constant defines the time duration for cross-fading the death animation, set to 0.1 seconds. It ensures smooth transitions between animations.

5. int deathHash: This field stores the hash value of the "Death" animation string, used to trigger the death animation in the animator component efficiently.

6. Awake(): This method attempts to retrieve and assign the WarriorStateMachine component from the same game object. If the component is not found, it logs an error message and exits the method

CHAPTER 4   ARCHITECTING MELEE COMBAT: BUILDING THE CORE FRAMEWORK

to prevent further execution. If the component is successfully found, it logs a message indicating the successful initialization of the W_DeathState. This setup ensures that the state machine is properly linked, allowing the NPC's death state to function correctly within the broader state management system.

7. OnStateEnter(): This method is responsible for executing specific actions when the NPC enters the death state. Its purpose is to stop the NPC's movement, disable its pathfinding agent, deactivate its melee weapon, and trigger the death animation. The method begins by checking if the pathfinding agent is enabled; if not, it exits early. If the agent is enabled, it stops the agent, clears its current path, and disables the agent to prevent further movement. It then sets the isNpcDead flag to true, finds the NPC's melee weapon by its tag, and disables its collider to prevent further interactions. Finally, it plays the death animation with a smooth crossfade and logs a message indicating the NPC has entered the death state. This method ensures that all necessary steps are taken when the NPC dies, making the transition into the death state seamless and visually consistent.

8. OnStateUpdate(): This method is designed to be called every frame while the NPC is in the death state. Its purpose is to monitor the isNpcDead flag and, if the NPC is confirmed dead, attempt to switch the state to the idle state. The method begins by checking if isNpcDead is true, indicating that the death state has been fully activated. If true, it

searches for the idle state (W_IdleState) within the state machine using the FindState() method. If the idle state is found, it logs a message indicating the transition and then switches the state machine to the idle state using the SwitchState() method. This method ensures that the NPC can transition smoothly from the death state to an idle state when appropriate, allowing for dynamic state changes during gameplay.

9. OnStateExit(): This method is triggered when the NPC exits the death state. Its primary purpose is to ensure the NPC's game object is properly cleaned up and removed from the scene after the death sequence. This method begins by logging a message indicating that the NPC is exiting the death state. It then schedules the destruction of the NPC's game object with a delay specified by the destroyDelay field, using the Destroy(gameObject, destroyDelay) method. This delay allows for any necessary animations or effects to be completed before the game object is removed. By managing the clean-up process, the OnStateExit() method ensures that the NPC is appropriately handled when transitioning out of the death state, maintaining the game's performance and visual coherence.

The W_DeathState class manages the NPC's death state by handling the transition into this state, performing necessary actions like stopping the NPC, disabling its melee weapon, and playing the death animation. It also checks if the NPC can switch to the idle state and eventually destroys the NPC game object after a delay. The class ensures that the NPC's death is handled smoothly and appropriately within the state machine.

Summary

This chapter was dedicated to crafting a sophisticated melee combat system akin to those found in today's most immersive action games. This chapter serves as your gateway into designing a dynamic and fluid combat system that enhances gameplay through strategic enemy interactions and customizable combat mechanics.

CHAPTER 5

Architecting Player Parkour Movement

In the realm of modern game design, the integration of dynamic and fluid player movements significantly enhances the gaming experience. Parkour, a discipline rooted in overcoming obstacles with speed and efficiency, has become a quintessential movement mechanic in many contemporary video games. This chapter, titled "Architecting Player Parkour Movement," dives into the design and implementation of a parkour system within a Unity-based project, aiming to provide players with a seamless and responsive movement experience.

The allure of parkour in video games lies in its ability to grant players a sense of freedom and mastery over the game environment. From scaling objects to vaulting over barriers and swinging between rooftops, parkour movements can transform static game worlds into playgrounds of possibility. To achieve such dynamic interactions, a robust architectural foundation is necessary. This chapter will guide you through setting up the foundational elements of a parkour movement system, discussing the interaction mechanics that make parkour both possible and exhilarating in a game setting.

The recipes in this chapter will cover topics such as environmental interaction and adaptive parkour mechanics, where the system responds intelligently to varying types of obstacles. By integrating these elements, developers can create a more intuitive and engaging player experience that rewards skill and creativity.

CHAPTER 5 ARCHITECTING PLAYER PARKOUR MOVEMENT

> **Note** The animations provided as part of this chapter download are those that have been made freely available for educational use. Consequently, these animations lack the fluidity characteristic of high-budget "AAA" games. Achieving the level of finesse required for such fluid animations extends beyond the scope of this chapter, as it necessitates professional design and meticulous refinement. The focus of the recipes in this chapter is on building the core Parkour framework.

To fully engage with the recipes in Chapter 5, please ensure you download the completed Unity project available for this chapter. This will enable you to directly apply the concepts discussed and effectively explore the intricacies of the parkour system within a functioning Unity environment.

Recipe 5-1: Exploring the Parkour Environment and Player Armature Game Object

Problem

Creating an engaging parkour system in a game requires a well-designed environment with various obstacles and a player character equipped with the necessary components to interact dynamically with these obstacles. The challenge lies in setting up the parkour environment with climbable structures and configuring the player character with the appropriate sensors and managers to detect and perform parkour actions seamlessly.

Solution

To address this challenge, you will utilize the third-person controller playground scene as your parkour environment that has been populated with obstacles created using simple cubes. The player character, represented by the Player Armature game object, will be enhanced with three key components: the Obstacle Sensor, Parkour Manager, and Line Renderer. The Obstacle Sensor will detect nearby climbable objects, the Parkour Manager will manage and execute parkour actions, and the Line Renderer will visualize the path for a parkour maneuver. This setup ensures the player can fluidly interact with the environment, providing a dynamic parkour experience.

How It Works

Begin by downloading the resource provided as part of Chapter 5. Start by opening the Playground scene for the ThirdPersonController that is available within Assets/StarterAssets/ThirdPersonController/Scenes.

Open the Playground scene and observe the central step-like structure composed of five cubes of varying heights. Select any of these cubes in the scene to display the corresponding object in the hierarchy. These cubes are named Step_0 through Step_4. Each step is equipped with a Nav Mesh Obstacle component (Figure 5-1), and the scene has been re-baked to incorporate these obstacles into the navigation mesh. Each of these cubes has been tagged as "Obstacle" and assigned to the "Obstacle" Layer. The height (Transform – Scale – Y value) of these steps ranges from 0.5 for Step_0 to 2.0 for Step_4. This variation in height ensures that the player character utilizes different parkour movements, such as stepping up, jumping, climbing, and vaulting, to traverse these obstacles, enhancing the dynamic nature of the parkour experience.

CHAPTER 5   ARCHITECTING PLAYER PARKOUR MOVEMENT

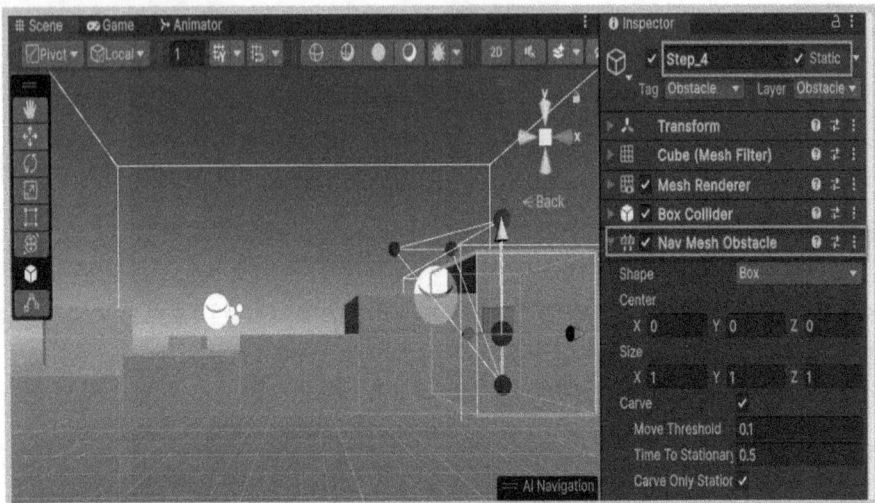

Figure 5-1. *Five cubes comprising the central step-like structure and Nav Mesh Obstacle*

Select the Player Armature game object in the hierarchy, which represents your player character. You will note that it has been fitted with three additional components, namely, Obstacle Sensor, Parkour Manager, and Line Renderer (Figure 5-2).

The ObstacleSensor script, attached to the PlayerArmature game object, detects obstacles in front of the player using raycasting. It uses a ray cast from the player's knee height in the forward direction to identify obstacles within a specified distance. When an obstacle is detected, the script gathers information such as the obstacle's height and the rotation needed for the player to face the obstacle. The script also visually represents the raycast using the LineRenderer component, providing immediate feedback in the game view on whether an obstacle is detected. The obstacle detection leverages a designated obstacle layer to ensure precise and relevant hits.

The ParkourManager script, attached to the PlayerArmature game object, manages the player's parkour movements within the game environment. It detects obstacles using the ObstacleSensor and executes appropriate parkour actions from a list of behaviors when an obstacle is

Chapter 5 Architecting Player Parkour Movement

encountered. This script handles the transition into and out of parkour mode, initiates the relevant parkour animations with root motion, and ensures the player is correctly oriented toward obstacles during these actions. It leverages Unity's animation system and target matching to smoothly integrate parkour movements into the gameplay. Upcoming recipes in this chapter explore these components in detail.

Figure 5-2. Newly added Player Armature, Parkour System Components

Recipe 5-2: Implementing the Obstacle Sensor

Problem

Detecting obstacles in real time is crucial for enabling dynamic parkour movements in a game environment. The challenge lies in accurately identifying obstacles in the player's path and determining their height and position to facilitate appropriate climbing actions. Without a reliable detection mechanism, the player character cannot perform seamless parkour moves, leading to unrealistic and unresponsive gameplay.

Solution

The ObstacleSensor class addresses this challenge by using a raycast from the player's knee height to detect obstacles in the forward direction. Upon detecting an obstacle, it gathers detailed information such as the obstacle's height and the necessary rotation for the player to face the obstacle. This data is encapsulated in a HitInfo struct. This information is visually represented using a LineRenderer, aiding in debugging and visualization. The collected data is then used to trigger appropriate parkour actions, ensuring fluid and realistic player movements over obstacles.

How It Works

The ObstacleSensor class, in conjunction with the HitInfo struct, provides a robust mechanism for detecting obstacles in the player's path and gathering essential information needed for dynamic parkour actions. By casting a ray from the player's knee height forward, it identifies obstacles tagged as "Obstacle" and gathers crucial details such as obstacle height and the rotation needed for the player to face the obstacle.

Listing 5-1. ObstacleSensor script

```
using UnityEngine;
//This script is attached to the PlayerArmature game object.

public struct HitInfo
{
    public bool hitObstacle; //determines if an obstacle was
                             //encountered
    public RaycastHit hitData; //provides information about
                               //the hit obstacle
    public float obstacleHeight; //provides the height of the
                                 //hit obstacle
    public Quaternion targetRotToFaceObstacle; //Players
               //rotation to face obstacles to climb upon
}

[RequireComponent(typeof(LineRenderer))]
public class ObstacleSensor : MonoBehaviour
{
    [Tooltip("The approx knee height of the Player
    representing the height from which the ray is cast
    forward.")]
    [SerializeField] private float kneeHeight = 0.35f;
    [Tooltip("The length of the ray in the forward
    direction.")]
    [SerializeField] float rayLength = 0.75f;

    private Vector3 rayOrigin; //Define the ray's origin

    private LayerMask obstacleLayerMask;

    private HitInfo hitInfo = new HitInfo();

    private LineRenderer lineRenderer;
```

CHAPTER 5   ARCHITECTING PLAYER PARKOUR MOVEMENT

```csharp
private void Start()
{
    obstacleLayerMask = LayerMask.GetMask("Obstacle");

    //Get the LineRenderer component, it is guaranteed to
    //be present by RequireComponent attribute
    lineRenderer = GetComponent<LineRenderer>();
}

public HitInfo ObstacleDetected()
{
    rayOrigin = transform.position + Vector3.up *
    kneeHeight;

    hitInfo.hitObstacle = Physics.Raycast(rayOrigin,
    transform.forward, out hitInfo.hitData, rayLength,
    obstacleLayerMask);

    if (hitInfo.hitObstacle)
    {
        //Debug.DrawRay(rayOrigin, transform.forward *
        //rayLength, Color.green);

        Utils.DrawRay(rayOrigin, transform.forward,
        rayLength, Color.green, lineRenderer);

        // Calculate the height of the object hit
        Collider hitCollider = hitInfo.hitData.collider;
        hitInfo.obstacleHeight =
        hitCollider.bounds.size.y;
        hitInfo.targetRotToFaceObstacle =
        Quaternion.LookRotation(-hitInfo.hitData.normal);

        Debug.Log($"Obstacle detected with height:
        {hitInfo.obstacleHeight}");
    }
```

```
        else
        {
            //Debug.DrawRay(rayOrigin, transform.forward *
            //rayLength, Color.red);
            Utils.DrawRay(rayOrigin, transform.forward,
            rayLength, Color.red, lineRenderer);
        }

        return hitInfo;
    }
}
```

1. The HitInfo struct is used to store information about the detected obstacle. It contains the following fields:

   - bool hitObstacle: Indicates whether an obstacle was hit.

   - RaycastHit hitData: Stores detailed information about the hit, such as the point of impact, the normal at the point of impact, and the collider of the obstacle.

   - float obstacleHeight: Stores the height of the detected obstacle.

   - Quaternion targetRotToFaceObstacle: Stores the rotation needed for the player to face the obstacle.

2. The line of code [RequireComponent(typeof(LineRenderer))] is an attribute in Unity that ensures the LineRenderer component is always present on the same GameObject to which this script is attached. When you add the ObstacleSensor script

CHAPTER 5 ARCHITECTING PLAYER PARKOUR MOVEMENT

to a GameObject, Unity automatically adds a LineRenderer component to that GameObject if it doesn't already have one. This guarantees that the ObstacleSensor script has access to a LineRenderer component, which is essential for its functionality.

3. [SerializeField] private float kneeHeight: Represents the height from which the ray is cast forward. The default is set to 0.35f.

4. [SerializeField] float rayLength: The length of the ray to be cast out in the forward direction. The default is set to 0.75f.

5. private Vector3 rayOrigin: Defines the origin point of the ray.

6. private LayerMask obstacleLayerMask: Specifies the layer mask used to identify obstacles while invoking the Physics.Raycast() method.

7. private HitInfo hitInfo: An instance of the HitInfo struct used to store the hit information of the obstacle the player is attempting to traverse.

8. private LineRenderer lineRenderer: A reference to the LineRenderer component used to visually represent the raycast in the game view, using the provided Utils.DrawRay() method.

9. Start(): The Start() method initializes the obstacleLayerMask by retrieving the layer mask for obstacles using the layer name "Obstacle." It then gets the LineRenderer component attached to the same GameObject. The RequireComponent attribute ensures this component is always present.

CHAPTER 5 ARCHITECTING PLAYER PARKOUR MOVEMENT

10. ObstacleDetected(): The ObstacleDetected() method casts a ray from the player's position to detect obstacles and returns a HitInfo struct with the information about the obstacle. It calculates the origin of the ray by adding the knee height to the player's position. It casts a ray from the ray origin in the forward direction for the specified length, checking for collisions with objects in the obstacleLayerMask, and storing the result in hitInfo.hitData. If an obstacle is hit by the ray, it uses the utility function DrawRay() to draw the ray in green in the game view. It retrieves the collider of the hit object, followed by calculating the height of the hit obstacle from its collider's bounds. It then calculates the rotation needed to face the obstacle by using the negative normal of the hit point. Finally, it logs the height of the detected obstacle for debugging purposes. In the event no obstacle was hit, the utility function DrawRay() is used to draw the ray in red in the game view.

The ObstacleSensor class is a crucial component for detecting obstacles in front of the player. It uses raycasting to identify obstacles, gather information about them, and determine the necessary adjustments for the player's orientation. The LineRenderer component visually represents the raycast, aiding in debugging and visualization. The HitInfo struct encapsulates all relevant data about the obstacle, making it easy to handle and use elsewhere in the game logic.

The DrawRay() method is a utility function that is part of the provided Utils class. It visually represents a ray in the Unity game view, using a LineRenderer component. It takes the starting position, direction, length, color, and a LineRenderer as parameters and draws a line from the start point in the specified direction and length with the specified color.

CHAPTER 5   ARCHITECTING PLAYER PARKOUR MOVEMENT

This method ensures the LineRenderer component is correctly configured and used to represent the ray you see within the game view.

Listing 5-2. Utils.DrawRay() method

```
public static void DrawRay(Vector3 start, Vector3 direction,
float length, Color color, LineRenderer lineRenderer)
{
    if (lineRenderer == null)
    {
        Debug.LogError("LineRenderer is null. Please provide a
        valid LineRenderer.");
        return;
    }

    // Set the color for the ray
    lineRenderer.startColor = color;
    lineRenderer.endColor = color;

    // Set the width for the ray
    lineRenderer.startWidth = 0.1f;
    lineRenderer.endWidth = 0.1f;

    // Set the material for the LineRenderer
    lineRenderer.material = new
    Material(Shader.Find("Sprites/Default"));

    // Define the ray's start and end points
    Vector3 end = start + direction * length;

    // Update the positions of the LineRenderer
    lineRenderer.positionCount = 2;
    lineRenderer.SetPosition(0, start);
    lineRenderer.SetPosition(1, end);
}
```

1. This method first checks to see if the provided LineRenderer is null, in which case it logs an error message and exits the method early.

2. If the LineRenderer is not null, it sets the starting and ending color of the line to the specified color.

3. It then sets the starting and ending width of the line to 0.1 units.

4. It then sets the material of the LineRenderer to a new material using the default sprite shader. This ensures the line is visible with the specified color.

5. It calculates the end position of the ray by adding the direction vector, scaled by the length, to the start position.

6. The number of positions in the LineRenderer is set to 2, representing the start and end points of the line.

7. It then sets the first position of the LineRenderer to the start point and the second position of the LineRenderer to the endpoint.

Recipe 5-3: Implementing the ParkourManager

Problem

The ParkourManager class needs to address the challenge of enabling dynamic parkour actions for the player character within the game environment. This includes detecting obstacles, initiating appropriate parkour animations, and ensuring smooth transitions between different

CHAPTER 5   ARCHITECTING PLAYER PARKOUR MOVEMENT

states such as entering and exiting parkour mode. The complexity arises in managing player input, obstacle detection, and animation synchronization to create a fluid and responsive parkour system.

Solution

The ParkourManager class solves this problem by integrating player input, obstacle detection, and animation control. It utilizes an ObstacleSensor component to detect obstacles and determine the appropriate parkour actions from a list of ParkourBehavior scriptable objects. Upon detecting an obstacle and determining a viable parkour action, the class triggers the relevant animations, ensures proper player rotation, and handles events to notify other scripts when entering and exiting parkour mode. This setup creates a seamless and immersive parkour experience, enhancing player interaction with the game environment.

How It Works

The ParkourManager class operates by first initializing references to required components such as the Animator, ObstacleSensor, and Keyboard in the Awake method. During the Update method, it listens for player input (the "c" key) and, if no parkour action is currently in progress, uses the ObstacleSensor to detect any nearby obstacles. If an obstacle is detected, the class iterates through the list of parkour behaviors to find a suitable action, triggering the OnEnterParkourMode event and enabling root motion for accurate animation playback.

The PerformTargetMatching method ensures the player's position and rotation are correctly aligned with the obstacle during the parkour action. The ParkourAction coroutine handles the execution of the parkour animation, waiting until it is nearly complete before resetting the relevant flags and triggering the OnExitParkourMode event. The IsAnimationNearlyComplete method assists in this process by checking

CHAPTER 5   ARCHITECTING PLAYER PARKOUR MOVEMENT

if the animation has reached a specified threshold and performing target matching to ensure smooth transitions. This cohesive approach ensures that the player character performs realistic and responsive parkour actions, enhancing the overall gameplay experience.

Listing 5-3. ParkourManager script

```
using UnityEngine;
using UnityEngine.InputSystem;
using System;
using System.Collections.Generic;
using System.Collections;

//This script is attached to the PlayerArmature game object.
public class ParkourManager : MonoBehaviour
{
   //Below events being listened for in ThirdPersonController
   //script.
    public event Action OnEnterParkourMode, OnExitParkourMode;

    [Tooltip("Drag and Drop all Parkour Behavior Scriptable
    Objects into this List")]
    [SerializeField] private List<ParkourBehavior>
    parkourBehaviors;

    private ObstacleSensor obstacleSensor;
    private Keyboard keyboard;
    private Animator anim;
    private bool inParkourAction;
    private float rotSpeed = 500f;
    private Quaternion targetRotation;//Rotates Player to face
                                      //Obstacle to be climbed
```

CHAPTER 5 ARCHITECTING PLAYER PARKOUR MOVEMENT

```
private void Awake()
{
    anim = GetComponent<Animator>();
    obstacleSensor = GetComponent<ObstacleSensor>();

    keyboard = Keyboard.current;
    if (keyboard == null)
    {
        Debug.LogError("Keyboard Not found");
        return;
    }
}

private void Update()
{
    if (keyboard.cKey.wasPressedThisFrame &&
        !inParkourAction)
    {
        HitInfo hitInfo =
        obstacleSensor.ObstacleDetected();

        if (hitInfo.hitObstacle)
        {
            Debug.Log($"Obstacle hit was:
            {hitInfo.hitData.transform.name} - Its Height
             is: {hitInfo.obstacleHeight}");

            foreach (ParkourBehavior action in
            parkourBehaviors)
            {
                if (action.ParkourActionPossible(hitInfo,
                    transform))
```

```
            {
                OnEnterParkourMode?.Invoke(); //Event
                //being listened for in
                //ThirdPersonController script.
                anim.applyRootMotion = true;
            StartCoroutine(ParkourAction(action,hitInfo));
                break;
            }
        }
      }
    }
}

private void PerformTargetMatching(ParkourBehavior action,
HitInfo hitInfo)
{
    if (anim.isMatchingTarget) return; //if Target
                    //Matching is already in progress.

    anim.MatchTarget(new
    Vector3(0f,hitInfo.obstacleHeight,0f),
    transform.rotation, action.AvatarTargetBodyPart,
    new MatchTargetWeightMask(action.TargetWeightMask, 0),
    action.StartTargetMatching, action.EndTargetMatching);
    Debug.Log("Performed Target Matching");
}

IEnumerator ParkourAction(ParkourBehavior action, HitInfo
hitInfo)
{
    inParkourAction = true;
    anim.SetBool("mirrorVault", action.Mirror); //ACC
    anim.CrossFade(Animator.StringToHash(
    action.AnimationName), 0.2f);
```

CHAPTER 5 ARCHITECTING PLAYER PARKOUR MOVEMENT

```
        yield return null;//Wait for the next frame, so
                    //animation is playing

    // Wait until the concerned animation is nearly
    //completed
    yield return new WaitUntil(() =>
    IsAnimationNearlyComplete(0.99f,action,hitInfo));
    anim.applyRootMotion = false;//Deactivate root motion.
    inParkourAction = false;
    OnExitParkourMode?.Invoke(); //Event being listened
                //for in ThirdPersonController script
}
private bool IsAnimationNearlyComplete(float threshold,
ParkourBehavior action, HitInfo hitInfo)
{
    targetRotation = Quaternion.LookRotation(-
    hitInfo.hitData.normal);//Rotation to face obstacle

    AnimatorStateInfo stateInfo =
    anim.GetCurrentAnimatorStateInfo(0); //Using Base
                                         //layer 0
    //Rotate the Player to face the obstacle
    transform.rotation =
    Quaternion.RotateTowards(transform.rotation,
    targetRotation, rotSpeed * Time.deltaTime);
    PerformTargetMatching(action, hitInfo);//Target
    //Matching being performed while waiting on animation
    //to complete
    return stateInfo.IsName(action.AnimationName) &&
    stateInfo.normalizedTime >= threshold;
}
}
```

CHAPTER 5   ARCHITECTING PLAYER PARKOUR MOVEMENT

1. public event Action OnEnterParkourMode, OnExitParkourMode: These events notify the ThirdPersonController script when the player enters or exits parkour mode, allowing for decoupling of functionality, enabling other scripts (ThirdPersonController) to react to changes in parkour state without being tightly integrated with the ParkourManager.

2. [SerializeField] private List<ParkourBehavior> parkourBehaviors: A list of ParkourBehavior scriptable objects that define different parkour actions. It provides a flexible way to define and manage multiple parkour actions that the player can perform.

3. private ObstacleSensor obstacleSensor: Reference to the ObstacleSensor component for detecting obstacles. It is essential to determine when and where parkour actions can be initiated.

4. private Keyboard keyboard: Reference to the Keyboard input device. It is used to detect player input for initiating parkour actions. You are encouraged to set up the StarterAssets (Input Action Asset) with a keyboard and joystick button combination for this Parkour action as was discussed in Chapter 2, "Unity's New Input System."

5. private Animator anim: Reference to the Animator component controlling the player's animations. It is necessary for triggering and controlling animations during parkour actions.

6. private bool inParkourAction: Indicates whether a parkour action is currently being performed, thus preventing overlapping parkour actions by ensuring only one action can be performed at a time.

7. private float rotSpeed = 500f: The speed at which the player rotates to face the obstacle, controlling the smoothness and responsiveness of the player's rotation during parkour actions.

8. private Quaternion targetRotation: The target rotation for the player to face the obstacle. It is used to smoothly rotate the player to the correct orientation before performing parkour actions.

9. Awake(): The Awake() method initializes references to required components and checks for the presence of the keyboard. It initializes the Animator and ObstacleSensor component references, followed by initializing the keyboard reference. In the event the keyboard is not found, it logs an error and exits the method.

10. Update(): The Update() method checks for player input and initiates parkour actions if an obstacle is detected. It checks if the "c" key was pressed and no parkour action is currently being performed, in which case it utilizes the obstacleSensor.ObstacleDetected() method to detect obstacles. The "if (hitInfo.hitObstacle)" conditional statement checks if an obstacle was detected, in which case information about the detected obstacle is logged to the console. The foreach loop that is encountered next iterates through the list of parkour behaviors and checks if

CHAPTER 5   ARCHITECTING PLAYER PARKOUR MOVEMENT

the current parkour action is possible based on the detected obstacle's hitInfo date (obstacleHeight). If the parkour action is possible, the OnEnterParkourMode event is invoked if there are any subscribers, followed by enabling root motion for the animation and starting the ParkourAction coroutine to perform the parkour action. Finally, as you have found an appropriate parkour action, you use the "break" statement to exit the foreach loop after initiating this parkour action.

11. private void PerformTargetMatching(ParkourBehavior action, HitInfo hitInfo): The PerformTargetMatching() method matches the player's position to the target (obstacle) position for the concerned parkour action. In game development, precise character movements such as jumping onto platforms can be achieved using Unity's Animator.MatchTarget() method. This method ensures a character's specific body part, like a foot or hand, lands at a predetermined position and time. For instance, in the animation clip named "StepUp," you can identify the moments when the character using its right foot starts to step up (at 30% or 0.3 normalized time) (Figure 5-3) and when they are about to land (at 54% or 0.54 normalized time) (Figure 5-4).

CHAPTER 5　ARCHITECTING PLAYER PARKOUR MOVEMENT

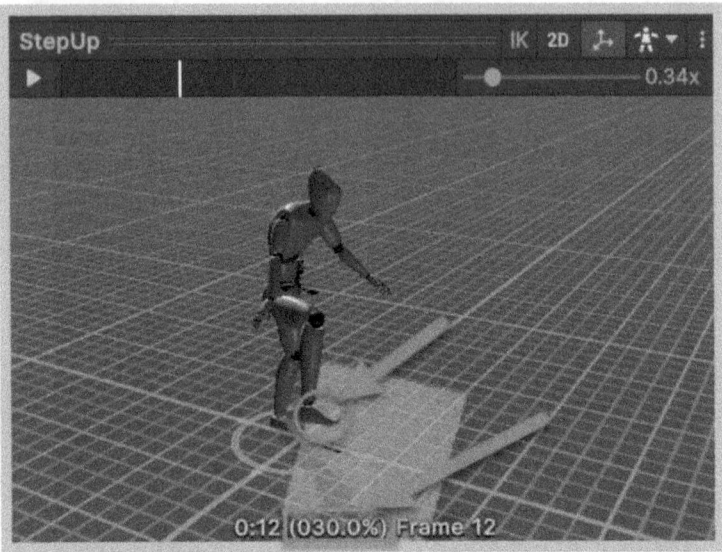

Figure 5-3. *Right foot StepUp animation at 30%*

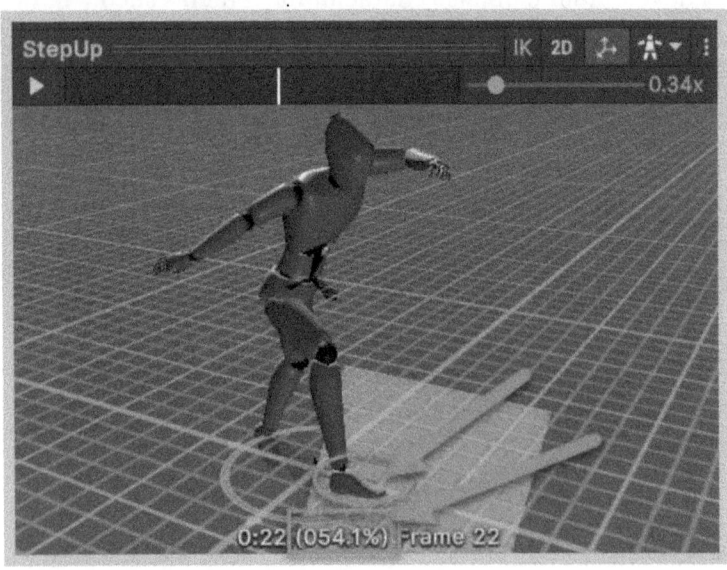

Figure 5-4. *Right foot StepUp animation at 54%*

CHAPTER 5   ARCHITECTING PLAYER PARKOUR MOVEMENT

By attaching this ParkourManager script to the PlayerArmature that calls MatchTarget() with these parameters, the character's right foot will precisely hit the designated target. The script responds to input, such as pressing a key, to synchronize the character's movement with the animation, ensuring realistic and intentional actions within the game, thus avoiding the need to have perfectly crafted animations for each obstacle that needs to be traversed. You also do not need to have these percentage values matched perfectly for foot placement in this case.

Note   Refer to the below link for Unity's documentation on Target Matching. https://docs.unity3d.com/Manual/TargetMatching.html

---

If target matching is already in progress, the statement "if (anim.isMatchingTarget) return;" exits the method. The anim.MatchTarget() method matches the player's concerned limb's position to the target (obstacle) position. Let's explore its parameters.

- new Vector3(0f, hitInfo.obstacleHeight, 0f): This parameter specifies the target position for the matching. In this case, it sets the target position to a point directly above the ground at the height of the detected obstacle (hitInfo.obstacleHeight), while keeping the x and z coordinates at 0 relative to the character's current position. This ensures that the character aligns vertically with the top of the obstacle during the animation and doesn't float above or clip through the obstacle.

499

- transform.rotation: This parameter specifies the target rotation for the matching. Here, it uses the current rotation of the character (transform.rotation), ensuring that the character maintains its current orientation while aligning with the obstacle.

- action.AvatarTargetBodyPart: This parameter specifies which body part of the character should be matched to the target position and rotation. The value comes from the ParkourBehavior scriptable object (action) and could represent either the AvatarTarget.RightHand, AvatarTarget.LeftFoot, etc., that should be aligned with the target position and rotation.

- new MatchTargetWeightMask(action.TargetWeightMask, 0): This parameter specifies the weight mask for the target matching, which determines how much influence the matched target (obstacle) has on the character's position and rotation. Here, it uses a weight mask defined in the ParkourBehavior scriptable object (action.TargetWeightMask), with a rotation weight that has been set to zero. This controls how strongly the character's position is influenced by the matched target. A weight of 1 means full influence, while 0 means no influence. The rotation weight of 0 means the character's rotation is not influenced by the target rotation.

- action.StartTargetMatching: This parameter specifies the normalized start time (0 to 1) of the target matching within the animation as

CHAPTER 5   ARCHITECTING PLAYER PARKOUR MOVEMENT

depicted in Figure 5-3. This value is stored in the ParkourBehavior scriptable object (action). If you select the "StepUp_SO" scriptable object available within Assets/Enemey_AI/Scripts/Parkour/ScriptableObjects, you will note that its StartTargetMatching value has been set to 30%, i.e., 0.3. This is the value being referred to by this parameter, which defines when during the animation the target matching should begin. A value of 0 means the start of the animation, while 1 means the end.

- action.EndTargetMatching: This parameter specifies the normalized end time (0 to 1) of the target matching within the animation as depicted in Figure 5-4. The value comes from the ParkourBehavior scriptable object (action). If you select the parkour behavior action "StepUp_SO," you will note that its EndTargetMatching value has been set to 54%, i.e., 0.54. This is the value being referred to by this parameter, which defines when during the animation the target matching should end. A value of 0 means the start of the animation, while 1 means the end.

Each parameter is carefully chosen to control the alignment process:

- The target position is set to the obstacle's height.
- The target rotation keeps the character's current orientation.
- The body part to align is specified by the parkour behavior.

- The weight mask determines the influence of the matching on the character's position.
- The start and end times define when the matching occurs during the animation.
- This precise control ensures smooth and realistic transitions during parkour actions.

12. IEnumerator ParkourAction(ParkourBehavior action, HitInfo hitInfo): The ParkourAction coroutine performs the parkour action animation and waits until it is nearly complete. It begins by setting the inParkourAction flag to true. It sets the "mirrorVault" boolean parameter available within the Animator to the value of the action "Mirror" property. This is used to mirror an animation and is used in the Vaulting parkour action discussed in Recipe 5-5. You then set in motion the animation for the parkour action using CrossFade(). It then waits for the next frame to ensure the animation has begun playing. The coroutine then waits until the animation is nearly (99%) complete, after which root motion is disabled. You then reset the inParkourAction flag to false and invoke the OnExitParkourMode event if there are any subscribers. This event is being listened to within the ThirdPersonController script.

13. private bool IsAnimationNearlyComplete(float threshold, ParkourBehavior action, HitInfo hitInfo): This method checks if the animation is nearly complete. It first calculates the player's target rotation to face the obstacle. It then retrieves the

current animation state information from the base layer. At this point, one of the Parkour animations will be playing. The player is then smoothly rotated to face the obstacle. The PerformTargetMatching() method is then invoked while the animation is playing, finally returning true if the animation is nearly complete based on the threshold.

14. OnEnterParkourMode and OnExitParkourMode: These events are listened for within the ThirdPersonController script. It allows the ThirdPersonController to perform additional actions when the player enters or exits parkour mode. Figure 5-5 depicts the code of the event listeners that have been set up for the OnEnterParkourMode and OnExitParkourMode events.

```
2 references
private void EnteredParkourMode() //CC
{
    inParkourMode = true;
    _controller.enabled = false; //disable CharacterController component
    Debug.Log("Entered Parkour Mode");
}

2 references
private void ExitedParkourMode() //CC
{
    inParkourMode = false;
    _controller.enabled = true; //enable CharacterController component
    Debug.Log("Exited Parkour Mode");
}
```

Figure 5-5. *Event listeners for events OnEnterParkourMode and OnExitParkour Mode*

A boolean variable "inParkourMode" has been declared at the beginning of the script, below the commented "animation IDs" section. Upon entering parkour mode, the CharacterController component is

CHAPTER 5 ARCHITECTING PLAYER PARKOUR MOVEMENT

disabled to ensure that no player interaction occurs when the concerned parkour animation is being played, which if allowed would result in weird behavior. Likewise, upon exiting parkour mode, i.e., when the parkour animation has completed playing, you give the character control back to the player by enabling the CharacterController component. The variable "inParkourMode" is used within the Update() method to ensure that while the player character is performing a parkour action, the Update() method simply exits without invoking any of the other methods listed within it. This has been depicted in Figure 5-6.

```
private void Update()
{
    if (inParkourMode) return; //CC

    _hasAnimator = TryGetComponent(out _animator);

    JumpAndGravity();
    GroundedCheck();
    Move();
    //Attack();
}
```

Figure 5-6. *The modified Update() method*

Some other minor additions to the code for the ThirdPersonController script can be noted within the Awake() method where GetComponent<ParkourManager>() is used to get access to the ParkourManager component, and within the OnEnable() and OnDisable() methods where you subscribe and unsubscribe to the events, namely, OnEnterParkourMode and OnExitParkourMode.

The ParkourManager class integrates player input, obstacle detection, animation control, and event handling to manage parkour actions in a game. It ensures smooth transitions between different states, such as entering and exiting parkour mode, and provides a flexible system for defining various parkour behaviors. The use of events allows for modular and decoupled code, making it easier to maintain and extend.

Recipe 5-4: Implementing Scriptable Objects for Parkour Actions

Problem

Implementing parkour actions in a dynamic game environment requires a flexible and scalable solution to manage various types of movements, such as climbing, vaulting, jumping, etc. Hardcoding these actions can lead to a rigid system that is difficult to maintain and extend. The challenge lies in creating a system where new parkour actions can be easily added, modified, or removed without altering the core logic, ensuring the game's extensibility and maintainability. Using Scriptable Objects to represent different parkour actions provides a modular approach, allowing for easy customization and reusability of parkour behaviors.

Solution

Using Scriptable Objects to represent different parkour actions, such as Step Up, Climb, Jump, and Vaulting, provides a flexible and modular approach to implementing parkour behaviors. Each action can be defined as a separate Scriptable Object, encapsulating its unique properties and logic. This allows for easy customization and extension of parkour behaviors without modifying the core gameplay code, ensuring a scalable and maintainable system that can be readily adapted to new parkour requirements.

How It Works

The ParkourBehavior class, defined as a Scriptable Object, encapsulates the properties and logic required to execute various parkour actions, such as Step Up, Climb, Jump, and Vaulting. Each parkour action is represented by an instance of this class, allowing easy configuration and management of different behaviors without altering the core code. Key properties include animationName, which must match the name in the Animator exactly, and minHeight and maxHeight to specify the height range of obstacles the action can handle. The class also manages target matching, crucial for aligning the player's avatar correctly during animations, with properties such as avatarTargetBodyPart, startTargetMatching, endTargetMatching, and targetWeightMask defining how and when the player's body should align with the target position. The method ParkourActionPossible() checks if the current obstacle's height falls within the specified range, determining the feasibility of the parkour action. This approach allows easy customization and extension by creating new or modifying existing Scriptable Objects, ensuring a scalable and maintainable system for implementing complex parkour behaviors. Ensure that every scriptable object parkour action you create and would like to use is dragged and dropped onto the Parkour Behaviors list, available as part of the ParkourManager component in the Inspector.

Note Code in Listing 5-4 that has been commented with //ACC has to do with the Vaulting behavior and will be discussed in Recipe 5-5.

Listing 5-4. ParkourBehavior script

```csharp
using UnityEngine;

[CreateAssetMenu(fileName = "NewParkourAction", menuName
= "Parkour/ParkourActionData", order = 1)]
public class ParkourBehavior : ScriptableObject
{
    [SerializeField] private string animationName;//Ensure the
        //animation name spelling in the SO exactly matches the
      //name in the Animator
    [SerializeField] private float minHeight;
    [SerializeField] private float maxHeight;
    [SerializeField] private string obstacleTag; //ACC

    [Header("Target Matching")]
    [SerializeField] protected AvatarTarget
     avatarTargetBodyPart;
    [SerializeField] private float startTargetMatching;
    //Percentage into the animation when target matching should
    //commence
    [SerializeField] private float endTargetMatching;
     //Percentage into the animation when the
     //avatarTargetBodyPart should reach a specific position
    [SerializeField] private Vector3 targetWeightMask = new
    Vector3(0f, 1f, 0f);

     //Properties
      public bool Mirror { get; set; } //ACC
     public string AnimationName => animationName;
     public AvatarTarget AvatarTargetBodyPart =>
     avatarTargetBodyPart;
     public float StartTargetMatching => startTargetMatching;
```

CHAPTER 5   ARCHITECTING PLAYER PARKOUR MOVEMENT

```
public float EndTargetMatching => endTargetMatching;
public Vector3 TargetWeightMask => targetWeightMask;

public virtual bool ParkourActionPossible(HitInfo hitInfo,
Transform player)
{
    if(!string.IsNullOrEmpty(obstacleTag) &&        //ACC
    !hitInfo.hitData.transform.CompareTag(obstacleTag))
        return false;

    if (hitInfo.obstacleHeight < minHeight ||
        hitInfo.obstacleHeight > maxHeight)
    {
        return false;
    }
    return true;
}
}
```

1. [CreateAssetMenu(fileName = "NewParkourAction", menuName = "Parkour/ParkourActionData", order = 1)]: This Unity attribute provides a convenient way to create instances of the ParkourBehavior scriptable object from within the Unity Editor. This attribute adds a menu item in the Unity Editor under the "Assets/Create" menu, allowing developers to create new instances of the ParkourBehavior scriptable object. Its parameters include:

    - fileName = "NewParkourAction": This specifies the default file name for new instances of the ParkourBehavior scriptable object. When you

CHAPTER 5 ARCHITECTING PLAYER PARKOUR MOVEMENT

create a new instance using this menu item, the default name of the scriptable object asset will be "NewParkourAction." You can rename the asset later if needed.

- menuName = "Parkour/ParkourActionData": Defines the path and name of the menu item that appears in the Unity Editor's "Assets/Create" menu. It creates a nested menu structure, so the menu item for creating a new ParkourBehavior scriptable object will appear under "Assets/Create/Parkour/ParkourActionData."

- order = 1: Here you specify the order in which the menu item appears in the "Assets/Create" menu relative to other items. An optional parameter that can be used to control the position of the menu item within the "Assets/Create" menu. A lower number places the item higher on the list.

2. [SerializeField] private string animationName: Stores the name of the animation clip used for the parkour action. It ensures the correct animation is triggered during the parkour action. The name must match exactly with the one in the Animator.

3. [SerializeField] private float minHeight: Defines the minimum height of obstacles for which this parkour action is applicable. It ensures that the parkour action is only performed on obstacles that meet this minimum height requirement.

4. [SerializeField] private float maxHeight: Defines the maximum height of obstacles for which this parkour action is applicable. It ensures that the parkour action is only performed on obstacles that meet this maximum height requirement.

5. [Header("Target Matching")]: Adds a header in the Unity Inspector for better organization, thereby improving the readability and organization of the serialized fields in the Unity Editor.

6. [SerializeField] protected AvatarTarget avatarTargetBodyPart: Specifies which body part should match the target position during the animation. It controls which part of the character's body aligns with the obstacle during the animation. The different body parts available for selection are the Root, Body, Left Foot, Right Foot, Left Hand, and Right Hand (Figure 5-7).

CHAPTER 5   ARCHITECTING PLAYER PARKOUR MOVEMENT

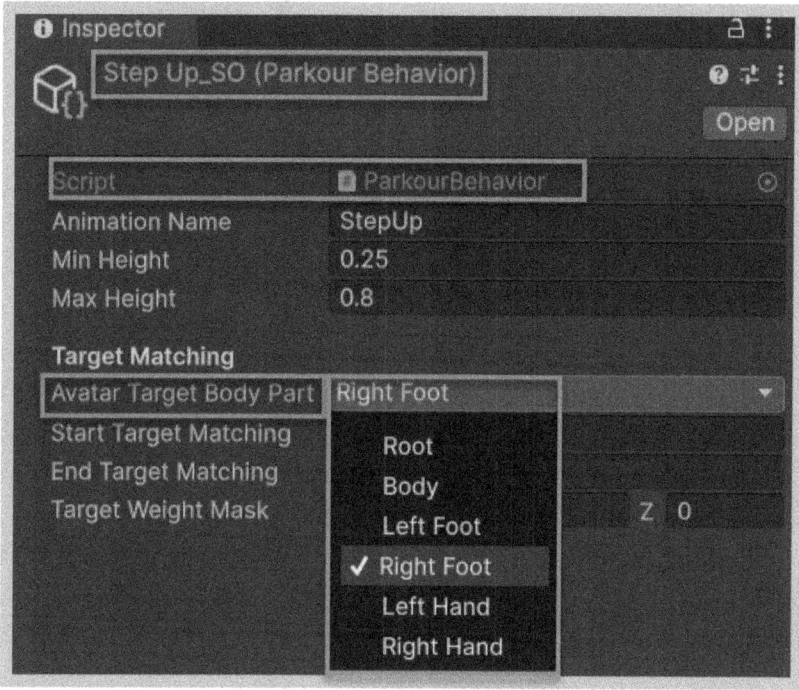

Figure 5-7. AvatarTarget body parts

7. [SerializeField] private float startTargetMatching: Defines the normalized start time for target matching within the animation. It specifies when to start matching the body part to the obstacle position during the animation.

8. [SerializeField] private float endTargetMatching: Defines the normalized end time for target matching within the animation. It specifies when to complete matching the body part to the obstacle position during the animation.

CHAPTER 5 ARCHITECTING PLAYER PARKOUR MOVEMENT

9. [SerializeField] private Vector3 targetWeightMask: Defines the weight of the matching in each axis (x, y, z). It controls how much influence the matching has on each axis of the body part's position.

10. public string AnimationName => animationName: Exposes the animationName field, allowing other scripts to retrieve the name of the animation associated with this parkour behavior.

11. public AvatarTarget AvatarTargetBodyPart => avatarTargetBodyPart: Exposes the avatarTargetBodyPart field, allowing other scripts to retrieve the body part to be matched during the animation.

12. public float StartTargetMatching => startTargetMatching: Exposes the startTargetMatching field, allowing other scripts to retrieve the start time for target matching.

13. public float EndTargetMatching => endTargetMatching: Exposes the endTargetMatching field, allowing other scripts to retrieve the end time for target matching.

14. public Vector3 TargetWeightMask => targetWeightMask: Exposes the targetWeightMask field, allowing other scripts to retrieve the weight mask for target matching.

15. public bool ParkourActionPossible(HitInfo hitInfo, Transform player): This method determines whether the parkour action can be performed based on the height of the detected obstacle. It returns a boolean value indicating if the parkour action is possible based on the provided HitInfo and player's Transform. It checks to see if the height of the

detected obstacle is outside the range defined by minHeight and maxHeight, in which case it returns false, indicating that the parkour action cannot be performed. However, if the obstacle height is within the acceptable range, it returns true, indicating that the parkour action can be performed. You will note that this method is invoked from within the Update() method of the ParkourManager script.

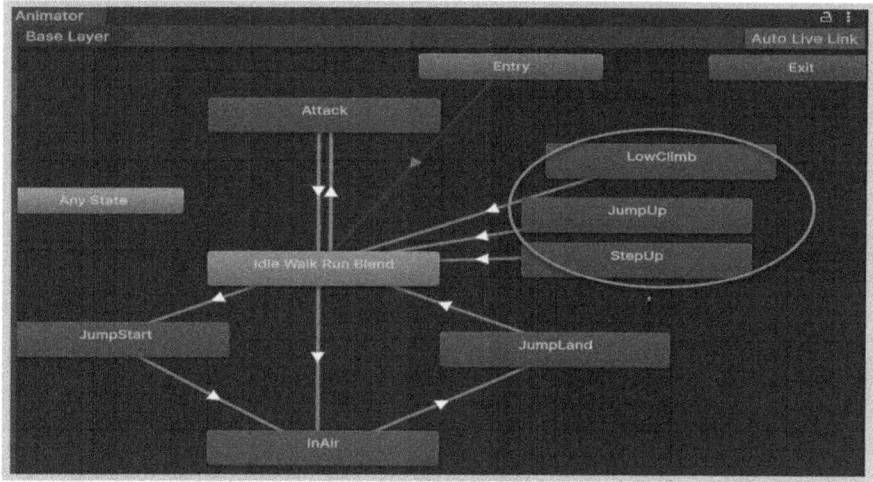

Figure 5-8. *The various parkour animations*

Figure 5-8 illustrates the three parkour animations corresponding to the created Scriptable Objects. These animations are invoked using the CrossFade() method, as seen in the ParkourManager script. Their transitions are one-way into the "Idle Walk Run Blend" tree, with HasExitTime checked. Consequently, once any parkour animation finishes, the player character seamlessly returns to the Idle state.

CHAPTER 5   ARCHITECTING PLAYER PARKOUR MOVEMENT

Navigate to the Assets/Enemy_AI/Scripts/Parkour/ScriptableObjects folder. Here, you will find four pre-configured Scriptable Objects with the suffix "SO." Although these objects have been set up for you, feel free to adjust their values as needed. In this recipe, you will explore three of these Scriptable Objects—StepUp_SO, LowClimb_SO, and JumpUp_SO—to understand their different field value settings.

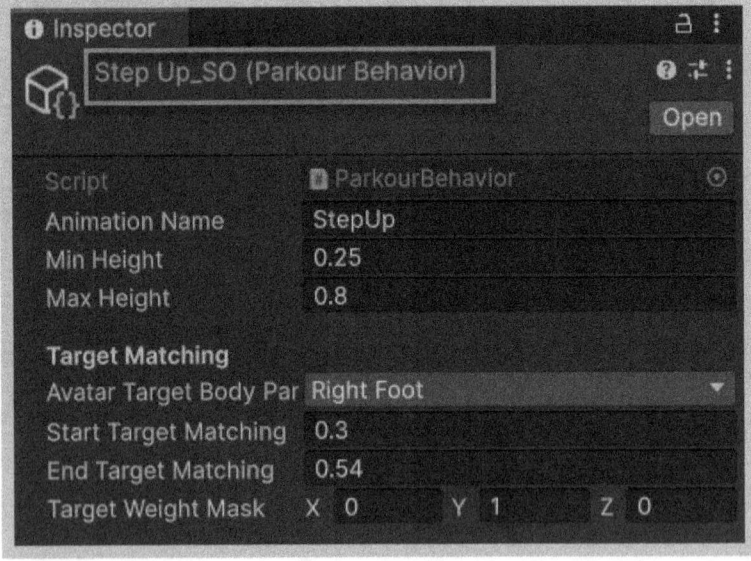

Figure 5-9. The StepUp_SO scriptable object

Figure 5-9 shows the StepUp_SO Scriptable Object. The animation name is set to "StepUp," matching the name used in the Animator exactly. To utilize the StepUp parkour action, the obstacle must be between 0.25 and 0.8 units in height. If the obstacle's height falls outside this range, the StepUp action

CHAPTER 5 ARCHITECTING PLAYER PARKOUR MOVEMENT

cannot be used. In such cases, a LowClimb or JumpUp action might be appropriate, depending on the obstacle's height. In the scene view, Step_0 has a height of 0.5 units, and Step_1 has a height of 0.75 units. Therefore, the StepUp action will be performed when the player character approaches these obstacles and the "C" key is pressed. Recipe 5-3 explained how to obtain the target matching values for the fields Avatar Target Body Part, Start Target Matching, and End Target Matching, as illustrated in Figures 5-3 and 5-4. For the StepUp action, the Avatar Target Body Part is set to the right foot based on the animation. The Target Weight Mask indicates that weight is applied only in the Y direction since the animation involves a simple vertical step up with no horizontal or forward movement, thus the X and Z components are set to zero. Unity's implementation for target matching uses the Target Weight Mask to control how much influence the target matching has in each axis, allowing precise control over the character's movement.

CHAPTER 5   ARCHITECTING PLAYER PARKOUR MOVEMENT

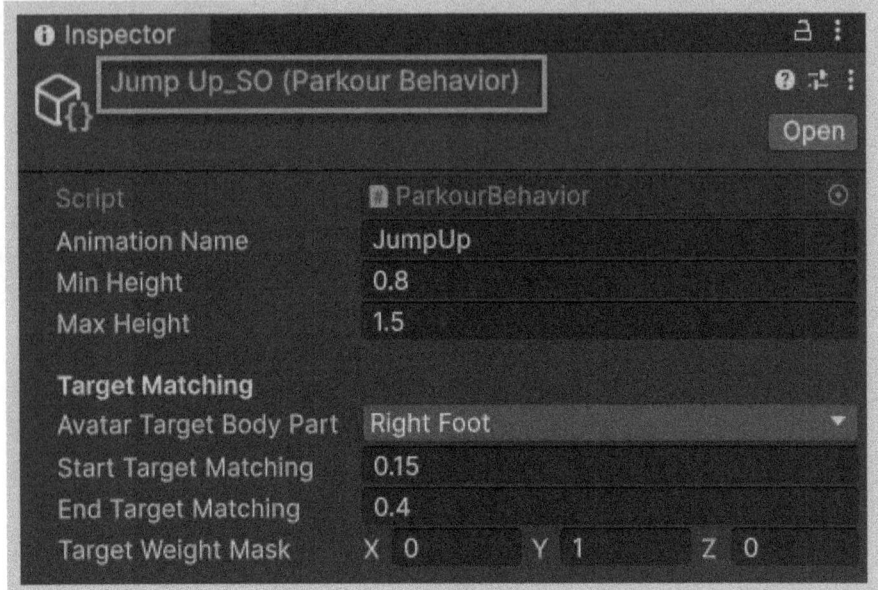

Figure 5-10. The JumpUp_SO scriptable object

Figure 5-10 shows the JumpUp_SO Scriptable Object. The animation name is set to "JumpUp," matching the name used in the Animator exactly. To utilize this parkour action, the obstacle must be between 0.8 and 1.5 units in height. In the scene view, Step_2 has a height of 0.5 units, and Step_3 has a height of 1.5 units. Therefore, the JumpUp action will be performed when the player character approaches these obstacles and the "C" key is pressed. You will note that the Avatar Target Body Part is set to the right foot based on the animation used. The field Start Target Matching has been set to 0.15 and End Target Matching has been set to 0.4. You could adjust these values to your liking should you want to. The Target Weight Mask indicates that

516

weight is applied in the Y direction only since the animation involves a simple vertical step-up with no horizontal or forward movement; thus, the X and Z components are set to zero.

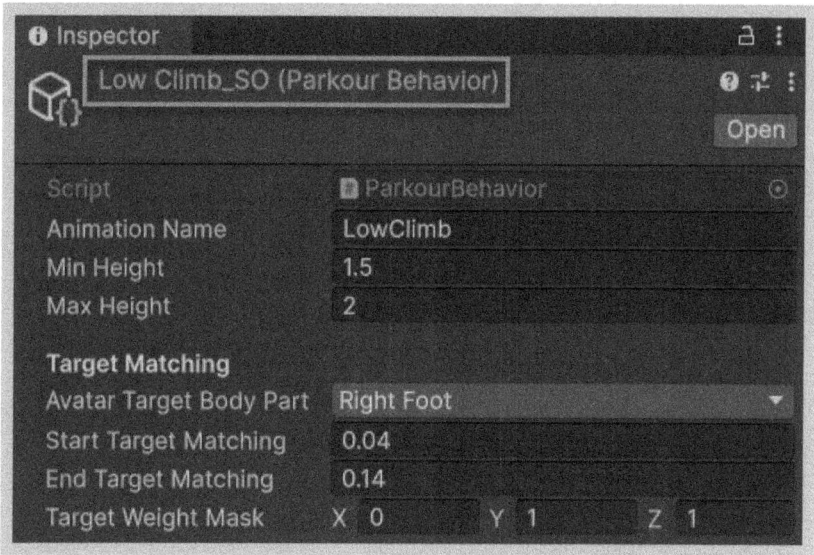

Figure 5-11. *The LowClimb_SO scriptable object*

Figure 5-11 shows the LowClimb_SO Scriptable Object. The animation name is set to "LowClimb," matching the name used in the Animator exactly. To utilize this parkour action, the obstacle must be between 1 and 2 units in height. If the obstacle's height falls outside this range, the LowClimb action cannot be used. In the scene view, Step_4 has a height of 2 units. Therefore, the LowClimb action will be performed when the player character approaches this obstacle and the "C" key is pressed. For this action, the Avatar Target Body Part is set to the right foot based on the animation. The Target Weight Mask indicates that weight is applied in both the Y and Z directions since the animation involves a forward movement in addition to a vertical step up with both forward and horizontal movement; thus, only the X component is set to zero, while the Y and Z components are set to one. Unity's implementation for target matching uses the Target Weight Mask to control how much influence the target matching has in each axis, allowing precise control over the character's movement.

Unity's Target Matching allows a single animation to be used for multiple target (obstacle) objects if the animation is crafted well. This ensures that different animations are not required for each new obstacle encountered. For effective target matching without having the character clip into obstacles, animations must be professionally crafted, and the values for Start Target Matching and End Target Matching must be precisely fine-tuned.

Recipe 5-5: Implementing a Vaulting Parkour Action

Problem

The need for a vaulting parkour action arises from the necessity to traverse mid-height obstacles efficiently, a common mechanic seen in many parkour-related games. Without a specific action for vaulting, player movement is restricted, reducing the fluidity and realism of parkour

CHAPTER 5 ARCHITECTING PLAYER PARKOUR MOVEMENT

sequences. Implementing a dedicated vaulting action ensures smooth and dynamic navigation over barriers that are too high to step over and too low to climb, enhancing the overall gameplay experience.

Solution

Implementing a custom vaulting behavior is essential for this parkour action. Vaulting can use either the right or left hand to support the object being vaulted over. The solution must handle scenarios where the player can approach the hurdle from the left or right corner. If approaching from the left corner, the player should use the right hand, and vice versa. Additionally, the system must account for the direction the player is facing relative to the hurdle's Z axis. If the player's Z axis is aligned with the hurdle's Z axis, it indicates a rear approach, while opposite Z directions indicate a front approach. The hand used to grasp the obstacle must adjust accordingly to ensure a smooth and realistic vaulting action.

How It Works

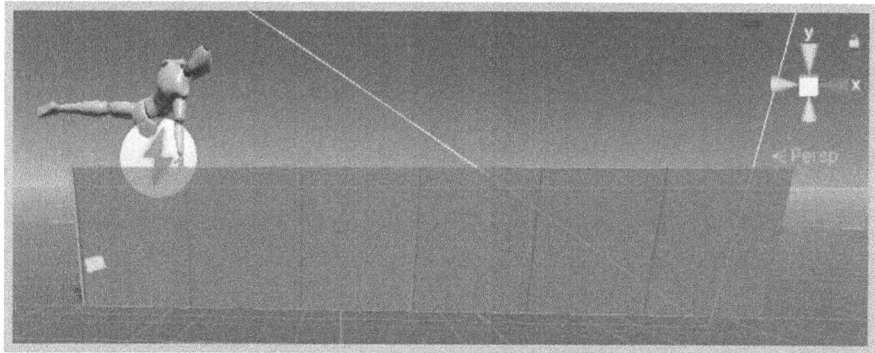

Figure 5-12. *Rear approach from the left corner – Right hand used to perform vault action*

CHAPTER 5   ARCHITECTING PLAYER PARKOUR MOVEMENT

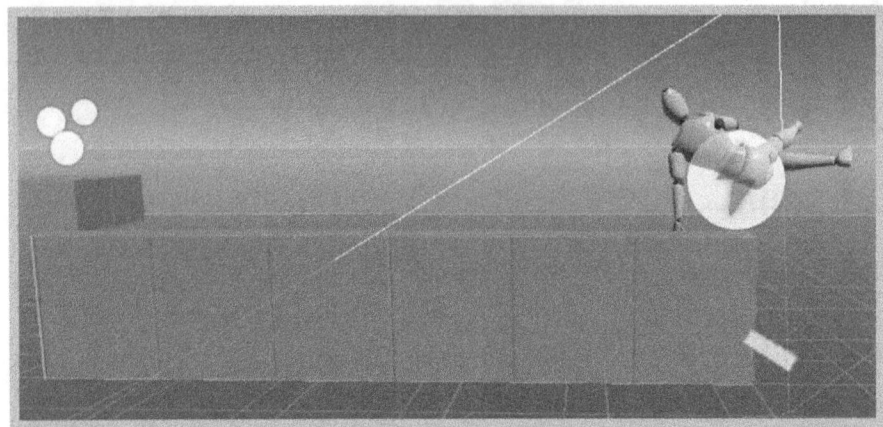

Figure 5-13. *Rear approach from the right corner – Left hand used to perform vault action*

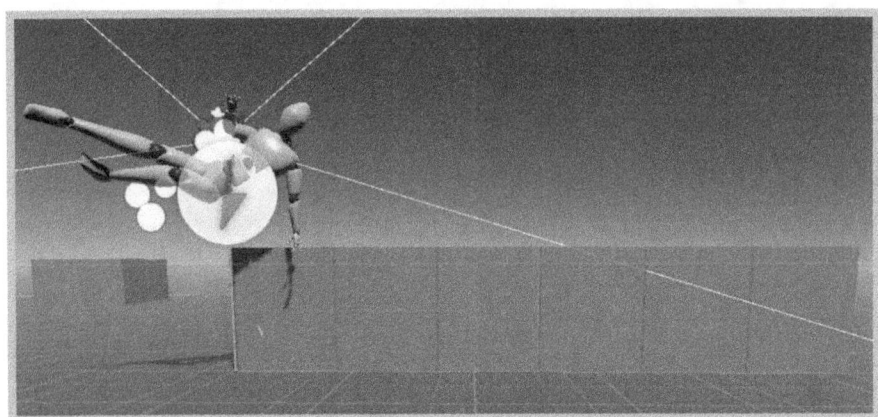

Figure 5-14. *Frontal approach from the left corner – Left hand used to perform vault action*

CHAPTER 5 ARCHITECTING PLAYER PARKOUR MOVEMENT

Figure 5-15. *Frontal approach from the right corner – Right hand used to perform vault action*

Figure 5-16. *x < 0 left of center and x > 0 right of center*

Listing 5-5. VaultBehavior script

```
using UnityEngine;

[CreateAssetMenu(fileName = "NewVaultAction", menuName =
"Parkour/ParkourVaultActionData", order = 2)]

public class VaultBehavior : ParkourBehavior
{
    public override bool ParkourActionPossible(HitInfo
```

```
    hitInfo, Transform player)
    {
        if(!base.ParkourActionPossible(hitInfo, player))
            return false;

        Vector3 hitPointLocalSpace = hitInfo.hitData.transform.
        InverseTransformPoint(hitInfo.hitData.point);

        if ((hitPointLocalSpace.z < 0 && hitPointLocalSpace.x
            < 0) || (hitPointLocalSpace.z > 0 &&
            hitPointLocalSpace.x > 0))
        {
            Mirror = true; //mirror the animation using the
                            //right hand
            avatarTargetBodyPart =AvatarTarget.RightHand;
        }
        else
        {
            Mirror = false; //Don't mirror the animation - use
                            //default left-hand set in the
                            //Vault_SO scriptable object.
            avatarTargetBodyPart = AvatarTarget.LeftHand;
        }
        return true;
    }
}
```

The VaultBehavior class extends the ParkourBehavior class and specializes it to handle vaulting actions within the parkour system. It adds additional logic to determine if a vaulting action is possible based on the position of the obstacle and whether the vaulting animation should be mirrored based on the relative position of the hit point. This design allows for flexible and reusable parkour behaviors that can be easily

CHAPTER 5   ARCHITECTING PLAYER PARKOUR MOVEMENT

managed and configured through the Unity Editor. This class overrides the ParkourActionPossible() method to include these specific checks and behaviors.

1. The VaultBehavior class inherits fields from the ParkourBehavior class and does not add new fields. The inherited fields are:

    - animationName: The name of the animation clip used for the parkour action.

    - minHeight: The minimum height of obstacles for which this parkour action is applicable.

    - maxHeight: The maximum height of obstacles for which this parkour action is applicable.

    - avatarTargetBodyPart: Specifies which body part should match the target position during the animation.

    - startTargetMatching: Defines the normalized start time for target matching within the animation.

    - endTargetMatching: Defines the normalized end time for target matching within the animation.

    - targetWeightMask: Defines the weight of the matching in each axis (x, y, z).

2. The ParkourActionPossible() method in VaultBehavior overrides the method in ParkourBehavior to include additional checks specific to vaulting actions. It declares an overridden method that returns a boolean value indicating if the vaulting action is possible based on the provided HitInfo and player's Transform.

523

- if (!base.ParkourActionPossible(hitInfo, player)) return false: Calls the base method to check if the generic parkour action is possible (based on height constraints). If the base method returns false, this method also returns false, ensuring the vaulting action only proceeds if the basic height requirements are met.

- Vector3 hitPointLocalSpace = hitInfo.hitData. transform.InverseTransformPoint(hitInfo.hitData. point): Converts the hit point from world space to the local space of the hit object, which allows for determining the position of the hit point relative to the obstacle, which is crucial for deciding whether to mirror the animation.

- if ((hitPointLocalSpace.z < 0 && hitPointLocalSpace.x < 0) || (hitPointLocalSpace.z > 0 && hitPointLocalSpace.x > 0)): Checks the position of the hit point in local space. If both z and x are either positive or negative, it indicates a certain orientation relative to the player, determining if the vaulting animation should be mirrored based on the relative position of the hit point.

- Mirror = true: Sets the Mirror property available within the parent ParkourBehavior class to true, indicating that the animation should be mirrored. This ensures the animation is mirrored correctly if the player needs to use the right hand instead of the left.

CHAPTER 5   ARCHITECTING PLAYER PARKOUR MOVEMENT

- avatarTargetBodyPart = AvatarTarget.RightHand: Sets the target body part for the animation to the right hand, ensuring the right hand is used for the vaulting action when the animation is mirrored.

- When the conditions for mirroring are not met, the else block ensures that the default behavior is followed. The Mirror property is set to false to indicate that the animation should not be mirrored, ensuring that the animation uses the default left hand when not mirrored.

- avatarTargetBodyPart = AvatarTarget.LeftHand: Sets the target body part for the animation to the left hand, ensuring the left hand is used for the vaulting action when the animation is not mirrored.

- return true: Returns true, indicating that all checks have passed and the vaulting action can be performed.

A new scriptable object can now be created using this VaultBehavior script.

This scriptable object has already been created as part of the downloadable project provided and exists in the folder, Assets/Enemy_AI/Scripts/Parkour/ScriptableObjects. It has been renamed to Vault_SO, as illustrated in Figure 5-18. It is also important to note that the hurdle obstacle in scene view has been tagged as "Hurdle" in the Inspector.

Revisiting Listing 5-4 (the ParkourBehavior script), certain lines of code have been commented with //ACC that relate to the Vaulting behavior. Let's discuss these lines of code:

1. [SerializeField] private string obstacleTag: This field allows specifying a tag that an obstacle must-have for the vault action to be considered possible. This

ensures that the vault action is only performed on obstacles that match a specific tag, adding another layer of filtering beyond just height. You will note that the scriptable object VaultBehavior, as illustrated in Figure 5-18, has this field populated with the tag "Hurdle." All other scriptable objects have this obstacleTag field left empty.

2. public bool Mirror { get; set; }: This line of code declares a public property named Mirror with both a getter and a setter. The Mirror property is used to indicate whether the animation should be mirrored. In the VaultBehavior class, this property is set to true or false based on the relative position of the obstacle, allowing the vaulting animation to adapt dynamically by using either the left or right hand. Figure 5-17 illustrates the Animator window with its mirrorVault parameter, which is a boolean value. Also within the Inspector, you will note that for this Vault animation, its Mirror property has been checked and the parameter name has been set to mirrorVault. The value of the mirrorVault parameter is set to the value of the Mirror property from within the coroutine ParkourAction() which exists in the ParkourManager script. The value of the Mirror property is set from within the VaultBehavior script.

3. if(!string.IsNullOrEmpty(obstacleTag) && !hitInfo.hitData.transform.CompareTag(obstacleTag)): This line of code checks if the obstacleTag field is not null or empty and whether the tag of the obstacle hit, matches obstacleTag. This condition ensures that the vaulting action is only considered possible if the

CHAPTER 5 ARCHITECTING PLAYER PARKOUR MOVEMENT

obstacle has the specified tag (Hurdle in this case). If the obstacle's tag does not match, the method returns false, indicating that the vault action cannot be performed on this obstacle. This adds an extra check specific to certain types of obstacles (hurdles), enhancing the versatility and specificity of the parkour system.

By including these fields and conditions, the VaultBehavior class can implement more complex and context-specific logic for determining when and how vault actions should be performed. This enhances the flexibility and realism of the parkour system in the game.

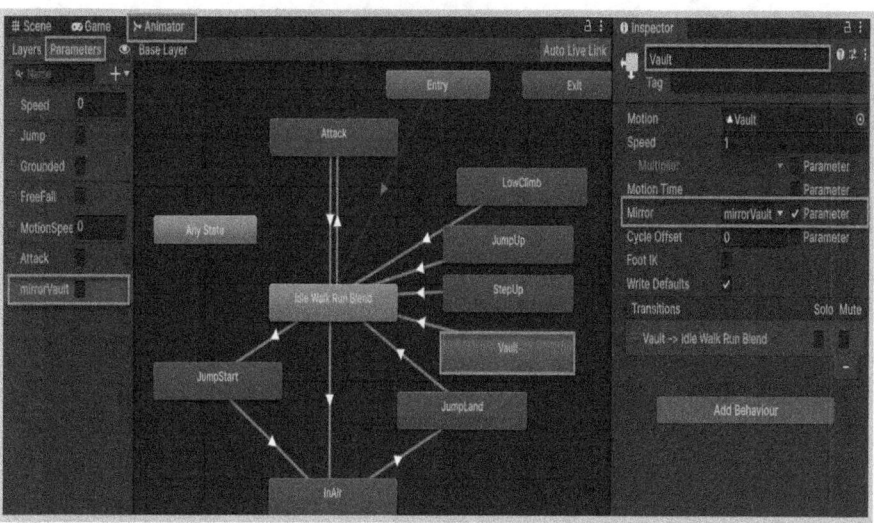

Figure 5-17. *The Vault animation, mirrorVault parameter, and Mirror setting*

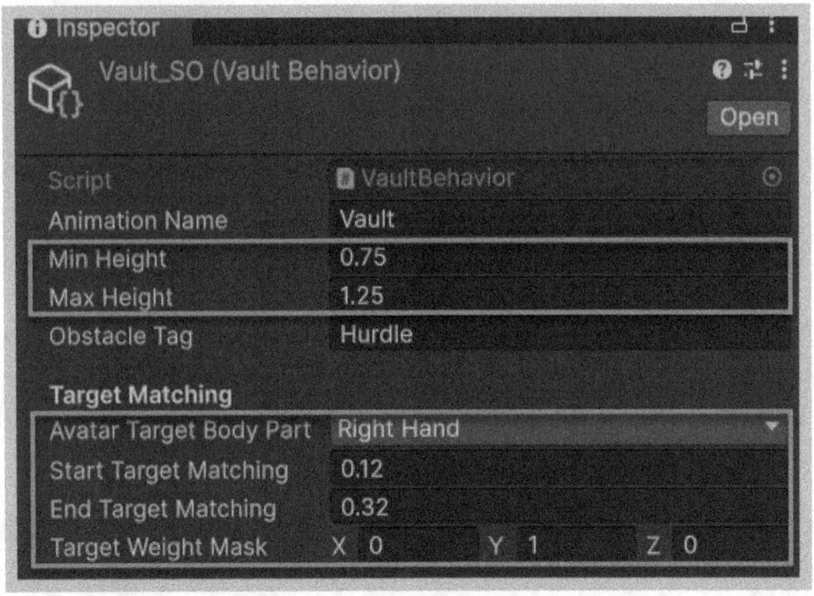

CHAPTER 5   ARCHITECTING PLAYER PARKOUR MOVEMENT

Inspector	
Vault_SO (Vault Behavior)	Open
Script	VaultBehavior
Animation Name	Vault
Min Height	0.75
Max Height	1.25
Obstacle Tag	Hurdle
Target Matching	
Avatar Target Body Part	Right Hand
Start Target Matching	0.12
End Target Matching	0.32
Target Weight Mask	X 0 Y 1 Z 0

Figure 5-18. The Vault_SO scriptable object property values

Lastly, you need to ensure that the Vault_SO scriptable object is added to the parkourBehaviors list of the ParkourManager component within the PlayerArmature game object, as illustrated in Figure 5-19. Also note that these scriptable objects have been arranged in ascending order of their minHeight field.

CHAPTER 5   ARCHITECTING PLAYER PARKOUR MOVEMENT

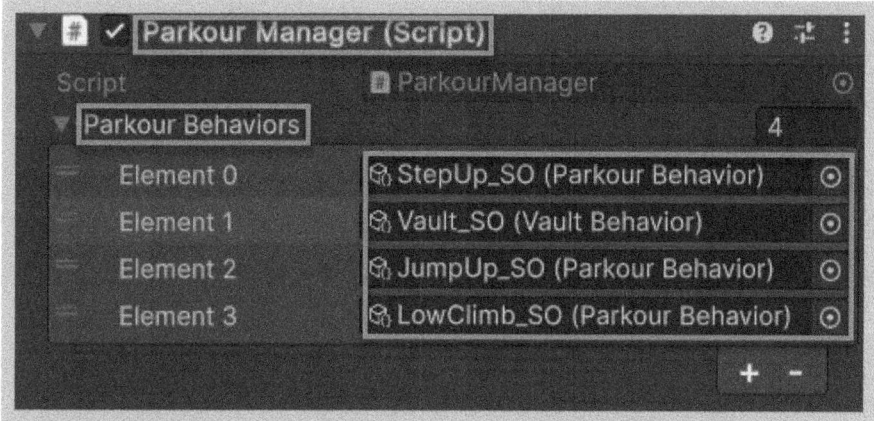

Figure 5-19. *parkourBehaviors list within the ParkourManager component*

Summary

In modern game design, dynamic and fluid player movements are essential to enhance the gaming experience, and parkour, rooted in overcoming obstacles with speed and efficiency, has become a quintessential movement mechanic. This chapter delves into the intricacies of implementing a parkour system, aiming to provide players with a seamless and responsive movement experience. Through a series of detailed recipes, this chapter covers essential topics such as environmental interaction, obstacle detection, parkour management, and the implementation of specific parkour actions using Scriptable Objects. By integrating these elements, developers can create intuitive and engaging player experiences that reward skill and creativity, transforming static game worlds into playgrounds of possibility.

Recipe 5-1: Exploring the Parkour Environment and Player Armature Game Object: This recipe addresses the challenge of creating an engaging parkour system by setting up a well-designed environment with climbable

CHAPTER 5 ARCHITECTING PLAYER PARKOUR MOVEMENT

structures and configuring the player character with the necessary components. The solution involves using a third-person controller playground scene populated with simple cube obstacles. The player character, represented by the Player Armature game object, is enhanced with three key components: the Obstacle Sensor, Parkour Manager, and Line Renderer. This setup ensures the player can fluidly interact with the environment, providing a dynamic parkour experience.

Recipe 5-2: Implementing the Obstacle Sensor: Detecting obstacles in real-time is crucial for enabling dynamic parkour movements. The ObstacleSensor class addresses this challenge by using a raycast from the player's knee height to detect obstacles in the forward direction. Upon detecting an obstacle, it gathers detailed information such as the obstacle's height and the necessary rotation for the player to face the obstacle. This data is visually represented using a LineRenderer, aiding in debugging and visualization. The collected data is then used to trigger appropriate parkour actions, ensuring fluid and realistic player movements over obstacles.

Recipe 5-3: Implementing the ParkourManager: The ParkourManager class integrates player input, obstacle detection, and animation control to enable dynamic parkour actions. It utilizes the ObstacleSensor component to detect obstacles and determine the appropriate parkour actions from a list of ParkourBehavior scriptable objects. Upon detecting an obstacle, the class triggers relevant animations, ensures proper player rotation, and handles events to notify other scripts when entering and exiting parkour mode. This setup creates a seamless and immersive parkour experience, enhancing player interaction with the game environment.

Recipe 5-4: Implementing Scriptable Objects for Parkour Actions: Using Scriptable Objects to represent different parkour actions provides a flexible and modular approach to implementing parkour behaviors. Each action can be defined as a separate Scriptable Object, encapsulating its unique properties and logic. This allows for easy customization and

CHAPTER 5   ARCHITECTING PLAYER PARKOUR MOVEMENT

extension of parkour behaviors without modifying the core gameplay code, ensuring a scalable and maintainable system that can be readily adapted to new parkour requirements.

Recipe 5-5: Implementing a Vaulting Parkour Action: The need for a vaulting parkour action arises from the necessity to traverse mid-height obstacles efficiently. Implementing a custom vaulting behavior ensures smooth and dynamic navigation over barriers that are too high to step over and too low to climb. The VaultBehavior class extends the ParkourBehavior class, adding additional logic to determine if a vaulting action is possible based on the position of the obstacle and whether the vaulting animation should be mirrored. This design allows for flexible and reusable parkour behaviors that can be easily managed and configured through the Unity Editor.

CHAPTER 6

Implementing Shooter Weapon Mechanics

In a shooting game, the weapon is a central component that needs to function seamlessly to ensure an immersive player experience. At first glance, a weapon may appear simple – point, click, shoot. However, a closer examination reveals a complex system with multiple responsibilities. In this chapter, you will meticulously outline and implement the essential mechanics required for a basic yet functional weapon, focusing on handguns such as pistols and revolvers. The functionality includes responding to trigger pulls, managing ammo, playing sound effects, and animating various actions, among others.

To achieve a polished result, the weapon must handle numerous tasks: reacting to trigger pulls, holding and using ammo, playing sound effects and muzzle flashes, animating trigger pulls and shots, reloading, checking for successful hits, and tracking remaining ammo. This intricate functionality necessitates well-organized code, distributed across several scripts that will be attached to the weapon. While the task may seem daunting, having a structured approach ensures that each aspect of the weapon mechanics is addressed efficiently.

As you delve into the development process, you will cover key areas such as animations, sound effects, ammo management, and reloading. Each responsibility, from firing and dealing with damage to providing feedback, will be explored in detail. By the end of this chapter, you will have a comprehensive understanding of how to implement robust shooter weapon mechanics in Unity, setting a solid foundation for more advanced weapon systems in your games.

Note For this chapter, a pre-included weapon model will be used to streamline the process, enabling you to focus on the coding aspects.

To fully engage with the recipes in Chapter 6, please ensure you download the completed Unity project available for this chapter. This will enable you to directly apply the concepts discussed and effectively explore the intricacies of weapon mechanics within a functioning Unity environment.

Recipe 6-1: Exploring the Player Weapon Setup

Problem

The implementation of shooter weapon mechanics is essential for creating an engaging and realistic player experience in a shooter game. This involves setting up the NPC and player's weapons, including aspects like firing rates, ammunition handling, and aiming systems. A well-defined weapon setup not only enhances gameplay but also ensures that weapons behave consistently and interact with other game elements, such as enemies, players, and the environment, believably. The challenge lies in integrating these mechanics seamlessly, balancing weapon attributes, and providing intuitive controls to enhance player immersion and satisfaction.

CHAPTER 6 IMPLEMENTING SHOOTER WEAPON MECHANICS

Solution

To address this challenge, you will set up a new handgun weapon equipped with various components essential for both player and NPC use. This recipe will guide you through the process of configuring this shootable weapon for your soldier NPC, covering aspects such as firing mechanics, raycasting, ammunition management, and sound effects. You can then adapt the same handgun weapon prefab for the player, with minor tweaks to ensure consistency in the gameplay experience. This approach not only streamlines weapon setup across different game characters but also enhances the overall game design by providing a cohesive and balanced weapon system.

How It Works

To get started, download the resource provided in Chapter 6. Open the Playground scene from Assets/StarterAssets/ThirdPersonController/Scenes. In the hierarchy, select the PlayerArmature game object. In the Inspector, scroll to the Health component. Note that the Current Health variable is public for testing purposes. After testing the NPC's weapon, set this variable to private in the Health script. This will allow you to observe how the player's health depletes when shot by the NPC within shooting range.

Expand the NPC game object in the hierarchy and select the Soldier_0 child object. In the Inspector, find the NPC Controller component. The arsenal array now includes two elements, with a new handgun weapon available for the NPC, showcasing shooter mechanics applicable to any weapon for both NPCs and players. The NPC currently uses the Sniper Rifle Controller, which can be replaced with a controller specifically designed for the handgun. The Right Gun property is set, ensuring the NPC holds the handgun in its right hand.

535

CHAPTER 6   IMPLEMENTING SHOOTER WEAPON MECHANICS

From within the Project pane, navigate to the Assets/Weapon folder, where you will find the handgun prefab that has already been set up with all required weapon components. The Scripts folder (Figure 6-1) you see here comprises all weapon-related scripts that have been attached to the handgun.

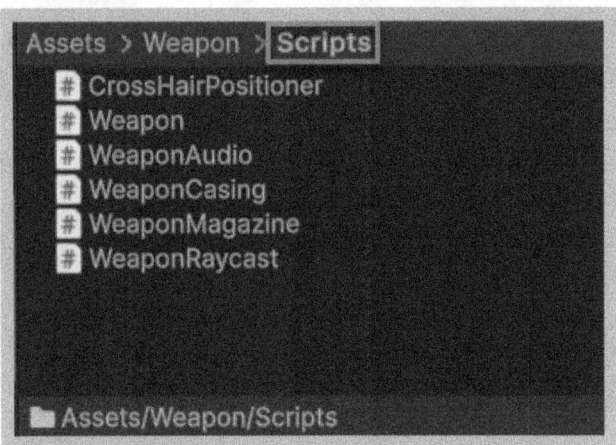

Figure 6-1.   Weapon-related scripts

Figure 6-2.   HandGun weapon with its related components

CHAPTER 6 IMPLEMENTING SHOOTER WEAPON MECHANICS

Open the handgun prefab and let's explore the various components that make up the handgun weapon. In the hierarchy select the root HandGun game object. Within the Inspector you will note that it comprises several components as illustrated in Figure 6-2.

The WeaponAudio class is a Unity component designed to handle and play various audio cues associated with a weapon in-game, enhancing the player's auditory experience. It requires an AudioSource component and is linked to a Weapon component, which it uses to trigger specific sounds. The class manages three primary audio clips: one for firing the weapon, one for dry firing (when the magazine is empty or absent), and one for loading or unloading a magazine. It subscribes to corresponding events from the Weapon component, such as OnWeaponFired, OnWeaponDryFired, OnMagazineAttached, and OnMagazineDetatched, to play the appropriate sound effects using the cached AudioSource. This setup provides a cohesive and immersive sound design, reflecting the weapon's state and actions during gameplay.

The Weapon class Unity component is designed to simulate a weapon's core functionality within a game, including firing, dry firing, and managing magazine attachments and detachments. It supports both NPC and player weapons, with conditional behaviors such as automatic reloading for NPC weapons and manual reloading for player-controlled weapons. The class utilizes events like OnWeaponFired, OnWeaponDryFired, OnMagazineAttached, and OnMagazineDetatched to communicate actions to other components, such as the WeaponAudio class, ensuring synchronized audio and visual feedback. The Weapon class also manages the weapon's firing rate through a configurable shootInterval, checks for available ammunition via a WeaponMagazine component, and handles the lifecycle of these actions by appropriately registering and deregistering event handlers. This implementation facilitates realistic weapon behavior and interaction within the game environment, enhancing the overall player experience.

CHAPTER 6   IMPLEMENTING SHOOTER WEAPON MECHANICS

The WeaponRaycast class is a Unity component responsible for simulating the trajectory and impact of a fired weapon by casting a ray from the muzzle point in the direction the weapon is aimed. It detects hits on objects within a specified distance (fireDist) and applies damage based on the target's layer, differentiating between headshots and body shots with configurable damage values. The class leverages the Unity Physics.Raycast() method to determine if the ray intersects with objects on defined shootableLayer layers, ensuring that only relevant targets are affected. It subscribes to the OnWeaponFired event from the Weapon class, triggering the CastRay() method whenever the weapon fires, and utilizes debug visualizations in the Unity Editor to assist with development and testing. This class enhances the realism and precision of shooting mechanics in the game, providing immediate and accurate feedback when a shot is fired.

The WeaponCasing class handles the visual and physical simulation of shell casings being ejected from a player's weapon when it is fired. This class can leverage object pooling through the ObjectPool<GameObject> to efficiently manage shell casing instances, optimizing performance by reusing objects rather than repeatedly creating and destroying them. It specifies the shell casing prefab, the ejection point, the ejection direction, the force, and the duration the casing remains in the world. When the weapon fires, the class activates a shell casing from the pool, positions it at the ejection point, applies a specified force in a defined direction using the Rigidbody component, and can then deactivate and return the casing to the pool after a set duration (as will be demonstrated in Chapter 7). This setup ensures a realistic and performant visual effect of shell casing ejection, enhancing the immersive experience in gameplay.

The WeaponMagazine class manages the ammunition and reloading mechanics for a weapon, simulating the behavior of a magazine in a firearm. It controls the maximum ammunition capacity (maxAmmoInMag), tracks the current ammo count, and handles the reloading process with a specified reloadTime. The class provides methods to check if ammo is available (HasAmmoInMag), use ammo (UseAmmo),

CHAPTER 6　IMPLEMENTING SHOOTER WEAPON MECHANICS

initiate reloading (Reload), and unload the magazine (Unload). It also includes a flag, IsReloading, to prevent the weapon from firing during the reloading process. By implementing an asynchronous coroutine for reloading (ReloadAsync), the class ensures that reloading matches the time required for corresponding animations, providing a realistic and immersive experience. Additionally, it tracks if a magazine has been used (isMagUsed) to prevent reloading once the magazine is unloaded. This class is essential for simulating realistic weapon functionality and managing ammunition in gameplay.

The upcoming recipes will explore each of these classes in detail.

Recipe 6-2: The Weapon Component

Problem

A Weapon needs to accurately simulate the behavior and mechanics of firearms within a game environment, including firing, reloading, and managing ammunition. This involves creating distinct functionalities for both NPC and player weapons, such as automatic reloading for NPCs and manual reloading for players. The system must handle various states and actions of a weapon, including firing, running out of ammo, and attaching or detaching magazines while ensuring these actions are communicated effectively across different game components.

Solution

The Weapon class provides a comprehensive solution for managing firearm mechanics in Unity. It incorporates a range of functionalities including firing, dry firing, and managing magazine attachments and detachment. By using events like OnWeaponFired, OnWeaponDryFired, OnMagazineAttached, and OnMagazineDetatched, the class communicates these actions to other components, such as WeaponAudio, to synchronize sound and visual effects. The class differentiates between NPC and player weapons, implementing automatic reloading for NPCs and manual reloading for players. Additionally, it controls the firing rate through the shootInterval parameter and integrates with the WeaponMagazine component to manage ammo levels, ensuring realistic weapon interactions and enhancing the overall gameplay experience.

How It Works

The Weapon class in Unity manages the core functionality of firearms, handling firing mechanics, ammo management, and interactions with other components. The class is designed to work with both NPC and player weapons, differentiating behaviors such as automatic reloading for NPCs and manual reloading for players. When a weapon is fired, the class reduces the ammo count using the WeaponMagazine component and triggers the OnWeaponFired event, which can be used by other components like WeaponAudio to play sound effects. If the magazine is empty and the weapon is an NPC weapon, the autoReload feature triggers a reload; otherwise, the OnWeaponDryFired event signals that the magazine is empty and needs manual reloading. The class also handles the attachment and detachment of magazines with events like OnMagazineAttached and OnMagazineDetatched, which facilitate the synchronization of audio and visual cues for these actions. The shootInterval parameter controls the firing rate, preventing rapid firing unless explicitly allowed. This setup ensures that all aspects of weapon functionality are integrated and communicated effectively across the game, providing a realistic and immersive experience. Figure 6-3 illustrates the expanded Weapon class within the Inspector.

CHAPTER 6 IMPLEMENTING SHOOTER WEAPON MECHANICS

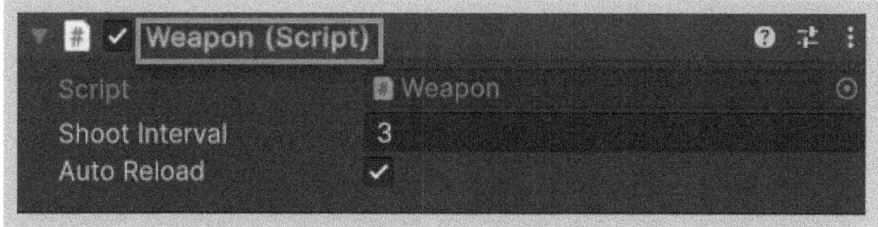

Figure 6-3. *The Weapon Component within the Inspector*

Listing 6-1. Weapon script

```
using System;
using UnityEngine;

[RequireComponent(typeof(WeaponAudio))]
public class Weapon : MonoBehaviour
{
    public event Action OnWeaponFired, OnWeaponDryFired,
    OnMagazineAttached, OnMagazineDetatched;

    [SerializeField] private float shootInterval = 2.0f;
    //Time between shots. If set to Zero weapons can rapid fire.

//Magazine will be auto-reloaded if it is an NPC weapon, the
//moment its ammo is over.
//For an NPC weapon set autoReload to true.
//For Player weapons autoReload should be false as the player
//needs to perform a reload action to load a magazine into the
//weapon.
    [SerializeField] private bool autoReload;

    private WeaponMagazine magAmmo;
    private float lastShotTime;
```

CHAPTER 6 IMPLEMENTING SHOOTER WEAPON MECHANICS

```csharp
    private void Start()
    {
    //Registering for the OnNpcAttack event needs  to be
    //done in the Start() method here as the NPC Weapon is
    //not preassigned to the NPC but is assigned to an NPC at
    //run time, so this event registration cannot be done
    //within OnEnable().
    //Ensure  that the weapon is an NPC's weapon tagged as
    //'NPC_Weapon'
        if (gameObject.CompareTag("NPC_Weapon"))
        {
            GetComponentInParent<AttackState>().OnNpcAttack +=
            TryFireWeapon;
            magAmmo = GetComponent<WeaponMagazine>();//For all
            //Weapons the Magazine script is a component of the
            //Weapon object.
        }
    }
    private void OnDestroy()
    {
        AttackState attackState =
        GetComponentInParent<AttackState>();
        if (attackState != null)
            attackState.OnNpcAttack -= TryFireWeapon;
    }
    private void FireWeapon()
    {
        magAmmo.UseAmmo(); //Reduce the ammo in the Magazine.
        lastShotTime = Time.time;
```

```csharp
      //Notify subscribers WeaponRaycast,WeaponAudio,
      //WeaponCasing, etc that weapon was fired.
      OnWeaponFired?.Invoke();
      Debug.Log("NPC Weapon Fired at Player");
 }
private void TryFireWeapon()
{
   if (magAmmo == null || magAmmo.IsReloading)
      return;

   if (magAmmo.HasAmmoInMag())
   {
      if (Time.time - lastShotTime >= shootInterval)
         FireWeapon();
   }
   else if (autoReload)
   {
      MagazineAttached();
   }
   else
   {
      OnWeaponDryFired?.Invoke();
      Debug.Log("NPC / Player Weapon Magazine is Empty - 
               Need to reload Mag");
   }
}

//Used with the Player's weapons only as the Players
//weapon magazines can be physically attached
public void MagazineAttached()
{
   if (magAmmo == null)
```

```csharp
    {
        Debug.LogError("magAmmo was Null");
        return;
    }
    OnMagazineAttached?.Invoke(); //Notify subscribers
//'WeaponAudio', script that mag was attached to a weapon
    magAmmo.Reload();
    Debug.Log("Weapon is Reloading");
}
//Used with Players weapons only, as only the Players
//weapon magazines can be physically detached.
public void MagazineDetatched()
{
    OnMagazineDetatched?.Invoke(); //Notify subscribers
    //'WeaponAudio', script that a mag was detached from
    //weapon
    magAmmo.Unload(); //Ensures the Magazine cannot be
                     //reused.
    magAmmo = null;
}
}
```

The Weapon class serves as a core component for simulating weapon behavior in-game, specifically focusing on firing mechanics, managing ammunition, and handling magazine-related actions. This class interacts closely with other components, such as WeaponAudio, WeaponRaycast, and WeaponCasing, to provide a comprehensive weapon system. It also differentiates behavior between NPC and player-controlled weapons, particularly regarding automatic reloading.

CHAPTER 6   IMPLEMENTING SHOOTER WEAPON MECHANICS

1. The [RequireComponent(typeof(WeaponAudio))] attribute is used to ensure that the WeaponAudio component is always present on the same GameObject to which the script (in this case, Weapon) is attached to. This attribute automatically adds the WeaponAudio component to the GameObject if it is not already present, or it will display an error if it cannot add the component for some reason. This guarantees that the required component is available for use, helping to avoid runtime errors and ensuring that the Weapon class can safely interact with the WeaponAudio component. This is particularly useful for maintaining dependencies and promoting better organization and error checking.

2. OnWeaponFired, OnWeaponDryFired, OnMagazineAttached, OnMagazineDetatched (Events): These events notify other components when specific actions occur, such as firing the weapon, attempting to fire with an empty magazine, attaching a magazine, and detaching a magazine. These are critical for synchronizing audio, visual effects, and other gameplay mechanics.

3. private float shootInterval: Defines the minimum time between consecutive shots. This prevents rapid firing unless explicitly allowed (e.g., setting to zero for rapid fire capability).

4. private bool autoReload: Determines whether the weapon automatically reloads when the ammunition is depleted. This is typically enabled for NPC weapons to streamline their behavior, while player weapons usually require manual reloading.

CHAPTER 6   IMPLEMENTING SHOOTER WEAPON MECHANICS

5. private WeaponMagazine magAmmo: Holds a reference to the WeaponMagazine component, available on this same game object, which manages the ammunition count and reloading mechanics.

6. private float lastShotTime: Stores the time when the weapon last fired. This is used in conjunction with shootInterval to control the rate of fire.

7. Start(): The Start() method initializes the weapon setup, particularly registering the TryFireWeapon() method to the OnNpcAttack event if the weapon is tagged as an NPC weapon. The statement if (gameObject.CompareTag("NPC_Weapon")) checks if the weapon is designated as an NPC weapon. If so the statement GetComponentInParent<AttackStat e>().OnNpcAttack += TryFireWeapon; registers the TryFireWeapon() method to the OnNpcAttack event, so the weapon fires when the NPC attacks. The OnNpcAttack event is invoked from the Attack state and listened for within this Weapon class as well as the Actions class. Lastly the statement magAmmo = GetComponent<WeaponMagazine>(); caches the WeaponMagazine component for managing ammunition.

8. OnDestroy(): This method unregisters the TryFireWeapon() method from the OnNpcAttack event when the weapon is destroyed, preventing potential memory leaks or null reference errors. The statement AttackState attackState = GetComponen tInParent<AttackState>(); retrieves the AttackState component from the parent object. It then checks

CHAPTER 6   IMPLEMENTING SHOOTER WEAPON MECHANICS

if the AttackState component exists using the statement if (attackState != null). If attackState is not null, it unregisters the TryFireWeapon() method from the OnNpcAttack event using the statement attackState.OnNpcAttack -= TryFireWeapon.

9. FireWeapon(): This method handles the actual firing logic, such as reducing the ammunition count and invoking relevant events. You begin by decreasing the ammunition count in the weapon's magazine, via the statement magAmmo.UseAmmo(). You then record the current time to manage the firing rate using the statement lastShotTime = Time.time. Finally, you invoke the OnWeaponFired event, notifying other components such as WeaponAudio and WeaponRaycast that the weapon has been fired, using the statement OnWeaponFired?.Invoke().

10. TryFireWeapon(): This method is responsible for determining whether the weapon can fire, needs to reload, or if it is out of ammunition and cannot fire. Here's a line-by-line breakdown of the code:

    - if (magAmmo == null || magAmmo.IsReloading): This checks if the magAmmo (a reference to the WeaponMagazine component) is null. If it is, it means the weapon does not have a magazine component attached or referenced, and the method should exit early. It also checks if the magazine is currently reloading. If true, the weapon should not attempt to fire. The method exits early if either condition is true, preventing further actions.

- if (magAmmo.HasAmmoInMag()): Here you check to see if the magazine has ammunition. If it returns true, there are bullets available to fire, in which case you check to see if the required time interval between shots (shootInterval) has elapsed since the last shot (lastShotTime). Time.time gives the current game time in seconds. If there is ammo and the required time interval has elapsed, the FireWeapon() method is called to fire the weapon, reducing the ammo count and triggering associated events like OnWeaponFired.

- else if (autoReload): This boolean field determines if the weapon should automatically reload when out of ammo. This is usually set for NPC weapons. If this statement evaluates to true, the MagazineAttached() method is called to reload the weapon. It typically involves playing reload animations and resetting the ammo count in the magazine. It also triggers the OnMagazineAttached event, which is used by the WeaponAudio component to play a sound.

- else: The final else block is executed if the magazine is out of ammo and the weapon is not set to auto-reload. The OnWeaponDryFired event is triggered to notify other components that the weapon tried to fire but was out of ammunition.

11. MagazineAttached(): This method handles the logic for when a magazine is attached to a weapon. It first checks if the magAmmo (a reference to the WeaponMagazine component)

CHAPTER 6   IMPLEMENTING SHOOTER WEAPON MECHANICS

is null. If it is, it means the weapon does not have a magazine component attached or referenced, and the method should exit early. It then invokes the OnMagazineAttached event, signaling other components like WeaponAudio that a magazine has been attached. It finally uses the magAmmo. Reload() statement to start the reloading process.

12. MagazineDetatched(): This method handles the logic for when a magazine is detached from a weapon. It invokes the OnMagazineDetatched event, notifying components like WeaponAudio. It then unloads the magazine which resets the ammo count. Lastly, it clears the reference to the WeaponMagazine.

The Weapon class serves as a central hub for weapon-related actions, coordinating with various other components to deliver a cohesive and immersive weapon system in the game. It ensures that all aspects of weapon functionality, from firing to sound and visual effects, are synchronized and managed efficiently.

Recipe 6-3: The Weapon Audio Component

Problem

The Weapon system requires a WeaponAudio class that addresses the challenge of providing immersive and context-sensitive audio feedback for weapon actions within a game. This includes playing sounds for firing, dry firing, and loading or unloading magazines. Ensuring that the appropriate audio cues are triggered accurately based on the weapon's state enhances the overall player experience and realism in gameplay.

Solution

To solve this problem, the WeaponAudio class integrates with Unity's AudioSource and the Weapon component to manage and play specific audio clips for various weapon actions. By subscribing to events like OnWeaponFired, OnWeaponDryFired, OnMagazineAttached, and OnMagazineDetatched from the Weapon component, the class can trigger corresponding sounds in real time. This setup uses serialized fields to assign audio clips and ensures that each action, such as firing a shot, dry firing, or loading a magazine, is accompanied by the appropriate sound effect. The approach enhances the auditory feedback in the game, providing a more engaging and realistic experience for players.

How It Works

The WeaponAudio class integrates with the Weapon component to provide specific audio feedback for various weapon actions, enhancing the player's auditory experience. Upon initialization, the class caches references to the Weapon and AudioSource components attached to the same GameObject. In the OnEnable method, the class subscribes to events from the Weapon component: OnWeaponFired, OnWeaponDryFired, OnMagazineAttached, and OnMagazineDetatched. These subscriptions are removed in the OnDisable method to prevent memory leaks. When the subscribed events are triggered, the class plays the corresponding audio clips using the cached AudioSource. For instance, it plays the firing sound when the weapon fires, the dry fire sound when the weapon attempts to fire without ammunition, and the magazine loading or unloading sounds when a magazine is attached or detached. The audio clips are assigned via serialized fields in the Unity Inspector, allowing for easy customization of the sound effects. This design ensures that each weapon action is accompanied by the correct audio feedback, enhancing the realism and immersion of the game. Figure 6-4 illustrates the expanded WeaponAudio class within the Inspector.

CHAPTER 6   IMPLEMENTING SHOOTER WEAPON MECHANICS

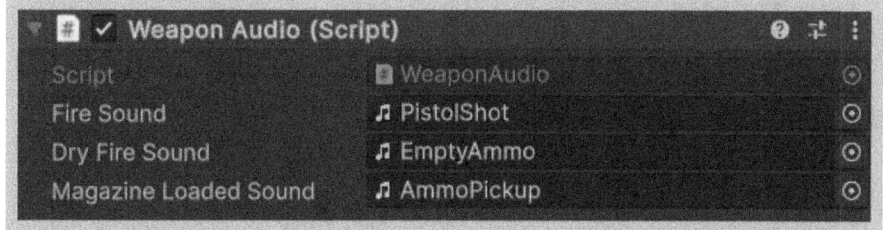

Figure 6-4. *The WeaponAudio Component within the Inspector*

Listing 6-2. WeaponAudio script

```
using UnityEngine;

[RequireComponent(typeof(AudioSource))]
public class WeaponAudio : MonoBehaviour
{
    //Different Audio sounds
    [SerializeField][Tooltip("Sound played when Weapon
     fires")]
     private AudioClip fireSound;
    [SerializeField][Tooltip("Dry Fire Sound played when
     Magazine empty or No Magazine in weapon")]
     private AudioClip dryFireSound;
    [SerializeField][Tooltip("Sound played when Magazine
     loads/Unloads within Weapon")]
     private AudioClip magazineLoadedSound;

     private Weapon weapon; //A reference to the Weapon
     //component on this game object that will be using this
     //script.
     private AudioSource audioSource;
```

CHAPTER 6   IMPLEMENTING SHOOTER WEAPON MECHANICS

```csharp
    private void Awake()
    {
        weapon = GetComponent<Weapon>(); //cache a reference
                                //to the weapon component.
    }
    private void OnEnable()
    {
        weapon.OnWeaponFired += WeaponFired; //this gets
                        //invoked when a bullet is fired.
        weapon.OnWeaponDryFired += DryFire;//Gets invoked when
                        //weapon has either no magazine or
                        //magazine has no bullets
        weapon.OnMagazineAttached += MagazineLoad; //this will
                    //be invoked when a magazine is loaded
        weapon.OnMagazineDetatched += MagazineUnLoad; //this
                //will be invoked when a magazine is unloaded
    }
    private void OnDisable()
    {
        weapon.OnWeaponFired -= WeaponFired; //this gets
                        //invoked when a bullet is fired.
        weapon.OnWeaponDryFired -= DryFire;//Gets invoked when
//weapon has either no magazine or magazine has no bullets
        weapon.OnMagazineAttached -= MagazineLoad;
        weapon.OnMagazineDetatched -= MagazineUnLoad;
    }

    void Start()
    {
        audioSource = GetComponent<AudioSource>(); //cache the
            //audio source as you will use it in various methods
    }
```

```
    void DryFire()//When the weapon tries to fire without ammo
    {
        //Debug.Log("Playing Dry Fire - No Magazine/Ammo
                    Sound");
        audioSource.PlayOneShot(dryFireSound);
    }

    void MagazineLoad() //When magazine is loaded into  weapon
    {
        audioSource.PlayOneShot(magazineLoadedSound);
    }

    void MagazineUnLoad() //When magazine is unloaded from
                        //weapon
    {
        audioSource.PlayOneShot(magazineLoadedSound);
    }

    void WeaponFired()
    {
        //Debug.Log("Sound of Weapon Fired");
        audioSource.PlayOneShot(fireSound);
    }
}
```

The WeaponAudio class is designed to manage and play audio effects for various weapon-related actions, such as firing, dry firing (when out of ammo), and magazine loading/unloading. It ensures that appropriate sounds are played in sync with the weapon's actions, enhancing the player's auditory experience and providing feedback during gameplay.

CHAPTER 6   IMPLEMENTING SHOOTER WEAPON MECHANICS

1. The [RequireComponent(typeof(AudioSource))] attribute is used to ensure that the AudioSource component is always present on the same GameObject to which the script (in this case, WeaponAudio) is attached.

2. private AudioClip fireSound: Stores the audio clip that plays when the weapon fires. Enhances realism and provides immediate feedback when the player or NPC fires the weapon.

3. private AudioClip dryFireSound: Stores the audio clip that plays when the weapon tries to fire without ammo. Alerts the player/NPC that the weapon is out of ammunition, prompting a reload.

4. private AudioClip magazineLoadedSound: Stores the audio clip that plays when a magazine is loaded or unloaded. Provides feedback during the reloading process, making it clear that the action has been completed.

5. private Weapon weapon: References the Weapon component on the same game object. Allows the WeaponAudio class to subscribe to weapon-related events and trigger corresponding audio effects.

6. private AudioSource audioSource: The AudioSource component that plays the audio clips. Handles the actual playback of audio clips, enabling the weapon to produce sounds.

7. Awake(): This method initializes the Weapon component reference. It retrieves the Weapon component attached to the same game object and

CHAPTER 6 IMPLEMENTING SHOOTER WEAPON MECHANICS

assigns it to the weapon field. This ensures that the WeaponAudio class can interact with the Weapon component.

8. OnEnable(): This method subscribes to weapon events when the script is enabled:

    - weapon.OnWeaponFired += WeaponFired: Subscribes the WeaponFired() method to the OnWeaponFired event. This ensures that the firing sound is played when the weapon is fired.

    - weapon.OnWeaponDryFired += DryFire: Subscribes the DryFire() method to the OnWeaponDryFired event. This ensures that the dry fire sound is played when the weapon is out of ammo.

    - weapon.OnMagazineAttached += MagazineLoad: Subscribes the MagazineLoad() method to the OnMagazineAttached event. This ensures that the magazine load sound is played when a magazine is attached.

    - weapon.OnMagazineDetatched += MagazineUnLoad: Subscribes the MagazineUnLoad() method to the OnMagazineDetatched event. This ensures that the magazine unload sound is played when a magazine is detached.

9. OnDisable(): Here you ensure that when the script is disabled you unsubscribe from the above-subscribed weapon events.

10. Start(): Here you cache the AudioSource component reference. You retrieve the AudioSource component attached to the same game object and assign it to the audioSource field. This ensures that the WeaponAudio class can play audio clips.

11. DryFire(): Plays the dry fire sound when the weapon tries to fire without ammo. It plays the dryFireSound audio clip using the AudioSource component. This provides feedback when the weapon is out of ammo.

12. MagazineLoad(): Plays the magazine load sound when a magazine is attached. Using the AudioSource component, the magazineLoadedSound audio clip is played, providing feedback that a magazine has been loaded.

13. MagazineUnLoad(): Plays a magazine unload sound when a magazine is detached. However, here you are using the same magazineLoadedSound audio clip using the AudioSource component. This ideally provides feedback when a magazine is unloaded.

14. WeaponFired(): Plays the weapon firing sound when the weapon is fired. Plays the fireSound audio clip using the AudioSource component. This provides feedback when the weapon is fired.

15. The WeaponAudio class directly interacts with the Weapon class by subscribing to its events (OnWeaponFired, OnWeaponDryFired, OnMagazineAttached, and OnMagazineDetatched). These events trigger the corresponding audio methods to play appropriate sounds.

CHAPTER 6　IMPLEMENTING SHOOTER WEAPON MECHANICS

By managing and synchronizing audio effects with weapon actions, the WeaponAudio class significantly enhances the player's experience by providing immediate and appropriate auditory feedback.

Recipe 6-4: The Weapon Raycast Component

Problem

In a game environment, accurately simulating the trajectory and impact of a fired weapon is essential for realism and player immersion. The challenge lies in determining if a shot hits a target, applying appropriate damage based on the hit location, and ensuring only relevant objects are affected. This requires a mechanism to detect hits and differentiate between various target areas, such as the head or body, each with distinct damage values.

Solution

The WeaponRaycast class addresses this challenge by casting a ray from the weapon's muzzle point in the aimed direction whenever the weapon fires. By using Unity's Physics.Raycast() method, the class detects hits on objects within a specified range and applies damage based on the object's layer, differentiating between headshots and body shots. The class integrates with the Weapon component, subscribing to the OnWeaponFired event to trigger the CastRay() method. It also includes debug visualizations to assist with development and testing, ensuring precise and accurate shooting mechanics.

CHAPTER 6   IMPLEMENTING SHOOTER WEAPON MECHANICS

How It Works

The WeaponRaycast class enhances shooting mechanics by casting a ray from the weapon's muzzle point whenever the weapon fires, detecting hits on objects within the specified fireDist. It uses the Physics. Raycast() method to determine if the ray intersects with objects on defined shootableLayer layers. If a hit is detected, the class searches for a Health component in the hit object or within its parent hierarchy. It then applies damage based on the target's layer, with higher damage for headshots and a lower damage value for body shots. The class subscribes to the OnWeaponFired event from the Weapon component to trigger the CastRay() method, ensuring accurate and immediate feedback when a shot is fired. Debug visualizations in the Unity Editor help with development and testing, making it easier to fine-tune shooting mechanics.

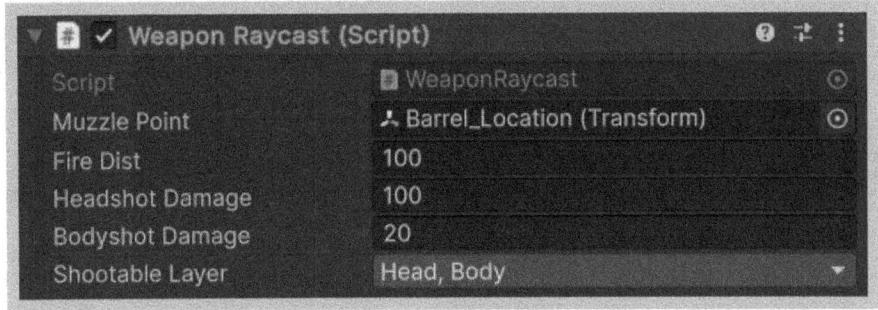

Figure 6-5. *The WeaponRaycast Component within the Inspector*

Listing 6-3. WeaponRaycast script

```
using UnityEngine;

[RequireComponent(typeof(Weapon))]
public class WeaponRaycast : MonoBehaviour
{
    [SerializeField]
```

```csharp
[Tooltip("A transform that determines where the raycast
 starts")]
private Transform muzzlePoint;

[SerializeField]
[Tooltip("Max distance the shot can hit a Target")]
private float fireDist = 100f;

[SerializeField]
[Tooltip("The amount of damage caused by a Head Shot")]
private int headshotDamage = 100;

[SerializeField]
[Tooltip("The amount of damage caused by a Body Shot")]
private int bodyshotDamage = 20;

//Ensure you assign shootableLayer in the Unity editor to
//match the layers of your shootable objects.
//This code assumes that all shootable objects are
//assigned specific shootable layers you define.
//Examples of your shootableLayer could be 'Head', 'Body',
//'Wall', 'Floor', 'Crate', 'Container', 'Door' etc

[SerializeField]
[Tooltip("Layer mask to specify which layers the raycast
 should hit")]
private LayerMask shootableLayer;

private void OnValidate()
{
    if (muzzlePoint == null)
        Debug.LogWarning($"muzzlePoint : {gameObject.name}
        : You have not setup its value in the Inspector");
}
```

CHAPTER 6 IMPLEMENTING SHOOTER WEAPON MECHANICS

```csharp
    private void OnEnable()
    {
        GetComponent<Weapon>().OnWeaponFired += CastRay;
    }
    private void OnDisable()
    {
        GetComponent<Weapon>().OnWeaponFired -= CastRay;
    }
    private void CastRay() //Method is called only when Weapon
                          //is fired.
    {
        Ray ray = new Ray(muzzlePoint.position,
                        muzzlePoint.forward);

        #if UNITY_EDITOR
            Debug.DrawRay(muzzlePoint.position,
            muzzlePoint.forward * fireDist, Color.red, 2f);
        #endif

        if (Physics.Raycast(ray, out RaycastHit hit, fireDist,
            shootableLayer))
        {
            //Start searching for the Health component within
            //the game object that the collider is attached to
            //and continue searching upwards through its parent,
            //grandparent, and so on, until it either finds a
            //Health component or reaches the root of the
            //hierarchy. If a Health component is found at any level
            //in this hierarchy, it will be returned; if not, null is
            //returned.
            Health targetHealth =
            hit.collider.GetComponentInParent<Health>();
```

```
if (targetHealth != null)
{
    if (hit.collider.gameObject.layer ==
        LayerMask.NameToLayer("Head"))
    {
        targetHealth.TakeHealth(headshotDamage);
        //Headshot
    }
    else if (hit.collider.gameObject.layer ==
            LayerMask.NameToLayer("Body"))
    {
        targetHealth.TakeHealth(bodyshotDamage);
        //Body shot
    }
}

#if UNITY_EDITOR
    Debug.DrawRay(hit.point, hit.normal,
                Color.green, 5f);
#endif
        }
    }
}
```

CHAPTER 6   IMPLEMENTING SHOOTER WEAPON MECHANICS

Figure 6-6. *PlayerArmature Upper Chest game object has been assigned to the layer Body*

As illustrated in Figure 6-6, note that the Upper Chest for the PlayerArmature (player) has been fitted with a box collider and its layer has been set to Body. This setup is required to ensure that when the NPC shoots at the player's chest (body shot) the damage dealt will be a value of 20 (Figure 6-5).

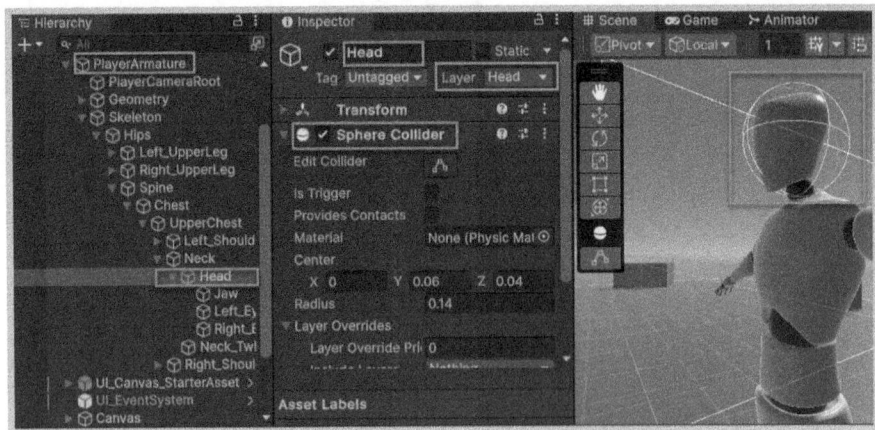

Figure 6-7. *PlayerArmature Head game object has been assigned to the layer Head*

CHAPTER 6 IMPLEMENTING SHOOTER WEAPON MECHANICS

As illustrated in Figure 6-7 note that the Head for the PlayerArmature (player) has been fitted with a sphere collider and its layer has been set to Head. This setup is required to ensure that when the NPC shoots at the player's head (headshot) the damage dealt will be a value of 100 (Figure 6-5).

The WeaponRaycast class is responsible for simulating the shooting mechanics of a weapon by casting a ray to detect hits on targets. When the weapon fires, this class determines whether a target has been hit, applies damage accordingly, and provides visual debugging aids. The class integrates with other components, such as Weapon, Health, and WeaponAudio, to create a cohesive shooting experience.

1. The [RequireComponent(typeof(Weapon))] attribute is used to ensure that the Weapon component is always present on the same GameObject to which the script (in this case, WeaponRaycast) is attached.

2. private Transform muzzlePoint: Determines the starting point of the ray cast, usually at the weapon's muzzle. It ensures that the raycast originates from the correct position, simulating a realistic firing direction.

3. private float fireDist: Defines the maximum distance the ray cast can travel. It limits the range of the weapon, ensuring that it cannot hit targets beyond this distance.

4. private int headshotDamage: Specifies the amount of damage dealt by a headshot. Differentiates between headshots and body shots, allowing for higher damage for headshots.

5. private int bodyshotDamage: Specifies the amount of damage dealt by a body shot. Provides a standard damage value for non-headshot hits.

6. private LayerMask shootableLayer: Defines the layers that the ray cast should interact with. It ensures that only relevant targets (e.g., enemy and player objects) are considered by the ray cast.

7. OnValidate(): Ensures that the muzzlePoint is assigned in the Unity editor. It logs a warning message if muzzlePoint is not set, reminding the developer to assign it.

8. OnEnable(): Subscribes the CastRay() method to the OnWeaponFired event, ensuring that the ray cast is performed whenever the weapon fires.

9. OnDisable(): Unsubscribes the CastRay() method from the OnWeaponFired event, preventing ray casts when the script is disabled.

10. CastRay(): Performs the ray cast to detect hits and applies damage. Here's a line-by-line breakdown of this method.

    - Ray ray = new Ray(muzzlePoint.position, muzzlePoint.forward): Creates a new ray starting at the muzzlePoint position and extending forward in the direction the muzzle is facing.

    - #if UNITY_EDITOR: Conditional compilation directive to include code only in the Unity Editor.

CHAPTER 6   IMPLEMENTING SHOOTER WEAPON MECHANICS

- Debug.DrawRay(muzzlePoint.position, muzzlePoint.forward * fireDist, Color.red, 2f): Draws a debug ray in the Unity Editor to visualize the raycast path.

- #endif: Ends the conditional compilation block.

- if (Physics.Raycast(ray, out RaycastHit hit, fireDist, shootableLayer)): Performs the ray cast and checks if it hits an object within the specified fireDist and on the shootableLayer.

- Health targetHealth = hit.collider.GetComponentInParent<Health>(): In the event the above if() condition is true, it searches for a Health component within the hit object's hierarchy.

- if (targetHealth != null): Checks if a Health component is found.

- if (hit.collider.gameObject.layer == LayerMask.NameToLayer("Head")): Checks if the hit object's layer is "Head" for headshots.

- targetHealth.TakeHealth(headshotDamage): Applies the headshot damage value if the hit object's layer is "Head."

- else if (hit.collider.gameObject.layer == LayerMask.NameToLayer("Body")): Checks if the hit object's layer is "Body" for body shots.

- targetHealth.TakeHealth(bodyshotDamage): This applies the body shot damage value if the hit object's layer is "Body."

CHAPTER 6   IMPLEMENTING SHOOTER WEAPON MECHANICS

- Lastly, the conditional compilation directive for editor-only code draws a green debug ray in the Unity Editor to visualize the hit point and normal direction.

11. The WeaponRaycast class subscribes to the OnWeaponFired event from the Weapon class. This ensures that the CastRay() method is called whenever the weapon is fired.

12. The WeaponRaycast class interacts with the Health class to apply damage when a ray cast hits a target. The Health class handles reducing health points and triggering death-related events.

The WeaponRaycast class integrates seamlessly with the weapon system, ensuring that firing a weapon results in accurate hit detection and appropriate damage application, all while providing visual debugging aids in the Unity Editor.

Recipe 6-5: The Weapon Casing Component Problem

Simulating realistic shell casing ejection in a game enhances immersion but can be performance-intensive if each casing is created and destroyed repeatedly. The challenge is to manage these ejected shell casings efficiently while ensuring they provide a realistic visual and physical effect when the player's weapon fires.

Solution

The WeaponCasing class addresses this challenge by using object pooling to manage shell casing instances. By reusing objects from a pool rather than creating and destroying them, the class optimizes performance. It specifies parameters like the shell casing prefab, ejection point, direction, force, and duration the casing remains in the world. When the weapon fires, it activates a casing from the pool, applies the necessary force, and then returns the casing to the pool after a set duration, ensuring both performance and realism.

How It Works

The WeaponCasing class attaches to the player's weapon and manages the ejection of shell casings when the weapon fires. It uses an ObjectPool<GameObject> to handle the shell casings, initializing the pool with a specified capacity and max size. When the weapon fires, the OnWeaponFired event triggers the EjectCasing method, which retrieves a shell casing from the pool, positions it at the ejection point, and applies force to simulate ejection. The Rigidbody component on the shell casing handles the physical simulation. After a set duration, the casing is returned to the pool, ready to be reused. This method ensures efficient management of resources, providing a realistic visual effect without impacting performance.

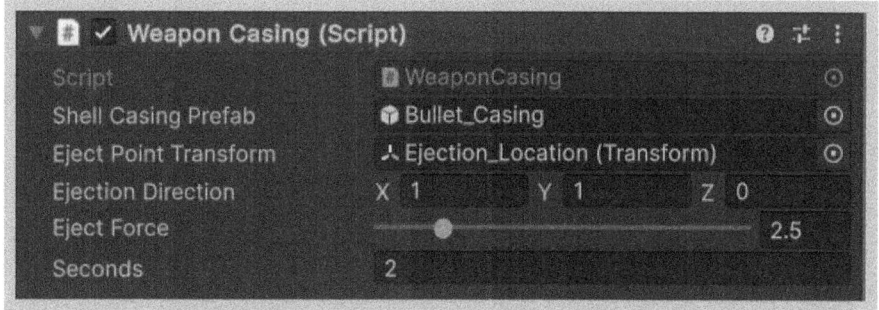

Figure 6-8. The WeaponCasing Component within the Inspector

CHAPTER 6 IMPLEMENTING SHOOTER WEAPON MECHANICS

Listing 6-4. WeaponCasing script

```
using System;
using System.Collections;
using UnityEngine;
using UnityEngine.Pool;

//Ideally attach this script only to the Player weapon to
//keep performance optimized. Using it on NPC Weapons won't
//have much of a visual effect and will deteriorate
//performance.
public class WeaponCasing : MonoBehaviour
{
    [SerializeField][Tooltip("The Shell Casing belonging to
      this Weapon")] private GameObject shellCasingPrefab;
    //Where to have the bullet casing eject from
    [SerializeField][Tooltip("Location from where the Bullet
      Shell Casing should be Ejected")] private Transform
      ejectPointTransform;
    // Serialized field for ejection direction
    [SerializeField]
    [Tooltip("Direction in which the shell casing will be
      ejected. Adjust in local space relative to the eject
      point transform.")]
    private Vector3 ejectionDirection = Vector3.right;
    //Eject force to be applied to the shell casing
    [SerializeField][Tooltip("Ejection Force for Shell
      Casing")][Range(1.0f, 10.0f)]
     private float ejectForce = 2.5f;
    //How many seconds should the shell casing last before
    //being removed.
```

CHAPTER 6   IMPLEMENTING SHOOTER WEAPON MECHANICS

```csharp
[SerializeField][Tooltip("How many seconds should the
 shell casing last in the World")]
 private float seconds = 1.5f;

private Weapon weapon;

private ObjectPool<GameObject> shellCasingPool;

private void OnValidate()
{
    if (shellCasingPrefab == null)
      Debug.LogError($"[Weapon Casing -
      {gameObject.name}] : The property 'Shell Casing
       Prefab cannot be left empty. It needs to be
       assigned a Prefab");

    if (ejectPointTransform == null)
      Debug.LogError($"[Weapon Casing - {gameObject.name}]
       : The property 'Eject Point Transform' cannot be
       left empty. It needs to be assigned a Transform that
       represents the Position from where the Bullet Casing
       should be Ejected");

    if (seconds <= 0)
      Debug.LogError($"[Weapon Casing - {gameObject.name}]
       : The property 'Seconds' cannot be a Zero or
       Negative value.");
}

private void Awake()
{
    weapon = GetComponent<Weapon>();
```

CHAPTER 6   IMPLEMENTING SHOOTER WEAPON MECHANICS

```
        // Initialize the object pool
        shellCasingPool = new ObjectPool<GameObject>(
            createFunc: CreateShellCasing,
            actionOnGet: OnGetShellCasing,
            actionOnRelease: OnReleaseShellCasing,
            actionOnDestroy: OnDestroyShellCasing,
            collectionCheck: false,
            defaultCapacity: 100,
            maxSize: 500);
    }

    private void OnEnable()
    {
        weapon.OnWeaponFired += EjectCasing;
    }

    private void OnDisable()
    {
        weapon.OnWeaponFired -= EjectCasing;
    }

    private GameObject CreateShellCasing()
    {
        return Instantiate(shellCasingPrefab);
    }

    private void OnGetShellCasing(GameObject shellCasing)
    {
        shellCasing.SetActive(true);
    }

    private void OnReleaseShellCasing(GameObject shellCasing)
    {
        shellCasing.SetActive(false);
    }
```

```csharp
private void OnDestroyShellCasing(GameObject shellCasing)
{
    Destroy(shellCasing);
}
void EjectCasing()
{
    GameObject shellCasing = shellCasingPool.Get();
    Rigidbody rb = shellCasing.GetComponent<Rigidbody>();
    shellCasing.transform.position =
    ejectPointTransform.position;
    shellCasing.transform.rotation =
    ejectPointTransform.rotation;

    // Apply force in the specified ejection direction,
    //transformed to world space
    Vector3 worldEjectionDirection =
    ejectPointTransform.TransformDirection
    (ejectionDirection.normalized);
    if (rb != null)
        rb.AddForce(worldEjectionDirection * ejectForce,
                    ForceMode.VelocityChange);
    else
    {
        Debug.LogError("Shell Casing does not have a
        Rigidbody component attached.");
        //Release back to the pool to prevent leakage.
        shellCasingPool.Release(shellCasing);
        return;
    }
```

```
    // With object pooling in place, you would activate and
    //then deactivate after a delay, instead of destroying.
    StartCoroutine(ReturnToPoolAfterDelay(shellCasing,
    seconds));
}

private IEnumerator ReturnToPoolAfterDelay(GameObject
shellCasing, float delay)
{
    yield return new WaitForSeconds(delay);
    shellCasingPool.Release(shellCasing);
}
}
```

The WeaponCasing class in Unity is responsible for simulating the ejection of shell casings when a weapon is fired. It uses an object pool to manage the shell casing objects efficiently, ensuring optimal performance. This class is intended to be attached to player weapons to provide a visual effect when the weapon is fired. However, for testing purposes, it has been attached to the NPC's handgun as the weapon system is being tested using the NPC.

1. private GameObject shellCasingPrefab: Stores the prefab for the shell casing object. This prefab is instantiated and ejected from the weapon when it is fired, creating a visual effect of shell casings being ejected.

2. private Transform ejectPointTransform: Determines the position from which the shell casing is ejected. It ensures that the shell casing appears to be ejected from the correct point on the weapon, enhancing visual realism.

3. private Vector3 ejectionDirection: Specifies the direction in which the shell casing is ejected. It controls the trajectory of the ejected shell casing, which can be adjusted relative to the eject point.

4. private float ejectForce: Defines the force applied to the shell casing when it is ejected. This determines how far and fast the shell casing travels when ejected, contributing to the realism of the effect.

5. private float seconds: Specifies the duration for which the shell casing remains in the world before being returned to the pool. This controls the lifespan of the shell casing objects, preventing them from cluttering the game world and affecting performance.

6. private Weapon weapon: Holds a reference to the Weapon component on the same game object. It allows the WeaponCasing class to subscribe to the OnWeaponFired event, triggering the ejection of shell casings when the weapon is fired.

7. private ObjectPool<GameObject> shellCasingPool: Manages the pool of shell-casing objects. It enhances performance by reusing shell casing objects rather than instantiating and destroying them repeatedly.

8. OnValidate(): Ensures that the necessary fields are set up correctly in the Unity Editor. Appropriate errors are logged to the console if the fields shellCasingPrefab and ejectPointTransform are not set, reminding the developer to assign them. Also logs an error if the field seconds is set to zero or a negative value.

9. Awake(): Within the Awake() method you initialize the Weapon component reference and set up the object pool. Here's a line-by-line breakdown of this method.

- weapon = GetComponent<Weapon>(): Retrieves the Weapon component attached to the same game object and assigns it to the weapon field.

- shellCasingPool = new ObjectPool<GameObject>(...): Initializes the object pool with specific functions for creating, getting, releasing, and destroying shell casing objects.

- createFunc: CreateShellCasing: Function to create a new shell casing object.

- actionOnGet: OnGetShellCasing: Function to activate a shell casing object when it is retrieved from the pool.

- actionOnRelease: OnReleaseShellCasing: Function to deactivate a shell casing object when it is returned to the pool.

- actionOnDestroy: OnDestroyShellCasing: Function to destroy a shell casing object when the pool is reduced in size.

- collectionCheck: false: Disables collection checks for optimization.

- defaultCapacity: 100: Sets the default number of objects in the pool.

- maxSize: 500: Sets the maximum number of objects in the pool.

CHAPTER 6   IMPLEMENTING SHOOTER WEAPON MECHANICS

10. OnEnable(): Subscribes the EjectCasing() method to the OnWeaponFired event, ensuring that shell casings are ejected when the weapon fires.

11. OnDisable(): Unsubscribes the EjectCasing() method from the OnWeaponFired event, preventing shell casings from being ejected when the script is disabled.

12. CreateShellCasing(): Instantiates a new shell casing object from the shellCasingPrefab and returns it.

13. OnGetShellCasing(GameObject shellCasing): Sets the shell casing object to active, making it visible and interactable in the game.

14. OnReleaseShellCasing(GameObject shellCasing): Sets the shell casing object to inactive, hiding it in the game and preventing interactions.

15. OnDestroyShellCasing(GameObject shellCasing): Destroys a shell casing object when the pool is reduced in size, freeing up resources.

16. EjectCasing(): Ejects a shell casing from the weapon when it is fired. Here's a line-by-line breakdown of this method.

    - GameObject shellCasing = shellCasingPool.Get(): Retrieves a shell casing object from the pool.

    - Rigidbody rb = shellCasing.GetComponent<Rigidbody>(): Gets the Rigidbody component attached to the shell casing object.

CHAPTER 6   IMPLEMENTING SHOOTER WEAPON MECHANICS

- shellCasing.transform.position = ejectPointTransform.position: Sets the position of the shell casing to the ejectPointTransform position.

- shellCasing.transform.rotation = ejectPointTransform.rotation: Sets the rotation of the shell casing to the ejectPointTransform rotation.

- Vector3 worldEjectionDirection = ejectPointTransform.TransformDirection(ejectionDirection.normalized): Transforms the local ejection direction to world space.

- rb.AddForce(worldEjectionDirection * ejectForce, ForceMode.VelocityChange): Applies force to the Rigidbody component to eject the shell casing.

- As part of the else block, an error is logged to the console if the shell casing object does not have a Rigidbody component, followed by releasing the shell casing object back to the pool since it does not have a Rigidbody component. The method then returns early.

- If the shell casing object does have a Rigidbody component, and after applying force using its Rigidbody component, a coroutine is started to return the shell casing object to the pool after a time delay as specified by the seconds field.

CHAPTER 6   IMPLEMENTING SHOOTER WEAPON MECHANICS

17. ReturnToPoolAfterDelay(GameObject shellCasing, float delay): This coroutine returns the shell casing object to the pool after the specified delay. Here's a line-by-line breakdown of this coroutine.

    - yield return new WaitForSeconds(delay): Waits for the specified delay before proceeding.

    - shellCasingPool.Release(shellCasing): Releases the shell casing object back to the pool, making it available for reuse.

18. The WeaponCasing class subscribes to the OnWeaponFired event from the Weapon class. This ensures that the EjectCasing() method is called whenever the weapon is fired.

The WeaponCasing class integrates seamlessly with the weapon system, ensuring that firing a weapon results in the realistic ejection of shell casings, all while managing these objects efficiently using an object pool to maintain optimal performance.

Recipe 6-6: The Weapon Magazine Component

Problem

Managing ammunition and reloading mechanics in a game is critical for ensuring realistic weapon behavior. The challenge is to simulate a firearm's magazine, including tracking ammo count, handling reloading with accurate timing, and preventing the weapon from firing during the reload process, all while aligning with in-game animations.

CHAPTER 6   IMPLEMENTING SHOOTER WEAPON MECHANICS

Solution

The WeaponMagazine class addresses this challenge by managing the maximum ammo capacity, current ammo count, and reloading mechanics for a weapon. It implements a coroutine to handle reloading asynchronously, ensuring the process aligns with animation timings. The class includes methods to use ammo, check if ammo is available, and unload the magazine, with safeguards to prevent firing during reloads. It also tracks whether a magazine has been used to ensure realistic reloading behavior.

How It Works

The WeaponMagazine class initializes with no ammo loaded and manages the ammo count and reloading state for a weapon. When the weapon fires, the ammo count decreases via the UseAmmo() method. If the magazine is empty, the Reload() method initiates an asynchronous reloading process, temporarily disabling firing until reloading completes. The class also handles unloading the magazine, resetting the ammo count, and marking the magazine as used. This setup ensures a realistic and immersive weapon experience, with reloading times that align with game animations and accurate ammo management.

Figure 6-9. The WeaponMagazine Component within the Inspector

Listing 6-5. WeaponMagazine script

```
using System.Collections;
using UnityEngine;

public class WeaponMagazine : MonoBehaviour
{
    [SerializeField]
    [Tooltip("The Max amount of Ammo the Weapons Magazine can
     have")]
    private int maxAmmoInMag = 25;
    [SerializeField]
    [Tooltip("How long it takes for the weapon to reload.
     While reloading Weapon can't be fired. (should match
     animation time)")]
    private float reloadTime = 1f;
    private int ammoCount;
    private bool isMagUsed = false;

    public bool IsReloading { get; private set; }

    private void Awake()
    {
        ammoCount = 0; // Initialize ammo count to Zero as
            //Weapons start with no Magazines loaded.
    }

    public bool HasAmmoInMag() => ammoCount > 0;

    public void UseAmmo() => ammoCount--;

    public void Reload()
    {
        if (!IsReloading)
            StartCoroutine(ReloadAsync());
    }
```

CHAPTER 6   IMPLEMENTING SHOOTER WEAPON MECHANICS

```
    public void Unload()
    {
        IsReloading = false;
        ammoCount = 0;
        isMagUsed = true;
        Debug.Log("Magazine Detatched from Weapon");
    }
    private IEnumerator ReloadAsync()
    {
        if (!isMagUsed)
        {
            IsReloading = true;
            yield return new WaitForSeconds(reloadTime);
            ammoCount = maxAmmoInMag; //Refill ammo after
                                      //waiting.
            IsReloading = false;
            Debug.Log("Magazine Loaded into Weapon");
        }
    }
}
```

The WeaponMagazine class is responsible for managing the magazine of a weapon, including tracking the ammunition count, handling reloading, and unloading the magazine. It ensures that the weapon can only be fired if there is ammunition available, and it prevents firing during the reloading process. The class plays a crucial role in simulating realistic weapon behavior in a game by managing the state of the weapon's magazine.

1. private int maxAmmoInMag: Defines the maximum amount of ammunition that the magazine can hold. It limits the number of shots a player can fire before needing to reload, simulating real-life weapon constraints.

CHAPTER 6   IMPLEMENTING SHOOTER WEAPON MECHANICS

2. private float reloadTime: Specifies the time required to reload the magazine. Introduces a delay during which the weapon cannot be fired, adding a layer of strategy and realism to gameplay.

3. private int ammoCount: Tracks the current amount of ammunition left in the magazine. It ensures the weapon cannot be fired if there is no ammunition left, controlling the availability of shots.

4. private bool isMagUsed: Indicates whether the magazine has been used and unloaded. It prevents the magazine from being reloaded again once it has been unloaded, ensuring that each magazine is used only once.

5. public bool IsReloading {get; private set;}: A property that indicates whether the weapon is currently in the process of reloading. It is used to prevent the weapon from firing while reloading is in progress, ensuring proper weapon behavior during reloading.

6. Awake(): Sets the initial ammo count to zero, indicating that the weapon starts with no magazine loaded. This ensures that the player must load a magazine before being able to fire the weapon.

7. public bool HasAmmoInMag() => ammoCount > 0: Returns true if the ammoCount is greater than zero, indicating that there is ammunition left in the magazine. Returns false if the magazine is empty.

CHAPTER 6   IMPLEMENTING SHOOTER WEAPON MECHANICS

8. public void UseAmmo() => ammoCount--:
    Decreases the ammoCount by one each time the
    weapon fires, representing the consumption of
    ammunition. This method is called by the Weapon
    class when the FireWeapon() method is executed.

9. Reload(): Checks if the weapon is currently
    reloading. If not, it proceeds to start the reloading
    process by initiating a coroutine to handle the
    asynchronous reloading process, preventing the
    weapon from being fired while reloading.

10. Unload(): Unloads the magazine, resetting the
    ammo count to zero and marking the magazine as
    used. It sets IsReloading to false, then resets the
    ammoCount to zero, indicating that the magazine
    has been emptied, followed by setting isMagUsed to
    true which marks the magazine as used, preventing
    it from being reloaded again.

11. private IEnumerator ReloadAsync(): This method
    handles the asynchronous reloading process,
    refilling the magazine after the specified reload
    time. It first checks to ensure that the magazine has
    not been used. If it has been used, the reloading
    process is not allowed. IsReloading is then set to
    true, indicating that the weapon is in the process
    of reloading. The coroutine is then paused for the
    duration specified by reloadTime, simulating the
    time it takes to reload the weapon. After the reload
    time has elapsed, the magazine is refilled to its
    maximum capacity. Finally, IsReloading is set to
    false, indicating that the reloading process has been
    completed and the weapon is ready to fire again.

12. The Weapon class relies on the WeaponMagazine to determine if the weapon can be fired (HasAmmoInMag()), to reduce the ammo count (UseAmmo()), and to manage the reloading process (Reload()). The Weapon class calls WeaponMagazine methods during its firing and reloading logic.

The WeaponMagazine class plays a pivotal role in controlling the ammunition and reloading mechanics of the weapon in the game. It ensures that the weapon's firing behavior is realistic by enforcing rules around ammo consumption, reloading times, and magazine usage. By managing these aspects, it provides a robust foundation for other weapon-related components, ensuring that the weapon operates within the constraints of its design.

Summary

In this chapter, you explored the critical components and mechanics necessary for implementing a realistic shooter weapon system in Unity. From setting up a common mechanic that can be used with both the player and NPC weapon to handling audio feedback, firing accuracy, and reloading mechanics, each recipe provides a comprehensive guide to creating a robust and immersive weapon experience. By following these detailed instructions, developers will be equipped to build weapons that not only function seamlessly within the game environment but also enhance the overall player experience with precise interactions and authentic feedback.

Recipe 6-1: This recipe addresses the foundational setup of shooter weapon mechanics within a game, focusing on configuring weapons for both player and NPC characters. The solution involves setting up a new handgun with essential components such as firing mechanics, raycasting, ammo management, and sound effects. By using a unified setup for both player and NPC weapons, this approach ensures consistency and balance in gameplay, enhancing the overall player experience.

CHAPTER 6　IMPLEMENTING SHOOTER WEAPON MECHANICS

Recipe 6-2: In this recipe, the focus is on the Weapon class, which manages the core functionalities of a firearm, including firing, reloading, and managing ammo. The class handles the firing rate, differentiates between NPC and player weapons, and communicates with other components like WeaponAudio to synchronize sound effects. This setup ensures realistic weapon interactions and seamless integration of weapon mechanics into the gameplay.

Recipe 6-3: This recipe introduces the WeaponAudio class, which is responsible for providing immersive audio feedback for various weapon actions, such as firing, dry firing, and reloading. By integrating with the Weapon component and subscribing to specific events, the class ensures that each weapon action is accompanied by the appropriate sound effect, enhancing the auditory experience and realism in gameplay.

Recipe 6-4: The WeaponRaycast class, covered in this recipe, is crucial for simulating the trajectory and impact of a fired weapon. It casts a ray from the weapon's muzzle to detect hits on targets, applying appropriate damage based on the hit location. This class ensures accurate shooting mechanics, providing immediate feedback when a shot is fired and includes debug visualizations for development and testing.

Recipe 6-5: In this recipe, the WeaponCasing class is introduced to manage the ejection of shell casings when a weapon is fired. Using object pooling, the class efficiently handles the visual effect of shell casing ejection, ensuring both performance optimization and realism. This method enhances the immersive experience by simulating realistic shell casing behavior without impacting game performance.

Recipe 6-6: The final recipe focuses on the WeaponMagazine class, which manages ammunition and reloading mechanics. This class tracks ammo count, handles reloading with accurate timing, and prevents the weapon from firing during the reload process. By ensuring that reloading times align with animations and managing ammo usage, this class plays a critical role in simulating realistic weapon behavior in the game.

CHAPTER 7

Implementing Efficient Object Pooling

In the world of game development, creating immersive experiences often demands the frequent creation and destruction of objects – bullets whizzing by in a heated battle, casings clattering to the ground, and explosions peppering the landscape. However, this dynamic creation and destruction can exert a significant toll on performance, introducing dreaded lag and frame rate drops that can break the spell of immersion. Enter the concept of object pooling, a crucial optimization technique that stands as a sentinel of performance in the bustling world of interactive experiences. This chapter delves into the art and science of implementing efficient object pooling, a method that recycles objects instead of letting them fall into the abyss of creation and destruction. By exploring the principles behind object pooling, examining practical implementations, and understanding its impact on game performance, you will be equipped with the knowledge to harness this powerful technique. Whether you're a seasoned developer or new to game creation, mastering object pooling is a step toward crafting seamless, efficient, and engaging digital worlds.

CHAPTER 7   IMPLEMENTING EFFICIENT OBJECT POOLING

The Performance Impact of Object Creation and Destruction

Object creation and destruction are fundamental aspects of game development in Unity or in any real-time game development engine and can significantly impact performance, thus necessitating careful management. It is a critical consideration for developers aiming to maintain high frame rates and smooth gameplay experiences. At the heart of this issue are two main factors: garbage collection (GC) and CPU overhead.

In Unity, which uses C# as its primary programming language, memory management is handled through garbage collection (GC). Garbage collection automatically frees up memory that is no longer in use by the application, which is beneficial for developer productivity but comes with performance costs. When objects are frequently created and destroyed, each new object requires memory allocation. If objects are constantly being created, the system has to allocate new memory spaces frequently, which is a relatively costly operation. Also, every time an object is destroyed, it becomes garbage that the garbage collector must collect. Significant garbage generation leads to garbage collection cycles. When the garbage collector runs, it can cause frame rate drops and stutters in gameplay because it needs to pause the application to inspect and free unused memory. These pauses are particularly noticeable in games that require real-time performance, such as fast-paced action or VR experiences.

Creating and destroying objects also incurs CPU overhead. Beyond just allocating memory, instantiating an object involves calling constructors and initializing state, which can be CPU-intensive, especially for complex objects. Similarly, destroying objects can involve finalizer calls and other cleanup operations, further using CPU cycles.

Object pooling is a pattern used to mitigate these performance issues by reusing objects instead of frequently creating and destroying them. By reusing objects from a pool, the number of new allocations (and consequently, the amount of garbage generated) is drastically reduced. This means the garbage collector runs less frequently, reducing GC-induced stutters. Reusing objects means initialization and destruction processes are minimized. Only the essential state reset is performed when an object is recycled, saving significant CPU time. Object pooling helps keep memory usage predictable and under control, as the total number of objects in use at any given time is capped by the pool size. This predictability is crucial for performance tuning and optimization.

Common Applications in Game Development

Some common applications of object pooling in game development:

- **Particle Systems**: Particle systems often involve the generation of numerous small objects to create effects like explosions, fire, smoke, or magic spells. These objects are typically short-lived, making them ideal candidates for object pooling to avoid the performance hit of constantly instantiating and destroying them.

- **Bullets and Projectiles**: In shooting games, bullets or projectiles are generated at a high rate. Using object pooling for bullets allows for rapid firing without the performance penalty of instantiating new bullet objects for each shot and efficiently handles their lifecycle from firing to impact or expiration.

- **Enemies and NPCs**: In games with many non-player characters (NPCs) or enemies that appear and disappear throughout gameplay, object pooling can manage these entities more efficiently. Pooling is particularly beneficial in scenarios like wave-based attacks where large numbers of enemies are spawned and then removed from the scene.

- **Collectibles and Power-Ups**: Games often feature collectible items or power-ups that players can pick up. These items can be pooled, especially in games where they spawn frequently and disappear once collected, to reduce the instantiation cost and manage their lifecycle efficiently.

- **UI Elements**: Dynamic UI elements such as notifications, floating text (e.g., damage numbers), or menu items that appear and disappear frequently can benefit from object pooling. This reduces the overhead associated with creating and destroying UI components, leading to smoother transitions and interactions.

- **Terrain Chunks and Tiles**: In large open-world games or games using procedural generation, terrain chunks or tiles are loaded and unloaded as the player moves through the world. Object pooling can be used to reuse these chunks or tiles, significantly reducing the cost associated with generating new terrain pieces on the fly.

- **Audio Source Objects**: For games that play many short audio clips (e.g., sound effects for actions, hits, or ambient sounds), pooling audio source objects instead of creating new ones for each sound play request can reduce overhead and improve audio playback performance.

- **Decals**: Decals (such as bullet holes, scorch marks, or blood splatters) that are projected onto surfaces can be managed via object pooling. This is especially useful in shooters or action games with a lot of environmental interaction.

Recipe 7-1: Implementing Object Pooling for Enhanced Performance

Problem

Frequent creation and destruction of game objects in Unity, such as bullets or enemies, can lead to significant performance issues due to the overhead associated with memory allocation and garbage collection. This can result in frame rate instability and increased CPU usage, especially in resource-intensive scenes and games.

Solution

Object pooling is an effective solution to manage and optimize resource usage in Unity. By pre-allocating a pool of objects at the start of the application and recycling these objects throughout the game's lifecycle, you can minimize the performance costs associated with runtime instantiation and destruction. Unity's ObjectPool<T> class provides a robust framework for implementing object pooling, allowing developers to manage any type of object with customizable creation, activation, and destruction behaviors. This approach enhances game performance, reduces memory usage, and ensures smoother frame rates.

How It Works

The core idea behind object pooling is to pre-allocate a "Pool" of objects at the start of the application or scene and then recycle these objects instead of frequently creating and destroying them during runtime. This approach significantly reduces the overhead associated with memory allocation, garbage collection, and the CPU cycles needed for object instantiation and destruction. Object Pooling works as follows:

- Initialization: At the start, the object pool is created with a fixed number or a dynamic range of objects. These objects are instantiated and stored in a collection, typically a list or a queue, and are initially set to an inactive or "available" state.

- Acquiring an Object: When the application needs an object (e.g., a bullet is fired, or an enemy spawns), it requests one from the pool. The pool checks for an available (inactive) object, activates it, updates its properties if necessary, and then hands it over for use in the game scene.

- Releasing an Object: After the object has served its purpose (e.g., a bullet disappears after hitting a target, or an enemy is defeated), it is returned back to the pool. Its state is reset to ensure it doesn't retain any previous usage data (like position, health, or visual effects), deactivated, and marked as available for reuse.

- Expansion and Contraction (Optional): Depending on the implementation, an object pool might support dynamic resizing. If all objects are in use and another is requested, the pool can either create new objects (if expansion is allowed) or deny the request. Similarly, objects can be permanently removed from the pool if they are no longer needed, reducing the pool's size.

Key Components of an Object Pool

- Pool Container: A data structure (like a List, Queue, or Stack) that holds the pooled objects. The choice of container affects how objects are managed and accessed (FIFO, LIFO, or random access).

- Prefab or Object Template: A template object from which all pooled objects are instantiated. In Unity, this is typically a GameObject prefab with predefined components and properties.

- Create Function: A method or delegate that defines how to instantiate new objects when initializing the pool or when expanding the pool size.

- Acquire/Release Functions: Methods or delegates that define the logic for activating and deactivating objects, including any necessary state reset or initialization when an object is acquired from or returned to the pool.

- Active/Inactive State Management: Logic to track whether objects are in use or available, often involving activating or deactivating GameObjects or components.

- Optional Expansion and Contraction: Logic that allows the pool to grow by creating new objects beyond its initial capacity (if allowed) and to shrink by destroying objects that are no longer needed.

By leveraging these components and mechanisms, object pooling minimizes the runtime costs associated with object management, leading to smoother frame rates, reduced memory fragmentation, and an overall more efficient use of system resources.

From Unity 2021 onward, Unity has provided built-in support for object pooling as part of its Application Programming Interface (API). With the introduction of the ObjectPool<T> class as part of the UnityEngine.Pool namespace, Unity has simplified object pooling for developers.

The following sections explore the use of Unity's object pooling API and guide you through developing your custom generic object pooling system.

Unity's ObjectPool<T> Class

Unity's ObjectPool<T> class, part of the UnityEngine.Pool namespace, is a powerful and flexible system designed to help developers manage object pooling within their Unity applications. It addresses the common performance issues associated with the frequent creation and destruction of objects, especially in scenarios requiring high performance, such as in video games or real-time simulations. The ObjectPool<T> class provides a generic way to pool objects of any type, making it broadly applicable across different types of projects.

Unity's ObjectPool<T> class offers a robust and efficient way to implement object pooling, significantly enhancing performance and resource management in Unity projects. By customizing the pool's behavior through its flexible API and delegates, developers can tailor pooling strategies to fit their specific needs and scenarios. However, developers should ensure that objects are properly reset when returned to the pool and that the pool's capacity aligns with the expected usage patterns to avoid unnecessary allocations or memory wastage.

Key Features and API Methods

- Generic Type <T>: The ObjectPool<T> class is generic, meaning it can manage pooling for any type of object. In the context of Unity, this is particularly useful for GameObjects, Components, or any custom class you might need to pool.

- Constructor: The constructor for ObjectPool<T> allows you to specify several important behaviors through delegates:

    - createFunc: A delegate that defines how new instances of the object are created when the pool needs to grow.

    - actionOnGet: A delegate that is called every time an object is taken from the pool. This is often used to reset the object's state or activate it.

    - actionOnRelease: A delegate invoked when an object is returned to the pool, commonly used to deactivate the object or clean up its state.

    - actionOnDestroy: A delegate called when an object is permanently removed from the pool and destroyed, allowing for custom cleanup logic.

- Additional parameters include collectionCheck (for debugging purposes to ensure an object isn't returned to the pool twice), defaultCapacity (initial size of the pool), and maxSize (maximum size of the pool).

- Get() Method: Retrieves an object from the pool. If the pool has available objects, it returns one; otherwise, it creates a new object using the createFunc delegate, assuming the pool hasn't reached its maxSize. If the pool is at its maxSize, the behavior depends on the pool's configuration and might not return an object.

- Release(T obj) Method: Returns an object to the pool. The actionOnRelease delegate is called to reset or deactivate the object as needed. If the object doesn't belong to the pool or the pool has reached its maximum size and cannot accept more objects, the actionOnDestroy delegate is invoked to properly dispose of the object.

- CountActive, CountInactive, and CountAll Properties: Provide information about the number of active (currently used), inactive (available in the pool) objects, and the total number of active and inactive objects, respectively, helping developers gauge the usage and efficiency of the pool.

- Clear() Method: Empties the pool, calling the actionOnDestroy delegate for each object. This method is useful for cleaning up when the pool is no longer needed, such as when changing scenes or shutting down the game.

Setting Up Your First Object Pool

Let's create a WeaponCasing class for your existing weapon system that is responsible for handling the ejection and management of shell casings when a weapon is fired. This class that is solely responsible for shell casing

CHAPTER 7 IMPLEMENTING EFFICIENT OBJECT POOLING

ejection will utilize Unity's ObjectPool<T> class to manage the pooling of shell casings. This script needs to be placed on your weapon game object. Listing 7-1 comprises the code for the WeaponCasing class that uses the object pooling pattern.

Listing 7-1. Object Pooling for shell casing ejection

```
using System;
using System.Collections;
using UnityEngine;
using UnityEngine.Pool;
public class WeaponCasing : MonoBehaviour
{
    [SerializeField]
    [Tooltip("The Shell Casing belonging to this Weapon")]
    private GameObject shellCasingPrefab;

    //Where to have the bullet casing eject from
    [SerializeField]
    [Tooltip("Location from where the Bullet Shell Casing
     should be Ejected")]
    private Transform ejectPointTransform;

    //Serialized field for ejection direction
    [SerializeField]
    [Tooltip("Direction in which the shell casing will be
    ejected. Adjust in local space relative to the eject point
    transform.")]
    private Vector3 ejectionDirection = Vector3.right;
        //Eject force to be applied to the shell casing
    [SerializeField]
    [Tooltip("Ejection Force for Shell Casing")]
    [Range(1.0f, 10.0f)]
```

CHAPTER 7 IMPLEMENTING EFFICIENT OBJECT POOLING

```csharp
    private float ejectForce = 2.5f;
    //How many seconds should the shell casing last before
    //being destroyed.
    [SerializeField]
    [Tooltip("How many seconds should the shell casing last in
     the World")]
    private float seconds = 1.5f;
    private Weapon weapon;
    private ObjectPool<GameObject> shellCasingPool;
    private void OnValidate()
    {
       if (shellCasingPrefab == null)
           Debug.LogError($"[Weapon Casing -
           {gameObject.name}] : The property 'Shell Casing
           Prefab' cannot be left empty. It needs to be
           assigned a Prefab");

       if (ejectPointTransform == null)
           Debug.LogError($"[Weapon Casing -
           {gameObject.name}] : The property 'Eject Point
           Transform' cannot be left empty. It needs to be

       assigned a Transform that represents the Position from
       where the Bullet Casing should be Ejected");

       if(seconds <= 0)
           Debug.LogError($"[Weapon Casing -
           {gameObject.name}] : The property 'Seconds' cannot
           be a Zero or Negative value.");
    }
    private void Awake()
    {
        weapon = GetComponent<Weapon>();
```

```csharp
    // Initialize the object pool
    shellCasingPool = new ObjectPool<GameObject>(
        createFunc: CreateShellCasing,
        actionOnGet: OnGetShellCasing,
        actionOnRelease: OnReleaseShellCasing,
        actionOnDestroy: OnDestroyShellCasing,
        collectionCheck: false,
        defaultCapacity: 100,
        maxSize: 500);
}
private void OnEnable()
{
    weapon.OnWeaponFired += EjectCasing;
}
private void OnDisable()
{
    weapon.OnWeaponFired -= EjectCasing;
}
private GameObject CreateShellCasing()
{
    return Instantiate(shellCasingPrefab);
}
private void OnGetShellCasing(GameObject shellCasing)
{
    shellCasing.SetActive(true);
}
private void OnReleaseShellCasing(GameObject shellCasing)
{
    shellCasing.SetActive(false);
}
```

```csharp
private void OnDestroyShellCasing(GameObject shellCasing)
{
    Destroy(shellCasing);
}

void EjectCasing()
{
    GameObject shellCasing = shellCasingPool.Get();
    Rigidbody rb = shellCasing.GetComponent<Rigidbody>();
    shellCasing.transform.position =
    ejectPointTransform.position;
    shellCasing.transform.rotation =
    ejectPointTransform.rotation;
    // Apply force in the specified ejection direction,
    // transformed to world space
    Vector3 worldEjectionDirection = ejectPointTransform.
    TransformDirection(ejectionDirection.normalized);
    if(rb != null)
       rb.AddForce(worldEjectionDirection * ejectForce,
       ForceMode.VelocityChange);
    else
    {
       Debug.LogError("Shell Casing does not have a
       Rigidbody component attached.");
       //Release back to the pool to prevent leakage.
       shellCasingPool.Release(shellCasing);
       return;
    }
    //With object pooling in place, you would activate
    //and then deactivate after a delay, instead of
    //destroying.
```

CHAPTER 7   IMPLEMENTING EFFICIENT OBJECT POOLING

```
    StartCoroutine(ReturnToPoolAfterDelay(shellCasing,
    seconds));
}

private IEnumerator ReturnToPoolAfterDelay(GameObject
shellCasing, float delay)
{
    yield return new WaitForSeconds(delay);
    shellCasingPool.Release(shellCasing);
}
}
```

Let's walk through the code provided as part of Listing 7-1. This script is attached to a player's weapon to handle the visual effect of ejecting shell casings every time the weapon fires. It utilizes Unity's physics system, object pooling for performance optimization, and event handling. Here's a breakdown of each significant part of the script:

1. Namespace Imports:

    - System: Contains fundamental classes and base classes that define commonly used value and reference data types, events, and event handlers, among others.

    - System.Collections: Provides interfaces and classes that define various collections of objects, such as lists, queues, bit arrays, hash tables, and dictionaries.

    - UnityEngine: The main namespace for Unity game engine classes.

    - UnityEngine.Pool: Namespace for Unity's object pooling utility, which helps manage collections of reusable objects.

CHAPTER 7   IMPLEMENTING EFFICIENT OBJECT POOLING

2. Class Definition and Metadata:

    - public class WeaponCasing : MonoBehaviour: Defines the WeaponCasing class that inherits from MonoBehaviour, allowing it to be attached to GameObjects in Unity and utilize Unity's lifecycle methods like Awake, OnEnable, OnDisable, etc.

3. Serialized Fields:

    - [SerializeField] private GameObject shellCasingPrefab;: A reference to the shell casing prefab. SerializeField allows this private field to be set in the Unity Editor.

    - [SerializeField] private Transform ejectPointTransform;: The transform on the weapon from where the shell casing will be ejected.

    - [SerializeField] private Vector3 ejectionDirection = Vector3.right;: The local direction in which the shell casing will be ejected. Defaulted to the right side.

    - [SerializeField] [Range(1.0f, 10.0f)] private float ejectForce = 2.5f;: The force applied to eject the shell casing, with a range constraint for the editor.

    - [SerializeField] private float seconds = 1.5f;: The duration before the shell casing is returned to the pool.

4. Private Fields:

    - private Weapon weapon;: A reference to the Weapon component on the same GameObject.

    - private ObjectPool<GameObject> shellCasingPool;: An object pool for shell casing GameObjects to optimize performance.

CHAPTER 7   IMPLEMENTING EFFICIENT OBJECT POOLING

5. Validation Method:

    - OnValidate: This method is called in the editor when the script is loaded or a value is changed. It checks for necessary references and logs errors if they are missing. Here it is checking to ensure that variables shellCasingPrefab and ejectPointTransform are not null and the variable seconds is not less than or equal to zero.

6. Initialization:

    - Awake: Called when the script instance is being loaded. It initializes the weapon reference and the shellCasingPool with specified actions for creating, getting, releasing, and destroying pooled objects.

    - ObjectPool<GameObject>();: The initialization of Unity's ObjectPool<T> via its constructor is a comprehensive example of setting up a custom object pool in Unity, particularly for managing the instantiation and lifecycle of GameObjects (i.e., shell casings in this case). Let's break down each parameter in the constructor to understand their roles and the methods they invoke.

    - createFunc: CreateShellCasing: Here createFunc is a delegate that defines how a new object (i.e., shell casing) is created when the pool needs to expand. The CreateShellCasing method assigned to this delegate will be called whenever the pool does not have any available objects (i.e., shell casings) to return and needs to create a new one. This method should return a new instance of the object type the pool manages, in this case, a new GameObject that represents a shell casing.

- actionOnGet: OnGetShellCasing: actionOnGet is a delegate that is called every time an object is retrieved from the pool with the **Get** method. The OnGetShellCasing method provided here will be executed on a shell casing GameObject when it is taken out of the pool. Typically, this method is used to set up or initialize the object in a specific state, such as activating it or resetting its properties to a default state. In this case, it activates the shell casing game object.

- actionOnRelease: OnReleaseShellCasing: actionOnRelease is a delegate that is called when an object is returned to the pool using the **Release** method. The OnReleaseShellCasing method assigned to this will be called on a shell casing GameObject when it is returned to the pool. This method is usually used for cleanup or resetting the object's state, such as deactivating it or clearing any data to prepare it for the next time it is used. In this case, the shell casing game object is being deactivated.

- actionOnDestroy: OnDestroyShellCasing: actionOnDestroy is a delegate that defines how an object should be destroyed when the pool itself is being cleared or when the pool shrinks below its maxSize. The OnDestroyShellCasing method will be called on a shell casing GameObject when it needs to be permanently removed and destroyed. This method should handle any necessary cleanup specific to the object's destruction, ensuring no memory leaks or other issues. In this case, the shell casing game object is being physically destroyed.

CHAPTER 7　IMPLEMENTING EFFICIENT OBJECT POOLING

- collectionCheck: false: collectionCheck is a boolean parameter that, when set to true, enables the pool to check if the object being released is already in the pool, throwing an exception if so. This is useful for debugging to ensure objects are not accidentally released multiple times. Setting it to false improves performance by skipping this check, under the assumption that the code correctly manages the pool objects.

- defaultCapacity: 100: defaultCapacity sets the initial size of the pool. This value indicates how many objects the pool should preallocate. Preallocating objects can improve performance by reducing the need for real-time instantiation. A capacity of 100 means 100 shell casings can be managed before any new instantiations are required.

- maxSize: 500: maxSize sets the maximum number of objects the pool can hold. If the pool reaches this size and an attempt is made to return another object to it, the excess object will be destroyed using the method provided in actionOnDestroy. A maxSize of 500 ensures that the game does not keep an unlimited number of shell casings, which could lead to memory usage issues.

7. Event Subscription and Unsubscription:

    - OnEnable and OnDisable: Subscribe and unsubscribe the EjectCasing method to the weapon.OnWeaponFired event, respectively, which implies that Weapon has a delegate-type event named OnWeaponFired. When the weapon fires,

CHAPTER 7 IMPLEMENTING EFFICIENT OBJECT POOLING

it triggers this event, causing EjectCasing to be called. This mechanism allows for loose coupling between the weapon firing mechanism and the casing ejection, facilitating easy adjustments and extensions. This setup ensures that EjectCasing is called every time the weapon fires.

8. Object Pooling Methods:

   - The CreateShellCasing, OnGetShellCasing, OnReleaseShellCasing, and OnDestroyShellCasing methods define how the pool creates new instances, activates them, deactivates them, and destroys them, respectively. Point (6) above explains their working.

9. EjectCasing Method:

   - The EjectCasing method is responsible for creating the visual effect of ejecting a shell casing from a weapon when it is fired. It does this by utilizing an object pool to manage the instantiation and reuse of shell casing objects, applying physics to simulate ejection, and ensuring efficient use of resources by returning the objects to the pool after use. Here's a detailed breakdown of each line within this method:

     1. GameObject shellCasing = shellCasingPool. Get();: This line retrieves a shell casing GameObject from the shellCasingPool, an object pool designed to manage instances of shell casings. If the pool has available objects, one is returned; otherwise, a new one is instantiated based on the pool's creation function.

CHAPTER 7   IMPLEMENTING EFFICIENT OBJECT POOLING

2. Rigidbody rb = shellCasing. GetComponent<Rigidbody>();: This line attempts to get a Rigidbody component attached to the shellCasing GameObject. The Rigidbody component is necessary for applying physics forces to the casing, simulating the ejection.

3. shellCasing.transform.position = ejectPointTransform.position;: Sets the position of the shell casing to the position of ejectPointTransform. ejectPointTransform represents the location on the weapon from where the casing should appear to be ejected.

4. shellCasing.transform.rotation = ejectPointTransform.rotation;: Sets the rotation of the shell casing to match the rotation of ejectPointTransform, ensuring the casing is oriented correctly as it is ejected from the weapon.

5. Vector3 worldEjectionDirection = ejectPointTransform.TransformDirection(ejectionDirection.normalized);: Calculates the world space direction of ejection based on a local direction vector (ejectionDirection). TransformDirection converts a direction from local space to world space, and normalized ensures the direction vector has a magnitude of 1.

CHAPTER 7   IMPLEMENTING EFFICIENT OBJECT POOLING

6. if(rb != null): Checks if the Rigidbody component was successfully retrieved from the shell casing. This is crucial because the next step involves applying a physics force, which requires a Rigidbody.

7. rb.AddForce(worldEjectionDirection * ejectForce, ForceMode.VelocityChange);: Applies a force to the casing's Rigidbody in the direction (i.e., worldEjectionDirection) calculated earlier, multiplied by ejectForce, which determines the strength of the ejection. ForceMode.VelocityChange is used to apply the force as an immediate change in velocity, ignoring the mass of the object. The ejectionDirection was transformed from local to world space to ensure it behaves consistently regardless of the weapon's orientation.

8. else: This branch is taken if no Rigidbody component is found on the shell casing. It's a fallback to handle the case where the shell casing is not set up correctly. It logs an error message indicating that the shell casing lacks a Rigidbody component.

9. shellCasingPool.Release(shellCasing);: If no Rigidbody is found, the shell casing is immediately returned to the pool to prevent it from remaining active without proper physics behavior. The EjectCasing method is also exited to avoid running the coroutine if the shell casing doesn't have a Rigidbody. This ensures that only properly set up casings are processed further.

CHAPTER 7   IMPLEMENTING EFFICIENT OBJECT POOLING

10. StartCoroutine(ReturnToPoolAfterDelay(shellCasing, seconds));: Starts a coroutine that waits for a specified duration (seconds) before returning the shell casing to the object pool. This delay allows the casing to exist in the scene for a short time, simulating the appearance of a casing falling to the ground after being ejected.

10. Coroutine – ReturnToPoolAfterDelay: A coroutine that waits for a specified delay before returning the shell casing to the pool. This mimics the temporary presence of a shell casing in the world.

ObjectPool<GameObject> is considered a generic in C# and Unity. The ObjectPool<T> class itself is a generic class provided by Unity for object pooling, where T is the type of objects it will manage. In the case of ObjectPool<GameObject>, the generic type parameter T is specified as GameObject, indicating that this particular instance of ObjectPool will manage GameObjects.

Generics in C# are a powerful feature that allows you to define a class, structure, interface, or method with placeholders for the type of its fields, parameters, or return values. This provides a way to create reusable, type-safe classes and methods without committing to a specific data type.

The ObjectPool<T> class makes use of generics to provide a flexible and type-safe way to implement object pooling for any type of object, not just GameObjects. This is particularly useful in Unity for managing instances of GameObjects, components, or any other class instances that might be expensive to instantiate and destroy frequently due to the performance overhead associated with these operations.

By using ObjectPool<GameObject>, you are essentially creating an object pool that is specifically designed to handle GameObjects, benefiting from the type safety and reusability that generics provide.

Recipe 7-2: Implementing a Centralized Object Pooler

Problem

Managing multiple types of objects, such as shell casings, bullets, and decals, in a game can lead to performance issues due to the high costs associated with frequent instantiation and destruction. This results in increased memory usage and CPU overhead, affecting overall game performance, especially in scenarios involving high-frequency object generation.

Solution

Implementing a centralized object pooling system in Unity offers a scalable and efficient solution for managing multiple object types. By using a single CentralizedObjectPooler script attached to an empty GameObject, you can initialize and manage pools for various prefabs, which can be accessed by other systems (like WeaponCasing, BulletSystem, or DecalSystem). This approach allows for objects to be reused rather than destroyed, significantly reducing instantiation costs and improving memory and CPU efficiency. The centralized pooler can maintain a dictionary of object pools, each configured for specific game object types, facilitating easy retrieval and return of objects, thus optimizing performance across different systems within the game.

How It Works

A generic object pool is implemented in a way that it can manage objects of any type. So far, the object pool created managed just one type of GameObject, i.e., shell casings, and was tied down to the WeaponCasing script. In this section, you will learn to create a centralized object pooling

CHAPTER 7　IMPLEMENTING EFFICIENT OBJECT POOLING

system that centrally manages pools for different types of game objects (like casings, bullets, decals, particles, sounds, etc.) and allows other systems (e.g., WeaponCasing, BulletSystem, DecalSystem, etc.) to request and return objects by type. This would allow using a combination of generic object pools with a nongeneric manager. This approach would simplify interaction with the centrally created pool by using type or prefab as a key to retrieve or return objects while maintaining the flexibility and efficiency of Unity's ObjectPool<T>.

To implement a centralized Object Pooler that manages multiple object types, this CentralizedObjectPooler script is attached to an empty GameObject in your scene and initializes pools for each specified prefab. Other scripts (like WeaponCasing, BulletSystem, DecalSystem, etc.) request objects from this centralized object pooler by specifying the prefab. Listing 7-2 lists the code for this CentralizedObjectPooler class.

Listing 7-2. Centralized Object Pooler

```
using System.Collections.Generic;
using UnityEngine;
using UnityEngine.Pool;

[System.Serializable]
public class PoolItem
{
    [Tooltip("Prefab of the Object You want Pooled")]
     public GameObject prefab;
    [Tooltip("Default Pool Size for above Prefab")]
     public int poolSize; //The default size of this items
                         //pool.
    [Tooltip("Max Pool Size for above Prefab")]
     public int poolMaxSize; //The Max size this item pool can
                            //grow to.
}
```

CHAPTER 7 IMPLEMENTING EFFICIENT OBJECT POOLING

```csharp
public class CentralizedObjectPooler : MonoBehaviour
{
    public static CentralizedObjectPooler Instance;

    [SerializeField][Tooltip("Total Number of Items in
    Game that need to be Pooled")] private List<PoolItem>
    itemsToPool;

private Dictionary<GameObject, ObjectPool<GameObject>> pools;

private void Awake()
{
        Instance = this;
        InitializePools();
}
private void InitializePools()
{
 pools = new Dictionary<GameObject, ObjectPool<GameObject>>();
        foreach (var item in itemsToPool)
        {
            var pool = new ObjectPool<GameObject>(
                createFunc: () =>
                {
                    var instance = Instantiate(item.prefab);
            // Make the CentralizedObjectPooler the parent
            instance.transform.SetParent(this.transform, false);
                    return instance;
                },
                actionOnGet: (obj) =>
                {
                  obj.SetActive(true);
```

CHAPTER 7   IMPLEMENTING EFFICIENT OBJECT POOLING

```
                // Optionally reset the parent to none when
                //getting the object
                obj.transform.SetParent(null);
            },
            actionOnRelease: (obj) =>
            {
            obj.SetActive(false);
            // Make the CentralizedObjectPooler the parent
            //again
            obj.transform.SetParent(this.transform, false);
            },
            actionOnDestroy: (obj) => Destroy(obj),
            collectionCheck: false,
            defaultCapacity: item.poolSize,
            maxSize: item.poolMaxSize
          );
       pools.Add(item.prefab, pool);
    }
  }
  public GameObject GetObject(GameObject prefab)
  {
      if (pools.TryGetValue(prefab, out var pool))
      {
          return pool.Get();
      }
Debug.LogError($"No pool found for prefab: {prefab.name}");
      return null;
  }
```

```
    public void ReturnObject(GameObject prefab, GameObject obj)
    {
        if (pools.TryGetValue(prefab, out var pool))
        {
            pool.Release(obj);
        }
        else
        {
Debug.LogError($"No pool found for prefab: {prefab.name}");
        }
    }
}
```

Let's walk through the code provided as part of Listing 7-2. This script is attached to an empty game object in the scene that you could name: CentralizedObjectPooler.

1. Namespace Imports:

    - System.Collections.Generic: Used for collections like lists and dictionaries.

    - UnityEngine: The main namespace for working with Unity Engine.

    - UnityEngine.Pool: Provides access to Unity's object pooling utility.

2. PoolItem Class:

    - The [System.Serializable] attribute makes PoolItem visible in the Unity Inspector, allowing for easy assignment and adjustments of its public fields.

    - public GameObject prefab;: Reference to the prefab that will be pooled.

CHAPTER 7   IMPLEMENTING EFFICIENT OBJECT POOLING

- public int poolSize;: The default size of the pool for this prefab.

- public int poolMaxSize;: The maximum size of the pool for this prefab.

3. CentralizedObjectPooler Class:

    - Inherits from MonoBehaviour, allowing it to be attached to a GameObject (i.e., CentralizedObjectPooler) and utilize Unity's event system (like Awake).

    - public static CentralizedObjectPooler Instance;: A public static instance of the class, implementing the Singleton pattern to ensure only one instance exists and is easily accessible.

4. Serialized Fields:

    - [SerializeField] private List<PoolItem> itemsToPool;: A list of PoolItem objects set in the Unity Inspector. Each item specifies a prefab and its default and maximum pool size. You need to ensure that these values are populated and not left blank. You could write an OnValidate method to ensure that these values are not left blank should you want to.

5. Private Fields:

    - private Dictionary<GameObject, ObjectPool<GameObject>> pools;: A dictionary to map each prefab to its corresponding object pool.

CHAPTER 7   IMPLEMENTING EFFICIENT OBJECT POOLING

6. Awake method:

    - Instance = this;: Initializes the Singleton instance.

    - InitializePools();: Calls the method to create pools for each specified prefab.

7. InitializePools method:

    The InitializePools method is designed to set up and initialize object pools for each type of GameObject specified in the itemsToPool list. It's a crucial component of the CentralizedObjectPooler class.

    - pools = new Dictionary<GameObject, ObjectPool<GameObject>>();: This line initializes pools, a dictionary that maps a GameObject (the prefab to pool) to an ObjectPool<GameObject>. Each ObjectPool manages instances of that prefab.

    - foreach (var item in itemsToPool): This foreach loop iterates over each PoolItem in the itemsToPool list. itemsToPool is expected to be a list of PoolItem objects, you populate within the Inspector, each specifying a prefab and the size of its pool.

    - Inside the loop, a new ObjectPool<GameObject> is instantiated for each item within the itemsToPool list. The ObjectPool constructor is called with several parameters that define its behavior:

        - createFunc: () =>

            {

            vvar instance = Instantiate(item.prefab);

            instance.transform.SetParent(this.transform, false);

CHAPTER 7 IMPLEMENTING EFFICIENT OBJECT POOLING

  return instance;

}, : This lambda function is called whenever the pool needs to create a new instance of the object. It instantiates the prefab, sets the CentralizedObjectPooler GameObject within the hierarchy as its parent (keeping the hierarchy organized and not affecting the global scale and position due to the false argument in SetParent), and returns the new instance.

- actionOnGet: (obj) =>

    {

    obj.SetActive(true);

    obj.transform.SetParent(null);

    }, : This action is performed when an object is retrieved from the pool. It activates the GameObject (obj.SetActive(true)) and optionally detaches it from the CentralizedObjectPooler GameObject in the hierarchy (obj.transform.SetParent(null)), making it independent in the scene hierarchy. This detachment is optional and based on whether you want pooled objects to be children of the pooler when active.

- actionOnRelease: (obj) =>

    {

    obj.SetActive(false);

    obj.transform.SetParent(this.transform, false);

615

}, : This action is executed when an object is returned to the pool. It deactivates the GameObject (obj.SetActive(false)) and reattaches it to the CentralizedObjectPooler GameObject in the hierarchy. This ensures that inactive pooled objects are kept organized under the pooler in the scene hierarchy.

- actionOnDestroy: (obj) => Destroy(obj), : Defines how an object should be destroyed when it is removed from the pool permanently. This straightforwardly calls Unity's Destroy method on the object.

- collectionCheck: false, : When set to true, the pool checks if an object is already in the pool before adding it, throwing an exception if a duplicate is found. This is set to false for performance reasons, as it assumes proper usage of the pool without duplicates.

- defaultCapacity: item.poolSize, : Specifies the initial number of objects to instantiate and keep in the pool. This is set based on the poolSize property of the PoolItem.

- maxSize: item.poolMaxSize : Defines the maximum number of objects the pool can hold. When the number of active objects returned to the pool exceeds this number, surplus objects will be destroyed rather than returned to the pool.

- pools.Add(item.prefab, pool); : After creating the object pool for a prefab, this final line within the foreach loop adds the pool to the pools dictionary with the prefab as the key. This allows for easy retrieval and management of pools based on the prefab.

  This method effectively sets up a separate pool for each type of object you want to manage.

8. GetObject Method:
   - Takes a prefab as input and attempts to retrieve the corresponding pool from the pools dictionary using the prefab as the key. If found, it returns an object from that pool. If not, it logs an error and returns null.

9. ReturnObject Method:
   - Takes a prefab and a GameObject as input, attempting to find the corresponding pool. If found, the GameObject is returned to the pool. However, if the pool is not found, it logs an error.

Using the CentralizedObjectPooler

The CentralizedObjectPooler that you have created can be used in other scripts like a WeaponCasing, BulletSystem, or DecalSystem script, which can all simultaneously interact with the CentralizedObjectPooler to get and return the concerned pooled game objects. This approach centralizes object pooling management, making it easier to expand and maintain across different types of objects and systems within your game.

In this section, you will use a modified version of the WeaponCasing script provided as part of Listing 7-1 to work with the CentralizedObjectPooler, which obtains pooled casing shells to be ejected by a weapon when fired. The modified WeaponCasing script provided as part of Listing 7-3 demonstrates how to utilize the CentralizedObjectPooler to manage shell casing GameObjects.

Listing 7-3. Modified WeapnCasing Script used with the CentralizedObjectPooler script

```
using System;
using System.Collections;
using UnityEngine;

public class WeaponCasing : MonoBehaviour
{

[SerializeField][Tooltip("The Shell Casing belonging to this Weapon")]
private GameObject shellCasingPrefab;
//Where to have the bullet casing eject from
[SerializeField] [Tooltip("Location from where the Bullet Shell Casing should be Ejected")]
private Transform ejectPointTransform;
// Serialized field for ejection direction
[SerializeField]
[Tooltip("Direction in which the shell casing will be ejected. Adjust in local space relative to the eject point transform.")]
private Vector3 ejectionDirection = Vector3.right;
//Eject force to be applied to the shell casing
[SerializeField] [Tooltip("Ejection Force for Shell Casing")]
[Range(1.0f, 10.0f)] private float ejectForce = 2.5f;
```

CHAPTER 7 IMPLEMENTING EFFICIENT OBJECT POOLING

```csharp
//How many seconds should the shell casing last before being
//destroyed.
[SerializeField] [Tooltip("How many seconds should the shell
casing last in the World")] private float seconds = 1.5f;

private Weapon weapon;

private void OnValidate()
{
  if (shellCasingPrefab == null)
    Debug.LogError($"[Weapon Casing - {gameObject.name}] :
      The property 'Shell Casing Prefab' cannot be left empty.
      It needs to be assigned a Prefab");

  if (ejectPointTransform == null)
    Debug.LogError($"[Weapon Casing - {gameObject.name}] :
      The property 'Eject Point Transform' cannot be left
      empty. It needs to be assigned a Transform that represents
      the Position from where the Bullet Casing should be
      Ejected");

  if(seconds <= 0)
    Debug.LogError($"[Weapon Casing - {gameObject.name}] : The
      property 'Seconds' cannot be a Zero or Negative value.");
}

private void Awake()
{
        weapon = GetComponent<Weapon>();
}

private void OnEnable()
{
        weapon.OnWeaponFired += EjectCasing;
}
```

CHAPTER 7 IMPLEMENTING EFFICIENT OBJECT POOLING

```
private void OnDisable()
{
        weapon.OnWeaponFired -= EjectCasing;
}
void EjectCasing()
{
 // 1
 var shellCasing = CentralizedObjectPooler.Instance.
 GetObject(shellCasingPrefab);
 Rigidbody rb = shellCasing.GetComponent<Rigidbody>();
 shellCasing.transform.position = ejectPointTransform.position;
shellCasing.transform.rotation = ejectPointTransform.rotation;
// Apply force in the specified ejection direction,
//transformed to world space
 Vector3 worldEjectionDirection = ejectPointTransform.Transform
 Direction(ejectionDirection.normalized);
 if(rb != null)
    rb.AddForce(worldEjectionDirection * ejectForce, ForceMode.
    VelocityChange);
 else // 2
 {
   Debug.LogError("Shell Casing does not have a
   Rigidbody component attached.");
   // Release back to pool to prevent leakage.
   shellCasingPool.Release(shellCasing);
   return;
 }

// With object pooling in place, you would activate and then
//deactivate after a delay.
```

CHAPTER 7 IMPLEMENTING EFFICIENT OBJECT POOLING

```
StartCoroutine(ReturnToPoolAfterDelay(shellCasing, seconds));
}

private IEnumerator ReturnToPoolAfterDelay(GameObject
shellCasing, float delay) // 3
{
yield return new WaitForSeconds(delay);
CentralizedObjectPooler.Instance.ReturnObject
(shellCasingPrefab, shellCasing);
}

}
```

You will note that most of the code provided as part of Listing 7-3 is identical to Listing 7-1. The new additions to the code in Listing 7-3 to ensure that WeaponCasing utilizes the CentralizedObjectPooler have been explained below:

1. Object Retrieval:

    - var shellCasing = CentralizedObjectPooler. Instance.GetObject(shellCasingPrefab); : The script requests a shell casing object from the CentralizedObjectPooler by passing the prefab it needs. The pooler checks if it has an available instance of the specified prefab and returns it. If not available, it instantiates a new one (depending on the pooler's implementation and capacity).

2. EjectCasing method – else block:

    - CentralizedObjectPooler.Instance. ReturnObject(shellCasingPrefab, shellCasing); The else block here handles the case where no Rigidbody is found as part of the shellCasing.

It logs an error and returns the casing to the pool immediately, preventing it from being incorrectly left active without physics behavior. If a Rigidbody is found, a coroutine is initiated that waits for a specified time (seconds) before returning the casing to the pool. This delay allows the casing to remain visible and interact with the game world before being deactivated and reused.

3. Returning to Pool:
   - After a delay (seconds), the shell casing is returned to the pool for future use. This delay simulates the casing's presence in the world before it's considered "spent" and ready for reuse.

BulletSystem and DecalSystemscripts can utilize the CentralizedObjectPooler in a similar manner, optimizing the management of bullets and decals within a game.

1. BulletSystem:
   - When firing a weapon, the BulletSystem can retrieve a bullet from the pool instead of instantiating a new one.
   - After setting the bullet's position and direction, it's propelled forward. Physics or raycasting can be used to handle impact detection.
   - Upon impact or after a certain time, the bullet is returned to the pool for reuse.

2. DecalSystem:

    - Decals (e.g., bullet holes and blood splatters) are often created in large numbers. Using a pool to manage them can significantly reduce instantiation costs.

    - When an object is hit, a decal is retrieved from the pool and placed at the impact point, properly oriented to match the surface applied to.

    - Decals might fade out or simply be removed after some time or when there's a need to free up resources, at which point they're returned to the pool.

Summary

This chapter focused on a vital optimization technique in game development aimed at minimizing the performance overhead associated with the constant creation and destruction of objects within a game. This practice is especially crucial in scenarios where objects like bullets, casings, and particles are frequently generated and disposed of, potentially leading to significant frame rate drops and a less immersive gaming experience due to garbage collection pauses and CPU overhead. Object pooling addresses these issues by reusing objects from a predefined pool, thereby reducing memory allocations and the need for garbage collection and optimizing CPU usage through minimized instantiation and destruction processes.

Index

A

AI, *see* Artificial intelligence (AI)
API, *see* Application Programming Interface (API)
Application Programming Interface (API), 592
Artificial intelligence (AI)
    attack state, 304–310
    chase state, 298–304
    cover state, 316–331
    death state, 331–335
    HitState class, 310–315
    Idle State, 278
    NavMesh agents, 224
    patrol state, 284–290
    wander state, 291–298

B

Binding models
    abstract actions, 73
    button south, 82–84
    composite type, 74
    control schemes, 74, 88–92
    groups, 74
    interactions, 74
    key aspects, 73
    left stick, 76, 77
    path/processors, 74
    pointer delta, 78–80
    right stick, 79–81
    shift key, 84–86
    spacebar, 81, 82
    sprint action, 84
    trigger, 86, 87
    WASD, 75, 76

C

Central Processing Unit (CPU), 586
Character controllers
    advantages, 3
    Assets/StarterAssets folder, 4
    character model
        animations/control schemes, 54
        animator component, 56, 57
        Avatar's configuration, 57
        Banana Man, 55
        compatible scale, 55
        humanoid model, 54, 56
        prerequisites, 55
        rig tab, 56
        swapping character model, 56, 58

INDEX

Character controllers (*cont.*)
    testing/fine-tune, 57
    T-pose model, 55
  dynamic object interaction
    BasicRigidBodyPush, 32, 34
    canPush, 35
    CharacterController, 33
    implementation, 32
    key components, 33
    layer mask, 33
    pushable object, 34
    pushing obstacles, 32
    push layers, 35
    push objects, 33
    Rigidbody component, 34
    strength, 33
    strength value, 35
  first-person player
    actions asset, 29
    analog/binary inputs, 26
    analog inputs, 27
    analogMovement setting, 27
    auto-switch property, 30
    behavior, 30
    binary inputs, 27
    BottomClamp, 23
    camera movements/
      rotation, 14
    camera object, 31
    camera systems, 9
    Capsule game object, 10
    center/radius, 12
    CharacterController, 11, 13
    Cinemachine, 15

Cinemachine virtual
  camera, 22
component, 13, 16, 24
control schemes, 27
core elements, 9
customization/
  extensibility, 8
default map/scheme, 30
factors, 8
FallTimeout, 19
features, 7
FirstPersonController, 13
functionalities, 8
fundamental structure, 9
game designs, 20
Gizmos, 15
gravity/jumping
  system, 14
gravity value, 18
ground detection, 21
grounded check, 14
handling input, 8
immersive/dynamic
  game, 7
input system, 15, 24
interaction, 7
JumpHeight, 18
JumpTimeout, 19
jump variable, 26
keyboard/gamepad input, 28
key properties, 29
LayerMask, 22
look variable, 25
minimum distance, 12

INDEX

mobile gaming, 8
mouse cursor settings, 28
movement-handling scripts, 25
movement/interaction, 13
movement/sprinting, 14
MoveSpeed, 16
move/sprint variables, 24
PlayerInput, 15
playground scene, 9
properties, 16, 20, 22
radius, 21
RotationSpeed, 17
script captures/ processes, 24
setup, 10
SpeedChangeRate, 17
SprintSpeed, 17
sprint variable, 26
StarterAssets (Input Actions) window, 28, 29
StarterAssetsInputs, 15
steeper slopes, 11
step offset/skin width, 12
TopClamp, 23
UI input module, 31
variables, 25
fundamental concepts/ components, 1
gamepad contorls
   accessibility/user satisfaction, 51
   actions, 51
   input methods, 52
   jumps/leaps, 53
   look action leverages, 52
   move action, 52
   preconfiguration, 52
   sprint action, 53
   testing, 53
ideal solution, 2
initial challenges, 2
input scripts, 95–112
input system, 64
mobile touch controls, 36–38
package manager, 4
render pipeline
   compatibility issues, 5
   dropdown states, 6
   editor main menu, 6
   pink textures, 5
requirements, 2
technical aspects, 59
third-person, 38–50
URP package, 3
warrior game object, 341
Combat system design, 338
Control scheme
   definition, 88
   dropdown, 89
   duplication/delete, 90
   edit/add options, 89
   features, 88
   GamePad selection, 88
   XR controllers, 90–92
CPU, *see* Central Processing Unit (CPU)

INDEX

D

Dynamic icons/gamepad actions
- bindings control path, 220
- component, 216
- conditional icon replacement, 218
- control path parameter, 219
- element manipulation, 218
- event subscription, 218
- fallback visual representation, 220
- Gamepad bindings, 217
- GamepadIconExample script, 221
- GetSprite() method, 219
- OnUpdateBindingDisplay method, 218
- overview, 218
- switch statement, 219
- Xbox/PlayStation, 215

E

Enemy AI system
- AI (*see* Artificial intelligence (AI))

F

Finite state machines (FSMs)
- combat systems, 338
- decision-making process, 223
- NavMesh (*see* NavMesh agents)
- NPCs (*see* Non-player characters (NPCs))
- structured approach, 223

FSMs, *see* Finite state machines (FSMs)

G, H

Game development
- audio clips, 588
- bullets/projectiles, 587
- collectible items/power-ups, 588
- decals, 589
- dynamic creation/destruction, 585
- enemies/NPCs, 588
- input system (*see* Input system)
- object pooling (*see* Object pooling)
- optimization technique, 585
- particle systems, 587–589
- terrain chunks/tiles, 588
- UI elements, 588

Garbage collection (GC), 586

GC, *see* Garbage collection (GC)

I, J, K, L

Input system
- action asset
  - actions, 67–73
  - binding/callbacks, 69
  - jumping option, 71

INDEX

key components, 68
look type, 70
modular approach, 67
move type, 69
processors, 68
solitary action map, 66, 67
sources, 65
sprint action, 72
StarterAssets, 65, 66
binding (*see* Binding models)
character controller
    scripts, 95–112
dynamic icons/gamepad
    actions, 215–221
flexible/contextual
    configurations
    dynamic control schemes, 62
    migration, 63
    package manager, 64
    touchpads/gyroscopes, 62
    Unity Input System, 63
handling input
    behavior property, 94
    callback functions, 92
    direct handling, 93
    elements, 92
    methods, 93
    OnApplicationFocus/
      SetCursorState
      methods, 95
    OnAttack method, 94
    polling, 92
handling methods
    attackAction variable, 151

Awake method, 152
canceled phases, 150, 151
features, 147
IsAnimationNearlyComplete
    method, 155
lifecycle phases, 147
OnAttackComplete
    method, 150
OnAttack method, 148
OnAttackStart/
    OnAttackComplete
    methods, 153
OnEnable/OnDisable
    methods, 152
performance issues, 147
performed phase, 149, 150
phases, 148
started phase signals, 148, 149
System.Collections, 154
WaitForAnimation
    coroutine, 154
persist rebound controls
    ActionMapManager
      script, 215
    active game session, 211
    binding overrides, 213
    OnEnable() method, 214
    RebindSaveLoad script, 213
    RebindUISampleActions, 211
    StarterAssets, 212
player (*see* Player attack action)
re-bindable controls, 175–210
scalable/intuitive approach, 61
UI interactions, 157–174

INDEX

M

Melee combat systems
- attack process
  - attackDistance, 402
  - AttackPlayer() method, 410, 411
  - Awake() method, 403
  - CrossFadeInFixedTime(), 410
  - handling transitions, 395
  - If() statement, 404
  - IsAnimationNearlyComplete() method, 408–410
  - IsObstacleInPath() method, 404, 407, 408
  - MoveTowardsPlayer() method, 404–407
  - nested if() statement, 404
  - OnStateEnter() method, 403
  - OnStateExit() method, 411
  - OnStateUpdate(), 403
  - proximity/line-of-sight, 394
  - SetDestination() method, 406
  - W_AttackState class, 395–402
- chase state
  - Awake() method, 380
  - finite state machine, 374
  - IState interface, 374
  - OnStateEnter() method, 380
  - OnStateExit(), 381
  - OnStateUpdate() method, 381
  - playerDetectionSphereRadius, 380
  - stateMachine, 379
  - stopDist, 379
  - stopDistBuffer, 380
  - W_ChaseState class, 375–379
- circling movement
  - Awake() method, 391
  - components, 389, 390
  - distance/detection parameters, 382
  - durations/random directions, 382
  - if() statement, 391–393
  - key features, 382
  - OnStateEnter(), 391
  - OnStateExit(), 394
  - OnStateUpdate(), 391, 393
  - OnTriggerEnter(), 394
  - W_CirclingState class, 382–389
- cover state
  - account factors, 453
  - action/combat-based games, 452
  - Awake(), 464
  - FindClosestCover(), 465–468
  - FindFarthestCover(), 468
  - GameObjects, 463
  - lastHidingSpot, 463
  - npcSpeed, 463
  - OnStateEnter(), 464

INDEX

OnStateExit(), 465
transform player, 463
W_CoverState class, 453–463
death state
   Awake() method, 472
   crossFadeTime/
      deathHash, 472
   DeathState class, 469–472
   destroyDelay/
      stateMachine, 472
   implementation, 469
   IState interface, 469
   OnStateEnter() method, 473
   OnStateExit() method, 474
   OnStateUpdate()
      method, 473
dynamic/fluid combat
      system, 337
free-flow combat system, 337
health script
   action events, 437
   currentHealth/isDead, 438
   CurrentHealth property, 438
   Die(), 439
   health class, 434–437
   implementation, 434
   maxHealth (), 438
   Start(), 438
   TakeHealth(), 434, 439
   testing function, 434
   Update(), 440
hit state
   Awake() method, 444
   CrossFade(), 444
   HitHash/IdleHash, 444
   implementation, 440
   key features, 440
   OnStateEnter()
      method, 444
   OnStateExit() method, 445
   OnStateUpdate()
      method, 444
   previousState, 444
   W_HitState class, 440–443
implementation, 338
non-player characters
   attackTimeRange, 355
   Awake() method, 356
   aware/unaware, 349
   ClearAttackingNPC(), 357
   GetAttackingNPC(), 357
   HandlePlayerSpotted()
      method, 356, 357
   IsAnyNPCAttacking(), 357
   NPCManager class, 349–357
   npcsInRange/
      npcsInLevel, 355
   OnEnable()/
      OnDisable(), 356
   PopulateNpcsInLevel()
      method, 357
   RegisterInRangeNpc(), 357
   SetAttackingNPC(), 357
   singleton pattern, 349
   Start() method, 356
   UnregisterOutOfRange
      Npc(), 357
   Update() method, 356

Melee combat systems (*cont.*)
  retreat state
    Awake() method, 417
    implementation, 411
    methods/fields, 412
    OnStateEnter(), 412, 417
    OnStateExit(), 412, 420
    OnStateUpdate(), 412, 418
    retreatDistance, 417
    RetreatFromPlayer(), 412, 419, 420
    W_RetreatState class, 412–416
  wandering behavior
    Awake() method, 450
    crossFadeTime/ isTargetSet, 450
    implementation, 446
    IState interface, 446
    navigationRadius, 450
    OnStateEnter() method, 451
    OnStateExit(), 451
    OnStateUpdate() method, 451
    SetNewWanderTarget() method, 447, 451
    stateMachine, 450
    walkHash, 450
    W_WanderState class, 447–449
  warrior animation events
    activation/deactivation, 421
    Awake(), 423
    DisableSwordCollider(), 422, 424, 427
    EnableSwordCollider(), 422, 424, 427
    MeleeWeaponDamage component, 423
    proper collider management, 426–428
    proxy methods, 425, 426
    synchronization, 421
    WarriorAnimationEvents class, 421–423
    WSword prefab, 424
  warrior game object
    animator component, 340
    Attack State, 342
    Awake() method, 347
    Chase State, 342
    CheckPlayerVisibility() method, 348
    circling logic/ animations, 342
    cohesive behavior model, 339
    components, 340
    Cover State, 343
    Death State, 343
    finite-state machine, 339
    fundamental state machine, 341
    Hit State, 343
    Idle State, 341
    Nav Mesh Agent, 341

INDEX

OnTriggerEnter()
   method, 347
OnTriggerExit() method, 347
PlayerDetector
   script, 344–346
Playground scene, 340
retreat actions, 342
Rigidbody component, 343
trigger mode, 340
visibilityCoroutine, 347
Wander State, 343
warrior's animations, 343
WarriorStateMachine
   component, 347
warrior state machine
   AlertNearbyNPCs(), 358, 370
   animations, 357
   Awake() method, 368, 369
   CirclingTime, 367
   class methods, 358
   event-driven methods, 358
   FindState(), 373
   HasSpottedPlayer, 367
   InitiateAttackOn
      Player(), 370
   IsPlayerDead, 367
   IsPlayerVisible(), 370
   IState implementations, 366
   modular approach, 358
   NavMeshAgent, 367
   NpcDead(), 371
   OnDisable() method, 368
   OnEnable() method,
      367, 368
   OnPlayerSpotted
      event, 366
   PlayerDead() method, 371
   RotateToFacePlayer(),
      367, 371
   Start() method, 370
   TakeDamage() method,
      371, 373
   transform, 366
   visibleChaseAngle
      property, 366
   WarriorStateMachine
      class, 358–365
weapon damage behavior
   Awake(), 432
   collider component, 432
   collider management/
      detection, 428
   EnableCollider()/
      DisableCollider(), 432
   hasDealtDamage, 432
   MeleeWeaponDamage
      class, 429–431
   OnDisable(), 433
   OnTriggerEnter(), 433
   self-damage/damage, 428
   topMostParentTag, 432
Mobile touch controls
   implementation, 36
   input debugger
      window, 37, 38
   integration, 36
   testing process, 36
   Unity Editor, 36, 37

633

INDEX

N

NavMesh agents
  AI characters, 224
  bake button, 229, 230
  characters/agents, 224
  component, 234
  navigation package, 224
  NavMeshSurface component, 228, 229
  NPCs, 230
  object setup, 227
  PlayerArmature game object, 225
  un-baked object, 225
Non-player characters (NPCs), 588
  AllPatrolPoints game object, 231
  attack state
    AttackState class, 305–308
    Awake() method, 309
    component, 308–310
    NPCSpeed() method, 308
    OnNpcAttack() method, 308
    OnStateEnter() method, 309
    OnStateExit() method, 310
    OnStateUpdate() method, 309
    SwitchState() method, 309
    transitions, 304
    visible/patrol/wander, 305
  behavior/weapon arsenal animations, 236
    Arsenal element, 242
    component, 237–239
    controller setup, 236
    dynamic assignment/ management, 235
    elements, 241–243
    NPCController class, 235
    properties, 238, 239
    rightGunBone/ leftGunBone, 242
    robust/flexible approach, 235
    script management, 239–241
    SetArsenal() method, 242
  capsule collider setup, 233
  chase state
    aggressive pursuit mode, 299
    Awake() method, 303
    ChaseState class, 299–302
    component, 302–304
    game mechanics, 298
    OnNpcChase() method, 302
    OnStateEnter() method, 303
    OnStateExit() method, 304
    OnStateUpdate() method, 303
    stateMachine/ NPCSpeed, 303
  combat systems (see Melee combat systems)
  configuration, 230
  cover state
    Awake() method, 326
    component, 325–331
    CoverState class, 316–325

INDEX

CrouchingRun()
  method, 325
FindClosestCover()
  method, 327–329
FindFarthestCover()
  method, 330
implementation, 316
NavMeshAgent, 316
OnNPCSquat() method, 325
OnNpcTakeCover, 325
OnStateEnter() method, 327
OnStateExit() method, 327
OnStateUpdate()
  method, 327
stateMachine, 326
death state
  Awake() method, 335
  component, 334, 335
  DeathState class, 332–334
  destroyDelay, 334
  implementation, 331
  NPCStateMachine
    component, 334
  OnStateEnter() method, 335
  OnStateExit() method, 335
  OnStateUpdate()
    method, 335
  PlayNpcDeadAnim, 334
  termination, 331
health management system
  class differentiates, 253
  currentHealth, 258
  CurrentHealth
    properties, 258
  Die() method, 258
  isDead, 258
  maxHealth, 257
  Monobehaviour/
    implements, 256–259
  OnHealthDepleted, 257
  OnNpcDeath, 257
  OnPlayerDeath, 257
  requirements, 252
  script code, 254–256
  Soldier_0 game object, 253
  TakeHealth()/Start()
    methods, 258
  Update() method, 259
hit state
  Awake() method, 314
  component, 314, 315
  Damage() method, 314
  HitState class, 311–313
  isNpcHit, 314
  OnStateEnter() method, 315
  OnStateExit(), 315
  OnStateUpdate(), 315
  PlayNpcHitAnim, 314
  repetitive/stuck states, 310
  stateMachine, 314
  transitions, 311
Idle State, 278
  Awake(), 282
  chasing/patrolling/
    wandering, 279
  IdleState class, 279–282
  MonoBehaviour methods,
    282, 283

INDEX

Non-player characters
    (NPCs) (*cont.*)
        movement controls/
           employs, 278
        OnNpcIdle, 282
        OnStateEnter(), 282
        OnStateExit() method, 283
        OnStateUpdate(), 283
        SwitchState(), 282
    parameters, 230
    patrol state, 284
        Awake() method, 289
        component, 288–290
        FindNextPoint() method,
            284, 290
        lastWaypointIndex, 289
        OnNpcPatrol() method, 288
        OnStateEnter() method, 289
        OnStateExit() method, 290
        OnStateUpdate()
            method, 290
        PatrolState class, 284–288
        stateMachine, 289
    PatrolState component, 234
    primary issue, 230
    properties, 234
    SniperRifleController animator
        actions script, 246–250
        activities/reactions, 250
        animation state methods, 251
        Awake() method, 251
        base layer/parameters, 245
        countOfDamage
            Animations, 250
        damage layer, 245, 246
        features, 245
        lastDamageAnimation, 250
        OnDisable() method, 251
        OnEnable() method, 251
        seamless transitions, 244
        state events, 244
        switch animations, 250–252
        Unity Project tab, 245
    Soldier_0, 231
    state machine (*see* State
        machine system)
    structure, 232
    wander state
        Awake() method, 296
        behavioral states, 291
        component, 295–298
        implementation, 291
        navigationRadius, 295
        OnNpcWander() method, 295
        OnStateEnter() method, 296
        OnStateExit() method, 297
        OnStateUpdate()
            method, 296
        SamplePosition() method, 297
        stateMachine, 295
        WanderState class, 291–295

O

Object pooling
    acquire/release functions, 591
    active/inactive state
        management, 591

INDEX

centralization
  awake method, 614
  CentralizedObjectPooler
    class, 609–613
  empty game, 612
  game objects, 609
  GetObject method, 617
  InitializePools
    method, 614–617
  namespace imports, 612
  performance issues, 608
  PoolItem class, 612
  private fields, 613
  ReturnObject method, 617
  scalable/efficient
    solution, 608
  serialized fields, 613
  systems, 609
CentralizedObjectPooler
  BulletSystem, 622
  DecalSystem, 623
  EjectCasing method, 621
  retrieval object, 621
  returning objects, 622
  utilization, 621
  WeaponCasing
    script, 617–621
Clear() method, 594
components/mechanisms,
  592, 593
constructor, 593
data structure, 591
effective solution, 589
expansion/contraction, 590
factors, 586
featues/behaviors, 593, 594
fundamental aspects, 586
game objects, 589
garbage generation, 586
Get() method, 594
memory access, 587
memory allocation/garbage
  collection, 589
memory management, 586
ObjectPool<T> class, 592–594
optional expansion/
  contraction, 591
performance costs, 589
prefab/object template, 591
recycle, 590
Release(T obj) method, 594
reusing objects, 587
script format, 599–607
  actionOnDestroy, 602
  actionOnRelease, 602
  class definition/
    metadata, 600
  collectionCheck, 603
  defaultCapacity, 603
  EjectCasing
    method, 604–607
  EjectPointTransform, 601
  event subscription/
    unsubscription, 603
  generics, 607
  get method, 602
  initialization, 601
  maxSize sets, 603

INDEX

Object pooling (*cont.*)
    methods, 604
    namespace imports, 599
    OnGetShellCasing
      method, 602
    private fields, 600
    release method, 602
    return value, 607
    rigidbody component, 605
    serialized fields, 600
    ShellCasingPrefab, 601
  shell casing ejection, 595–600
  source code, 595–600
  validation method, 600
  working process, 590, 591
OnStateUpdate(), 465

P, Q

Parkour system
  dynamic/fluid player
    movements, 477, 529
  environmental interaction/
    adaptive mechanics, 477
  obstacle sensor
    detecting obstacles, 530
    detection mechanism, 482
    DrawRay() method, 487
    HitInfo struct, 482, 485
    LineRenderer, 489
    ObstacleDetected()
      method, 487
    ObstacleSensor
      class, 482–485
    source code, 485, 486
    Start() method, 486
    Utils.DrawRay()
      method, 488–490
  ParkourManager class, 530
    alignment process, 501
    anim.MatchTarget()
      method, 499–501
    Awake() method, 496, 504
    components, 495, 496
    dynamic actions, 489
    IEnumerator
      ParkourAction(), 502
    IsAnimationNearlyComplete
      method, 490
    ObstacleDetected()
      method, 496
    ObstacleSensor
      component, 490–495
    OnEnable()/OnDisable()
      methods, 504
    OnEnterParkourMode/
      OnExitParkour mode, 503
    PerformTargetMatching()
      method, 490, 497, 498, 503
    StepUp animation, 498
    Update() method, 496, 504
  player armature game
    object, 530
    central step-like structure,
      479, 480
    components, 481, 482
    environment, 478
    key components, 479

INDEX

obstacle sensor, 479
playground scene, 479
raycasting, 480
scriptable objects, 530
    AvatarTarget body
        parts, 511–513
    CrossFade() method, 513
    flexible/scalable
        solution, 505
    JumpUp_SO object, 516, 517
    key properties, 506
    LowClimb_SO object,
        517, 518
    modular approach, 505
    parameters, 508, 509
    parkour animations, 513, 514
    ParkourBehavior
        script, 507–509
    StepUp_SO object, 514–516
    target matching, 518
    Update() method, 513
vaulting action, 531
    component, 529
    frontal approach, 520, 521
    handle scenarios, 519
    mirror property, 526
    obstacleTag, 525, 526
    ParkourActionPossible()
        method, 523–525
    ParkourBehavior class, 525
    rear approach, 519, 520
    scriptable object, 525
    smooth/dynamic
        navigation, 518
    vault animation/mirrorVault
        parameter/mirror
        setting, 527
    VaultBehavior class, 521–523
    Vault_SO scriptable
        object, 528
Player attack action, 112
    animation
        animIDAttack variable, 123
        AssignAnimationIDs
            method, 123
        attack() method, 124
        attack state, 122
        completion, 126
        conditions check, 125
        CrossFadeInFixedTime()
            method, 128
        Idle Walk Run Blend state,
            121, 122
        initiation, 125
        Kevin Iglesias directory, 120
        management, 126
        parameters tab, 120
        static method, 124
        string comparisons, 123
        ThirdPersonController
            script, 119, 128
        transition, 121
        WaitForAnimation()
            method, 128
    Attack() method, 118
    broadcast messages, 132
        action mappings, 133
        broadcasting mechanism, 133

INDEX

Player attack action (*cont.*)
    compile-time safety, 134
    considerations, 134
    GameObject
      hierarchy, 132
    hierarchical
      communication, 133
    Overbroadcasting, 134
    recursive method, 133
Gamepad control scheme,
    114, 115
implementation, 113
input component behavior
    broadcast messages
      option, 132–134
    components/scripts, 129
    dropdown menu, 130
    Invoke C Sharp Events
      option, 142–146
    Invoke Unity Events
      option, 135–142
    send messages
      option, 130–132
    strict performance
      constraints, 129
Invoke C Sharp Events option
    Awake() method, 144, 145
    encapsulation/
      separation, 143
    handling events, 143
    input actions, 143
    input events, 142
    OnAttackStart/
      OnAttackComplete, 146
    OnEnable/OnDisable
      methods, 145
    Start() method, 144
    subscribe methods, 143
Invoke Unity Events option
    advantages, 137
    Attack Unity Event, 141
    attack/update methods, 138
    behavior property, 135
    considerations, 137, 138
    event configuration, 135
    high customizability, 137
    invocation, 135
    modularity/flexibility, 135
    OnAttack method, 141
    StarterAssetsInputs script,
      140, 141
    strong decoupling, 137
    ThirdPersonController
      script, 138, 139
    unity event linkage, 135
KeyboardMouse control
    scheme, 113
keyboards/gamepads, 112
modification, 112
OnAttack method, 117
send messages option
    action mappings, 130
    advantages, 132
    considerations, 132
    error handling, 132
    message-passing system, 130
    OnJump method, 131
    send messages, 131

Starter Assets (input action asset), 113–115
StarterAssetsInputs script, 115–118
testing, 119
ThirdPersonController script, 118, 119
Update() method, 118

R
Re-bindable controls
ActionBindingIcon, 184
ActionMapManager script, 194–197
Awake() method, 198–200
bindings, 178
buttons, 189
Canvas game object, 185–187
component, 185, 186
comprehensive setup, 193
control rebinding actions, 190
dynamic control scheme, 175
features, 203–205
implementation, 175
import tab, 177
input system package, 176
interact action, 177
InteractRebind, 182
keyboard game object, 179
keyboard/mouse actions, 177
modal windows, 191, 192
MoveRebind, 179, 181, 183
OnClick() event, 193, 201, 202

OnEnable() and OnDisable() methods, 199
OnrebindControlsCanvas Close() method, 200
package manager, 176
PerformInteractiveRebind() method, 205, 207–211
RebindActionUI script, 201
ResetToDefault() method, 203
ResolveActionAndBinding() method, 206
restructuring game object, 188
samples tab, 176
StartInteractiveRebind() method, 202, 205
step-by-step guide, 176
text property references, 181
ToggleRebindControls, 187, 188
toggleRebindControls
  Action, 200
  UI elements, 200
variables, 198

S
Scripts
  character controller
    acceleration/deceleration, 102
    CameraRotation method, 95, 99–101
    ClampAngle method, 108, 109
    components, 95

INDEX

Scripts (*cont.*)
    deltaTimeMultiplier, 100
    GroundedCheck method, 98
    input direction, 103
    input.look property, 96
    JumpAndGravity
      method, 105–107
    jumping/falling
      dynamics, 107
    mode set/digital, 97
    move method, 97, 101–104
    normalization, 97, 98
    OnDrawGizmosSelected
      method, 110–112
    target speed, 102
  handle input actions, 92–95
Shooter weapon mechanics
  audio component
    AudioSource
      component, 554
    Awake(), 554
    DryFire(), 556
    dryFireSound, 554
    events, 550
    feedback, 549
    initialization, 550
    inspector, 550
    MagazineLoad(), 556
    magazineLoadedSound, 554
    MagazineUnLoad(), 556
    OnDisable(), 555
    OnEnable(), 555
    Start(), 556
    WeaponAudio class, 556
    WeaponAudio
      script, 551–553
    WeaponFired(), 556
    weapon-related actions, 553
  development process, 533
  game components, 539
  handle numerous tasks, 533
  magazine component
    ammoCount, 581
    ammunition/reloading
      mechanics, 577
    Awake() method, 581
    inspector, 578
    maxAmmoInMag, 580
    ReloadAsync(), 582
    reloading asynchronous, 578
    Reload() method, 582
    reloadTime, 581
    Unload(), 582
    WeaponMagazine class,
      578–580, 583
  player weapon setup
    aspects, 534
    AudioSource
      component, 537
    CastRay() method, 538
    components, 535
    HandGun weapon, 535, 536
    health script, 535
    project pane, 536
    resource, 535
    WeaponCasing class, 538
    Weapon class, 537
    WeaponMagazine class, 538

INDEX

WeaponRaycast class, 538
weapon-related scripts, 536
raycast component
  bodyshotDamage, 564
  CastRay() method, 557,
    558, 564
  cohesive shooting, 563–566
  head game object, 562
  headshots/body shots, 557
  OnDisable(), 564
  OnEnable(), 564
  OnValidate(), 564
  realism/player
    immersion, 557
  shootableLayer, 564
  Upper Chest game
    object, 562
  WeaponRaycast class, 566
  WeaponRaycast
    code, 558–561
shell casing ejection
  Awake() method, 574
  component, 566
  CreateShellCasing(), 575
  EjectCasing() method,
    575, 576
  inspector, 567
  object pool, 572–577
  object pooling, 567
  OnDestroyShellCasing(), 575
  OnDisable()/
    OnEnable(), 575
  OnGetShellCasing(), 575
  OnReleaseShellCasing(), 575
  OnValidate(), 573
  ReturnToPoolAfter
    Delay(), 577
  shellCasingPrefab, 572
  WeaponCasing class,
    567–572, 577
weapon component
  automatic reloading, 540
  autoReload, 545
  behavior/mechanics, 539
  components, 544, 545
  comprehensive solution, 539
  events, 539
  FireWeapon(), 547
  lastShotTime, 546
  MagazineAttached(), 548
  MagazineDetatched(), 549
  manual reloading, 540
  OnDestroy(), 546
  shootInterval, 540, 545
  Start() method, 546
  TryFireWeapon(), 546–548
  WeaponAudio
    component, 545
  WeaponMagazine
    component, 546
  Weapon script, 541–544
Starter Assets
  character controllers (*see*
    Character controllers)
State machine system
  abstract class, 263–265, 267
  abstract computational
    model, 260

643

State machine system (*cont.*)
  Awake() method, 274
  behaviors/modification, 260
  centralized approach, 273
  class/elements, 273–278
  clear definition/
      organization, 260
  currentState, 264
  Find() method, 278
  game events/
      conditions, 264–266
  game parameters, 272
  inheritance, 263
  interactions, 260
  IsPlayerAttackable()
      method, 275
  IsPlayerVisible() method, 275
  IState interface, 267
  NpcDead() method, 276
  NPCStateMachine class,
      262, 268–273
  OnEnable()/OnDisable()
      methods, 274
  OnStateEnter() method, 266
  OnStateExit() method, 267
  OnStateUpdate() method, 266
  Patrol/Wander states, 261
  previousState, 264
  RotateToFacePlayer()
      method, 275
  spherical linear
      interpolation, 277
  Start() method, 275
  StateMachine class, 262, 264

Super Mario, 260
SwitchState(), 265, 266
TakeDamage() method, 276
transitions, 261, 262
Update() method, 266

T

Text Mesh Pro (TMP), 158, 159
Third-person character controller
  animation integration, 43
  animator component, 48–50
  audio feedback, 43
  blend trees, 49
  camera angle override, 47
  components, 38, 41, 46
  comprehensive solution, 39
  development, 42
  directional movement/
      rotation, 50
  footsteps, 45
  game object, 40
  jump action, 50
  keyboard/gamepad inputs, 39
  landing audio clip, 44
  lock camera position, 47
  movements/actions, 42
  parameters, 48
  perspective/camera control, 43
  Player Armature, 41
  project tab, 40
  properties, 39, 44, 47
  real-time interaction, 40
  rotation smooth, 43, 44

setup, 41
speed parameter, 49

U, V, W, X, Y, Z

Unity's Starter Assets, 1
Universal Render
  Pipeline (URP), 5, 6, 55
User interface (UI) controls
  Canvas setup/TMP, 158, 159
  consolidate action maps, 164–168
    ActionMapManager
      script, 168–174
    Awake() method, 172
    DefaultInputActions, 164
    default map property, 168
    OnEnable()/OnDisable()
      methods, 172
  overlapping inputs, 166
  PlayerArmature game
    object, 165
  player input
    component, 166
  StarterAssets, 165
  ToggleUI action, 168–174
  ToggleUIPerformed, 173
  universal action
    map, 167
  variables/functionality, 171
  DefaultInputActions, 162
  event system, 160–163
  input contexts, 157
  keyboards/gamepads, 157
  module component, 161
  re-bindable controls, 175–210
  universal action map, 157

GPSR Compliance

The European Union's (EU) General Product Safety Regulation (GPSR) is a set of rules that requires consumer products to be safe and our obligations to ensure this.

If you have any concerns about our products, you can contact us on

ProductSafety@springernature.com

In case Publisher is established outside the EU, the EU authorized representative is:

Springer Nature Customer Service Center GmbH
Europaplatz 3
69115 Heidelberg, Germany

www.ingramcontent.com/pod-product-compliance
Lightning Source LLC
LaVergne TN
LVHW010331260326
834688LV00036B/656